DISORDERS
in the
KINGDOM

DISORDERS
in the
KINGDOM

Part I
A History of the Merger of the Congregational Christian Churches and The Evangelical and Reformed Church

A Documented, Eye-Witness Account by
Malcolm K. Burton

Revised and Updated

VANTAGE PRESS
New York / Washington / Atlanta
Los Angeles / Chicago

Other books by Malcolm K. Burton
Destiny for Congregationalism—1953
Constitution for Congregationalism?—1954
*A Comprehensive Analysis of the Proposed Constitution for
the United Church of Christ—1960*
*What Did the Courts Actually Say About The United
Church of Christ?—1964*
*To Revamp Protestant Worship—A Critique of The Lord's
Day Service—1965*
How Church Union Came—1966
Early Merger Pamphlets (Reprinted in book form)—1977
*Sermons on Special Days of the Church Year,
Volume I—1977*
Sermons on Special Days, Volume II—1980
Sermons on the Mysteries of Life and Death—1980
Sermons on Controversial Subjects—1981
Bible Sermons on God—1981
Bible Sermons with Unique Insights—1981

The following book by Mr. Burton's father was edited
by Malcolm K. Burton, and published posthumously:

The Message for Our Day—The Bearing of Science on Religious Faith—1975 by Charles Emerson Burton, D.D., LL.D.

REVISED EDITION
Updated to 1980

Published by Vantage Press, Inc.
516 West 34th Street, New York, New York 10001

Manufactured in the United States of America
ISBN 533-04751-X

Library of Congress Catalog Card No.: 80-52187

Dedicated in friendship
to all loyal Congregationalists
whether inside or outside
of The United Church of Christ

Contents

Foreword

The author, Rev. Malcolm K. Burton, was in attendance at every national meeting of the Congregational Christian Churches during all the years that the proposed merger with the Evangelical and Reformed Church was under consideration. He witnessed and took part in the discussions at every critical stage, as the minutes of those meetings will show.

Going as a voting delegate to all of the meetings of the General Council of the Congregational Christian Churches from 1942 through 1958 (except for one which he attended as a non-delegate), he received the official minutes of each meeting and also the *Advance Reports*. These he had kept and has had available for the writing of this book. He also kept the issues of *Daily Advance* published during the Council sessions for the meetings of 1944, 1946, and 1948. These give a running account of events as they took place.

In addition, Mr. Burton began voluminous pamphleteering on the merger in October 1945. His publications—often not more than a week or two apart—are almost like a diary of events as they took place, as well as being a commentary on many of the tactics used and the far-out claims made for the merger. In all, he published over 350 pamphlets, circular letters, leaflets, and books. Until November 1954 these were done under his own name. Occasionally friends cooperated with him, notably Rev. Alexander H. Abbott of Norwich, Connecticut.

In November 1954, Mr. Burton was elected Director—later called Executive Vice-Chairman—of the Committee for the Continuation of the Congregational Christian Churches. Most of his writings thereafter appeared in the publications of that committee.

Son of Dr. Charles E. Burton, who was Executive Secretary of all the national home missionary Societies from

1914 to 1921, and then successively the Executive Secretary of the National Council and of the General Council of the Congregational Christian Churches from 1921 to 1938, the author grew up among Congregational officials and knew many of the most prominent men personally.

At all times during the merger's development there were members of the Executive Committee of the General Council who were his intimate friends and who furnished him with reliable information on events that were not openly disclosed.

In 1947 the author was named as one of three persons to conduct a Forum on the Merger through the pages of the national magazine, *Advance*. The other two were Rev. John Phillips of Duluth, and Dr. Ronald Bridges, a former moderator. This committee was appointed by the Executive Committee of the General Council in an effort to offset the one-sided treatment of the merger by the editor, Dr. John Scotford. Under the general rules of the Executive Committee, all members of subcommittees were sent the minutes of the Executive Committee and its subcommittees. This committee for the Forum on the Merger was never discharged by the Executive Committee, but Dr. Scotford announced after a brief period of four months that he was "taking over" the Forum on the Merger. However, since the Forum committee was never officially discharged, Dr. Frederick L. Fagley continued to send Mr. Burton all of the previously mentioned Executive Committee minutes.

Thus, through personal attendance at General Council meetings, through all the official minutes of these meetings, through publications and information coming through members of the Executive Committee, the author of this book has a wealth of unimpeachable evidence for what he has written.

Any persons who may wish to defend the merger may take exception to some personal evaluations made by the author, or may object to the injection of personal recollections on certain matters. But no one can gainsay the solid evidence that the actions taken—or not taken—are true and unanswerable. Even if all personal evaluations were discounted or discarded, the facts set forth in this book, from the official records themselves and other historical documents, are sufficient to prove the main thesis and the basic conclusions here set forth.

In addition to the contacts mentioned above, Mr. Burton was elected by the Executive Committee to be a member of the Committee on Free Church Polity and Unity. From the year 1950 to 1954 this committee made the most exhaustive study ever made of the documents and practices of the churches, associations, conferences, boards, and General Council. This Committee then submitted its tentative findings to the state Superintendents and nearly 200 leading Congregationalists, asking in what respects, if any, Congregational practices had departed from the written documents. Surprisingly, the answers came back almost uniformly that there had been no departure from essential practices and principles as set forth in the constitutions and other official documents of our organizations.

Mr. Burton served not only on the Polity Committee as a whole, but was also a member of its Central Committee, which met more frequently, and of the subcommittee on polity. He was also the author in large part of the chapter of the report on various possible forms of church union.

As recorded in this book, Mr. Burton attended the Spiritual Conference of the Evangelical and Reformed Church in 1945 and 1946, each lasting about five days. This was early in the merger discussions, when ministers, and some officials, were willing to meet for frank and open discussions with Congregationalists who had their doubts about the merger. Later any such meetings became virtually impossible. As brought out in this book (chapter 11), it came to be thought a breach of etiquette for any Congregationalists to try to communicate directly with Evangelical and Reformed Church ministers in order to discover whether they had the same understandings as were being presented as "official" to the Congregational Church members.

When the Evanston Meeting met as the first organized resistance to the merger in November 1947, Mr. Burton was present but had taken no part in its organization. He was, however, placed on its Continuing Committee. This did not involve his writing any of its publications.

After the Oberlin Council in 1948, when the promerger people had tried to create the illusion that all problems had been solved, and when the Evanston meeting had officially voted to disband, since its members were not all of one mind regarding what had happened at Oberlin, it was Mr. Burton who sent out to the churches the first publication showing that there was still reason for opposition. His four-page leaflet, *What Really Happened at Oberlin*, was sent out to all the churches in early September. Almost immediately, Dr. James W. Fifield, Jr., pastor of First Congregational Church in Los Angeles—which was the largest church in our denomination—phoned Mr. Burton and asked that he republish the leaflet and send him 6,000 copies as soon as possible, and 6,000 of a supplementary pamphlet. Dr. Fifield then set about telephoning people all over the country and organizing the national "Anti-Merger" group, which later changed its name to The Committee for the Continuation of the Congregational Christian Churches in the U. S. From the first, Mr. Burton served on its Executive Committee.

When the Cadman Church, in Brooklyn, brought its lawsuit against the General Council in 1949, the author was asked on the first day of the trial to sit with the Cadman Church lawyer. Mr. Kenneth W. Greenawalt, attorney for the Cadman Church, had approached a group from the Continuation Committee who were present in the courtroom and asked if anyone might know those whom the defense lawyers were bringing into court as possible witnesses. The group indicated that Mr. Burton would be, perhaps, the best qualified. The result was that he sat at the attorney's table throughout the twenty-three days of trial and also assisted in finding documents and other evidence useful in prosecution of the case.

When a federal lawsuit was filed in June 1957, Mr. Burton and nine other individuals were among the plaintiffs, as well as four churches. Again the author worked with attorney Greenawalt throughout the thirty-one days of the trial.

Mr. Burton assisted other attorneys on cases brought against the merger, one in Toledo, another in Detroit, and most recently in Groton, in 1979.

The details of these court cases will not fall within the scope of this present volume. But much of the information does appear in the author's book, *Destiny for Con-*

gregationalism (Modern Publishers, 1953) and "How Church Union Came" (Continuation Committee, 1966). The Cadman case is covered in great detail in *Destiny for Congregationalism,* except for the final disposition of the case by the New York Court of Appeals, which came after the book was published. In like manner the federal lawsuit is treated quite fully in *How Church Union Came.* But again the most important decision in this case came a few months after this book was published. The Michigan Supreme Court in a thirty-six-page opinion swept aside and rejected the basis upon which Judge Dimock had dismissed the federal lawsuit, thus making it clear that no court had ever made a legal determination as to whether the *Basis of Union* was legal or whether it was consistent with Congregational polity.

That last statement should be qualified to this extent. Judge Steinbrink, the original and trial judge in the Cadman case, had made a sweeping decision against the *Basis of Union,* calling that document "a conglomeration of confusion and conflicting statements with a cacophony of ideas." He had issued sweeping injunctions against going ahead with the merger. The two higher courts in New York "reversed" the decision and judgment on the grounds that the Cadman church had no property rights in the General Council, and that, therefore, the civil courts could not make any determination. But the courts, both the Appellate Court and the Court of Appeals, specifically stated that they had not considered the ecclesiastical questions, and they did not reverse the findings of Justice Steinbrink on these matters, although asked to do so.

The reader of this book should guard against any preconceived ideas that the courts approved the merger or gave it legal sanction. In laymen's language, it can best be understood if we say that the courts merely turned their backs on the issues and let the merger leaders get away with anything they wanted.

Justice Steinbrink was the *only* judge who ever held a *trial on the merits* of the *Basis of Union.** In fact it was

---

*Another trial on the merits was held after the above was written. It began on August 27, 1979 at Norwich, Connecticut and involved the Groton Congregational Church. Decision was rendered June 25, 1980. See Appendix, Document 32.

only in his court that any opportunity was ever given to have both sides present their cases, and when sufficient time was given to bring out all the issues. Judge Steinbrink's decision was without the force of law once the case was thrown out for want of jurisdiction, but what Justice Steinbrink said in his opinion is of great significance intellectually and morally. No off-the-cuff comment by some lawyer or judge, here or there, was based on the kind of thorough interrogation and profuse testimony that stands back of Steinbrink's words. The promerger insistence on sweeping all this under the rug, and the oft-repeated assurances that the "courts have approved the merger," are among the more reprehensible things done in the whole merger history.

Therefore, even though the details of the lawsuits must wait for another volume, or for a study of other sources, it is important to the reader of this volume to free his mind of any of the false propaganda that was given out with regard to the lawsuits. The real issues might otherwise be clouded in his mind as he reads.

Mr. Frank Bean, who organized the League to Uphold Congregational Principles, asked Mr. Burton to meet with the Board of Directors of that organization at the time when its members considered whether to join in the fight against the merger. Previously that organization had been devoted only to opposing certain types of political action associated with the Council for Social Action. After several hours' discussion, the directors of the League voted to join in the merger action. Later it was the League to Uphold Congregational Principles that united with the Continuation Committee in calling the first meeting of the National Association of Congregational Christian Churches.

In May 1955, the Interim Committee of the Continuation Committee began the process of establishing a new missionary Society. Palmer D. Edmunds and Malcolm Burton wrote a preliminary set of articles of incorporation while the other members of the Interim Committee waited. Then all members of the Interim Committee agreed to become the original incorporators, including Mr. Burton.

Shortly afterward plans were made with leaders of the League to call the first meeting of the National Association for November 9 and 10, 1955. Mr. Harold S. Bailey obtained Rev. Russell J. Clinchy, his former pastor, to be key-note speaker. Mr. Burton wrote the call to the meeting, which went out over the names of the League and the Continuation Committee. It was left to Mr. Burton to make all of the arrangements for the meeting, which he did with the assistance of his good wife, Carol. And so, at last, the Congregational Christian Churches that wanted to continue in their time-honored freedoms and practices were assured of that choice and opportunity.

A. VAUGHAN ABERCROMBIE,
Formerly Executive Secretary of
The National Association of
Congregational Christian Churches

Preface

Several months after completing the writing of this book, it came quite forcibly upon me that this book does indeed constitute Part I of the merger story. It is still my hope to continue the account of later events in a second volume under the same title. But if time runs out on me, I can console myself that most of the later events have already been recorded in some of my other writings.

Destiny for Congregationalism, published in 1953, might well be considered as Part II. It deals especially with the period of the Cadman lawsuit, beginning in the fall of 1949. It was written while I was serving on the Committee on Free Church Polity and Unity, appointed under the authority of the General Council. Both through my research for evidence usable in the lawsuit and through my involvement in the Polity Committee work, *Destiny for Congregationalism* reflects the nature of true Congregationalism and the issues that were at stake in the merger, and it tells vividly what happened in the Cadman trial.

In 1954, at the New Haven General Council meeting, Dr. Douglas Horton tried to get the General Council to write a constitution for the "fellowship." He did not mention it, but this had become the key issue in any attempt to go on with the merger, since Dr. James E. Wagner had made it crystal clear in published statements that he would not accept the claims made in the Cadman trial that there would be no constitution for the United Church as a whole—but rather just a constitution for the General Synod and Boards.

In response to Dr. Horton's effort at New Haven, I wrote *Constitution for Congregationalism?* This was published in September of 1954 by Modern Publishers of Oklahoma City. This publisher was really Mr. Victor E. Harlow of the Harlow Publishing Company. Mr. Harlow had asked permission to sit in with the Polity Committee and had sat quietly in a corner throughout its discussions. Hence he was well informed of the issues involved in both of these first books, which he published under the name of Modern Publishers as a personal side venture. This *Constitution for Congregationalism?* might well be considered Part III of the merger story.

Next among my publications I would choose, I believe, the thirty-page booklet, *What Did the Courts Actually Say on the United Church of Christ?*, published by the Continuation Committee on January 11, 1964. This traced the findings and judgments of the New York courts in the Cadman case, and then took up the federal lawsuit as decided by Judge Dimock and later by Judge Clarke of the U.S. Court of Appeals. Judge Dimock insisted that the New York Court of Appeals *had* decided all of the issues of polity connected with the United Church of Christ, even though it had plainly affirmed, without modification, the Appellate Court's Judgment that no such issues had been decided. Judge Clarke, in writing the Appeals Court decision, side-stepped whether the ecclesiastical issues had been decided but let Judge Dimock's dismissal of the case stand. We later learned that Judge Clarke was a member of the United Church of Christ, but we have no way of knowing whether he was aware that his church had joined. This booklet, *What Did the Courts Actually Say on the United Church of Christ*, could be considered Part IV of the whole merger history. A copy is in the archives of the Congregational Library in Boston.

Finally, as a possible Part V of the total history of the merger, I could mention *How Church Union Came*, published in 1966 by the Continuation Committee. It summarizes, in just seven pages, the main events taken up in this present volume. Then it takes up briefly the story of the lawsuits and the manner in which the United Church of Christ was finally pushed through.

In retrospect, then, I realize that the first part of the merger story is what had been most neglected. This is what I have tried to cover in *Disorders in the Kingdom*.

Unfortunately none of the previous books was written after the Michigan Supreme Court, in August of 1966, laid to rest the arguments Judge Dimock had followed in his decision in the federal lawsuit. Possibly a dozen local lawsuits had also been thrown out on the same erroneous arguments of *res judicata*, based on the Cadman decision of the Court of Appeals of New York—but *not* based on the *judgment* of that court, and it is the *judgment that really counts*. The issues here involved were all treated in detail in my *How Church Union Came*, published just a few months before the Michigan Supreme Court decision. The arguments I used were, of course, not original with me. They came from attorneys Kenneth W. Greenawalt and Alfred Lindbloom—the latter being the lawyer for the plaintiffs in the Detroit Mayflower Church case.

As mentioned earlier in this preface, I still hope to write a part two of *Disorders in the Kingdom*, bringing together the essential facts treated in the publications mentioned above. There would be added some insights on the Polity Committee's work and also various things revealed in the later part of Dr. Palmer's file, especially the official reactions to the original decision in the Cadman case.

I have, however, some other things which I hope to accomplish, especially some writing on genuine religious concerns. It was my interest in these religious questions that prompted me, in the first place, to oppose the merger. I saw in the proposed United Church of Christ the danger of conventional church concepts and dogma becoming even more deeply entrenched, with the accompanying threat that honest and original insights would be even more stifled than in the past. I believe my apprehensions were justified, and from what I hear from the lips of United Church ministers (and others) the trend has been just what I feared.

I wish gratefully to acknowledge permission granted by the United Church Press to use copyrighted material from Dr. Gunnemann's book. Each quotation in this manuscript from his book should carry the notation: "Reprinted with permission from Louis H. Gunnemann, *The Shaping of the United Church of Christ: An Essay in the History of American Christianity*. Copyright © 1977 United Church Press."

I wish to express my deep gratitude also to the members of the Committee for the Continuation of the Congregational Christian Churches for their encouragement and support in the writing and publication of this book, and to others who read portions of the book during its writing and made valuable contributions and suggestions. Some were very instrumental in getting me to write the book, especially Rev. A. Vaughan Abercrombie and Mrs. A. Burnham Converse. Mrs. Converse also typed a good deal of the first draft which I had dictated on the tape recorder. I very much appreciate the recollections and added detail given me by Rev. Henry David Gray. As always, I have been indebted to my wife, Carol Berkemeier Burton, for her constant moral support and for the endless hours of work in proofreading, constructive criticism, and collating sheets of the preliminary printing of the manuscript. Rev. Philip W. Palmer furnished me with the letters from his father, Rev. Albert W. Palmer, who was moderator of the General Council during the fateful period of the Oberlin meeting in 1948. To all I give my very sincere thanks and appreciation.

—Malcolm K. Burton

Acknowledgments

The author and publishers wish to thank the following individuals and publisher for permission to use material from their files and publications.

Rev. Philip W. Palmer, of St. Andrews United Church, Blind River, Ontario, for letters from his file of the letters of Dr. Albert W. Palmer.

United Church Press, quotations by Dr. Gunnemann reprinted with permission from Louis H. Gunnemann, *The Shaping of the United Church of Christ: An Essay in the History of American Christianity.*

DISORDERS
in the
KINGDOM

1

Congregationalism: Merged or Submerged?

THIS will be the story of how the Congregationalists, the descendants of the Mayflower Pilgrims, were talked out of their historic and previously uncompromised freedom in local, self-governing churches. Also lost was their free and happy fellowship with other like-minded churches in associations and conferences owned and operated by the churches themselves, untrammeled by any dictates or regulations coming down from higher judicatories or officialdom.

Congregationalists were told from the beginning of the merger plan that "nothing would be changed" and that they would always remain simply Congregational churches. For the sake of future historians we need to keep the record straight.

The Constitution upon which the churches were induced to vote, in order to join, contained assurances that their autonomy was inherent and could not be abridged by any action of United Church bodies:

> Nothing in this Constitution and the Bylaws of the United Church of Christ shall destroy or limit the right of each local church to continue to operate in the way customary to it; nor shall be construed as giving to the General Synod, or to any conference or association now, or at any future time, the power to abridge or impair the autonomy of any local church in the management of its own affairs. . . . . ."

This passage went on directly to enumerate certain specific rights of crucial importance which have apparently been largely ignored by United Church of Christ officials:

> ... which affairs include, but are not limited to, the right to retain or adopt its own methods of organization, worship and education; to retain or secure its own charter and name; to adopt its own constitution and bylaws, to formulate its own covenants and confession of faith; to admit members in its own way and to provide for their discipline or dismissal; to call or dismiss its pastor or pastors by such procedure as it shall determine; to acquire, own, manage and dispose of property and funds; to control its own benevolences; and to withdraw by its own decision from the United Church of Christ at any time without forfeiture of ownership or control of any real or personal property owned by it.

Significantly the United Church of Christ has actively participated and promoted the larger plan of union, known as COCU (Consultation on Church Union) in which virtually none of the rights here set forth would prevail according to a published draft of the plan. But in addition we can cite the following pressures exerted against the specific rights set forth above.

Hardly had the United Church come into being before a statement of faith was adopted and pressed on the churches for their use. There came also an elaborate booklet entitled, "The Lord's Day Service" containing orders of worship highly liturgical in nature and completely foreign to the very simple and straightforward services most common among Congregationalists. An elaborate and very detailed desk calendar for ministers was published and sent out, telling ministers when to start their planning for various activities—especially, it seemed to me, on when and how to start raising money for the denomination. It also had all the old ideas of the Christian year, with the ancient emphasis and name for each Sunday, such as the "Seventh Sunday after Trinity," and so forth. Goals for the giving by local churches are set officially, both for the per capita dues and for general benevolences. These goals are "voluntary," but ministers know that it is in their interest to see that the goals are met.

New Sunday school materials were brought forth, some of the first being very radical and teaching children to become activists, even to the point of opposing the forces of law and order, for "conscience sake."

A suggested or "model" constitution for the local church was prepared and sent out, with a form of organization in sharp contrast to the usual Congregational form for the local chuch.

In the one state with which I was familiar (Michigan) attempts were made to get churches to change their charters and incorporation, giving up their status under the special statute for Congregational churches and incorporating instead under a general statute that would permit change.

More recently the United Church of Christ has set up the Office for Church Life and Leadership. This was part of an overall centralization of powers in the General Synod which is discussed in Chapter 9. This amounts to a new board for the denomination, on a par with the Board for World Ministries and the Board for Homeland Ministries. It absorbs the functions of five or six former commissions, committees and councils. This new Office for Church Life and Leadership is aimed at the local churches, the ministers and the laymen. It is to help provide leadership for the United Church, with the realization that the churches must supply the support for the denomination.

Already this Office for Church Life and Leadership has published a slick eight-and-one-half by eleven-inch booklet of seventy-four pages telling the churches, the ministers, the associations and the conferences how to operate. In one inconspicuous place there appears, without comment or emphasis, the paragraph from which we quoted above guaranteeing the autonomy of the local church and its right to manage its own affairs. But in page after page of the manual no recognition is given to these provisions, even as alternate possibilities. Instead there appear dogmatic statements as to what churches and ministers are to do, backed up by countless quotations from bylaws with the notation at the bottom of each page: "United Church of Christ Constitution and Bylaws" (with notation of article and section). This all appears as so much *law* and as though it were *binding* upon churches and ministers. Possibly some of the officials actually believe this to be true. Note this from page 1 of this manual:

All guidelines and procedures suggested here should be read

with the knowledge that where they are not constitutionally mandated they are not binding.

Since the publication of this manual, a lawsuit was heard in Norwich, Connecticut, in which the lawyer for the United Church of Christ insisted that none of the provisions of the constitution and bylaws were binding upon the local church. Judge Hendel, in his decision and judgment handed down on June 25, 1980 also decided that none of the provisions we have been discussing were actually binding on a local church and that churches were free to ignore the advice and regulations of officials and Bylaws alike. But the pressures to make the Congregational churches over, and to get them to conform to standards set by the United Church of Christ, will, conceivably, continue.

Omitted entirely from the manual on the ministry, so far as I can discover, is any quotation of paragraph 3 of the Preamble of the Constitution, which has been greatly relied upon by lawyers to get lawsuits against the United Church of Christ dismissed:

The provisions herein define and regulate the General Synod and those instrumentalities of the United Church of Christ which are recognized, established by or responsible to the General Synod, *and describe the free and voluntary relationships which the local churches, associations, conferences and ministers sustain with the General Synod and with each other.* The pattern of relationships so described is recommended to local churches, associations, conferences and ministers, to enable them more effectively to accomplish their tasks and the work of the United Church of Christ.

Not all Congregationalists were taken in by the assurances given to them, either in the Constitution or in the previous Basis of Union. They were deeply concerned about the superstructure proposed for the United Church, by the over-all Constitution, and by the loss of the free kind of fellowship which Congregationalists have always enjoyed.

As early as 1949, a lawsuit was filed by Cadman Memorial Church against the General Council to prevent the consummation of the merger.

Several groups of churches refused to go along, notably

those in the National Association of Congregational Christian Churches which celebrated its twenty-fifth anniversary in June, 1980. The Conservative Congregational Christian Conference was started a few years sooner, and other churches have stayed out of the United Church of Christ without aligning themselves with any denomination.

Some may look upon the controversy caused by the creation of the United Church of Christ as the biggest "church fight" of the century, starting officially in 1942 and lasting to the present time.

This controversy involved more than a dozen lawsuits, two of them on the national level and taking up more than sixty days in court. These lawsuits settled none of the fundamental issues, and nothing has ever been determined as to whether the United Church of Christ really has a Presbyterian, and not a Congregational polity or structure. The United Church of Christ has never said what it was on this crucial issue.

In the Cadman lawsuit, where the trial judge held against the formation of the United Church of Christ, the higher courts dismissed the case on the ground that the plaintiff church had failed to show a property interest in the General Council. Many other cases were dismissed on the assumption that the first case had decided all the issues involved—even though the actual Judgment of the two highest courts had specifically disavowed any consideration of the questions of polity and the details of the plan for union.

Finally, in 1966, the Michigan supreme court reviewed carefully the previous cases and declared, in a careful 36-page decision, that *res judicata* did not apply and that the Cadman case did not stand as a bar to lawsuits seeking answers to the merger question. But then the U.S. Supreme Court handed down a decision in a Georgia church case that seemed to say that no court in the land could consider any church case. Later it was understood that this meant that courts could not go into religious questions but must decide church cases on "neutral principles of law."

Thus, the opponents of the merger were left holding the bag until just recently, with nothing to show for their efforts until Judge Hendel's decision in the Groton case. The impact of this decision has yet to be fully assessed. There is no way of knowing whether the United Church of Christ will find some way around it. This decision could conceivably force curtailment of some far-reaching policies and methods of the United Church of Christ.

Judge Hendel has put it into his decision and judgment that nothing in the United Church of Christ Constitution and bylaws is *binding* upon the local churches. Churches are therefore free to ignore rules and regulations written into the Constitution and bylaws. They do not have to call their ministers in the fashion set forth in the Manual on the Ministry and elsewhere. Furthermore Judge Hendel ruled that the United Church of Christ does not have the legal power to amend its Constitution and bylaws in any way that would curtail the freedom and autonomy of local churches, associations or conferences. Among other things this could prevent the United Church of Christ from following through on the plan for a much larger union—that contemplated in the Consultation on Church Union—a plan ardently supported by the United Church of Christ. (See Appendix, document 32 for the relevant portions of Judge Hendel's decision.)

How far the Congregationalists were from recognizing the plan of union for what it was going to be can be further understood from the following. At the 1948 meeting of the General Council of the Congregational Christian Churches, at which the Basis of Union was approved, Dr. Albert W. Palmer, the moderator, summed up the character of the United Church as he saw it or thought it ought to be. He was an ardent supporter of Congregational principles and also of the plan for union:

> All organizations through which the fellowship is expressed and implemented, such as associations, conferences, councils, boards and synods, must be voluntary and autonomous— subject only to the churches which create them as vehicles of their cooperative desires and necessities. That is to say, they are to be controlled democratically from below, not by centralized organization from above. (Page 84, Minutes of 1948 General Council)

Quite contrary to Dr. Palmer's idea of what the United Church would be, Chapter 9 of this book shows that it has been shaped and reshaped into a more and more centralized superstructure. With numerous quotations from Dr. Louis Gunnemann, who was one of those who helped shape this superstructure and refers to it as highly sophisticated, we have shown how Congregationalists like Dr. Palmer were completely misled as to the real import of the overall constitution and the powers it placed in the General Synod and its ability to get amendments that would enhance its powers.

In his book, *The Shaping of the United Church of Christ*, Dr. Gunnemann has enumerated the steps by which these changes were made. As Dr. Gunnemann says, the General Synod is now recognized as the decision-making body for the denomination. The Executive Council, greatly enlarged to include representative state executives, is the "General Synod *ad interim*," charged with carrying out the decisions of the General Synod and has for its own budget approximately one million dollars a year. The president of the Church, according to Dr. Gunnemann, is no longer dependent upon his personality and persuasive powers but is now the chief executive officer with authority to engage sufficient staff to carry out his duties. Budgets for the state conferences have been greatly increased until they receive approximately half of the income received at the national level. Their staffs have been correspondingly increased to cover many new functions. The new Office of Church Life and Leadership is discussed in detail. Dr. Gunnemann laments that many local churches have not learned to accept their "identity" as parts of the United Church of Christ. From advertisements that I have seen of comprehensive new Sunday school materials for the United Church I would say that the drive is on to make the church people, including the children, stop thinking of themselves as Congregational or Evangelical and Reformed but only as United Church of Christ. It would seem likely that this is also an objective of the Office of Church Life and Leadership.

Thus the promises given to Congregationalists about remaining "Congregational" seem definitely out of the picture. In recent years efforts have been made to get the Congregational Christian Historical Society, with an office in Boston, to merge with the Evangelical and Reformed historical group into the new United Church of Christ Historical Council. This effort has been rejected, with the firm belief that history of the past should remain with those who know it best and cherish it the most. The executive committee of the historical society is made up, however, of persons who are members of the United Church, with one or two exceptions. The projected plan called for closing the New England office and having regional offices elsewhere for the United Church of Christ Historical Council.

One of the most extreme departures from Congregationalism is evidenced on page 11 of the Manual on the Ministry. There under the heading "Responsibilities of the Governing Board" is this:

> When a pastor has resigned, the governing board of the congregation:
> —accepts the resignation, and sees that all members of the congregation have been notified.

This directive is not in the Constitution or bylaws, and furthermore Congregational Churches have not, traditionally or ever in my experience or to my knowledge, had governing boards. The Episcopalians have their Vestries which rule their congregations, and the Presbyterians have their elders. But with Congregationalists all important decisions rest with the church in properly called meetings. In at least two states in which I served, state laws also required that for the dismissal of a Congregational pastor a meeting of the church had to be called, with the purpose plainly stated in the call, which in turn had to be read from the pulpit for two Sundays before the meeting. Elsewhere this has also been required in church bylaws.

More than once, while attending national church meetings, I have had some layman come up to me and confidentially ask, "How can we quietly get rid of our minister without everybody knowing about it?" I have always replied that it could not be done. We Congregationalists have tried to be open and above-board.

The practice set forth in the Manual on the Ministry would permit a small group of persons, on a governing board, to harass a minister until he resigned, or to demand his resignation for reasons not known to the membership of the church. This has not been the Congregational way. This one illustration goes a long way to tell how far the United Church of Christ has sought to submerge Congregationalism.

Some day Congregationalists are likely to wake up and ask, "What in the world has happened to our Congregational Churches?" Just their penchant for reading history, especially in New England, would refresh their minds on what Congregationalism has always been.

The following pages represent an effort to set forth clearly, and with authoritative evidence all along the way, what happened to the Congregational Christian Churches in regard to the merger with the Evangelical and Reformed Church.

The initial momentum for this plan undoubtedly started in the seminaries, which were preaching "unity" and "ecumenicity" for twenty years or more prior to the onslaught of this merger push. Great things were claimed for this idea of union. The plan evolved for the Congregational merger openly spoke of "looking forward to further unions" of the churches so that "they all might be one." It was always claimed that this was the "will of Christ" or the "will of God." It was, however, certain denominational officials who translated this loose talk about unity into a specific plan for union and then relentlessly pushed it.

The plan went through many revisions. First, the *Basis of Union* was published in March of 1943, and there were eight or more revisions. A final edition was approved by the Executive Committee of the General Council in the spring of 1947 and sent to the churches, associations, and conferences for a vote.

The churches were inundated with a flood of materials from denominational headquarters, and, to a lesser extent, from critics of the plan. As the proposal dragged on through many years, the denominational agencies took full advantage of their superior organization and their access to almost unlimited funds. They did not hesitate to use monies that were given to "Our Christian World Mission" to bury the churches with propaganda, promises, assurances, and even subtle threats—and some not so subtle. Never were the really solid facts revealed or admitted. There was a great deal of evasion, denial of the truth, and cover-up.

The denominational leaders, on both the national and state levels, took advantage of the many years of merger negotiation to carry out a relentless attrition of ministers who were opposing the merger. Even among the Congregational churches there were state superintendents (or "conference ministers") who had considerable influence in placing ministers in churches looking for pastors. It was easy enough for up-and-coming ministers to realize that they stood little chance of recommendation from the "higher-ups" if they opposed the union. And, with a twenty-year lapse between the beginnings of the merger fight and the final consummation of the "United Church of Christ" it takes little imagination to understand why most churches had ministers who were working hard for the merger.

Ostensibly the churches themselves voted on the plan on two occasions. The first was on the *Basis of Union*, which was the preliminary plan. This was supposed to receive a 75 percent approval from the conferences voting, the associations voting, the churches voting, and the individual members voting. This was the representation upon which the *Basis of Union* was presented to everyone for a vote. But when the deadline came for this vote to be completed, in April of 1948, it fell far short of the 75 percent, with only approximately 56 percent approval of the churches and members voting. And so the officials extended the time for voting to June 1948 and renewed their pressures for a favorable vote. Again they failed. So at the General Council meeting at Oberlin, Ohio, in late June 1948, they had a Committee of Fifteen elected to "get the vote," and gave the committee money to proceed for that purpose. Once more the period for the voting was extended until the following February. Still they failed to get the 75 percent approval. Yet the national body, the General Council of the Congregational Christian Churches, which by that time had become rather easily manipulated by the pro-merger forces, voted to go ahead anyway.

In the years which followed, there were many times when it was thought that the merger proposal was dead, and when many leaders in the denomination said that the plan should either be completely rewritten or scrapped altogether. The story that follows will show some of the manipulations that took place to keep reviving the "dead horse." This story will have many shocking details and many statements which may seem extreme. But it will be thoroughly documented. The writer was at the very heart of things during the whole long controversy. He wrote more than 350 pamphlets, circular letters, and books on the subject. These documents in themselves form practically a diary of merger happenings, having been written within a week or two of the time when events took place. They cover many incidents that the writer himself would not remember today without refreshing his memory from these sources. The writer was also called in on the various lawsuits to work with the attorneys and to help furnish information on all aspects of Congregational history and of the merger proceedings. He sat at the attorney's table for twenty-three days of trial in the Cadman Church case. Again he sat with the attorneys through the thirty days of the federal lawsuit, both of which will be explained in further chapters. One of the author's books was written shortly after the Cadman lawsuit of 1949 and goes into great detail as to evidence presented in court and the testimony of leaders on both sides (*Destiny for Congregationalism*, 1953).

It shall be my purpose to give something of a sketch of some of the personalities who were involved, and this will be done in part by quotations from their letters and statements at critical times.

Perhaps I should state that part of my reason for setting forth this account is that various students in universities across the country have attempted to write doctor's theses or master's theses on the history of the merger controversy. They were not present at the time that events took place, and their knowledge is exceedingly partial and limited. Furthermore, there are many things I knew along the way but never publicized and which ought to be told. These would be lost unless I put them in the record.

I should explain my own background a little further by saying that I not only grew up in a Congregational household, but that my father became Executive Secretary of all the home missionary societies of the denomination, on the national level, in 1914. Then in 1921 he became the Executive Secretary of the National Council of the Congregational Churches, which in 1931 became the General Council of the Congregational Christian Churches, after many of those Christian Churches joined with the Congregational. Thus, during my boyhood I came to meet many of the leaders of the denomination and to know firsthand the executives of the national Boards. Incidentally, several of these executives were strongly opposed to the merger at the beginning, but were whipped into line by manipulations at General Council meetings.

I would like to mention also the purely volunteer status I had throughout all of the merger controversy. I was never employed, nor did I ever receive any financial remuneration for books or for speaking engagements on the merger; or for the work of writing pamphlets; or for my work sitting as an ecclesiastical "expert" through several lawsuits; or for my work with the Continuation Committee. I wrote always while employed full-time as a pastor. During the first part of the merger discussion, I was pastor of a 500-member church at New London, Connecticut, and carried on all of my duties as pastor in addition to whatever writing or speaking I was doing. After that I was pastor, from 1952 until 1971, of the First Congregational Church at Pontiac, Michigan—a church of more than 1,000 members with an almost hopeless building program on its hands when I went there. I managed to carry on all of my duties as pastor and to see the Pontiac church through the completion of a beautiful Gothic structure during the same ten years that I was most actively engaged in the writing of pamphlets and in the consultation with lawyers in New York. My financial remuneration was solely that of a pastor of churches.

This story will tell, as I said before, how the Congregational Christian Churches were talked into the United Church of Christ. I realize that in laying bare these facts I may also give an outline for procedures that might be used by the executives of other congregationally-organized denominations to subvert their free churches and take them into an authoritarian structure. But by the same token I am writing an account that should be a warning and a help to the members of such other free churches. It may help them avoid the pitfalls that ensnared the Congregationalists. It will be a shocking story. So much so, in fact, that when the Watergate scandals began to break in our national affairs, those of us who had been through the merger controversy, and had seen the tactics used and the cover-ups along the way, felt that Watergate was a pretty tame affair. The word *cover-up* could be used a hundred times or more with regard to the merger negotiations and manipulations. And for us there was no Judge Sirica before whom we could lay the facts; nor was there any power of subpoena by which we could compel the executives to answer questions under threat of the charge of perjury if they did not tell the truth.

The one word of warning that should be given to church members everywhere is: "Don't be taken in by the plea that you should trust your leaders."

The first pamphlet that I wrote and distributed regarding the merger bore the title, "Is the Merger Being Put Over on Us?" From that time on, I was told that my "biggest mistake" was in attacking the leaders. Yet I am content to let history speak on the issue of whether the merger was "put over" on the Congregationalists, and whether they were deceived into giving up their historic and heretofore inalienable right of freedom.

Let me now set the record straight on one more point before we get into the details of it. Not once in all of the merger negotiations did the leaders permit those who were critical of the plan to sit down with them, with the leaders of both denominations present, and have opportunity to make sure that the issues were being faced openly and honestly. I always had the feeling that if the right questions were asked, and answers insisted upon, the merger would have been dropped then and there. But the one thing that the leaders never permitted was an open confrontation, in any meaningful way, of the officials who were responsible for the actual plan of union and the articulate critics of the plan. No real opportunity was given to the opponents to question for themselves the leaders of both denominations to bring forth the underlying answers. For instance, at a very critical time in 1946, at the General Council meeting, a few leaders of the Evangelical and Reformed Church sat on the platform. The Council delegates had already been whipped into a frenzy of promerger hysteria. A single crucial question was addressed to the Evangelical and Reformed leaders. An involved and evasive answer was given (which we shall discuss later). The promerger majority accepted this confusing statement as a gesture of compromise and burst into loud applause. No opportunity was given to follow up with intelligent inquiry as to what the answer really meant, if anything, and that was the extent to which any confrontation was ever permitted.

Slowly, however, the truth leaked out, as this account will show. Almost always the truth was at first denied. Then, once it began to be admitted the implications would be twisted and contradicted with a barrage of explanations. Words that had betrayed the true meaning of the plan were changed and more evasive ones substituted. But in spite of all this, the truth would come out. It is there for all who are willing to look at it to see. A few plain and simple facts are enough to prove this.

The whole experience of this merger controversy boiled down to one of intellectual honesty and integrity. I do not mean this in the way that most people might think of it—namely, that the leaders did not, on the whole, mean well or that they did not believe what they were saying. I mean intellectual honesty in depth, where a person makes sure that he knows what he is talking about. I can recall using an illustration in one of my sermons almost fifty years ago. If a salesperson in a large department store said that a certain garment was made of silk, when in fact it was rayon, she would not have the kind of intellectual integrity that I am talking about, even if she honestly thought that it was silk or her manager had said that it was. When the Better Business Bureau checks upon a store like Marshall Field's in Chicago, it does not stop with someone's assertion that "I thought it was true." The sad thing in the whole merger affair was that most ministers and others who favored the merger spent precious little time checking up to see whether the things they were saying could be verified, or even whether they made sense. A store is held responsible if the goods it sells are not, in fact, what they were claimed to be. It is up to the store to make absolutely sure that it knows what it is talking about. This is the kind of intellectual integrity and intellectual honesty I am referring to in this book. In the merger discussions we found absolutely no way to hold anyone responsible, from the top leaders down to the average pastor and lay persons, for what they claimed were facts in the merger plan.

Twice in public debates I had state conference ministers claim that the courts had made certain decisions which I knew they had not. One claimed that the United States Supreme Court had declared the United Church of Christ to be Congregational. Actually the Supreme Court had never agreed to review any merger court case, and a refusal to hear a case is not a decision. Furthermore, no lower court had ever made such a judicial determination. The other conference minister claimed that Judge Dimock had made certain determinations. I knew Judge Dimock's decision backwards and forwards and had a copy right in my hand as I sat by him as he spoke. I asked him to show me the passage. He merely stuck his nose in the air and said, "It's there." But it wasn't. These are but two illustrations of the unfounded statements that were made throughout the whole merger controversy, and there were hundreds and hundreds of such misrepresentations that went unchecked.

I remember also one minister who had served two years as the moderator of our national body, the General Council. After having served that term, right at the height of the merger controversy, he admitted that he had favored the Basis of Union and had spoken in its behalf, but that he had never read the document himself. This sort of thing is appalling and almost unbelievable.

We move on now to a simple statement of the inescapable issue that is at the heart of the whole merger plan; it will show that churches joining the United Church did thereby compromise their freedom, and did give up the inalienable right to remain truly Congregational.

2

The Issue in a Nutshell

THE whole question of whether The United Church of Christ is Congregational or not, and whether the local Congregational Churches that joined it will continue indefinitely to be "Congregational," hinges upon the document known as the Constitution of the United Church of Christ. A constitution is, by definition, "the fundamental law" of the organization for which it is adopted. Now this particular constitution has many so-called guarantees or disclaimers in it, which say that certain provisions shall be "descriptive only" of the "free and voluntary relationships" between certain of the bodies within the United Church of Christ. The constitution also contains a paragraph, No. 21 as originally adopted, which has all sorts of assurances in it to the effect that Congregational Churches would continue to have certain freedoms they have previously enjoyed. But there is one catch in all of this, i.e., that the constitution can be amended without any action by the local church, or churches. This is the overriding consideration that would make null and void the so-called guarantees upon which many Congregationalists have relied implicitly.

The constitution provides that it can be amended by action of the General Synod, followed by the approval of two-thirds of the state conferences. Nothing has been specifically excluded from possible amendment. Anything that is now in the constitution can, presumably, be removed at a later time by a simple amendment. Or the General Synod and state conferences may vote to join another denomination and would then adopt a whole new Constitution for the new union, and treat it as an amendment to the present one.

Neither of these possibilities can be considered an idle conjecture. Attempts were made by some Congregationalists, at the time that the United Church Constitution was being written, to have provision made that certain parts of this constitution would not be subject to amendment but would stand permanently as inalienable rights. But that proposition was turned down. It is no secret that paragraph 21 has been repugnant to many people in the United Church, especially from the Evangelical and Reformed Church side. Some considered its adoption a sign of weakness and a compromise made just to get the union put through.

As for the possibility of another church merger, there are three possibilities that loom right now. The United Church magazine, *A.D.*, in its December 1976 issue, reports:

> Noting already existing common ministries, the Executive Council recommends that our General Synod next July begin formal talks with the Christian Church (Disciples of Christ) pointing toward a possible 1983 decision to unite.

A second possibility would be with the Presbyterians, with whom the United Church is already involved through joint publications, bookstores, etc.

The third possibility of a church union is the grandiose COCU scheme for uniting a large number of denominations and obliterating most of the distinguishing characteristics of each. This plan, in which ten denominations are now listed as participants, would pool the resources and membership of five or more local congregations of different backgrounds, different social strata, and ethnic groups into single parishes. All property would be owned by the overall church but managed by the "parishes," which would govern clusters of local congregations of worshippers. Ministers would be assigned by the bishops. Every vestige of Congregational freedom, autonomy, and self-government would be gone. The parish, made up of several worshipping congregations, would govern all of these worshipping groups. There would be no such thing as a local church owning its own property, electing its own officers, selecting its own minister, or deciding upon its own manner of worship.

The United Church of Christ has been steadfastly taking part in the development of this plan and in helping to keep it alive. This ambitious scheme started officially in 1962, and many years have gone into writing out plans and details for it. Early in the deliberations it was reported that a showdown had come on the question of the power of the bishops. It was reported in newspapers that the Methodist Church, which was the largest among the participants, gave the ultimatum that it would quit the deliberations unless it was agreed that bishops would appoint the ministers to their churches. That was agreed to by the participants, and the United Church of Christ has stayed right in there as a participating denomination.

In 1970 a tentative Plan of Union For The Church of Christ Uniting was sent out for study to the nine denominations then participating, including such old-line churches as the Methodist, Presbyterian, Episcopal, and Christian churches, and the United Church of Christ. When comments came back from these churches in 1972, some newspaper accounts reported that there was so much adverse comment on the plan that it was as good as dead. But the negotiators have persisted, and the United Church of Christ never reported the adverse reactions in any very forthright manner. Instead it spoke of a change of emphasis, which would seek to work from the ground up and to create union first on the local level, along lines set forth in the Plan.

Since 1972, the COCU Plan has continued to receive notices in United Church of Christ publications, although brief and infrequent. "Keeping You Posted" has carried quite a number of these. COCU has kept a low profile, and many people have supposed that it was no longer being seriously considered. Not so in official United Church of Christ circles, as the following recent announcement indicates. In the 1 December 1976 issue of "Keeping You Posted," we read:

COCU NEARS THEOLOGICAL CONSENSUS FOR UNION

The 13th plenary session of the Consultation on Church Union dealt with theological issues of church union and issued a document entitled "In Quest of a Church of Christ Uniting."
The theological statement, billed as an "emerging consen-

sus," is essentially a revision of the first seven chapters of the 1970 draft of the COCU Plan of Union. It will be made available to congregations late this year. Chapters dealing with controversial structural issues will not be reconsidered until after theological consensus is reached. . . .

The National Council of Community Churches was admitted as the tenth member of COCU, the first new addition since 1967.

In the light of the persistent and continuing support given by the United Church of Christ to the COCU plan, and now with the possible union with the Christian Church (Disciples of Christ), any thought that former Paragraph 21 (now Section 15) of the present United Church Constitution has lasting validity does seem naive, to say the least.

As I have said, the fact that the constitution of the United Church of Christ can be amended without the consent of the individual churches, means that the Congregational Churches that joined the United Church of Christ gave up their "inalienable" rights. It is the inalienable character of these rights that has been taken away, and that is really all-important—not the fact that temporarily the churches are being allowed to continue more or less as they have been in the past.

Besides this power of amendment there are many other provisions in this constitution and its bylaws that should have disturbed any Congregationalist who read it carefully. Most of the argument over the proposed union centered simply upon the autonomy of the local church. Nothing was said about the right of private judgment by the individual member—a right that had been stressed and reemphasized over and over again among Congregationalists. Furthermore the right of the minister to complete freedom was also overridden in the discussions, even though the subject did come up. One attempt was made at the time that the Basis of Union was given its final revision to "guarantee" the freedom of the ministers. But a forthright statement on this was watered down to say that the rights of the ministers were "presupposed." Then, when the Constitution of the United Church of Christ was written, the subject was omitted entirely, and instead a whole series of "recommended procedures" regarding ministers was adopted.

Thus we see, in the bylaws and in the constitution itself, provisions for the installation of all pastors, which in itself means that the calling of a pastor must be approved by the local Association. We find also a whole string of "recommended procedures" by which a church is to report immediately to its state conference whenever its pastor resigns and is then to receive from the state conference a list of ministers recommended to it and from which it is supposed to make its choice.

To be sure, there are contradictory provisions in the constitution, such as a statement in Section 15 that a church is free to call or dismiss its minister in any way that it chooses. But this gets at the problem from only one side. As far as the minister is concerned, he will be in disfavor (and he knows it) if he accepts a call to a church without going through the "recommended procedures." If he comes from another denomination, he is supposed to get a "privilege of call" before accepting a call to a local church. All this in spite of the fact that the constitution, paragraph 21, says that a church is free to call or dismiss its minister in any way that it chooses.

It should be easy to see that the higher-ups in the United Church of Christ have their finger on the minister of the local church—just as they do, for that matter, in the Methodist church. Through the minister they have indirect pressure upon each local church as well. Who, then, can say that the local church really has the freedom which it formerly enjoyed in the Congregational fellowship?

But again, the one determining issue is this overall constitution, and the fact that it can be amended by the General Synod and two-thirds of the state conferences, without consent of the local churches. And do not overlook this important legal technicality: any church that approved the Constitution of the United Church of Christ did thereby approve this procedure for its amendment.

It was always difficult, even impossible, to get this sort of critical information to the average member of the Congregational Christian Churches before he voted. The officials certainly did not give the churches warnings of what was involved—like the "warnings" posted in New England villages when a town meeting has a proposal before it. It is doubtful that most Congregational Church members ever saw a copy of the constitution. If they did see it the chances are that it was far too involved to think the matter through.

Under the present circumstances, with paragraph 21 still in force as Section 15, the churches would have the alternative of voting themselves out of the United Church of Christ if an amendment were proposed that would obliterate their present rights. But they would have to know about the impending change and would have to act quickly. They could get out, and that is all that they could do to protect themselves and to retain Congregational prerogatives they had supposed were "guaranteed" to them.

But most church members might never know that sweeping amendments were pending. The churches are supposed to be informed of any proposed amendments to the United Church constitution, even if they cannot vote on them. But often such information goes to the minister, or possibly to the minister and the church clerk. A conspiracy of silence, or just plain carelessness and indifference, would mean that the members themselves would never know that an amendment was in the offing. The rights they think they carried with them into the United Church of Christ could disappear in just a matter of a year or two. Silence on the part of the pastors and other church officers during the time that the amendment was pending would mean that the members would not even know that anything had happened, possibly for years to come.

If anyone believes that this matter of an overall constitution was not part of a carefully laid plan, which was pressed with great determination over many years, they should read carefully the rest of this story. From the first, the Evangelical and Reformed Church leaders were hard bargainers and they knew what they wanted. They made it absolutely evident from time to time that they were demanding certain things. One of them was this matter of the overall constitution. Another was the matter of the installation of pastors, which meant that no minister would be received as a pastor of a church without approval by an association or conference. As a compromise of sorts, paragraph 21 was finally put into the constitution, even though it contradicts many of the recommended procedures that appear in other places. While Congregationalists were encouraged to believe that this paragraph guaranteed their Congregationalism and "was all they needed to know," Evangelical and Reformed people viewed it differently, as witness the following.

Dr. James E. Wagner expressed himself on the meaning of paragraph 21 in a little book, *Perspectives for a Local Church Officer*, published in 1965 by the United Church Press. Dr. Wagner was president of the Evangelical and Reformed Church and then one of the original co-presidents of the United Church of Christ in the interim before the constitution was adopted. He was also one of the chief bargainers for the Evangelical and Reformed Church during the final negotiations on the union. He summarizes the meaning of paragraph 21 by taking it in the context of the paragraph that immediately precedes it and the one which follows it, paragraphs 20 and 22. He heads his discussion by referring to "where autonomy and obligation meet." Paragraph 20 speaks of the "god-given" responsibility of the local church for the United Church of Christ and its work, and also of the "god-given responsibility" of the denomination for the "well-being" of its local churches. Paragraph 22 says that actions, or decisions or advice emanating from the General Synod, a Conference, or an Association, should "be held in highest regard by every local church." From these two paragraphs, one preceding and one following paragraph 21, Dr. Wagner speaks of paragraph 21 as being "hedged about." He further states that it might be argued by an "irresponsible" person that a local church could, under paragraph 21, "do just as it pleases." But, says Dr. Wagner, "Nothing could be farther from the truth."

This statement by Dr. Wagner is only one of many in the long history of the merger in which the Evangelical and Reformed Church leaders made plain their sentiments. They did not believe in the congregational form of government. They did not believe that it had any future. They considered their way better and argued that the United Church should choose the "better way." And there were, quite obviously, some in the top Congregational Christian leadership who agreed with them. The problem was to devise a document that would win a favorable vote among the Congregational Christian Churches. However, right up to the final decision to go ahead with this union, at a crucial meeting in October 1954, there was a deadlock over this issue of the overall constitution.

Along the way leaders in the Congregational ranks tried to explain the constitution away. Witnesses for General Council in the Cadman trial (November 1949–January 1950) testified with monotonous regularity that "there will be no Constitution for the United Church as a whole, but only for the General Synod, Boards and instrumentalities." Later, when the General Council at Claremont in 1952 recommended the writing of a constitution prior to going on with the union, the vote limited this as in the testimony at the Cadman trial, to a "Constitution for the General Synod" of the United Church.

Both the testimony at court and the Claremont Resolution greatly disturbed the leaders of the Evangelical and Reformed Church, and in published statements they kept hammering away against them. They wanted to know if the representations made to the courts were "binding" on them, and on the future United Church. A higher sense of honor would have ruled out such a question altogether. Similarly, they wanted to know what the General Council meant (as if they did not know) by requesting that the constitution be written for the "General Synod." These issues came to a head finally in a meeting of the two executive committees of the two denominations on 13 October 1954. For many hours the realities of the situation were laid bare. Persons present have said that it looked during all that time as though the merger were dead.* Dr. Wagner had read a very forthright statement that laid the issues on the line. But then, amidst the gloom, someone suggested that they all have a period of prayer together. Following their prayers together, an Evangelical and Reformed leader asked why they should let "little things" stand in the way. So the two groups issued a joint statement declaring that "Christ calls us to mission and to unity." The "little things" of course were the things for which Congregationalism has always stood and which the

---

*Dr. Howell D. Davies and I sat just outside the conference room and received almost hourly reports of what was going on from Mrs. Claude Kennedy, a member of our Executive Committee.

leaders of the Congregational Christian churches had promised their people would be preserved. This was really the final sellout. Everything after that came pretty much as a matter of course and as an anticlimax. The issue was the matter of an overall constitution, which would naturally have to provide a method for its own future amendment.

The Congregationalists had never had an overall constitution. Each local church had its own constitution and was always a complete legal entity in itself. Each district association had its own constitution, and so did each state conference. None of these were expected to be in conformity with a national constitution. (One exception to this, which has misled some people, might be the fact that the General Council made its own rules as to how delegates would be elected to it. The associations and conferences might then include in their rules provisions that conformed to those of the General Council. But this obviously was a case of the General Council's controlling its own affairs and setting forth the terms of its own existence. It was not a case of the General Council's attempting to dictate or control the nature, purposes, or operation of any associations or conferences).

Besides the final showdown on 13 October 1954 there had been many previous ones, on which we shall report in further chapters. The issues were essentially the same all along. But while many Congregationalists fought valiantly along the way, it was the Evangelical and Reformed members who always managed to come out on top—with the help, of course, of some highly placed Congregational leaders who were willing to see the end of Congregationalism or at least to see it "watered down."

A much fuller discussion of this issue of a constitution may be found in my 1954 book, entitled, *Constitution for Congregationalism?* Likewise much of the testimony of General Council witnesses in the Cadman trial is included in my longer book, *Destiny for Congregationalism*, published in 1953. Both books were published by Modern Publishers, Oklahoma City.

Copies of hundreds of pamphlets and photocopies of many important letters written during the merger controversy are in the archives of the Congregational Library in Boston, as are also complete records of the Cadman lawsuit and the federal suit, Burlington Church and others v. The Evangelical and Reformed Church, and others.

As we get into more of the detail of the merger's history, and as we present documentation from important letters and pronouncements of the leaders on both sides, remember the simple fact that we have set forth in this chapter. The real issue is the overall constitution and the fact that it can be amended without consent of the local churches. Churches that went into the union have, to all intents and purposes, signed a "blank check." They can now be taken into other mergers without having the right to vote on such propositions. It was approval of this constitution that meant the end of the "inalienable rights" of Congregational Churches that went into the United Church of Christ. Meanwhile, paragraph 21 has already been subject to amendment and is now section 15 with the same wording.

POSTSCRIPT TO THE ABOVE

All of the foregoing was written several years prior to a decision on the Groton Congregational Church, Groton, Connecticut. Trial began on August 27, 1979. The decision and judgment was handed down on June 25, 1980.

It must therefore be admitted that arguments similar to those set forth in this chapter were presented during the trial by the Plaintiffs' attorney. I was also put on the stand and questioned directly by Judge Hendel on some of these matters.

Regarding the many so-called recommended procedures in the Constitution and Bylaws of the United Church of Christ, Judge Hendel asked if these were absolutely binding. In one case I answered that it was more a matter of pressure. In another instance I remarked they were not binding at present but might be made so by future amendments. He then questioned me on the Constitution and its possible amendment.

I now report, therefore, that Judge Hendel made a finding that no church is compelled to follow the recommended procedures:

Based upon all the evidence during the trial and the arguments of law made by the parties on the merits of the present action, the court holds that the United Church of Christ does not have the ability to bind the church or to demand contributions from the church in violation of the charter of the church. (See also Document 32 in the Appendix)

As regards the Constitution and its possible amendment Judge Hendel reviewed provisions of paragraph 21 (now listed as Section 15), and also provisions affecting possible amendments. Judge Hendel then held;

> Based upon the clear provisions and intent of the United Church of Christ Constitution, the court cannot accept the plaintiff's argument that the United Church of Christ Constitution hypothetically could be amended in the future to affect the property or inherent autonomy of a local church.

In suggesting that the constitution might be amended in the future, I had referred to the section in the Constitution referring explicitly to amendments, paragraph 88 in the edition before the court. The judge, however, quoted first from paragraph 21 and then from the section stating the powers of the General Synod, with certain explicit limitations against any abridgment of the autonomy of Conferences, Associations and churches. This statement limiting the powers of the General Synod precedes the provision on amending the Constitution and by-laws. (See Appendix 32)

From Judge Hendel's decision it would appear that the General Synod could not even take up or pass upon any amendment that would affect the autonomy of the Conferences, Associations, or churches. This could have extremely far-reaching consequences.

How, under Judge Hendel's decision, can the United Church of Christ continue in the negotiations of the Consultation on Church Union? Many years ago the Consultation agreed under pressure from the United Methodist Church that Bishops would appoint all the ministers. This would certainly violate provisions of paragraph 21 and the autonomy of the local church. So also would other suggested provisions for churches to turn over their properties to larger parishes and be controlled, as mere worshipping congregations, by officers elected on the parish level. How could the United Church of Christ possibly continue to negotiate with other COCU members, in good faith, when faced with the decision and judgment of Judge Hendel?

Whether the officials of the United Church of Christ

can find some way around this decision is a matter on which I would not hazard a guess. The United Church of Christ was made a party to this suit, against its will. I was present several years ago when a motion was being argued that would bring the United Church of Christ in as a party. It would seem that being a party to the suit the judgment stands as a bar to such actions as Judge Hendel has decided against. To be sure, this is a decision in a single state and in a lower court. But how can the United Church of Christ appeal the decision when it has *won* the case and when its own attorneys used the same arguments and cited the same passages as Judge Hendel? Or, again, how could the United Church of Christ amend its Constitution so as to affect all the churches except those in Connecticut? Worst of all, even the attempt to obliterate the safeguards for churches, Conferences and Associations would show bad faith and a lack of integrity on the part of United Church of Christ.

Certain larger aspects of this picture deserve careful evaluation.

This court did not get into the larger question of the overall polity of the United Church of Christ. The lawyers and the judge all endeavored from the start to avoid larger issues which might make a very lengthy and involved trial. There was no pretense of comparing congregational and presbyterian polities, or even to go into the nature of the former Evangelical and Reformed Church.

It would be quite impossible to claim that Judge Hendel declared the United Church of Christ to be Congregational. The most that he declared was to the effect that a local church could not be *bound* by rules and regulations made by the United Church of Christ. At one point he emphasized that the church could, by rejecting the assistance of the United Church of Christ, remain "independent." This is a far cry from a Congregational Church enjoying the wonderful fellowship of its former wider bodies, themselves dedicated to the Congregational ideals and concept of a free church, each under the direct headship of Christ.

We are including in our Appendix, as Document 33, a Bill of Rights sponsored at several stages of its development by Rev. Henry David Gray. Dr. Gray was a member of the Committee on Free Church Polity and Unity and chaired its subcommittee on polity, doing a tremendous amount of research and study. No other study shows with such complete documentation behind it what real Congregationalism was. The Bill of Rights here presented reflects all this background. Most significantly it is also the statement presented to, and presumably by, the chairman of the United Church of Christ subcommittee for the writing of Paragraph 21. A comparison of the two shows how much of the spirit and real purpose of Congregationalism was left out of paragraph 21 and the Constitution as a whole.

To say that a church is still "free" simply because it can still defy, reject, and resist the pressures of higher officials and rules laid out systematically for its behavior, and to suffer the ostracism inevitable for such defiance, is a pathetic commentary on the United Church of Christ or its claim to preserving the Congregationalism of any of its member churches.

I should add to the foregoing that I had always been perfectly aware that paragraph 21 had said that the autonomy of the local church could not be abridged "now or at any future time." But the very fact that the leaders of the United Church of Christ had carried on participation in the Consultation on Church Union for many years, as I have discussed previously in this chapter, showed no apparent regard for the express limitations set forth in the Constitution. This was enough to convince me that they believed they could either ignore paragraphs 21 and 50 or could amend them away. After all, the Constitution of our old General Council carried over express limitations against acting as a legislative or judicial body. So there was no right to approve the Basis of Union. Considering the way that courts ignored such issues, how were we to know that one judge would, finally, pull up the reins and place strict construction on expressed conditions laid down in the United Church Constitution and hold church leaders to the letter of the printed word as Judge Hendel has done?

I might add further that I do not believe that the United Church of Christ Constitution has the right or power to say that the autonomy of the local church "is modifiable by its own action." This is tantamount to saying that a local church is free to change from one kind of church to any other kind at will. This is contrary to long-standing legal precedents. The Groton Church case could have been decided in favor of the Plaintiffs if it could have been proved that the church had lost its power to act independently—albeit that such independence must often be exercised in defiance of pressures coming from officials.

3

Some of the Principal Personalities

THE one individual most responsible for pushing the union through was undoubtedly Dr. Douglas Horton, Minister of the General Council of the Congregational Christian Churches. He was the one who started writing about the union in articles in the national magazine *Advance* as early as June 1942. It was he who "saved" the merger on several occasions when it would otherwise have been dropped. He was certainly a spokeman and a leading architect of the plan. According to one account, which I heard from a member of the joint committee that drew up the Basis of Union, Douglas Horton was elected secretary of the group and sat with a portable typewriter on his lap, typing out the individual passages of the Basis of Union after the subjects had been discussed by the joint committee. If that is true, and I believe it is, then the actual phrasing and wording of the Basis of Union at least passed through Douglas Horton, if indeed they were not created in large part by him.

The title *Minister of the General Council* is one which Dr. Horton insisted upon when he took the position as head of the General Council. He was in fact my father's immediate successor; but the position was previously known as *Executive Secretary*. The former title suggested that the office was one devoted primarily to carrying out the purposes and directives of the General Council.

After the title was changed to *Minister*, Dr. Horton used to tell people that the word *bishop* and the word *minister* were both possible translations of a single Greek word used in the New Testament, thereby more or less equating the two.

There will be many incidents in our story as it unfolds that will reveal the personality of Dr. Horton in much fuller detail; but in large measure the responsibility for things as they developed was his.

Next in importance was Dr. Truman Douglass, who became the head of the combined missionary societies known as The Board of Home Missions. According to his own testimony during the Cadman trial, the first actual suggestion for this merger came through himself and Dr. Samuel Press of the Evangelical and Reformed Church. At that time Dr. Douglass was pastor of a church in St. Louis and had become acquainted with the Evangelical and Reformed men in the area. It was out of that relationship that a telegram was sent to the General Council meeting at Beloit in 1938 suggesting a possible union. But the telegram arrived too late to be considered at that meeting.

As head of the Board of Home Missions, Dr. Douglass was the one who could exercise the most clout from the standpoint of organizational power. There were over 1,000 churches that had grant mortgages from the Church Building Society, one of the subsidiaries of the Board of Home Missions. The future pensions of ministers were under the Annuity Fund, which was another subdivision of the Board. Despite official denials of any such intentions in some later actions of the General Council, the suggestion was made at various times by Dr. Horton and others that a minister would lose his active status in the Annuity Fund if he did not go along with the merger. In like manner, at least one widely circulated publication sent out by the General Council indicated that churches with grant mortgages would have to pay up, with back interest from the time that the grants were made if they did not go into the United Church.

It was under the Board of Home Missions, too, that the Office of Communications was set up, and this became the chief propaganda arm for the merger, sending out innumerable press releases to give the proposal a favorable public image and create the impression that everything was all settled long before it was. This agency also undertook during the last few years of decision-making to send out a mailing every two weeks to hundreds of members in local churches with propaganda in behalf of the union.

Next we might take the name of Dr. John Scotford, who was the editor of the Congregational national magazine *Advance*. He played a very important role in the early stages of the merger discussion. We will have more to say about how he did it, but in all probability he was one of those persons who made it possible to stir up a mob psychology at the 1946 General Council meeting and prejudice the whole future course of events. It was that meeting that whipped many state superintendents and several national secretaries into line.

On the Evangelical and Reformed side, the top leaders at the beginning included Dr. Louis W. Goebel, who was president of the Evangelical and Reformed Church through the time of the historic 1948 General Council meeting at Oberlin, Ohio. Certainly as important, if not more so, was the first president of the Evangelical and Reformed Church, Dr. George W. Richards. He was, during the formative stages of the negotiations, head of the Evangelical and Reformed committee on the union. He knew what he wanted and did not hesitate to tell some of us that he had no use for the Congregational form of government. There were times when he said that his "ardor had died down" for the union. But the next thing we knew he came up with what he called a *tertium quid*, or a "third way" out of a seemingly insoluble dilemma.

Next on the Evangelical and Reformed side was Dr. James E. Wagner, who became the president of the Evangelical and Reformed Church after Dr. Louis Goebel. He was, in my estimation, a realist and was more inclined to "call a spade a spade" than anyone else in the top echelon on either side—so much so that he came nearer to wrecking the union plan than anyone else. But actually all that he was doing was the sort of thing that the head of a labor union might do during contract negotiations. He carried on a tough line and then would seem to relax a little to permit some sort of compromise that actually would not rob him of his ultimate objectives.

Now we consider the attorney for the General Council of the Congregational Christian Churches, Mr. Loren N. Wood. Mr. Wood had been at Carleton College at the same time as my father, and both were members of the same literary society. He himself told me that it was my father who coached him on some of his first debates at Carleton. I am sure that he was called in at the time that the Board of Home Missions was set up to be the attorney for the General Council in working out the structural and legal details of forming the overall Board. Having done so he was the natural choice as a lawyer to defend the General Council and its Boards at the time that the Cadman Church case was brought in Brooklyn. Mr. Wood worked out a defense of the plan of union that claimed that the United Church of Christ would not be an invasion of any Congregational principle and that its structure would be essentially Congregational. He also injected a note of independence for the boards, and the defense witnesses in the Cadman trial were apparently coached to say that the Congregational Churches had no interests in the boards they had founded, and that the boards were not Congregational in any legally binding sense, but could work for churches of any denomination. Incidentally, his own church, at the time that he was on its Board of Trustees, finally voted not to go into the United Church of Christ.

Dr. William F. Frazier was the first head of the Board of Home Missions after the seven previous missionary societies had been brought together. Then he became the treasurer of the Board. He was often thought to be the brains of the legal defense in the Cadman trial. It was he who most emphatically insisted that there would be no constitution for the United Church of Christ as such, but only for the General Synod and the Boards and Instrumentalities. His rationale was that the interpretations of the Basis of Union that had been adopted at Oberlin in 1948 had said that the Constitution would be descriptive only of "the free and voluntary" relationships of the churches, conferences, and associations. By definition, said Dr. Frazier, a constitution must be a governing document. Therefore some provisions of the Interpretations made it less than an overall constitution. What we shall see as we trace the events as they transpired is that this kind of argument proved entirely unacceptable to the Evangelical and Reformed Church leaders.

Other officials of various parts of the Board of Home Missions were Dr. Frank Scribner of the Annuity Fund and Mr. William K. Newman of the Church Building Society.

Both were witnesses in the Cadman trial. Dr. Scribner was also a frequent speaker and debater in behalf of the merger. I debated against him at an association meeting in Concord, New Hampshire.

Another person who featured in the Cadman trial was Dr. Wilhelm Pauck, who was put on the stand as one who had been on the committee that drew up the Basis of Union. He was presented as an authority on Congregationalism, even though he told the court that he had been born in Germany and was a member there of the Evangelical Church of East Prussia. He first learned about Congregationalism, he said, by studies at the University of Berlin. He was a professor at Chicago Theological Seminary, and the first time that I heard the word *ecumenical* was when I was sitting in as an auditor in one of his courses. The impression that I got as he used the word *ecumenical* was that there was some very special aura to it. His application was in terms of the early church councils. He seemed to take the attitude that decisions made by the early councils, "before the church was divided," had a very special authority. This is similar to the attitude of the Roman Catholic Church, which apparently considers the actions of these early bodies as almost a third Testament of the Bible. His testimony on the stand in the Cadman trial, as we shall show later, reduced the principles of Congregationalism to the point of the ridiculous.

Another on our list of prominent leaders was Dr. Ferdinand Blanchard, who was Moderator of the General Council in 1944 when the first presentation of a definite plan of union was up for discussion. Immediately afterward he was made chairman of the Committee on Interchurch Relations, which was handling the details of the merger. In that capacity he gave some very dogmatic answers as to the meaning of the Basis of Union and how "Congregational" it was.

Dr. Ronald Bridges, a layman, will come into our story at two or three very critical points. He first made his prominence in the denomination as a very gifted speaker for men's groups, and he was made head of the Laymen's Fellowship. Then he was chosen Moderator of the General Council and presided at the 1946 meeting in Grinnell, Iowa. At that meeting a serious question had been raised ahead of time as to whether some fast move would be made by the merger proponents, catching the denomination off guard, and voting the merger through then and there— before the plan was finalized and when no one knew that such a move was possible. Dr. Bridges as moderator pulled a very neat trick, which almost no one knew about and which prevented this from happening. Both he and various members of the Executive Committee felt that it would be a mistake to let the merger be rushed through prematurely. But two years later, when the merger plan was bogged down by some other difficulties, it was Ronald Bridges who pulled another trick, this time paving the way for the Oberlin Council to pull the same kind of surprise and vote approval of the Basis of Union, even though the Executive Committee had previously recommended that no action be taken at that meeting because the vote on the Basis of Union had fallen so very far short of the recommended percentages. Details on both meetings will be given later.

Dr. Albert W. Palmer succeeded Ronald Bridges as Moderator of the General Council and presided at the 1948 General Council at Oberlin, where the delegates not only approved the Basis of Union but also adopted a set of Interpretations that they claimed were in keeping with the Basis of Union. These Interpretations came solely from the Congregational side and had not been acted upon by the Evangelical and Reformed Church. Dr. Goebel was present and said something to the effect that he felt the Evangelical and Reformed Church leaders would approve them. Exactly the opposite took place a few months later. Confusion and trouble followed for many years. And the constitution that was finally adopted deviates in many crucial respects from both the Interpretations and the Basis of Union.

Before we give a picture of some of the opponents of the merger, it may prove helpful to mention the names of some prominent persons who either kept a neutral position, or who tried to form a bridge between the two sides and to exercise a reconciling influence. The list would include: Dr. Frederick L. Fagley who was the Associate Secretary of the General Council; Judge Meier Steinbrink, who heard the Cadman lawsuit; Dr. Alfred Grant Walton, who drew up the original "Comments on the Basis of Union," which was the forerunner of the Oberlin Interpretations; Dr. Howard Conn, who was opposed to the union, then went along with the *Comments*, but finally wound up against the union. Dr. Henry David Gray, whom we always considered opposed to the merger seemed to meet with promerger people through the time of the 1956 Council, trying to form a bridge of understanding. He was also a very important member of the Committee of Free Church Polity and Unity. He was, he has told me, the original author of the former paragraph 21 of the United Church Constitution, which he had been asked to submit as a suggestion of what the opponents wanted. He included in the paragraph, however, one provision that was omitted: the right of a local church to ordain its own minister, a right Congregational churches had always enjoyed in the past. He was one who urged that certain things, including what he had written, be in a preamble or otherwise placed so that it would not be subject to future amendment.

Dr. Gaius Glenn Atkins assiduously avoided getting into the conflict (his age at the time would be excuse enough), but he wrote the little history of Congregationalism, *Adventure in Liberty,* in an attempt to shore up the love and respect of Congregationalists for their heritage.

Dr. L. Wendell Fifield, pastor of the Plymouth Church of the Pilgrims in Brooklyn, became the chairman of the Committee on Free Church Polity and Unity. He was a member of the Executive Committee of the General Council, and did not become an active participant in the antimerger movement, although he did become a sharp critic of some of the procedures that took place after the 1954 meetings. The Committee on Free Church Polity and Unity came (1950–1954) during a lull in the merger controversy, when the original court decision in the Cadman case had stopped the merger dead in its tracks. In a very sweeping and precise condemnation of the merger plan, Justice Meier Steinbrink had enjoined the Congregational bodies from going ahead. His was the only court that ever accepted the merger question for a trial on the merits, and he was the only judge who ever heard testimony or wrote a decision on the merits of the plan for union. Higher courts later threw his decision out on the technical grounds that the courts could not take such a case unless it was proved that a property interest was involved. They decided that the Cadman Church had no property interest in the General Council or its funds and therefore reversed Justice Steinbrink, throwing the case out of court and making it of no legal effect. But they did not reverse any of the findings on the merger plan, because, as they said, they did not consider any of the ecclesiastical questions or matters of polity.

It was four years before the General Council was free to go ahead again, and in that cooling-off period there was considerable desire for a healing of the breach in the fellowship and for a reaching of hands across from pro-merger and antimerger sides. Dr. Fifield was responsible for having suggested a careful study of Congregationalism, and of what part it could rightfully play in the ecumenical movement. He was named chairman of a committee of twenty-one persons, which then met for four years, with at least two meetings a year of the full committee, each meeting lasting several days.

One of the above names deserves additional comment at this time in order to understand many of the events that followed and something of the moral support I received along the way during the long and bitter merger controversy. Dr. Frederick L. Fagley was an exceedingly colorful individual with a tremendous capacity for work and a gifted personality with a brilliant mind, all behind a seemingly commonplace exterior and homey manner. He told me that he had been the private secretary to the political boss of Ohio before he entered the ministry, and he had some experience in the Methodist denomination. He was such a competent typist that he said he had known only one secretary who could keep up with him, and I have known him to go out before breakfast to bang out 100 letters on his typewriter in a little cabin in the woods back of his Sunapee cottage. He was the man who handled the business details of the General Council meetings and knew how to get along with head waiters and all the other functionaries of big hotels and convention centers. Within the denomination he was known as the "Jim

Farley" of the fellowship because of his tremendous acquaintance with people and his knowledge of what was going on in all parts of the denomination.

As head of the Department of Evangelism and Devotional Life, he wrote some very down-to-earth books on how a minister builds a church through the steady processes of "parish evangelism." He was coauthor with Dr. Gaius Glenn Atkins of the *History of American Congregationalism* published in 1942. It was he who finally persuaded Dr. Gaius Glenn Atkins to write the choice little book *Adventure In Liberty,* so useful with pastors' classes and for new church members. He also had Dr. Atkins prepare each year, from 1933 to 1946 the devotional booklet, "Fellowship of Prayer."

During his long tenure as Associate Secretary of the General Council, Dr. Fagley set up many seminars for Commissions of the General Council, and some of these were held at Lake Sunapee in one of the large hotels that were there then. I was privileged to sit in on several of these as an onlooker.

My father was elected general secretary in 1921, and shortly afterward Dr. Fagley became his associate. In 1924 father built a cottage on Lake Sunapee in order to be near Dr. Fagley, so that the two of them could have frequent conferences together during the summers. When I finished my freshman year at college, I came to Sunapee for the first time and spent the first night at Dr. Fagley's home. In the years that ensued, my contacts with Dr. Fagley were many and of very deep significance. While I was a student at the seminary, he pressed into my hands a copy of Karl Barth's work, *The Word of God and the Word of Man.* After I had read a little of it, I indicated to him that I did not have much use for that kind of loose theological mumbo-jumbo, with its careless use of words. But I can still see the meaningful way in which he looked at me and said, "You read it!" I knew there must be something back of his insistence, and I read it. But I did not come to accept Barth's point of view. I was, however, deeply grateful in years to come for having gotten this background on what later became an important part of the theological atmosphere with which I had to contend during the time of my ministry. Little did I know that Dr. Horton, who was the translator of this book by Barth, would figure so prominently in the affairs of my life. Whether Dr. Fagley sensed that something was afoot that I ought to know, in terms of our own denomination, I cannot guess.

Dr. Fagley used to gather together, for each General Council session, a group of a dozen or fifteen younger ministers to act as ushers at the meetings, as errand boys, and to serve in various other capacities. I became part of his "team" at the 1929 National Council meeting in Detroit and again in 1934 and 1936.

In the historic 1934 Oberlin meeting, when the Council for Social Action was set up, I was assigned to Rev. Herbert D. Rugg, who was responsible for the daily bulletin that reported all the events of the previous day. I was the "runner" who took the copy to the printer, read proof, and later hurried back with the printed copies and saw that they were distributed—this among many other duties. While at that 1934 Council I saw the rabble-rousing techniques employed by the proponents of the Social Action movement, who literally tore the whole Council program apart in order to get their way. I never expected to see grown men crying, with tears streaming down their cheeks, insisting that they could not support the mission programs of the denomination unless they could have this new and radical agency, the Council for Social Action, set up. That should have prepared me for some of the techniques later used on the merger.

In 1936, at the South Hadley Council meeting, I was again on Dr. Fagley's staff. In all of these meetings I got to know a great many of the leaders in the denomination.

Back in 1928 I had found myself questioning the relationship that I might have in the ministry. I felt irritated and out of place with much of the conventionalism that was so prominent at the seminary—not among the professors, but among most of the young fellows studying for the ministry, who were trying to put on preacher airs. In those days this involved wearing spats, carrying a cane, and wearing black velvet on the lapels of their topcoats. These outward signs were insignificant compared to the conventionalism of their thinking. Any time that the professors gave us something new to think about, and especially if it was something most church people never knew, they would be inclined to lay down their pencils and look aimlessly out of the window. I, on the other hand, felt that the professors were giving us "great stuff." I had come to wonder if an ordination council would turn me down if I came out full-fledged in support of the finest insights of the Old Testament and New Testament scholars I had known. I communicated my uneasiness to Dr. Fagley, and told him that I wouldn't want to finish a seminary education and then be rejected. His reply was something like this: "Well, that's easy. Just go ahead and get ordained now, and then you'll know." He also proceeded to guide me, step by step, through the process. Remember that he was the head of the department on the ministry, among other official positions, and it was the preachment of the fellowship that only college and seminary graduates should be permitted ordination. But he told me how to go about having the Newport Church in New Hampshire call the Council (for which I typed the letters at his direction). I discussed the matter with my father, who did not express disapproval.

Incidentally, many prominent Congregationalists summered around Lake Sunapee at that time, and these ministers were also invited to be members of the Association's Ecclesiastical Council, including my father, Rev. Archibald Black, who preached my ordination sermon, my home pastor, Rev. Warren Wheeler Pickett of the Church in the Gardens, Long Island, New York, and seven or eight other leading clergymen, among whom was Dr. Luther Weigle, who had just been elected Dean of Yale Divinity School.

Previously, during that summer and the year before, Dr. Fagley had sent me out doing summer supply preaching, twice in quite a large church. He let me get a real taste of being a preacher, and probably he had received reports on how I was doing. I had majored in public speaking at Carleton College, and I preached the first Sunday out of college at my home church in Forest Hills, on Long Island, New York. The preaching came easily enough. Dr. Fagley had become like a second father to me, and that relationship continued throughout the merger struggle. I frequently met with him at his home, or had lunch with him in a restaurant near the office, besides our many visits at Lake Sunapee.

Dr. Fagley told me more than once that he considered it his duty to help anyone on either side of the controversy who needed information, in so far as he was free to give it. He tried officially to maintain a neutral attitude. He made two or three important contributions to the merger literature, as we shall see. I realized that he was "sworn to secrecy" on some things, and I did not try to press him on these. (Not infrequently persons at Executive Committee meetings were told that certain matters were "privileged" and not to be divulged to anyone.)

In the summer of 1945 I indicated that I wanted to start writing against the merger. He told me that it was no use. He said that he had never been in favor of the 1931 union with the Christian denomination. He said very pessimistically that he had lived long enough to know that some things in this world you just can't stop, even if you'd like to. Nevertheless, when I did start writing, he sent me a list of one hundred names of important people who, he said, should receive my material, and he sent me a contribution (among the first) to help me with postage. And many were the notes and letters of encouragement which he sent me after that.

Years later, during his final illness, Dr. Fagley said to me "Malcolm, you have a lot of friends." I knew that I had a good many bitter enemies, and that I had friends in the antimerger group. Perhaps I passed his remark off too lightly. He reached out his hand to me and with a tight squeeze and great feeling, he said most emphatically, "Malcolm, you have a lot of friends." This was the last time I saw him, and, if I remember correctly, it was only a matter of weeks before he died. His funeral, as with my father, was held in South Church, Newport, New Hampshire, where I had been ordained.

Let me mention now some of the persons opposed to the merger who figured prominently in national affairs. I shall not attempt to give the list of antimerger people who were leaders in various parts of the country, but I do want to identify those who enter into our story on the history of the merger procedures from a national standpoint.

I have sometimes been singled out as the original opponent to the merger, but this certainly is not true. Dr. Theodore M. Shipherd was in there fighting long before I saw the light. He was a member of the Executive Committee of the General Council at the time that the first activities were going on behind the scenes, getting ready for the original proposition on the union. He and Rev. Alexander H. Abbott were pastors in Norwich, Connecticut, a few miles from my pastorate in New London. Those two men headed up nationally the Associates in Reading, a group interested in getting ministers to read more serious books. Our county ministers' association met frequently with them. I had found myself sometimes at odds with Dr. Shipherd on some of the books we read, and so, when he first injected some comments about a merger in the offing, I was more or less bored. Mr. Abbott chimed in once about the differences in doctrine and theology between the Evangelical and Reformed Church and ourselves. But it still made little impression on me. Both of these men, however, came to be my very close friends and associates in my merger work. Dr. Shipherd gave me, during the early years of the merger controversy, the inside story of what was going on. After I started my writing in October 1945, Mr. Abbott spent many hours with me, going over every document I was writing, paragraph by paragraph and even down to individual words. He was a brilliant scholar and very well versed in theological and philosophical questions.

Three men should be mentioned together, for they were leaders in the Cadman Church, which brought the first lawsuit: Mr. Raymond Fiero, Mr. Joseph D. Fackenthal, and Rev. Arthur Acy Rouner. Mr. Fackenthal planned the lawsuit against the General Council, wrote the pleadings in the case, and secured Mr. Kenneth W. Greenawalt as trial attorney. Mr. Fiero was chairman of the Board of Deacons of the church and was also a member of the Executive Committee of the General Council, overlapping in part Dr. Shipherd's term on the committee. He became my inside informant on some crucial matters that Dr. Fagley was not free to divulge. Dr. Rouner, as pastor of the church, became a star witness in the trial and a kind of anchorman on the meaning of Congregationalism.

Dr. Marion J. Bradshaw, Professor of the Philosophy of Religion and Ethics at Bangor Theological Seminary for thirty years, became one of the early pamphleteers. We used to work together, sending out joint mailings that would include things which he had written at the same time that I was sending out mine.

Partly on that local scene, two laymen in Illinois got out frequent mimeographed letters about the merger that they mailed to people throughout the state of Illinois. They were Mr. J. E. Juttemeyer and Dr. Palmer D. Edmunds. Dr. Edmunds was a professor of law at John Marshall Law School (where in 1976 he completed fifty years on the faculty), and he became an advisor to all of the antimerger people in regard to legal issues involved and gave advice on what steps could be taken.

The first organization opposed to the merger on a national scale was called together as the Evanston Meeting by Dr. Neil E. Hansen, Dr. Arthur Cushman McGiffert, Jr., and Dr. Hugh Elmer Brown. Dr. Hansen was secretary of the Chicago Missionary Society; Dr. McGiffert was president of Chicago Theological Seminary; and Dr. Hugh Elmer Brown was pastor of the First Congregational Church of Evanston, Illinois, where the meeting was held. The meeting they called brought together people from all over the country in November of 1947, and adopted a statement protesting the Basis of Union and the plan of the merger.* Care was taken that my name not be associated with the calling of the meeting or the planning of it; nor was I a speaker there. Its leaders wanted a fresh image of opposition. I did loan them my mailing list, and I noted at the time that approximately two-thirds of the persons present had been receiving my material. The meeting elected a Continuing Committee that did extensive pamphleteering from November until the following June, up to the time of the Oberlin Council meeting of 1948. I was elected to that committee. Mr. S. T. Roberts was chairman of this committee. He was an incisive writer, and my impression is that Dr. McGiffert, Rev. Neil Hansen, and Mr. S. T. Roberts were jointly responsible for writing the letters and reports which went out. The findings of the Evanston Meeting were drawn up and acted upon at the time of the meeting itself. Mr. Roberts was a layman from the Philadelphia area.

*See Appendix.

Dr. Howell D. Davies came into the scene in 1950, when he retired as Regional Secretary for the Missions Council in the Chicago office. Dr. Harry Johnson, who was for many years Superintendent of the Intermountain District, was the only superintendent to take an active position on the side of the continuing churches. In 1955, upon his retirement from his superintendency he became the first Executive Secretary of the National Association of Congregational Christian Churches, when it was set up in November of 1955.

Dr. Max Strang was very active in Iowa and helped to start a Continuation Committee in that state. Later, in the fall of 1948, he became Director of the Antimerger group, with an office in Chicago. The name changed in January, 1949 to The Committee for the Continuation of the Congregational Christian Churches in the U.S. Rev. Harry R. Butman and Rev. Joseph J. Russell were active in Massachusetts and were the organizers and officers of the Continuation Committee for the state, as well as becoming members of the national committee. Dr. Warren S. Archibald was the key figure in organizing the Continuation Committee for Connecticut.

Mrs. Claude (Gladys) Kennedy became a member of the General Council's Executive Committee after Raymond Fiero went off. She was acknowledged as an antimerger person before she was elected and was put on as the active representative of those opposed to the union. By that time the Executive Committee had become stacked almost solidly with promerger adherents. She was an excellent observer and kept extremely careful notes of what was going on, and at some critical times she was our only source of information on closed-door sessions where a good deal of secret manipulating was going on; the outside world was not supposed to know the real issues that were being discussed or the deals that were being made. She was also a very valuable member of the Executive Committee of the Continuation group and of its Interim Committee at the time that a new Missionary Society was set up and the National Association was called into being, both in 1955.

Rev. James W. Fifield, Jr., was the one who started the national Continuation Committee. After the debacle at

Oberlin in 1948, when the opposition to the merger was supposed to have been erased, he got on the phone in October and lined up prominent people all over the country to serve on the national committee, first called Anti-Merger. He assumed a large part of the responsibility for raising funds for the Committee, its publications, and the financial support it gave to the Cadman Church in its lawsuit. He was chairman of the Executive Committee of the Continuation Committee through the fateful years to 1956, after the Omaha Council. A brother of L. Wendell Fifield, he was pastor of First Congregational Church, Los Angeles, the largest Congregational Church in the country.

4

Hidden Pressures for the Merger

THERE were several hidden pressures that helped to force the merger through. They seldom if ever surfaced, and certainly the average church members knew absolutely nothing about them when the Basis of Union and Constitution were voted on.

One, which was probably very clear in the minds of those who wanted it, was the desire to have a denomination that could speak out on social action questions and not have the people say that the leaders had no right or power to speak for them. For some years the representatives of the Council for Social Action had been wont to appear before the Congressional and Senate committees and say that they were speaking for 1,300,000 Congregationalists. They were taken to task for this, and in 1954 the General Council meeting in New Haven said that they had no right, in Congregationalism, to do it.

With us it had long been recognized that councils and other ecclesiastical bodies had no legislative or judicial powers, and that any resolutions adopted had "no authority beyond the weight of their own wisdom, backed by the significance of the delegation from which they issue" (1936 *Manual* of the Congregational Christian Churches, p. 53).

The advocates of social action kept a low profile throughout the merger discussions, and certainly did not make social action one of the announced objectives of the merger; yet probably those who had these interests in mind were the chief beneficiaries of the United Church of Christ as it finally came forth.

The censure of the Council for Social Action by the 1954 meeting at New Haven, and all the tradition of Congregationalism regarding its General Council *not* having the right to speak for the churches and of its *not* being a "representative" or legislative body, became a thing of the past the moment that the United Church of Christ was set up and its Constitution adopted. Although most Congregationalists were not alert enough to see it, or to sense its importance, the Constitution of the United Church of Christ definitely states that the General Synod "is the representative body of the United Church of Christ."

Even these words, *representative body*, are key words in a presbyterial setup, indicating delegated authority from the churches to the higher body and are directly contrary to Congregational principles. In Congregationalism we have had a New England type of democracy, as typified in the town meeting—the purest form of democracy. In the representative system you have a "republic," where the people elect representatives to "rule over them," at least to some extent. This is a point clearly made by Dr. James E. Wagner in his book, *Perspectives for a Local Church Officer*, from which we quoted previously.

In one fell swoop, then, the constitution of the United Church of Christ gave the adherents of the social action group just what they had been denied under Congregational polity. During the merger discussions the advocates of social action were probably laughing up their sleeves all along, knowing that the rebuke of the New Haven Council would soon be a thing of the past.

Anyone acquainted with the activities of the United Church of Christ since its formation can see that the social action people have had a field day. The pronouncements of the United Church of Christ—and there have been many of them—have been very largely in this field of social concerns. If the denomination had such expertise that all of its pronouncements made sense, or programs that it advocated would really work, this might not be too bad. But the United Church of Christ has been taking positions in the political and social realms where there is wide room for honest differences of opinion, and where, in many cases, the problems involve extremely intricate questions of business, finance, foreign policy, public housing, and minority rights, and where well-meaning ministers and their associates do not know all of the answers. The positions officially taken by the United Church of Christ do not necessarily reflect the opinions or desires of the people in the churches, but now there is no way for the folks back home to put a check on these far-reaching pronouncements. The people in the pew can no longer argue that "in Congregationalism you cannot do this in our name"—because the United Church of Christ is not Congregational.

This is just one more illustration of the change that has been made and of what it means.

We might say that the ecumenical movement was a second of the hidden pressures working to force the merger through. In this case the ecumenical slogans were often mentioned, but nobody knew, or could ever find out, what kind of church was implied by the oft-quoted claim that "Christ prayed that they all might be one." And with nothing specific to discuss, there was nothing that could be debated or appraised on its merits.

The frequent and emotional use of this claim that Christ prayed, in the night that he was betrayed, that "they all might be one," displayed at its best sloppy thinking and at its worst just plain dishonest scholarship and lack of intellectual integrity. The phrases recorded in John 17, verse 21, are: "That they all may be one; as thou, Father, art in me, and I in thee, that they also may be one in us; that the world may believe that thou hast sent me." Individual Christians can have that kind of oneness with other people everywhere, and they do not even need to be members of any church. There is nothing whatever in this passage to suggest union of church organizations, much less that everybody in the world must be forced into one tremendous "organic" structure. The Roman Catholic Church has been guilty for years of using the first part of this verse as the basis of its claim that there can be only one true church and that all Protestants should "return to Rome."

We tried throughout the merger controversy to pin down the folks who kept using the sentimental plea "that they all might be one," but to no avail. What kind of church did they have in mind—going, that is, beyond the immediate merger to any kind of ultimate objective? They would disclaim immediately any suggestion of an authoritarian church, or one where liberty of conscience would be curtailed. In vague terms they would talk of "unity in diversity." But never was there anything specific or definite.

In the four years in which I served on the Committee on Free Church Polity and Unity, I frequently pursued this question. But the promerger people, who constituted three-fourths of the committee, seemed empty of suggestions. Our committee was supposed to come up with suggestions on various possible forms of church union. Guess who finally wrote that chapter? I did—and I was not one pushing for union.

Because it was such an emotional appeal, and because there was absolutely nothing specific or tangible that the churches could examine or discuss when their members voted, the constant use of this claim that "Christ prayed, in the night that he was betrayed, that they all might be one" was nothing less than a hidden pressure forcing the merger through—hidden because its real implications could not be examined.

The third of these hidden pressures on the merger was probably the most subtle of all, but again the ministers who were committed to its point of view probably knew or believed that this was involved in the merger. It was something that we could feel but could not prove. It never became a part of the proposition as voted upon by the churches. Yet in many ways it meant the most sweeping abrogation of the fine intellectual standing that Congregationalism had attained under great leaders like Horace Bushnell, Washington Gladden, Lyman Abbot, Henry Ward Beecher, Charles E. Jefferson, S. Parkes Cadman, and many, many more.

Here was a hidden purpose for a change of doctrinal viewpoint to conform with the Barthian and Neo-orthodox theologians who were so prominent at the time.

I am indebted to Steven W. Bailey for bringing to my attention the following information. In his paper on the merger controversy, written for a class at Harvard Divinity School and later selected as an award-winning paper of the Congregational Foundation for Theological Studies of the National Association, Steven Bailey quotes a statement of Dr. Horton's, written thirty years after the experience which he describes. The moment I saw this statement, I wished that we could have had some such statement from the pen or lips of Dr. Horton when we were arguing the merger question. It would have put a new light, it seemed to me, on why we had the whole long struggle through which we passed. But not until after the United Church was set up did this surface.

Here is the statement, written by Dr. Horton when he was Dean of the Harvard Divinity School:

> It was a generation ago that I ran across the German text, published under the title *Das Wort Gottes und die Theologie.*... Only those who are old enough to remember the particular kind of desiccated humanism, almost empty of other-worldly content, which prevailed in many Protestant areas in the early decades of this century, can understand the surprise, the joy, the refreshment which would have been brought by the book to the ordinary and, like myself, somewhat desultory reader of the religious literature of that time. To question evolutionary modes of thought in that day was something like questioning the Ptolemaic theory in the time of Copernicus, with the stupendous difference that Copernicus seemed at first to shut the transcending God out of the world and Barth seemed immediately to let him in.

The work with which Dr. Horton was so elated became *The Word of God and the Word of Man* when Dr. Horton translated it at that time into English, and that was the book which Dr. Fagley had given me shortly after it was published, and which he was so insistent that I read. To me it was filled with innumerable generalities, very sweeping in nature. Barth's insistence that the divine-human encounter was one in which God took all the initiative, and was not one in which man could reach out and find God at the same time that God was reaching toward him, seemed arbitrary nonsense. So did much else in Barth's wordy and exaggerated language.

But I see this statement by Dr. Horton in the light also of events that took place at the Durham Council meeting in 1942.

My first experience of going to a General Council meeting as a voting delegate was this 1942 meeting, held at the University of New Hampshire. I attended the business sessions quite faithfully and vividly recall the many hours of debate spent on pacifist resolutions, where Dr.

Albert W. Palmer was the leader. This, remember, was during the Second World War. But I do not recall the action taken that initiated the merger struggle. It was a single small paragraph, which must have passed without much comment and with no debate. But I do remember some other events which I have long suspected were part of the groundwork for the merger. They could have served as a trial balloon to see whether the matter of doctrine could safely be brought out into the open with respect to a merger.

At that Durham meeting a small ad hoc group, claiming no official connection, had nailed up some posters on tree trunks and telephone poles in typical electioneering fashion. I still have one and shall include a copy of it as a page here in this book.* It advertised evening meetings that were to take place after the regular business sessions, under the name of *Christus Victor*. Ostensibly, according to statements of its leaders, this group was one committed to an open inquiry on serious theological questions in the hope that Congregationalists might deepen their perspectives and their understandings in this field. Frankly, I was in favor of that as a general purpose.

The leaders of the group started out as though they had no predetermined objectives, that they were open-minded and wanted to be seekers and searchers with the rest of us. But under prodding it soon became evident that they "had all the answers." It seemed obvious that they simply wanted to put their ideas and beliefs over on other people. I have the distinct recollection that one of the leaders intimated that they hoped that the day would come when all Congregationalists would have to subscribe to a uniform creed or statement of faith. It was at that time that I became somewhat involved by saying that if they were planning on anything like that, it was my hope that they would not have a statement that would exclude the views of such persons as the Quakers and the Unitarians in the way that the Federal Council of Churches had done—leaving them, as it were, as non-Christians. This nearly blew the lid off. One of the leaders, who later became one of the secretaries of the National Council of Churches, arose and with intense vehemence shouted at

*See Appendix Document 1.

me, "Why, why, that is Arminianism!" I attended at least two of the evening sessions but was eventually invited, quite emphatically, to leave—which I did.

Dr. Horton was not only at the meetings, but I remember him as being all smiles about what was going on. Later, in an article in *Advance* (July, 1943), he commented favorably on Christus Victor, saying, "Another evidence that we mean to improve our education is the grass-roots movement among Congregational Christian adults called 'Christus Victor.'"

There were others present who felt very strongly, as I did. Among them I remember two men who later supported the merger. I doubt that they ever made a connection between what went on at Christus Victor meetings and the merger plan as publicly presented. One, Dr. Frank M. Sheldon, was on the committee that drew up the Basis of Union. In 1947 he wrote me a letter where he again stressed the fact that he was a "liberal" theologically, and that he had so stated in meetings with Evangelical and Reformed leaders. Later, in 1954, Dr. Wagner said that they (Evangelical and Reformed people) had been "concerned about doctrine." Dr. Wagner then went on to say that it should be noted "that if both communions were once affected by the breezy modernism and liberalism of the past half-century or more, both of them have now been affected, and to some extent been transformed in their theological character, by the recent resurgence of Biblical theology and of the sterner doctrinal assumptions readily associated with such names as those of Barth, Brunner and Reinhold Niebuhr...."

This statement by Dr. Wagner came too late to affect the merger outcome, as did that of Dr. Horton's when he was Dean at Harvard Divinity School. But the statements are worth comparing for their rejection of the solid and scientific scholarship that had marked biblical studies for seventy-five years, and for their enthusiastic embrace of the old "other-worldly" Calvinistic dogmas that were revived by the pseudo-Calvinists, and of the medieval orthodoxy masquerading in modern dress as "Neo-orthodoxy."

Many people think of Dr. Washington Gladden as either a great pioneer in trying to bring a Christian social

order, or only as the author of the hymn, "O, Master, Let
Me Walk with Thee." Few know that he wrote two very
scholarly books on the Bible, incorporating much of the
finest critical scholarship as it had developed up to his
time, and these were intended for lay people in the
churches. One, *Who Wrote The Bible?—A Book for the
People*, was published in 1892. The other, *How Much Is
Left of the Old Doctrines?*, was published in 1899. As an
early follower of Horace Bushnell, Dr. Gladden had long
since rejected the Calvinistic doctrines that had been espoused in this country by Jonathan Edwards and many
others. Would Dr. Wagner characterize him as a "breezy
modernist?" Or, would Dr. Horton find Barth's "other-
worldly" concerns preferable to Dr. Gladden's down-to-
earth approach to the Gospel and to the Bible?

The spokesmen at these first Christus Victor meetings
faded out of the Congregational limelight in a few years,
but two years after the Durham meeting, Christus Victor
had a fifteen-minute presentation one morning during the
Grand Rapids General Council meeing in June, 1944. That
evening there was a much longer session at which Dr.
Wilhelm Pauck and others spoke. I remember walking
out in disgust after the morning presentation. Right behind me was Dr. Hugh Elmer Brown, pastor of the First
Congregational Church of Evanston, Illinois. He was in a
rage, and with swear words, that took me aback—coming
from him,—he wanted to know "where those fellows came
from." He said that what they were saying was the kind of
old, narrow-minded religion from which he had rebelled
many years before, and he thought that it was dead in
Congregationalism. He, as I have mentioned, was later one
of the three men who called into existence the first organized resistance to the merger, the Evanston Meeting of
November 1947.

From the time of the 1944 General Council I can recall
no public exposure of the Christus Victor group. But I received a communication at least two years later that
would indicate that it had gone underground. I received a
letter from a minister unknown to me. He enclosed an invitation to a Christus Victor retreat that had been sent to
him by mistake. It had been sent to his address but with
another minister's name on it. Apparently the person ad-

dressing the invitation had taken the wrong address from the Year Book. The note said that a selected group of ministers were being invited "again this year" to the retreat, and that "again this year, as last" Dr. Truman Douglass would be their esteemed leader. This is the last that I heard of the Christus Victor movement as such, but it is not too much to guess that there was within the leadership of the Congregational Christian Churches a kind of *sub rosa* movement whose members knew perfectly what they wanted. In fact, for a number of years Dr. Horton led some "ashram" type of meetings for selected friends and leaders at retreats in New Hampshire.

In 1955 Dr. Marion J. Bradshaw brought out his book, *Baleful Legacy,* in which he put forth the thesis that one purpose of the merger was to create a new denomination which would become the vehicle of neo-orthodoxy. With great care Dr. Bradshaw outlined the principal positions of the men whom Dr. Wagner had mentioned—Barth, Brunner, and Reinhold Neibuhr—and called attention to the fact that the leaders of neo-orthodoxy in this country were most of them concentrated in the Evangelical and Reformed Church and the Congregational Christian fellowship. Certainly many of our pastors at that time were taken up with neo-orthodoxy as "the latest thing" and could hardly preach a sermon without quoting Barth, Niebuhr, Tillich, Brunner, or Kierkegaard.

Stephen Bailey points out in his paper that Dr. George W. Richards, chairman of the Evangelical and Reformed committee on the merger and formerly the first president of the Evangelical and Reformed Church, was also an interpreter of Barth, having translated some of his work, just as Dr. Horton had done.

For the uninformed on these theological matters, let me merely say that the impression that I got, first from reading Barth and then Niebuhr, was that almost everything was in general terms; that you could not pin anything down with any degree of exactitude; and that inconsistencies and paradoxes were considered as virtues, rather than as signs of careless thinking or inadequacy. Here was the opposite of the scientific method.

Karl Barth disclaimed any idea that every word of the Bible was to be taken literally as the "word of God."

Nevertheless, he insisted that the Bible is the Word of God. In fact he seemed to make his interpretation of "the Christ" as God's "Word," and His only word to us—although with anyone who wrote as many volumes as Barth did, and frankly changed his mind so freely, it is hard to make any statement for sure. Dr. Barth had studied under some of the great modern biblical scholars, but he claimed that he was "going beyond" them. Actually he turned his back on them and on all that careful scholarship had meant with its honest and scientific use of words and facts.

The title *Christus Victor* is from Kierkegaard. The leaders of the group at Durham insisted that it meant that "Christ has overcome the world"—not that he will overcome the world, or that his ideas will ultimately be victorious, but that he has *already* overcome the world. When I reported this to Dr. William S. Beard, one of my father's closest associates, he quipped, "Well, something has surely slipped up somewhere." Maybe that is just an illustration of the difference between the down-to-earth and realistic approach that formerly characterized much of Congregationalism and the "other-worldly" approach of Barth, Kierkegaard, and others.

Neo-orthodoxy seemed to downgrade, or even to spurn, the idea of the historical Jesus, which the great biblical scholars had endeavored so patiently and so honestly to reveal. Instead they wanted the other-worldly "Christ," which they presented as a preexistent being who had been with God from the beginning. Christ, not God, according to some of them, created the world. This whole idea started back in the early centuries when the text of the first verse of John's gospel was blown up out of all proportion and had been the sole source ever since for this kind of theological nonsense. The author of the fourth Gospel had used some of the clever semantics invented by Philo of Alexandria, a great Jewish scholar who lived about the time of Jesus. Philo was trying to reconcile Jewish scripture with the thinking of the Greek world. The Greeks objected to any idea of God as a big man creating the world with his hands. But they did have a philosophical concept of a great, creative, undergirding force in the universe, which they denoted with the word *Logos*.

Philo, anxious to bridge the gap between Greek and Jewish thought, seized upon a second use of the Greek *logos*. It also meant just plain *word*. So, turning to the book of Genesis, Philo said, "Look: the Bible does not say that God made the world with his hands. He merely *said*, 'Let there be light; let the earth bring forth its increase, and so on.' Hence it was just God's *word* that did everything. And *word* and *logos* are the same thing." The author of the fourth gospel was also trying to speak to the Greek world. He borrowed the clever semantics from Philo and went one step further. Christ became the *Logos*, or the "word." Theologians have spun many a fine web of dogmatism on this flimsy and very dubious use of language, of which the ancient Athanasian creed is but one example.

And so we find Barth rejecting the historical Jesus and turning entirely to this other-worldly concept of "the Christ."

Michel Vallon, in his book *Apostle of Freedom*, says (p. 202):

> Christian faith, according to Barth, is by no means based on the impression made by the personality of Jesus. The New Testament shows no interest in it. Moreover, the attempt to write the life of Jesus or reconstruct his personality has, in Barth's view, no relevance whatsoever to faith in Christ. He goes so far as to assert that behind the New Testament picture of Jesus there is nothing very God-revealing, but only the Rabbi of Nazareth, rather a commonplace figure alongside many of his fellow teachers. In his own words (Barth says): "Even in that function that is most surely His own, the teaching of the people, the training of His disciples, he does not achieve any aims, indeed He does not appear to have so much as striven for any definite aims.... Even in personality He does not appear to have had anything like so convincing and winning an effect as an amiable Christian journalism and rhetoric in recent days delight to represent."

This quotation from Barth reminded me, in its low esteem for Jesus, of the learned men of Abraham Lincoln's day who considered his Gettysburg Address a "flop" and a disgrace to our presidency.

And so Congregationalism was asked, partly through the merger and for its sake, to sell its fine intellectual birthright and outstanding leadership for a mess of theological pottage. Just when the great scientists were coming to believe, along with the best informed religious thinkers, that the "natural" universe is so great, so marvelous, so inexplicable that there is no need for the word *supernatural*, we were suddenly asked to go back to the child's play of "other-worldliness"—as though the universe were not, after all, "one," and as though the laws of the universe were entirely different and apart from the truths of religion and of God's revelations to us.

Religious people today should wake up to the real world in which they are living. As one of the early Russian cosmonauts remarked upon his return from outer space, "I didn't see any angels up there."

Steven Bailey in his paper maintained that Dr. Horton wanted to follow Barth's idea of the church. From reading Barth's early work I can see reference to "the Church" where Barth obviously was accepting without question the kind of "church" represented in his Reformed Church in Germany. But one of the ironies of Barth and of his influence is that toward the end of his life Barth was widely quoted as saying that the best hope for Christian unity would be in the Congregational form of church government! This brought him to the same position as that of Henry Martyn Dexter, the great authority on Congregational polity of one hundred years ago. How far things can go in full circle!

Before we leave the subject of the hidden pressures, we should look back over the world scene of international councils of churchmen. Steven Bailey in his paper calls attention to the fact that Douglas Horton had attended ecumenical conferences in Britain (at Oxford and Edinburgh) in 1937, just a year before he became head of our General Council. Then in 1954 the World Council of Churches met at Evanston, Illinois, in September, just at the time that the merger was stalled and faced its final great crisis, which came a month later. By building up great emotional pressure again for ecumenicity, the World Council of Churches became one of the most persuasive reasons why the two groups of merger leaders decided that they simply had to go ahead with the merger, just when a full and honest appraisal of the facts had made it plain that they should not. "There is no doubt," wrote Dr. James E. Wagner, "but that the spirit of Evanston. . . . hovered over the Cleveland meeting from the moment it convened." (*The Messenger*, of the Evangelical and Reformed Church, 2 November, 1954)

These worldwide meetings of churchmen were only a few of a long successsion of world conferences where missionary leaders and others dreamed their dreams of a unified approach to all of humankind, with the simplistic notion that beliefs could all be compromised and whittled down to some sort of "simple" approach that would include everything and satisfy everybody. Actual attempts at a synthesis of beliefs have produced nothing simple, but rather words and more words, with a result appealing to very few. Witness COCU's latest "Statement of Emerging Theological Consensus," 3-6 November, 1976 (Eighty-five typewritten pages).

Why the ecclesiastical leaders feel that they have a right to push everybody else around, and to try to force millions upon millions of humble souls into their schemes for church grandeur and power, is a question worth pondering. The argumentative booklet prepared as a guide to and for the promotion of the COCU plan carries the very presumptuous title "What Does God Require of Us Now?" Who gave the relatively small clique of persons who prepared the COCU Plan of Union the right to say what *God* requires of us? Would they try to speak *ex cathedra* for God, just as the pope claims to do for Christ?

In Congregational churches, it has always been insisted that each individual church seeks guidance directly for itself, with Christ the head for each congregation. The early New England slogan for state and church was: "A State without a King, and a Church without a Bishop."

We have outlined above some of the hidden pressures that were working to force the merger through: the desire of the social action people for a church that could speak for the people on all sorts of social questions; the ecumenical drive with its sentimental plea that "Christ prayed, in the night that he was betrayed, that 'They all might be one' "; and the deep undercurrent of doctrinal bias of those others loosely classified under the name of neo-orthodoxy.

5

The Beginning Period, 1942–1944

AMONG the dozens of resolutions adopted at the General Council meeting at Durham, New Hampshire, in June of 1942, appears this motion in a single paragraph on page 21 of the minutes:

> Voted: That the General Council authorizes its Commission on Interchurch Relations and Christian Unity jointly with the Commission on Closer Relations with Other Churches of the Evangelical and Reformed Church to explore the possibilities of organic union between the Evangelical and Reformed Church and the General Council of the Congregational Christian Churches.

It should be noted that this resolution gave authorization merely for the exploration of the possibilities of "organic union" between the Evangelical and Reformed Church and the *General Council*. (But in October 1954, the Executive Committee quoted this resolution in its "Letter Missive" as referring to an organic union with the *Congregational Christian Churches*.)

There is nothing to indicate that the members of the 1942 General Council had the slightest idea of what "organic union" with the Evangelical and Reformed Church would mean, and if it was only to involve our General Council then our fellowship would remain essentially as it had been. They certainly had nothing before them to suggest that this resolution meant that our free churches were to be swallowed up in a presbyterial type of overall "Church." The delegates were probably unaware of the form of organization represented in the Evangelical and Reformed Church, and they certainly did not know that even the words *organic union* had a special connotation to members of that communion.

In the Constitution and Bylaws of the Evangelical and Reformed Church appeared these words in regard to the act of incorporating a congregation in that Communion:

> 10. Whenever a congregation desires to become an incorporated body, a draft of the proposed Articles of Incorporation and the constitution of the congregation shall be submitted to the Synod, or to the Synodical Council, for approval before the charter is presented to the civil authorities. A charter shall not be approved that does not bind the congregation to be an organic member of the Evangelical and Reformed Church, and to be governed by its constitution and bylaws. (p. 15, 1942 edition)

The top leadership of the two denominations had been carrying on conversations in regard to this possible union for two or three years before the action was taken at Durham, but the average delegate had no particular knowledge of the Evangelical and Reformed Church's organization. If the proposal had involved a union with the Presbyterian Church, the delegates would have known that the polity, or structure, of the other body was different from the Congregational. But in this case few of the ordinary delegates realized that this union would mean a merger with a body whose polity was fundamentally different from that of the Congregational Christian Churches. Whereas our churches enjoyed complete freedom and autonomy, the Constitution of the Evangelical and Reformed Church began with this statement, in its Preamble:

> For the maintenance of truth and order in the proclamation of the gospel of our Lord Jesus Christ and the advancement of the Kingdom of God in accordance with the Word of God, the Evangelical and Reformed Church ... ordains this constitution to be its fundamental law and declares the same to have authority over all its ministers, members, congregations, and judicatories.

Many attempts were made during the merger discussion to hide the difference between the two denominations, or to pretend that they were "just like us." Certainly there was no frank admission in the beginning that there was a fundamental difficulty, nor any forthright effort to meet head-on the problem of merging two dissimilar polities. Authority in the Congregational Christian Churches rested at the bottom, in the local church. In the Evangelical and Reformed Church it rested in the denomination as a whole and was controlled by its legislative bodies, called *judicatories*, starting at the top with the General Synod. The United Church now uses this term *judicatories*, as applying to associations, conferences and the General Synod.

The way that the differences in polity were glossed over from the first can be seen in the statement published in *A Primer of Union*, page 7, question 32:

> What kind of "polity" or church government do the two denominations employ? The Congregational Christian Churches may be said to have a congregational polity (ruled by congregations) with presbyterial elements (ruled by presbyteries, or committees representing groups of churches), and the Evangelical and Reformed Church a presbyterial polity with congregational elements. Both contain episcopal elements (ruled by the leaders chosen by conferences or synods) but without connotations of "apostolic succession."

The use above of the words *ruled by* is not always true to the facts as they existed in the Congregational Christian Churches.

After many years of merger discussion, we did in May 1955 receive from the Executive Committee of our General Council and the General Council of the Evangelical and Reformed Church, the following frank statement (in the leaflet, *United In Christ*):

> For the first time, two great churches of different cultural backgrounds—the one Continental European, the other British—and with dissimilar forms of polity—the one Presbyterian, the other Congregational—will join in a common fellowship. . . .

Not until 1955 did such a forthright statement appear, setting forth clearly and admitting for the first time the differences in polity and the real problem which had faced the Commission on Interchurch Relations from the start.

During most of the years of the merger discussion, this central issue of free churches joining with an authoritarian church was evaded and dodged. On every occasion when a full and careful discussion should have taken place, some other procedural moves were made the order of the day. The General Council meetings of 1944, 1946, 1948, and 1954 are all disgraceful examples, which we shall discuss as we get to them. It will be our purpose to trace the actual procedures used, showing the way in which the proposition was carried along from year to year without ever having a full discussion of the documents being presented, and with the really crucial decisions being made behind the scenes and without the General Council itself having the chance to decide. Thus the Basis of Union was sent out in 1947 to churches for a vote without decision from the General Council, and without the General Council having an opportunity to discuss its text, part by part, or paragraph by paragraph. In like manner the decision to go ahead again in 1954, after the merger had been held up in the courts for four years, was not presented to the General Council at New Haven in 1954. Instead the Executive Committee made that decision a few months later, and used the next two years to carry out a ruthless propaganda campaign to win support for the decision that it had already made.

A Basis of Union was worked out and printed in March of 1943 that bears little resemblance to the final draft prepared for submission to the churches in January 1947. The first draft was exceedingly general in its nature and gave way a few months later to a new edition in August of 1943. The main framework of the final Basis of Union was to be found in that draft, with two notable exceptions: one, the whole of Section VIII, dealing with the boards was not added until after the 1946 General Council; the other was any mention of the ascending series of judicatories, with the rights of complaint, appeal and reference, which were first introduced in the edition of April 1944.

Some indication of the early work in promoting the merger can be surmised from the following firsthand experience.

In February of 1943 a meeting of the Committee for War Victims was scheduled as a matter of convenience at Second Congregational Church, New London, Connecticut, because of the convenience of that city to both Boston and New York. Having been asked to make our church building available as a meeting place, I was also invited to attend the sessions. During an interlude in the meeting, Dr. Douglas Horton spoke to me about the proposed merger, saying something to this effect: "Here are a couple of books which I would like you to look over. They have to do with the Evangelical and Reformed Church. We have found that these folks are our kind of people. When it comes to the meetings of the Federal Council of Churches, and so on, they usually vote as we do and think as we do. That is why we are thinking of a union with them."

The two books which Dr. Horton gave me were the Constitution of the Evangelical and Reformed Church and a newly published textbook for confirmation classes entitled *My Confirmation*. It was quite a long time before I looked at the constitution. A few years later, too, I was told by some of the Pennsylvania Evangelical and Reformed men that they never used the *My Confirmation* book but preferred to stick by the Heidelberg Catechism. It was some time, too, before I learned that the Evangelical and Reformed representatives on the Federal Council voted against admitting the Quakers and the Unitarians to the Federal Council, whereas our representatives voted for admitting them—reflecting in my mind quite a difference in doctrinal rigidity and temperament.

But as a result of this personal contact from Douglas Horton, I became interested in the proposed union. I did what I suppose Dr. Horton wanted me to do, and I became an early proponent of the union. At the spring meeting of the New London Association of Congregational Churches and Ministers, held in May of 1943, I made my first speech on the merger—a speech in which I warmly advocated the Union. This was before I had seen any copy of the Basis of Union and when only the first edition had even been published. No details about what the merger might really mean were then known to any of us at the meeting. Probably other persons, in other parts of the country became interested in the merger in the same way that I did, and advocated it with much the same absence of solid information. But for me there was a rude awakening.

Something unusual, I am sure, transpired at that New

London Association meeting. Present in that group of ministers was one man who had served in the foreign mission field in close proximity to Evangelical and Reformed Church men. Immediately he gave his personal testimony, and I still remember how emphatic he was about differences in background and manner of thinking found among the representatives from that church. Another minister, Rev. Alexander H. Abbott, whose training in the history of religion and philosophy had once brought to him an offer to head a department of philosophy of the faculty at Amherst College, spoke up on the historic differences in theology and background of the Evangelical and Reformed Church from our own. Other ministers, well trained in the older traditions of Yale and Harvard, joined in questioning me in my advocacy of the union. Rev. Theodore M. Shipherd, a member of that association, was also a member of the Executive Committee of the General Council and brought to the association some insights on how the merger question was being handled and promoted at the top level. All told, it was a very disquieting afternoon for me, a proponent of the merger who had no real information on the issues at stake. A questioning process was set in motion in my mind and in that of many others. The whole association became alerted to the proposal in a way which few if any other associations in the country experienced.

Early in the following year, in either January or February of 1944, Dr. Wilhem Pauck, a member of the committee drafting the Basis of Union, was invited to a special meeting of the New London Association held at Park Church, Norwich, where Rev. Theodore M. Shipherd was pastor. Dr. Shipherd by that time was recognized as a critic of the union, within the Executive Committee at least. Out of fairness, he believed it proper to let a member of the merger committee come and speak in its defense, since he was openly opposing the merger. The moderator of the evening showed every deference to the outside speaker and did what he could to run interference for him. He arbitrarily ruled that no member of the association could ask more than one question. This, remember, was in the very beginning of public discussion on the merger, when very many questions had never been raised before. The evening proved memorable, however, in several ways. Dr. Pauck informed his audience, in a deep, guttural German accent, that "we Congregationalists must make great sacrifices" for the union. Nothing too definite was said as to what these sacrifices would have to be. In all the future discussion of the merger I can recall no instance when an exponent of the merger told us that there would be any sacrifices to be made. On the contrary, we were always assured that we would not be giving up anything.

Dr. Pauck took numerous notes on objections raised at the meeting of the New London Association. In March, a month or two later, a new edition of the Basis of Union was published, in which a number of phrases were changed apparently because of criticisms expressed at this meeting in Norwich. The changes, however, seemed only to make the document more evasive. They did not meet the objections of the members of the New London Association. This tendency to seek merely inoffensive wording, without really grappling with the problems at issue, always seemed to mark the procedure when it came to revising the Basis of Union. Never were critics of the document invited to sit in with the joint committee to express their misgivings or to pinpoint the difficulties as they saw them.

The 1944 edition of the Basis of Union carried with it an elaborate and careful outline of suggested procedures to be followed in the future, and the Associations and Conferences were asked to express their opinions on these procedures prior to the General Council Meeting that June at Grand Rapids. Most of these suggested procedures were very commendable and would have furnished a far more sound basis for going ahead than the procedures that were later devised. Instead of following the procedures approved at Grand Rapids, the game plan for advancing the union was constantly changed to suit the expediency of the moment, and never were the sound suggestions for full discussion of the plan of union carried out, even though they had been approved by the 1944 Council meeting.

The 1944 edition of the Basis of Union also carried the first mention of an ascending series of ecclesiastical courts, or judicatories, which were set forth consistently after that. These would be contrary to Congregational principles.

When it came time for the New London Association to

act in May 1944, this matter of judicatories added new fuel to the flames of questioning and discontent, because courts of this sort meant that higher bodies could pass judgment on actions of the local churches or decide what they "ought" to do. Therefore the New London Association adopted a resolution that dealt with the matter of proceeding further, and it went on to state some of the misgivings which had developed. In the light of my subsequent activities in the merger matter, some people would probably ascribe this resolution to me, and me alone. Actually the resolution was drawn up by a committee of three, and I had the least to say in regard to its wording. As I recall, Rev. George Avery Neeld was chairman. The other two were Rev. Alexander H. Abbott and myself. The resolution, as adopted, was:

> The members of the New London County Association of Congregational Churches believe in the promotion of Church Federation, and in the union of churches when historical backgrounds or essential characteristics are harmonious.
> We further believe that consideration of possible union of the Congregational Christian Churches and the Evangelical and Reformed Churches might be continued.
> But, we further believe that the proposed plan for merger creates implements that could be used far beyond the necessities of merger, and could radically impair the genius of Congregationalism.
> Therefore, we wish to register our insistent objection to the proposed plan of merger.

Although not primarily responsible for the resolution itself, I did write a supplementary sheet entitled "Reasons for Opposing the Merger." This was presented to the association and adopted along with the resolution.

When these two documents were sent to the General Council office, they drew an immediate response from Dr. Horton. He wrote more or less favorably of the resolution itself, but took issue with the first paragraph of the statement of "Reasons." This first paragraph, to which Dr. Horton took exception, read as follows:

> The proposed plan of merger represents a far-reaching trend toward centralization of control over our churches. The General Synod would be a smaller body than our present Council, much less representative, but with far more power.

Conferences would take from the local Associations their present power of election of delegates. The General Synod would have power to establish the standards and methods of ordination to the ministry, to draw up the Constitution for the United Church, and even TO CHANGE ANY PARTS OF THE PRESENT PROPOSED BASIS OF UNION. No assurances contained in this Basis of Union have, therefore, any binding effect.

Dr. Horton's letter, dated 27 May, 1944, was addressed to Rev. Howard Champe, registrar of the New London Association. It read as follows:

Dear Mr. Champe:

Thank you for your letter of May 22 enclosing the resolution of the New London Association.

The resolution seems to me to be intelligent and fair. You register your disapproval of the proposed Basis of Union—and it is expressions of judgment of this sort that we want from all over the country—and yet you do not close the door on further negotiations.

I am afraid, however, that the Association has misunderstood the meaning of the Basis of Union. None of the three statements in the first paragraph, for instance, represent the facts.

(1) The General Synod would not necessarily be a smaller body than the present Council.

(2) Conferences would not take from the local Associations their present power of election.

(3) The General Synod would not have power to change any parts of the proposed Basis of Union. Such authority belongs today neither to the General Council of the Congregational Christian Churches nor to the General Synod of the Evangelical and Reformed Church: it is inconceivable that either group would look favorably upon such a high degree of centralization.

Yours faithfully,
(signed) Douglas Horton

This letter had, I must confess, a very shocking and disillusioning effect upon me the moment that I read it. The Basis of Union, as then printed, provided that the General Synod could amend the Basis of Union after the union was consummated. That provision, incidentally remained unchanged through all subsequent revisions of the Basis of Union. The General Synod was to be composed of 300 delegates from each communion, whereas our General Council at that time had approximately 900 or 1,000 delegates. The Basis of Union did provide that the delegates to General Synod would be elected solely by the Conferences and that provision, as well as the two just mentioned, was never changed. This issue of election of General Council delegates by Conferences *only* was, right then, a "red hot" issue. The General Council of 1936 had, upon recommendation of the state superintendents, taken away the right of the associations to elect most of the delegates. But immediately amendments were proposed that would change things back again. In 1942 this was done, going further than any previous provisions and setting up "unit" delegates from the churches themselves. Churches were grouped into units of 1,000 members or more, and churches of more than 1,000 members could nominate their own delegates.

For Dr. Horton to say that our association had misunderstood the meaning of the Basis of Union, and that none of the three statements in our first paragraph "represent the facts" is beyond intelligent comprehension.

In the years that lay ahead, the same sort of contradiction and denial of plainly stated provisions of the plan of union became a proverbial pattern and a kind of stock in trade of those promoting the merger. To try to pin anything down became a constantly baffling and impossible task.

About two months later I had another disillusioning experience through another letter from Dr. Horton. All of this was before I had started any pamphleteering or publishing of articles against the merger. We shall go into further details on the second letter after taking up the 1944 General Council meeting at Grand Rapids.

But before leaving the subject of our New London Association resolution, it might be of interest to readers of this account to see the broad outline of our position which I had stated in the last paragraph of "Reasons for Opposing the Merger." Here it is:

Persons who do not appreciate the principles of Congregationalism may criticize us for our lack of uniformity in doctrine, our varying standards for the ministry, our loose and inefficient control over our church affairs. But our genius has been in the independency of our churches. This alone gave us the freedom that others lacked. This gave refuge to some of the best minds of other generations, and it accounted for our churches turning out a disproportionate share of great religious leaders. Our tolerance in matters of faith has made us a kind of nonsectarian denomination. Our churches have been genuinely community churches. We have had an ecumenical spirit that was virtually interdenominational. We have been ready to cooperate with any and all Christians, and we have welcomed to our communion persons from all kinds of denominational background. Any attempt to increase our mere size or efficiency or to clamp down uniform tenets or methods upon us, will fail to make us any more ecumenical. The proposed Basis of Union contains all the tools needed to destroy our Congregationalism, rather than to preserve and merge it.

This final paragraph laid down pretty well the basic issues of the entire merger controversy. I cannot take credit for the ideas, because we had discussed them among the ministerial members of our association, and particularly among people like Dr. Shipherd and Mr. Abbott.

It is very interesting, at least to me, to compare this statement for the values it expressed with the emphasis given by Dr. Gaius Glenn Atkins in the closing part of the little history of Congregationalism, *Adventure in Liberty*. I made the statement previously that Dr. Atkins had written this book as an attempt to shore up the love of Congregationalism among its adherents. I made that statement on the basis of a conversation I had with Dr. Fagley. But first let me quote the final page from *Adventure in Liberty* as it originally appeared in the January issue of the *Missionary Herald* in 1947. Part of this is identical to some statements in Atkins and Fagley's longer *History of American Congregationalism*.

If one stands far enough away from the massive and entangled action of Protestantism, he sees throughout its course a growing quest for the realization of the independence of the spirit-guided Christian life, both in theory and practice.

Protestantism was bound by the very genius of it, when the right time came, to try the experiment of the liberty of a Christian man with all its implications and issues, completely and at all costs.

Now no historian of the Congregational Christian way dares to say that in Leyden or New England Plymouth or Massachusetts Bay was the predestined issue of the Protestant Reformation, or the heirs "of all the ages in the foremost ranks of time." But it is true that historically the American Congregational Christian Churches have made the Congregational way of exercising the liberty of the Christian more consistently central than any other of the denominations whose polity is Congregational.

The polity itself, as one sees it in its entirety has always been a means to an end: the right and duty of the church member to administer his own church business with a direct control; a minimum of ecclesiastical machinery; willing obedience to majority discussions; and a disciplined respect for the rights of the minority.

Congregationalism believes this to be necessary to the liberty of a Christian man, and whatever else is built must be upon this foundation....

So much for more than three hundred years of history. These are not easy times, but when one considers all that this Fellowship has come through, he knows that they may face the future sustained with the past and unafraid—still Pilgrims seeking the order which hath foundations, whose builder and maker is God.

To me, this statement by Dr. Atkins stressed the same kind of permanent values in Congregationalism we tried to set forth two or three years earlier in the closing paragraph of "Reasons for Opposing the Merger." Many times, during my merger addresses and debates, I quoted some or all of the words from Dr. Atkins. Many people were Congregationalists more by accident of location than by conviction or understanding of what it meant. We were constantly having to argue *for* Congregationalism, besides having to show the dangers of losing it in the merger plan.

Getting back now to Dr. Fagley's telltale comment, let me explain that Dr. Fagley, who had coauthored with Dr. Atkins the longer *History* in 1942 tried for a long time, but without success, to get Dr. Atkins to write the shorter history. But finally Dr. Atkins agreed, saying, "I will do it as my lick against this——merger." Dr. Fagley, in telling me about this, said that it was the only time in his many years of intimate association with Dr. Atkins that he ever heard him use such a word. It is in contrast to the beautiful language that usually came from the pen and lips of Dr. Atkins, but it probably showed his very deep feeling in the matter.

I received through the years eight or nine handwritten letters from Dr. Atkins, including his strong endorsement of my *Destiny for Congregationalism*, which left no doubt of his true position on the merger. (Photocopies of most of these letters are in the collection at the Congregational Library in Boston.)

I quoted above from the original copy of *Adventure in Liberty*. The booklet was republished several times, and twice there is a notation that it was revised. The 1950 copy leaves off the final paragraph as quoted above. The 1961 edition carries the notation that it was revised by Dr. Horton.

It is indeed a sad and tragic irony that Dr. Horton should have gotten his hands on this little booklet after Dr. Atkins had died, and then taken the opportunity to change it to serve his own purposes in a very subtle way. There is no indication that any new material was inserted or where. There is nothing to alert future historians to the fact that some statements that appear just as though they had been written by Dr. Atkins were inserted afterward, presumably by Dr. Horton. Here was a recognized authority on the history of Congregationalism, and for anyone to insert a passage of his own, nearly two pages long, into which he slipped some of his own very controversial ideas, is to our way of thinking quite inexcusable.

The passage now in question from *Adventures in Liberty* is on pages 27, 28, and 29 of the 1961 edition, under the heading of, "The Meaning of Congregationalism." At issue was the claim made by Dr. Horton in his 1950 General Council address that the General Council was free to vote any way that it wanted, without reference to the wishes of the churches which had set it up and supported it. Advancing the theory that local Associations, Conferences, and General Council are "like the local churches" in their freedom to "seek the mind of Christ" for themselves, Dr. Horton had set forth his theory or "Congregationalism B" in an address with the title, "Of Equability and Perseverance in Well-doing." The same kind of arguments had been used by witnesses for the General Council in the Cadman lawsuit to justify the General Council in going ahead on its own to merge with the Evangelical and Reformed Church. Actually Dr. Horton's theory brought very little vocal support at the time, and many promerger people seemed embarrassed when the subject was brought up.

Much more is involved here than meets the eye. The

merger plan originally spoke of just a union of the General Council with the Evangelical and Reformed Church. But from the time of the publication of the first Basis of Union, the merger plan plainly stated the details for a complete union of the whole denomination. Throughout the merger discussion the pretense was frequently made that "it would be just the General Council acting for itself." But this was either hypocritical, since everyone knew that the plan involved the whole fellowship; or it was just a dishonest statement. The General Council controlled all the boards and mission societies that the churches had built up through more than a century. There was never any doubt that the Council intended, through its members, to take the boards with it. Further, it was perfectly evident that the plan contemplated that the churches would almost surely follow, whether they wanted to or not, if the Council voted to go ahead.

"Congregationalism B" was, in reality, an attempt to clothe the General Council with the appearance of authority—authority to "speak the mind of Christ" for the denomination, and authority to act in reality as a legislative body for the fellowship—something it was specifically forbidden to do. As we noted earlier in this book, the General Council was set up with the specific limitation that it could not act as a legislative or judicial body, or consent to act as a council of reference. We shall have occasion to come back to this central problem repeatedly. But for the present let us return to the insertion which was put into the 1961 edition of *Adventure in Liberty*.

Speaking of the local, state and national bodies, the text in this revised edition reads, on page 28:

... It was for the mid-twentieth century to realize that these bodies have a theological complexion similar to that of the local church in that, although they are made up of persons drawn not from the world like the members of ordinary congregations, their members are none the less, like the 'two or three' of scripture, gathered in the name of Christ, and for a sufficient period of time to develop a common mind in his presence. They therefore enjoy an authority over themselves (though not over the churches from which their members come) which derives from Christ. This new conception, advanced originally by Congregational thinkers in England, adds the capstone to the modern type of Congregationalism.

The travesty of making this appear as though it were an insight of the historian, Dr. Gaius Glenn Atkins, when in reality it bears all the evidence of Dr. Horton's specious claims, is bad enough. But when one considers the way that the General Council meetings were stage-managed, manipulated, high-pressured and stampeded, it is nothing short of sacrilege to pretend that their actions came after "seeking the mind of Christ." I was present at the Council meetings of 1942, 1944, 1946, 1948, 1949, 1950, 1952, 1954, 1956, and 1958. We shall go into pertinent details in later chapters and in a future volume; but even to suggest that these Councils met in open, objective, deliberative fashion, and in quietness and calm sought the "mind of Christ," would be the farthest thing from the truth that I can imagine. And no one had more to do with the handling of these meetings than Douglas Horton himself.

To add a final twist to Dr. Atkins's *Adventure in Liberty*, the following new paragraph was added to the 1961 edition, in place of the splendid last one by Dr. Atkins.

THE UNITED CHURCH OF CHRIST
Crowning all in the mid-twentieth century came the union with the Evangelical and Reformed Church. In that union two mighty ecclesiastical streams, one with its source on the Continent of Europe, the other deriving from the British Isles, met and shared their strength. It is a temptation to describe the uniqueness of this enterprise, its encouragement to other unions through the Christian world, and the new vitality it brought to the uniting communions; but that is matter for another history.

We readily grant that this final paragraph, relating as it does to the consummation of the merger, might be recognized by future historians as an addition from Dr. Horton. But the irony remains that a booklet written by Dr. Atkins, as his "lick against the merger," should finally be distorted so as to support the union.

In this chapter we have seen a small indication of the things to come. Already the portrayal of the leadership responsible for the merger procedures begins to reveal itself more clearly.

———— 6 ————

Procedures Approved at the 1944 General Council

OSTENSIBLY the only official business scheduled on the merger for the Council meeting at Grand Rapids in 1944 was the approval of certain *procedures* to be followed in the future in regard to the merger discussion and action. Actually, the Council meeting was utilized by the promerger leaders as a one-sided promotional event that was kept strictly under control and where nobody was allowed to bring forth a free discussion. Secondly, a number of reasonable-sounding procedures were authorized by the Council; but then the definitive parts of this procedure were never carried out.

According to the March 1944 edition of "The Basis of Union," each Association and Conference at its spring meeting was asked to vote upon the following resolution:

> RESOLVED that this Conference (or Association) approves the procedure hereinafter outlined in reference to the proposed union between the Congregational Christian and the Evangelical and Reformed Churches:

Then followed a series of paragraphs dealing with what this procedure was to be. First was the proposition that all churches, associations, conferences and national agencies:

> ....be asked during the coming biennium to seek every opportunity for fellowship with the corresponding groups of the Evangelical and Reformed Church and to enter into such types of cooperative endeavor as will engender mutual acquaintance.
> That this Council declare its willingness through its Executive Committee to unite with the General Synod or Gen-

eral Council of the Evangelical and Reformed Church (1) in promoting fellowship in areas where the two communions are both well represented, (2) in organizing the sending of leaders of either denomination into areas where the other denomination is not numerically strong, and (3) in aiding the churches, associations, conferences, and national agencies in such types of cooperative endeavor as will neither presuppose nor prejudice ultimate union between the denominations.

Then came the crucial matter of the way that the General Council would proceed. This provided that:

... this Council declare its willingness to be called into a joint three-day session with the General Synod of the Evangelical and Reformed Church for a general discussion of the implications of the proposed union in June, 1946, and

That immediately thereafter this Council meet to accept or reject the following resolution:

RESOLVED: (a) That the General Council approves the union of the Congregational Christian and the Evangelical and Reformed Churches upon the terms of the Basis of Union submitted by the Commission on Interchurch Relations and Christian Unity

(b) The General Council directs its secretary to submit the Basis of Union (1) to each of the churches of the fellowship, (2) to each of the Associations of the fellowship, (3) to each of the Conferences of the fellowship with the request that within twelve months they study it, discuss it, and finally approve or disapprove the union of the two denominations on the terms which the Basis of Union sets forth....

The next paragraph provided that the union would stand approved if an "overwhelming vote was affirmative," and would be dropped if it was overwhelmingly negative.

One change in the above procedure was made at the General Council meeting as a result of a motion which I made to amend the above proposal. We will come to that very shortly.

You will note from the foregoing that the procedures outlined did not suggest or call for a discussion, or presentation of any kind, of the Basis of Union itself at the 1944 General Council meeting.

What actually happened, however, was that the 1944 Council was itself used as a sounding board to start the bandwagon going, and to prejudice the issues before the churches had even had a chance to start getting acquainted with the other denomination or to study the Basis of Union.

A two- or three-hour session was held in which three or four of the leaders responsible for writing the Basis of Union were up in the chancel of Park Church, and a leader was appointed to handle questions coming from the audience. But these questions were not permitted orally. The only thing that the delegates at that Council could do was to write out a single question and hand it to an usher. These in turn were gathered together and handed to one person on the platform, who then looked them over and chose whichever questions he wanted, and then read them to the members of the Basis of Union committee to answer—with no limitation on the time permitted to these sponsors of the union. There was no chance to follow up on any question already asked; there was no way of knowing who had asked questions, so that questioners could then seek each other out; there was no chance to elucidate what a questioner had meant by his question if the point had been missed entirely; and there was simply no back-and-forth discussion.

I was the only person at the 1944 Council meeting who had the opportunity to speak with regard to the merger from a critical standpoint. This did not happen at the same session as the one in which the Basis of Union was "explained" by its sponsors.

As we noted above, all that the local associations and conferences had been asked to do, in advance of the 1944 General Council meeting, was to express their willingness to go forward with the procedures as outlined in the March edition of the Basis of Union. No expression of support or opinion on the plan had been suggested or requested. However, a few associations, representing a very small proportion of the total of 256 associations, sent in resolutions strongly endorsing the union as such. The leaders made the most of these. Again, one individual was given the resolutions and permitted to read the ones he wanted—maybe twenty-five or thirty. How many could have been read, and whether any of them recorded differing sentiments, we shall probably never know. Thus there were read a series of resolutions sounding forth with hearty endorsement of the plan for a merger. This, mind you, was before the plan had been finalized, before any General Council had discussed the meaning of the Basis of Union or sent it to the churches for a vote. (Actually, as it turned out, no General Council ever did discuss the Basis of Union before it was sent to the churches; and no General Council as such ever voted on sending the Basis of Union to the churches.) But at this 1944 meeting, as each resolution was read endorsing the union, considerable applause broke forth. Then, after this show of enthusiasm, our resolution from the New London Association was read, containing as it did some words of caution. It was greeted with loud "boos."

As we said earlier, the impetus for this merger probably started in the seminaries, long before this plan was suggested. It started in the big, fuzzy idea of the ecumenical movement, and it had been imbued in many of the younger ministers as a great and wonderful ideal. I still maintain that our New London resolution was very reasonable, calm, and objective. Let it be remembered that this was just the beginning—the very first time that the plan had come before any General Council after anything definite had been drawn up. Yet where was there any orderly procedure, or decent parliamentary presentation or consideration? The disorderly way in which it began was fairly typical of everything that was to follow in other years.

As a result of the way that our resolution was received at the meeting, I spoke to Dr. Horton personally and protested that we ought to have a right, in view of the behavior of the Council, to present our viewpoint. I was not only a member of the committee which drew up the resolution, but I had also been elected moderator of the association. Dr. Horton, at a time like this, was always quite reasonable in his manner, and he promised to take it up with the Executive Committee, which at that time was far from committed to the merger. He reported to me after lunch that the Executive Committee had approved my having fifteen minutes on the program to make my presentation. But, when I later went up to the pulpit to make my presentation, I was curtly told by Dr. Albert W. Palmer, who was moderating the session, that he was cutting my time in half.

Thus it was, however, that I became the one and only

person to speak against the merger at the 1944 General Council meeting. It meant that I became a marked man, both ways. Those supporting the merger recognized in me an opponent of their plan. Those who shared doubts and misgivings knew that I was one person whom they could contact for a sharing of ideas and viewpoint. I began getting considerable correspondence and building up a fairly wide acquaintance with people who were not sold on the merger.

Let us turn back now to the matter of the procedures and the one change that was made. As printed in the March 1944 Basis of Union, and also in the Advance Reports for the 1944 General Council, the paragraph dealing with the voting by churches, associations, and conferences was worded in terms of "finally approve or disapprove the union of the two denominations on the terms which the Basis of Union sets forth."

On the spur of the moment I had written out a brief amendment and presented it at the session when the motion on procedures came up. The words which I moved as an amendment, to be added to the above, were:

... with the distinct understanding that such action is in no way binding upon them.

Although offered as an amendment to the motion on procedures, these words of mine are not recorded as having been an amendment. Dr. Horton merely stated that he was sure my words would be acceptable as part of the original motion by other members of the committee. Only by comparing the wording as quoted in the March Basis of Union with that as printed in the minutes of the Council, on page 49, can anyone see that the motion was changed. My words are included. But that is not the whole story.

In July 1944, I received a letter from Dr. Horton, dated July 9, which read:

Dear Malcolm,

In going over the Minutes of the General Council I have come across several passages where our secretaries were not quite able to keep up to the debate and where, therefore, we are not dead certain of correct readings. One of these is your amendment to the "procedure" of the Basis of Union, accepted by Dr. Palmer and made part of his report. There are divergent readings of it as it was scribbled into the printed text.

Should it be "with the understanding . . ." or "with the distinct understanding . . . ?" Of course they both mean the same thing. I think the former is stronger, because it is simpler and more forthright, and accords with the sober tone of the rest of the document—but the question is, What really was it? Do you happen to remember? If you cannot remember, I shall leave out the word "distinct," which seems a little foreign to the context as one reads it over. Perhaps Dr. Palmer will remember though I doubt if he will, since it was written in such a hurry.

Another question: Would you not think it helpful to readers if a note were introduced (not as part of the text) to the effect that the churches and so forth would not be expected to take final action till the constitution as a whole was before them?

Ever yours,
(signed) Douglas Horton

At the time that I made my amendment, I had scribbled the wording down in the page of a little notebook, and for some reason took the precaution of making an exact copy before I went up to the rostrum to make my motion. As I left the rostrum, the assistant secretary reached out his hand for my slip of paper, and I gave him the copy from which I had read. As I recall it was Fred Alden, later superintendent of New Hampshire.

I wrote back to Dr. Horton that I had kept a copy, and that the wording "distinct understanding" was the way that I had given it. But that was not the end of this incident. I mentioned all this to Dr. Fagley almost immediately, while we were visiting at his cottage on Lake Sunapee, showing him the letter from Dr. Horton. He told me something more disturbing—namely, that Dr. Horton had suggested to him that they leave out entirely my suggested amendment so far as the official action was concerned, and that they merely have a footnote at the bottom suggesting that this was the "understanding." It was Dr. Fagley himself who was responsible for seeing the minutes actually printed, and he said that he told Dr. Horton, "No." My amendment had been accepted as part of the motion and would have to stay there. This may all be a small matter, but it shook my confidence in more ways than one. With the difficulty that we were to experience in getting anything "nailed down" for sure, this word *distinct* had real value to me, then and now.

As it turned out, this matter of the votes by the churches not being binding on them became one of the most vexing and troublesome problems for the merger strategists throughout the entire merger negotiations. It was the subject of extended discussion within the Executive Committee before the next Council session, and many different schemes were put forth trying to circumvent this "distinct" understanding. These attempts will show up periodically in our story.

As for the suggestion in Dr. Horton's last question, nothing could have been more helpful than an absolutely clear understanding that the churches would not be in the merger until they had approved the constitution. (This is the way that it finally turned out, but only after years of turmoil. For most of the intervening years we were dogged with all kinds of "official" pronouncements that our churches would be "assumed" to be in the merger, or that they would be in the merger unless they withdrew from their associations before the merger went through. It was not until the constitution of the United Church of Christ was drawn up that we ever got assurance that the churches would have to vote themselves in, and would not be in otherwise.)

It will bear repeating when we take up those events, but we might as well say right now that the best parts of the procedures were never carried out. First, there never was a joint session of our General Council with the General Synod of the Evangelical and Reformed General Synod, in the kind of face-to-face experience that I was soon to have at Allentown in 1945 and 1946. They never had the chance to discuss the matter and to find out if they both understood the same thing from the same wording.

Second, the General Council never openly considered the Basis of Union as a matter before the assembly for open discussion. There was always some motion on procedure before the house. They never permitted discussion paragraph by paragraph; or gave opportunity for questions as to the meaning of one passage or another; or gave any opportunity for any possible amendments before the document was sent out to the churches for a vote.

In these respects the procedures improvised along the

way were contrary to those voted in the 1944 Council meeting.

The provisions for getting better acquainted with the Evangelical and Reformed Church were carried out to some degree. There were leaders of the Evangelical and Reformed Church who came into the state of Connecticut, for instance, and addressed meetings of ministers; and there was a certain amount of back-and-forth questioning, but mostly from an uncritical viewpoint.

For me personally the most important exchange came when five of us Congregational ministers, selected, I presume, by Dr. Horton, went as guests to an Evangelical and Reformed Spiritual Conference, which they held annually at Cedar Crest College in Allentown, Pennsylvania. Pehaps it was because of my position as an opponent of the merger that I was invited to be one of the five. The others were, so far as I could judge, in favor of the union, even though they may have had a question or two to ask.

It was a memorable experience for me, and one that was both pleasant and at the same time deeply significant in all of my future stand on the merger.

As a slightly humorous touch, two things happened just as we were getting out of the car when we arrived. For one thing, the owner of the car carefully went around locking the doors on the car. One of the Evangelical and Reformed men standing by asked with a smile, "What's the matter; don't you trust us?" Another minister, who was still a pastor at the time, by name James E. Wagner, looked us over and said, "Well, I don't see any horns sticking out."

There were many things about the Spiritual Conference that were very enjoyable and might well be emulated by Congregational groups. In one sense it was a serious conference. In the mornings, and, I think, again in the evenings, there were some excellent addresses given by really good scholars. This was the serious part of the conference. But in the afternoons, unlike Congregational conferences that are jam-packed with business and meetings of all sorts, the Evangelical and Reformed men took off for the golf course or other places of recreation and fellowship together in a very leisurely way. I can highly commend it. Incidentally, the conference was four or five days long.

And these men in Pennsylvania were almost entirely from the "Reformed" side of the Evangelical and Reformed Church. Sometimes they spoke a bit critically of the "Evangelical" men as more regimented than they.

I found the Evangelical and Reformed ministers at that time exceedingly open, frank, and friendly. We would many times have discussions about the merger in which ten or fifteen of them would be gathered around, and all of them spoke very freely and frankly. Denominational officials present at the conference did not mix with us this way, and in public discussions were more inclined to be curt and officious. This does not apply to local synod presidents, who themselves were pastors and not full-time, paid executives. Some synod presidents were among those most open and friendly.

I liked the Evangelical and Reformed men personally. In fact one of them had so many things in common with me that I was happy to accept his invitation to come as his guest the following year to the next Spiritual Conference, in 1946. There were other Congregationalists who came that next year, but they were under the official auspices, with expenses paid by the denomination, as I had been in 1945.

The friend with whom I became so well acquainted, and whose methods of handling his church and methods of preaching seemed to be so nearly identical to my own, was Clement DeChant. He was elected to be the president of the Spiritual Conference for that following year. He passed away not many years later, for which I have always been sorry. But during the immediate period of our acquaintance we arranged to have an exchange of pulpits in which he was present when I preached in his church in Philadelphia, and I was present when he came to New London and preached at our church (Second Congregational). Ours was a very close association. The following year, in 1946, we roomed together, and we discussed various issues late into the night as we lay in the dark on our separate cots.

The first year, however, I began to get some rather definite impressions, and I am sure that these came from repeated statements made by many of these Evangelical and Reformed pastors, and later confirmed in great detail when the chairman of the Evangelical and Reformed committee on the merger was present, in 1946, for a very serious, well-attended discussion that lasted for a couple of hours.

I think back on these Evangelical and Reformed pastors as "young fellows." They were probably about my own age or a little younger in some cases. I had just turned forty. One of the most memorable things that happened, and that certainly played a part in my future understanding of things, was when a group of these young Evangelical and Reformed ministers were standing around—at least twelve or fifteen of them—and they told me how the merger had been presented to them first at their local synod meetings. One of them said, "We were told by our national leaders that you Congregationalists had come to the place where you felt that your system had broken down and that you had looked over all the other denominations and decided that our setup is the kind of thing which you want." The man who said this then turned to one minister after another and asked them for verification. He would turn to one man and say, "You are in a different synod than I am. Was that the way it was presented to you?" The answer was invariably Yes.

This was obviously contrary to all the fine assurances that we were being given that "nothing would be changed."

It was after attending this conference at Allentown that I went back, rather troubled in mind, to our summer cottage on Lake Sunapee and thought things over. On the one hand, I liked these young fellows. On the other hand, I was certainly troubled by the things which they had so openly told me. I knew that they spoke in favor of the presbyterian type of control, at least in so far as it related to ministerial standing—with its approval by the higher judicatory of any pastor selected by a local church before he could be called. It was at this time that I began to think in terms of some pamphleteering. To me it seemed perfectly obvious that something was wrong somewhere. I had the idea that if a few simple statements were sent out, laying the facts before some of the leaders in our denomination, that the right questions would be asked and the merger would be quickly dropped. It was at this time that I talked over with Dr. Fagley my idea of starting some pamphleteering. It was at that time that he said I could do it if I wanted, but there was simply no use. I remember his saying, "You can't beat city hall." I thought of that as simply an old cliche, but now I wonder how much more he knew about the inner workings, just then, than he was free to tell me.

I started my first writing of pamphlets in the middle of October 1945. I made up a list of approximately 200 names, mostly of state superintendents, members of the Executive Committee of the General Council, and so on. Dr. Fagley, in spite of his discouraging remarks, sent me one of my first contributions in the form of postage stamps to cover an enlarged mailing that would include 100 names that he sent me, mostly of prominent lay persons whom I would not have known about. And the third statement I sent out, which did not bear my name as author, was really written by Dr. Fagley as part of a report he made to the Executive Committee regarding the limited powers of the General Council. I did not include his recommendations about the steps that the General Council would presumably have to take if it were to clothe itself with the powers that the Basis of Union expected it to carry with it and turn over to the United Church in the event of union, which come up in the next chapter.

I got out one little mimeographed statement each week for the next seven weeks. These were somewhere between four and eight pages of half-sized sheets, done in small type on an old Hammond typewriter. On the basis of the 1944 General Council meeting, and of Dr. Horton's letter to the New London Association, in which he seemed intent upon squelching all opposition as soon as it appeared, I entitled my first pamphlet, *Is the Merger Being Put Over On Us?* The third pamphlet, containing one page besides what Dr. Fagley had written for the Executive Committee, I entitled *Documentary Evidence of the Fundamental Change Involved in the Basis of Union.* It bore neither his name nor mine. The fifth statement was written by Rev. Alexander Abbott, and bore his name. Its title: *Is the Name "Congregational" Important to Us?* The sixth statement, based especially upon conversations with Evangelical and Reformed men at Allentown, was entitled,

Will the Merger Involve Us in a Presbyterian System?

Incidentally, I also have the letters I wrote home from the 1944 General Council and from the next Council meeting at Grinnell in 1946. All of this material, in addition to the published minutes and reports of each Council from 1942 through 1958, give me opportunity to refresh my memory, if I need it, on any points that may arise.

With regard to the 1944 General Council it could be mentioned that the Massachusetts Congregational Conference, at its meeting a month earlier had adopted a resolution which included the following:

(1) The Massachusetts Congregational Conference recommends to the Executive Committee of the General Council that there be set up at the General Council meeting at Grand Rapids in June, a representative commission which shall be responsible for conducting hearings on the subject of the aforesaid Basis of Union. (p. 61, Minutes, 1944 General Council.)

Here was an effort toward an orderly and fair procedure. But no such commission was ever appointed, and at no General Council meeting was there ever a seminar set up where there could be informal discussion among interested parties regarding the Basis of Union—this in spite of the fact that seminars on many other topics were regular parts of Council programs. Everything was always kept strictly under control, and no general discussion ever permitted on the merger to be held at the 1946 General Council meeting. I personally sent a request for a seminar discussion on the merger to be held at the 1946 General Council meeting, and received a curt reply from Dr. Blanchard that there was no time for it.

One other thing happened at the '44 Council worthy of considerable note. Dr. Hugh Vernon White, one of the seven Congregational members of the committee that drew up the Basis of Union, wrote an article quite critical of the Basis of Union. It was written for our national magazine in plenty of time for inclusion before the Council met. But he was induced to withhold the article until the time of the Council meeting. Then he and Dr. Horton ostensibly joined in a statement coauthored by the two of them, making it appear that there was no disagreement within the committee. This statement was then published in the *Daily Advance*, which was received only by the Council delegates. It never did get national publicity.

This article initiated by Dr. White goes further in a forthright analysis of the plan of union than any statements emanating from the top level made before or after this time. Issues were ready to come forth at this early date; thus, note the emphasis placed in this article upon the matter of an overall constitution.

> The question for us to decide is whether the delegation of powers called for by the Basis of Union accords with the tradition and genius of our churches.
>
> A brief survey of practical differences which would be noted between our present and the proposed denomination will help us answer the question: (1) The entire denominational life would be described in a master constitution whereas at present we are operating under many constitutions knit together only by unwritten law. . . .
>
> (a) The relation between the General Synod, the Conferences, the Associations and the churches would undoubtedly be pointed up by the bringing together of what is now in the constitution of the General Council and what is now the material found in the "Manual." Standards of procedure for ordination would probably have greater influence upon usage if they were bound in with the accepted constitution and bylaws of the fellowship as a whole.
>
> (b) The relation between the General Synod and the Boards would also be closer than that which now exists between the General Council and the Boards. . . .
>
> . . . shall we now move on to a system defined in a written constitution heading up in a General Synod which would be both an ecclesiastical and an administrative body? We must decide whether this would constitute a desirable forward step in our denominational development or entail the loss of something essential in Congregationalism."

Numerous other admissions were made in this frank statement, the substance of which was later obscured by the innumerable assurances from Dr. Horton and others that "nothing would be changed." Even at the 1944 Grand Rapids meeting this frank statement was completely overshadowed by procedures that did not permit discussion of this or any other crucial facts.

Thus we see that, even though a fairly reasonable and open plan of procedures had been suggested and actually voted at the General Council meeting in 1944, the total result of the 1944 Council was quite other than a fair and objective beginning on merger discussion. The rigidly controlled discussion period, where Dr. Horton and Dr. Wilhelm Pauck "answered" people's questions at great length, and where no one could follow up with further questions, prevented any fair procedure at this Council. Then, in the following two years, the reasonable procedures for a joint meeting with the Evangelical and Reformed General Synod in 1946, and for a full discussion and vote upon the Basis of Union by a future General Council, before the churches were asked to vote on the Basis of Union, were never carried out. Instead, everything fell into a pattern of barnstorming, and political methods.

Let me hasten to add, however, that when sane and reasonable procedures were scrapped, as they were prior to the 1946 and 1948 Council meetings, it was not the result of evil conniving and intent on the part of the great majority of leaders in the fellowship. Instead the procedures that had been planned and announced were scrapped when the merger ran into very deep trouble, and when the saner and more decent leadership knew that delays were absolutely essential. But then, angered by the delays, some of the militant and more fanatical ecumenists, encouraged, we believe, by Dr. Horton, took things into their own hands and pushed all reasonable caution aside and demanded immediate action—without permitting any decent, objective and full discussion before forcing a vote. The actions they forced led the denomination into deep trouble, as we shall see.

7

Events Leading up to the Grinnell Council of 1946

THE three years immediately following the 1944 Council were extremely important, with plans being made and then cancelled, and new plans being made and changed again.

All the important issues came to the surface and were plainly set forth by one person or another by January 1947. At that time the Basis of Union was "finalized" and frozen into an unchangeable form. Yet never were the real issues met head-on, and never were clear or explicit answers given to basic questions sincerely asked and earnestly set forth. All of this will be evident as we proceed.

Any orderly procedures that would have led to a full discussion of the plan of union got lost in the shuffle (or maybe they were purposely scrapped to avoid an honest confrontation on the issues).

The General Council meeting at Grinnell, Iowa, in 1946, was supposed to have furnished a point by point, line by line discussion on the Basis of Union. This was to take place in a *joint* meeting of the Congregational Christian General Council and the Evangelical and Reformed General Synod. In preparation for this an edition of the Basis of Union was prepared with a separate number in front of each line of print, so that discussion could easily be drawn to any sentence, word, or provision in the document. This edition of the Basis of Union, dated September 1945, was marked, "Final Edition. To be submitted to the Congregational Christian General Council and the Evangelical and Reformed General Synod in June 1946."

But no such discussion of the Basis of Union ever took place. No meeting of the General Council ever presented the opportunity to ask the meaning of specific passages or to offer amendments to the plan before it was "finalized" and sent out for the votes of approval by conferences, associations, and churches. Much less was there ever a joint meeting of the General Council with the Evangelical and Reformed General Synod in a three-day joint session, where such an examination and discussion of the Basis of Union could take place. But as we shall see, once "finalized," the Basis of Union became the object of interpretations, explanations, assurances, promises, and weasel-worded casuistry from persons of high estate to low and from committees, conferences, and the General Council itself. And then the "comments" and "Interpretations" thus set forth became themselves the subjects of further interpretation and even of testimony in various courts as to what they meant.

To explain how all this irregularity of procedure came to pass will be the purpose of this chapter. The whole future pattern of the merger's promotion was established in this three-year period, and probably the disorderly and highly improper actions of the General Council at Grinnell really decided which way the merger would eventually go. From that time on, even without any honest and forthright discussion of the issues, the merger was considered a foregone conclusion by most officials in the denomination, including almost all of the state superintendents. This in turn made most ministers feel that they must be pro-merger if they were to be recommended for advancement to larger churches. What this meant in the next eleven years, when the United Church of Christ came into existence, is incalculable. Hence the tremendous importance of the events which we shall proceed to set forth.

Some of the events described in this chapter were complicated, and the various plans adopted by the Executive Committee, and then superseded by other plans, were exceedingly involved and lengthy. To make this chapter more readable I shall summarize where possible and then furnish the full text in the appendix.

EVENTS RIGHT AFTER GRAND RAPIDS

Troubles began to develop soon after the Grand

Rapids meeting. Some very fundamental problems had not been taken into account, and one by one they began to surface.

For one thing, the negotiations for the union had been conducted by one group: The Commission on Interchurch Relations and Christian Unity. But the Executive Committee of the General Council had to be brought into the picture, since it acted for the General Council between meetings. Questions began coming up in the Executive Committee. Some of these were referred back to the Commission on Interchurch Relations which in turn had to confer further with the similar committee of the Evangelical and Reformed Church. Thus we get the following sequence:

1. On 26 September, 1944, the Executive Committee voted to meet with the corresponding group from the Evangelical and Reformed Church to go over the plans. (*Advance Reports*, p. 8, 1946)

2. On 23 January, 1945, the Committee voted that the conferences be invited to study the Basis of Union and report their suggestions for improvements before June 1945. (*Advance Reports*, p. 10, 1946)

3. On 15 March, 1945 the order of business for the Executive Committee was "an unhurried discussion of the proposed merger" for the entire afternoon and evening, with five statements to be considered. Then they voted for six important studies and reports to be made and furnished in the future (*Advance Reports*, pp. 10–11, 1946). This was where things really began to get complicated, and we shall soon discuss the details.

4. On 19–22 June 1945, after general discussion the Executive Committee agreed to a new, slightly different timetable, in which the General Council would meet for three days "with representatives of the Evangelical and Reformed Church for discussion, with seminars and hearings." This did not say "with General Synod of the Evangelical and Reformed Church," and it did not provide for a vote of approval on Basis of Union, but only on "what steps should be taken and how the program of education should be financed looking forward to a final vote in 1948." (*Advance Reports*, 1946, p. 13)

5. On 6-7 December 1945, Executive Committee voted to adopt "the recommendation of the Joint Committee, that a joint meeting with the Evangelical and Reformed General Synod be held at Grinnell." (*Advance Reports*, 1946, p. 16)

6. On 29-30 January, 1946, it was voted:

   a. that before any churches, associations, conferences or the General Council be encouraged to vote finally upon the proposed union, time be taken to prepare a supplement to the Basis of Union covering matters not previously considered;

   b. that the vote at the General Council in June, 1946 not be upon the matter of reference to the churches, etc., but upon the preparation of such a supplement; and

   c. seven separate paragraphs dealing with matters to be included in the "supplement," especially with reference to financial matters and how the Boards would be united. (*Advance Reports*, 1946, pp. 17-18)

7. There was one final action on 31 January, 1945. The Executive Committee "VOTED: That we deem it inadvisable at this time, to take a straw vote, on the matter of the proposed merger with the Evangelical and Reformed Church." (*Advance Reports*, 1946, p. 18)

This final recommendation would seem wise under the circumstances, and certainly not unreasonable. Yet from all the information I received at the time, Dr. Horton promptly ignored this vote of the Executive Committee, and so did his most ardent followers. This marked the turning point. It meant the end of any careful, objective, honest facing of the issues. It marked the beginning of the use of mob psychology and bandwagon tactics on a wide and deliberate scale. The Grinnell Council meeting was its testing ground, and nothing was ever the same after that.

As for the other actions mentioned above, a great deal more lay behind them than might easily be supposed.

For one thing, the digest of minutes of the Executive Committee that was printed as part of the *Advance Reports*, for the General Council, was always greatly abbreviated. The members of the Executive Committee received the full minutes at the time, or soon after each meeting. I was privileged to see some of these. Even the digest of minutes referred to above mentions "A Statement on Constitutional Provisions, prepared by Dr. Fagley." This was on the agenda for discussion on 15 March, 1945. This document I have, and, as mentioned earlier, I used most of it in the third pamphlet which I printed. But there is no indication whether the Executive Committee ever studied it or discussed it. It was voted to refer it, however, to the Commission on Interchurch Relations. There are references to fifteen questions raised by Dr. Theodore M. Shipherd. But what these were is not indicated beyond the fact that Dr. Shipherd had gathered the questions which other members of the Exective Committee were raising.

Among the more serious matters voted upon were:
1. That there be a thorough study of the financial situation of each denomination.
2. The relationship that the Congregational Boards would have in the union. (This is what led to the recommendation that a supplement to the Basis of Union be prepared; eventually this simply became chapter VIII of the Basis of Union.)
3. A question as to whether any other mergers were possible. Dr. Horton said no.
4. The question as to the nature of the Evangelical and Reformed Church, with a vote that each member be sent a copy of its Constitution. (Rather late, it would seem to me, to start finding out what they were trying to merge with.)
5. That Dr. Shipherd's questions be submitted to the Commission on Interchurch Relations and that specific answers be received and circulated among the members before the June meeting. (Nothing about these is mentioned in the minutes of the June meeting, or any other place.)

Finally came the vote, which we mentioned above, on whether Dr. Fagley's statement on Constitutional provisions be sent to the Commission on Interchurch Relations. This statement went to the very heart of the matter as to whether the General Council had any power or right to carry out the Basis of Union. All of the above were on pages 10 and 11 of the *Advance Reports*. Incidentally, when Dr. Blanchard wrote his report for the Commission, appearing on page 38 of *Advance Reports*, he gives not the slightest indication of any awareness of the "Constitutional question." Certainly neither he nor anyone else ever made public any answer to the very serious questions Dr. Fagley raised, which will come into our discussion very shortly. They tie in with two other very significant factors which are definitely reflected in the minutes and the actions taken, even though the condensed minutes do not tell us everything that went on.

DISCUSSION OF VOTING PROCEDURE

One of the votes of the Executive committee mentioned above referred to the fact "that the Council is at present definitely limited in its actions under the vote of the Grand Rapids Council." This was part of the reason for giving up the original plan of a vote at Grinnell. Apparently it took a long time to realize that difficulty existed, because this vote was not until January 30 or 31 of 1946. By that time many other difficulties had also arisen.

Very little transpired in the closing months of 1944, relative to the merger, except the vote of September 26 that the two Executive Committees should get together—not just the Interchurch Relations groups. This was the closing period of the Second World War, and travel conditions were very difficult. The January minutes mention only the request that conferees send in suggestions for changes in the Basis of Union.

But somewhere along the line, the Executive Committee took considerable time for discussion of the "nonbinding" provision of the 1944 vote at Grand Rapids by the General Council. This, of course, referred to my "amendment," saying that conferences, associations, and churches, when voting on the Basis of Union, would vote "with the distinct understanding that such vote was in no way binding upon them." The abridged minutes of the Executive Committee, as published in the Advance Reports for 1946 do not show any record of these discussions, but they were fully revealed in the unabridged minutes, which were mimeographed and sent to members of the Executive Committee shortly after the meetings transpired.

The thought was advanced that two votes of the churches would be required because of this "non-binding" provision that was added to the procedures at the Grand Rapids Council. The first vote, it was suggested, would be "advisory," and then some later vote would have to be taken by which the churches, associations, and conferences would commit themselves to the union. In all the years that followed, nothing really definite and final was set forth on this until, in 1960, the final constitution for the United Church was prepared. For all those intervening years a great deal of scheming to avoid such a second vote went on, with all sorts of weasel-worded statements that churches would be assumed to be in, or that they would be in the union if their associations joined, or that they would have to vote themselves out of the "fellowship" to avoid being in. The greatest amount of friction and unpleasantness over the merger came over this issue of how churches could be gotten into the merger, as later discussions will show.

A great deal more was involved, however, than just my amendment at Grand Rapids. At issue was just how the General Council could proceed with the merger, what authority did it have to do so, and what steps would it have to take to make the procedure look even halfway legitimate. Let us go back and see the problem as it existed.

All editions of the Basis of Union, through the provisional drafts of March and August 1943, of March and October 1944, and of September, 1945, carried this very direct and simple provision:

XI. APPROVAL OF THE BASIS OF UNION

1. The Basis of Union shall be submitted to the national bodies of the Congregational Christian Churches and of the Evangelical and Reformed Church. Each shall proceed according to its own constitution in the approval or disapproval of the Basis of Union.

Now this was very simple for the Evangelical and Reformed Church, because its constitution had definite provision for making changes. The General Synod would first vote its approval; then the matter would go to the local synods. If two-thirds of the synods approved, then the

General Synod would declare the matter adopted at its next meeting.

For the Congregationalists no such provision existed. The Constitution for the General Council was not one having authority over Conferences, Associations or Churches. There was no provision for a merger of this kind. This was a very difficult and complex problem, but apparently only very simplistic and superficial solutions were sought in the 1944-46 period.

Later, during a lull in the merger controversy, when the General Council had been restrained by court action, the Committee on Free Church Polity and Unity was appointed in 1950 in accordance with the vote of the General Council to make a thorough study of the nature of Congregationalism with the specific task of finding out what kind of unions the Congregational Christian Churches could enter into, and just what authority the General Council would have. After calm, objective, and unhurried studies over a four-year period, the committee came up with six different theories. There simply was no clear-cut answer.

If one looks at the procedures voted at the 1944 General Council at Grand Rapids, it is easy to see that the original intent was to match the procedures of the Evangelical and Reformed Church. The General Council of Congregational Christian Churches would, under the plan, approve the Basis of Union at its meeting in June, 1946. So would the Evangelical and Reformed General Synod. The General Council, under the plan proposed at Grand Rapids, would then submit the Basis of Union to the conferences, association, and churches "with the request that within twelve months they study it, discuss it, and finally approve or disapprove the union of the two denominations on the terms which the Basis of Union sets forth. . . ." Meanwhile the local synods of the Evangelical and Reformed Church were to vote also on the Basis of Union. If the groups in both denominations gave sufficient approval, then the two national bodies were to meet in Columbus, Ohio, in the fall of 1947 and consummate the union.

The change in procedures made when I offered my amendment really upset the plan. Or did it? Had the original motion meant that when churches "finally approved" the Basis of Union that they were to give *final approval*, or did the words *finally approve* merely indicate the sequence in which each body would act? If the original procedure had intended "final approval," then it would seem to me in looking back upon the event that my "amendment" should have been declared out of order because it would destroy the intent of the original motion. It would appear that ultimately my proposed amendment accepted by Dr. Horton on behalf of the committee as part of the original motion did destroy the intent of the original motion in the minds of the Executive Committee at a later date, and that was one reason for not carrying out the original time-schedule.

I have always been somewhat puzzled by the alacrity with which Dr. Horton accepted my "amendment" and said that he was sure that the other members of the committee would accept the wording as part of the original motion. Or why did not Albert W. Palmer, who was chairman of the Commission on Interchurch Relations at the time, object? Dr. Palmer acted as moderator, as I recall, during the merger discussion, even though Dr. Blanchard was the real moderator. (The two men were switched around after the 1944 meeting: Dr. Blanchard became chairman of the Interchurch Relations Commission, and Dr. Palmer was to be moderator four years later, at Oberlin in 1948.)

Two possible explanations come to mind as to why my amendment was allowed to go through. For one thing Dr. Horton may have sought to avoid a showdown then and there. I have been told that in Executive Committee meetings and elsewhere, it was quite common for Dr. Horton to have a matter dropped for the time being if he sensed that he might lose in a vote of the committee. Then, at some other unannounced time, he would bring the same matter up in different guise, hoping to avoid a confrontation. He tried, I was told, to avoid all outright, open, and evident disagreements. Perhaps that is what motivated him when he so agreeably accepted something that later caused a lot of trouble.

But there is another possible explanation. Maybe both Dr. Horton and Dr. Palmer knew that they had a back-up plan in case the recommended procedures did not go through as planned. This was something that most people knew absolutely nothing about, even though it was openly part of the record, right in the minutes of the 1944 General Council meeting. I see no trace of any mention of it within the Executive Committee. I did not discover it until about May of 1946. Dr. Theodore Shipherd, who had been one of the most alert critics of the merger, confessed to me just before the Grinnell meeting that if he ever had known about it, he had quite forgotten that it was there.

Early in the 1944 General Council meeting at Grand Rapids, there had been proposed as an amendment to the General Council Constitution a whole series of provisions by which the General Council might pass an "act" affecting conferences, associations, or churches, and then the bodies would have twelve months in which to approve or disapprove the act. This proposed amendment to the constitution could not be acted upon finally for another two years, which would bring it up at the 1946 General Council meeting at Grinnell. The proposed amendments to the bylaws, which were to go with this amendment to the General Council constitution, would have the act go into effect if a *majority* of the bodies *voting* had approved it. The bodies voting would in each case be those that would be "affected" by the act of the General Council. (See *Advance Reports*, 1946, p. 116)

Here, it would appear at first glance (by persons not familiar with Congregational polity and the inherent limitations placed on the General Council at its inception) was the perfect answer to the procedural question. This would mean that the General Council could proceed "according to its own constitution" in approving the Basis of Union, just as the Basis of Union itself stipulated. The proposal would fit perfectly into the picture and would put the General Council on the same basis as the Evangelical and Reformed General Synod—only with the Congregationalists a mere majority of those *voting* in each category would be required. What a cinch! It would mean, too, that the procedures voted at Grand Rapids would be merely a duplication, except that they looked forward to "overwhelming" approval, not just a majority in each category. Was this possible back-up plan the reason why my amendment got by so easily? With this as a possibility they would not need the 1944 vote at Grand Rapids on procedures. In fact for them to follow the amendment route would ostensibly conform better to the provisions of the Basis of Union. Certainly this proposed amendment to the constitution fitted very neatly into the picture. But the question was, would it have any validity even if passed and adopted at Grinnell? To this deeper and more fundamental problem we turn now.

FACING THE CONSTITUTIONAL PROBLEM

We come logically now to the statement prepared at the request of the Executive Committee by Dr. Fred Fagley on "constitutional provision," mentioned on pages 10 and 11 of the 1946 *Advance Reports*, and to which I have frequently alluded. All but the last paragraph of this statement appeared in my own series of publications around the end of October 1945, although I did not attach Dr. Fagley's name to it. It was one of the documents I sent to all superintendents and other leading people in the denomination. This statement by Dr. Fagley showed very clearly that the General Council could not, under the express limitations placed on it at the time of its inception and recognized ever since, adopt the Basis of Union. For the same reason, I might add, it could not logically or with any authority amend its own constitution in the manner proposed in 1944 and which we have just been discussing.

I mentioned in an earlier chapter that the General Council had no legislative or judicial authority.

This paper by Dr. Fagley traces the history of this limitation. And if the General Council had no legislative authority, it could not pass any act that would affect conferences, associations or churches, either with or without ratification "by a majority of those voting within twelve months."

Dr. Fagley's paper was entitled, *Brief Statement on Constitutional Provisions.* It was mimeographed for the Executive Committee and bears his signature. He gave me a copy very soon after it was prepared, although I was in the U. S. Army (for three months until V. E. Day and the end of the European conflict) at the time that it is first mentioned in the Executive Committee Minutes for 15

March, 1945. This "brief" statement would take at least five pages to present in full in this book, but in terms of the tremendous amount of emphasis that its material had always received from Congregational historians and authorities on Congregational polity, his statement is indeed very brief. It states the things most commonly, and most sacredly, held among Congregationalists. I shall leave out some of the first part of Dr. Fagley's paper, but I shall now copy verbatim its most essential statements and conclusions, giving some brief comments of my own along the way.

Dr. Fagley starts with the National Council's first meeting in Oberlin in 1871. He notes that the call for the meeting stated, among other things, the proposition:

> That the churches withhold from the National Council all legislative or judicial power over the churches or individuals and all right to act as a council of reference.

Note that it was recognized that the churches themselves were setting up this Council, and it was they that were withholding all legislative authority.

Then Dr. Fagley quotes directly from the constitution, which was adopted after two days' discussion and which, with only minor revisions, was in force until 1913:

> The churches, therefore, while establishing this National Council for the furtherance of the common interests and work of all the churches, do maintain the Scriptural and inalienable right of each church to self-government and administration; and this National Council shall never exercise legislative or judicial authority, nor consent to act as a council of reference.

Dr. Fagley goes on to say:

> In the Council of 1913, when it was proposed to reorganize the missionary work and strengthen the Council, the question naturally arose—was there any encroachment on the fundamental principle of complete autonomy of the local church? . . .

The revised constitution of 1913, Dr. Fagley pointed out, included the following preamble and section on polity:

> The Congregational Churches of the United States, by del-

egates in National Council assembled, reserving all the rights and cherished memories belonging to this organization under its former constitution . . . and affirming our loyalty to the basic principles of our representative democracy, hereby set forth the things most surely believed among us concerning faith, polity, and fellowship:

POLITY. We believe in the freedom and responsibility of the individual soul, and the right of private judgment. We hold to the autonomy of the local church and its independence of all ecclesiastical control. . . .

"Under this revised constitution," declared Dr. Fagley, "the Council carried forward its work until 1931 when the proposal was made for the Council to unite with the Christian Church. It was then explained that in the Christian Church the principle of church government, resting completely with the local church which was absolute in its range, no portion of which had been delegated to any other body in that fellowship, was identical to that of the Congregational churches. Therefore, while the question was raised as to whether or not the delegates elected by the Congregational churches to the Council of 1931 possessed the right to vote on the question of merger with the Christian churches, the question was not pressed because the churches were not being asked to surrender any of their authority nor to confer upon the Council any rights beyond those possessed by the National Council under its previous constitution.

"The new constitution adopted in 1931 contained the following paragraph:

The Congregational Christian Churches of the United States by delegates assembled, reserving all the rights and cherished memories of their historic past and affirming loyalty to the basic principles of unity and democracy in church polity, hereby set forth the principles of Christian fellowship immemorially held by these churches. We hold sacred the freedom of the individual soul and the right of private judgment. We stand for the autonomy of the local church and its independence of ecclesiastical control. . . .

Dr. Fagley then quoted the opinions of Dr. William E. Barton, noted authority on Congregationalism, author of two minister's manuals and the book, *The Law of Congregational Usage*; and also from Dr. Charles E. Burton, executive secretary of the General Council at the time of the union with the Christian Church and author of the *Manual of the Congregational Christian Churches* of 1936:

Dr. Barton stated:
"The national Council is not an ecclesiastical court, and has no jurisdiction in matters of discipline, or ecclesiastical standing. It has no authority over any local church, association or conference...."
and Dr. Burton:
"The General Council is not a legislative body with ecclesiastical authority over the churches, the conferences, the associations, or the denominational societies. It does, however, pass recommendations addressed to any of these. It also bears testimony to its faith through approved statements or resolutions on various topics at its own will. These expressions carry with them no authority beyond the weight of their own wisdom, backed by the significance of the delegation from which they issue...."

Dr. Fagley then takes up two constitutional questions suggested from a study of the Basis of Union:

I. The Basis of Union provided under Article 2—*Practice*—that: "The government of the United Church shall be exercised through Congregations (Associations if desired), Conferences, and the General Synod in such wise that the autonomy of each shall be respected in its own sphere, each having its own rights and responsibilities...."
This section proposes that the delegates to the General Council shall establish a Synod which will have autonomy and authority, and the question arises—Do the delegates elected under our present constitution have any authority themselves which they can pass on and lodge with the agency they are asked to create?
II. In Article 4, Section 5, it is provided that: "The General Synod shall have power to receive overtures and petitions; to give counsel in regard to cases referred to it; and to maintain correspondence with other denominations."
But the original constitution specifically states that: "...this National Council shall never exercise legislative or judicial authority, nor consent to act as a council of reference."
This provision was reaffirmed, in general statements, in the constitution of 1913 and 1931.

The closing paragraph of Dr. Fagley's statement, which I did not include in the pamphlet I printed in October, raised the specific question as to things that might have to be done before the General Council tried to consummate the Basis of Union. Obviously this was just an exploratory effort on Dr. Fagley's part, with no claim to a final solution to a difficult question. Note that he refers to the *churches* conferring authority upon the General Council, instead of the naive notion of the General Council merely trying to vote authority to itself, through the proposed amendment we have been discussing.

Dr. Fagley's final paragraph was as follows:

> It would appear therefore, that to enable the delegates to the General Council to vote on the several proposals in the Plan of Union, the first step might be to seek a revision of the present constitution by which the churches would confer upon the General Council the necessary authority, clothing it with the rights and duties it would be expected to transfer to the proposed Synod. For if the free *churches* of our fellowship are to unite with *a church*, with a centralized authoritative nature, that these independent churches should first become *a church* themselves with corresponding authority, rights and duties comparable to the body with which they seek to unite. Then the Congregational Christian Church thus created could transfer to the new body, the General Synod, the autonomy in its own sphere and the authority over the boards and agencies of the fellowship which are implied in the Basis of Union.
>
> Respectfully submitted,
> Frederick L. Fagley

This, then, was the statement prepared by Dr. Fagley in response to the request of the Executive Committee regarding "constitutional provisions." As I have intimated, there is no indication that the Executive Committee ever got to a study and discussion of it. In the "unhurried" discussion of merger matters on 15 March, 1945, the statement was on the docket. But apparently all that was done was to refer it to the Commission on Interchurch Relations and to say "that the questions raised in the statement be kept on our agenda for future study." No further mention is made of it, nor is there any indication a report back was made by the Interchurch Relations Commission

I would believe that Dr. Shipherd and others tried to get a study of these issues, and Dr. Fagley's statement was intended to be a "thought-starter" that might bring the fundamental issues out into the open.

Knowing Dr. Fagley as well as I did, I cannot for one moment believe that he would want the churches to vote the kind of authority suggested in Dr. Fagley's last paragraph, nor would he want them to vote to become a "church." What is more, I feel sure that, being a realist, Dr. Fagley was quite confident that the churches, if asked to do these things, would never comply. His suggestions were for the sake of an honest facing of the facts, which was actually never done from start to finish of the merger presentation and discussion.

I remember that after a leisurely discussion with Dr. Fagley one afternoon at his cottage, we were walking slowly out to my car. As a kind of final summation of our discussion, Dr. Fagley made a wry face, as he was sometimes wont to do, and sweeping one hand in a wide circle from one side of his body to the other, he said, "Douglas doesn't care anything about a vote by the churches. If he can get the General Council's approval, that's all he cares about." He referred, of course, to Douglas Horton, and this was his summation of the way that he believed Dr. Horton was operating, and was planning to operate. It was a prophetic utterance.

It may have been at this same time that Dr. Fagley gave a bit of his homey philosophy on this same subject. He commented that as far as the churches were concerned, "Home is where the boards are, and if the General Council goes into the union it would take the boards with it, since its members control them." In other words, even if the churches would have to vote themselves into the union, they would be pretty sure to do it if the Boards and Council were already in.

PROBLEMS THAT DEVELOPED WITHIN OFFICIAL CIRCLES

As we noted, the questions that Dr. Shipherd had raised within the Executive Committee, and Dr. Fagley's statement on the constitutional provisions, were presented prior to the summer of 1945. There is no evidence of any thorough discussion having taken place on them, but the mere fact that they were presented means that some people must have become aware of certain difficulties.

The summer of 1945 was the occasion of my going, with four other Congregationalists, to the Spiritual Conference at Allentown, Pennsylvania. I had the feeling that the other Congregationalists went mostly with the desire to find out good things about the Evangelical and Reformed men and their church, and any questions I heard them ask were not too embarrassing.

I think that I found as many nice things about the Evangelical and Reformed men as they did, and, as I commented in the last chapter, I liked the men with whom I became acquainted. But I did ask questions, and some of these were on very fundamental matters. As I said before, the men were frank, open, and honest with me. We seemed mutually to understand that we had differences. It was on the basis of these discussions that I wrote some of my early pamphlets in the fall of 1945.

I have often wondered if my response to leisurely contact with the Evangelical and Reformed men had something to do with the abandonment, on the part of the leaders of the two denominations of any plan to have the General Synod of the Evangelical and Reformed Church and the General Council of the Congregational Christian Churches meet together for a three-day discussion of the Basis of Union. If one individual, like myself, meeting leisurely with Evangelical and Reformed men for five days, could come up with so many discoveries as to issues that were not being faced, and of presentations that were different as between the two denominations, what would have happened if 300 delegates of the Evangelical and Reformed Church had met with 1,000 delegates from the Congregational Christian Churches and had tried to go over the Basis of Union line by line and sentence by sentence? We can easily imagine what would happen if some Congregationalist tried to clarify some part of the Basis of Union, and the Evangelical and Reformed men wanted it just as it was, or else wanted it made stronger in the opposite direction.

Actually this is the sort of thing the Congregationalists later tried to do by themselves, after it was too late. Practically all of the discussion at the Oberlin Council in 1948 was an attempt to work over the wording of the interpretations and to get phrasing that would be satisfactory to Congregationalists in general. But it was then too late to have any changes made in the Basis of Union, and the Evangelical and Reformed General Synod was not present to make objections or opposite suggestions. Useless as it was, in any fundamental sense, the Oberlin Council fiddled along trying to get interpretations of the Basis of Union that would "sell" the merger to the churches that had voted against it or had not voted at all on the Basis of Union.

The futility of all this, from the standpoint of an honest and honorable approach to the union, was proven a few months later when the Evangelical and Reformed General Council (their equivalent to our Executive Committee) took the position that its members would not be bound by the Oberlin interpretations. At their meeting on 29 September, 1948, the Evangelical and Reformed leaders said that the Congregationalists could have any interpretations they wanted, but neither the Evangelical and Reformed Church nor the future United Church of Christ would be bound by them. Then the most disgraceful part of the whole merger deliberations took place. The Congregational Church Executive Committee tried to cover up the fact that the Evangelical and Reformed people had taken any such vote. They insisted on a joint meeting as soon as possible and put the pressure on the Evangelical and Reformed leaders to yield. "We can't get the votes for the Basis of Union," said the Congregational Church people, "unless you change your position." And so, having honestly stated their feelings, the Evangelical and Reformed leaders consented under duress, saying that they would go along. Years later Dr. Wagner was to bring the matter up again by saying that the Oberlin interpretations had always been repugnant to the Evangelical and Reformed Church.

Is this not proof enough that a joint meeting of the Congregational Church General Council with the Evangelical and Reformed General Synod for a three-day discussion of the Basis of Union, line by line, would have ended in disaster? From just reading minutes of Executive Committee action it might be supposed that the joint meeting merely got innocently lost in the shuffle. A realistic look at things makes such an interpretation look ridiculous. Did my visits at Allentown in 1945, and the discoveries I made in five days of visiting there, tip the leaders off? Is this why things became more and more a matter of sessions behind closed doors, with carefully worded releases covering up the real problems as they were being presented? Is this the reason for the "stiff-arm" tactics of keeping the opponents of the merger from ever getting in on the decision-making?

As I stated before, I started publishing my own statements on the merger in the middle of October 1945. Seven of them were printed before the midwinter meetings of 1946 of the Executive Committee and the Board officials. Another seven of them were published between that time and the Grinnell Council. These pamphlets were:

1. *Is the Merger Being Put over on Us?* This was based largely upon the way that the merger presentation was handled in 1944 at the Grand Rapids meeting.
2. *How Much Does the Ecumenical Church Require of Us?*
3. *Documentary Evidence of the Fundamental Change Involved in the "Basis of Union."* This was Dr. Fagley's statement, complete except for the omission of the last paragraph and of his signature.
4. *Are the Dangers of Regimentation Real?*
5. *Is the Name "Congregational" Important to Us?* This was a statement prepared by Rev. Alexander H. Abbott and bore his name as author, but was sent out on 8 November 1945 as one of my series.
6. *Would the Merger Involve Us in a Presbyterian System?* This document, sent out on 20 November 1945, was based almost entirely upon my conversations with the Evangelical and Reformed men at Allentown.
7. *Are We Temperamentally Suited to Unite?* This also was based upon conversations with the men at the Spiritual Conference in Allentown in 1945.

As I indicated before, these statements were sent out only to about three hundred individuals, but including all of the state superintendents, members of the executive committee, and others whose names Dr. Fagley had asked me to include.

I have no way of knowing what effect these pamphlets

had on the turn of events as they developed. At least two of the superintendents ordered quantities of some of these publications to send out to ministers in their states. On the whole I received only very civil and generally commendatory letters in response to them. Up to the time of the Grinnell Council everyone seemed to be very open and frank with me and tended to show me a great deal of respect. Everything changed after the Grinnell Council when the denominational officials began taking the attitude that everything was settled in favor of the merger. Many men who had been open and frank with me before would hardly speak to me or even nod their heads as we passed, from that time on.

One of the most articulate reactions which I received to my pamphlets came from Dr. George W. Richards. Dr. Richards had been professor of church history for many years at Lancaster Seminary, and most of the ministers of the previous Reformed Church had studied under him. He was later president of that seminary; he was chairman of the committee on merger for the Reformed church with the Evangelical; he was first president of the combined Evangelical and Reformed Church; and he was chairman of their Merger Committee since the beginning of the discussions with our fellowship. His letter follows:

May 13, 1946

Dear Brother Burton:

Thank you for sending copies of your pamphlets referring to the proposed union. You raise difficult questions which must be carefully considered. Of course the polity of the Evangelical and Reformed Church directly contradicts that of the Congregational and Christian Churches. If either of the negotiating parties is ready to yield to the other, we can unite so far as polity is concerned. Personally I think the union must be *either-or* not *both-and*. If one or the other method of polity is adopted with enthusiasm and voluntarily, union is possible; but union by compromise or surrender, I cannot endorse. I thought when we began negotiations there might be a third possible way; but according to your pamphlets that seems to be out of the question.

Sincerely yours,
Geo. W. Richards

By the time of the Grinnell Council Dr. Richards was again looking for "a third way," as we shall see. But his letter here was more perceptive and frank than any from leaders of the Congregational Christian negotiating team.

Other things that began to influence our own official group prior to the midwinter meeting of January 1946 were questions that were being raised by Dr. William F. Frazier, who said that two pushcart peddlers selling oysters on the streets of New York would not think of combining their businesses with as little attention to details of the financial arrangements and so on, as had been shown in the merger negotiations to date. This is what he was saying publicly in meetings in various states.

Sometime prior to the midwinter meeting I met with three men who drew up a petition to be presented to the Executive Committee, hopefully with many other signatures affixed, requesting that the merger be dropped. These men were Dr. Alfred Grant Walton, who was president of the Board of Home Missions; Dr. Russell Henry Stafford, who was president of the American Board of Commissioners for Foreign Missions; and Mr. Allen Burns, who was vice-chairman of the Executive Committee. I do not recall whether there were any others present but the four of us. I still have the full document they drew up. However, at the time of the midwinter meeting, there was so much sentiment against going ahead with the merger that I doubt if this petition was ever pushed, or many other signatures solicited.

These, then, were some of the forerunners of the midwinter meeting:

The questions raised by Dr. Shipherd;

The statement on the constitutional problem by Dr. Fagley;

My own pamphlets, which went to most of the official group;

The criticisms being made by Dr. Frazier and others;

And the pending petition from leaders in the American Board, the Home Board, and the Executive Committee.

When the midwinter meeting was held in January, all of the officials of the boards, commissions, and so forth were present, along with the state superintendents. Dr. Harry Johnson was president of the superintendents' conference that year, and he called the superintendents together and asked Dr. Frazier, treasurer of the Board of

Home Missions; Dr. Frank S. Scribner, secretary of the Annuity Fund, and Dr. Fred Field Goodsell, the executive vice-chairman of the American Board (the real Executive of the Board) to address the superintendents. When these three executives had explained the difficulties, problems, and inequities in the merger plan, word came out that the superintendents had now turned almost solidly against the merger. This was in January of 1946.

The atmosphere of the midwinter meeting became one of either pessimism about the chances of the merger, or of downright conviction that the whole thing should be dropped.

From that time on I kept receiving word from people "in the know" that the merger was dead. They said that I was foolish to waste any more time on it. Nevertheless, I did send out seven more leaflets before the Grinnell meeting in June.

MANIPULATING THE GENERAL COUNCIL MEETING

In the spring of 1946, prior to the General Council meeting, there was no issue before the churches, associations, or conferences on which they were supposed to take any kind of vote or express any opinion or desire. In fact they had been told *not* to take a straw vote on the merger at that time since additional work had to be done on the official plan before it was ready for consideration.

Nevertheless some unofficial activities were going on in various places. Dr. Douglas Horton was making speeches on the merger and, despite the official vote by the Executive Committee of the General Council that *no straw votes should be taken*, he would, I was told at the time, frequently ask his audience for a show of hands as to how many favored the union. Thus he would go, according to the information that I received, from place to place presenting only a promerger view. Then he would report that at his last meeting almost everyone was in favor of the union, and again he would call for a show of hands. In this way it was possible for him to claim that almost everyone favored the merger.

Dr. Shipherd reported to me at the time that Dr. Horton was very busy in the spring of 1946 journeying around the country, addressing groups wherever he could on the merger. Dr. Fagley reported that Dr. Horton was out "beating the bushes" for the merger.

Then *Advance*, our denominational paper, pulled a publicity stunt incomparably clever in giving the Executive Committee a "black eye" for its actions in delaying the merger, and at the same time whipping up emotional pressure for immediate action on the merger. The editor, Dr. John Scotford, had already been acting as one of the chief promoters of the merger, with glowing editorials for it in almost every issue. Before printing the official actions of the Executive Committee—which called for delay—he printed, on the same page (p. 36 of the April 1946 issue) and just before these official actions, a very inflammatory denunciation of "certain officials" responsible for the delay. This letter, titled "A Communication," addressed to Dr. Horton, reads in part as follows:

Dear Dr. Horton,

This message is being addressed to you and to the corresponding national leader of the Evangelical and Reformed church by the undersigned at the authorization of a group of twenty-five pastors of the Congregational and Christian and Evangelical and Reformed churches in Indiana, assembled for a fellowship luncheon at the recent Indiana Pastors Conference.

Reports were brought to us directly from our Cleveland midwinter meetings to the effect that many rumblings and rumors were being heard there unfavorable to the continuation of merger negotiations. It was indicated that top leaders in our denomination are raising objections, throwing up obstacles, and in various ways impeding and threatening the progress of these negotiations. From our Evangelical and Reformed brethren came reports of similar efforts at sabotage among responsible leaders in their denomination....

... To have this merger, already so far advanced, defeated now by unrepresentative action on the part of leaders in positions of power, would be a tragic blow to the cause of Christian unity as well as a betrayal of the confidence of the people of our churches whose elected representatives these leaders are.

May we depend upon you to share the sentiment and urgency of this letter with your colleagues in the offices of the General Council, the Missions Council, the American Board,

the Board of Home Missions, and the Council for Social Actions.

Shirley E. Greene, Congregational Christian
Merom, Indiana
Rev. John W. Myers, Evangelical and Reformed
Fort Wayne, Indiana

Here we see twenty-five ministers from the two denominations, representing nobody but themselves, deploring as "unrepresentative" the actions of the officially elected Executive Committee of the national body of our fellowship, the General Council. This was their reaction, entirely upon an emotional plane, to the honest, thoughtful, and carefully considered plans of many of the best minds in the denomination. But this letter, with its total disregard for an intelligent and honest facing of the facts, was the harbinger of things to come—if indeed it was not itself an important part of the procedures by which the General Council at Grinnell, in June 1946, was to be manipulated.

Because of my information about the way that Dr. Horton was promoting the merger when other people were telling me that it was dead; and because of Dr. Scotford's constant promotion of the merger, I prepared a very special pamphlet in May, 1946, entitled, *Warning: It Could Happen At Grinnell.*

I had just discovered the pending amendments proposed for adoption to the Constitution of the General Council, which I discussed previously and which could come up for adoption at the Grinnell Council meeting. These were the proposals that would ostensibly permit the General Council to pass an Act and then allow twelve months for churches, associations, and conferences to vote approval or disapproval. Putting two and two together, I realized that adoption of these proposed amendments would then make it appear possible to vote approval of the Basis of Union immediately after that. Churches, associations, and conferences would have just twelve months to vote approval or disapproval, and a mere majority would be sufficient to put the merger over.

This pamphlet, *Warning: It Could Happen at Grinnell*

was sent only to leading officials in the denomination. Its circulation was limited to just 100 persons. The manner in which it was received was largely that of an official "tut, tut" and, "how could you think any such thing?!" Nevertheless, a number of careful steps were taken to prevent its suggested prediction from coming true.

8

The Grinnell Council Meeting of 1946

THE decisive step toward the merger was taken at the Grinnell Council meeting, according to many commentators afterward. To get an accurate picture of what transpired at that meeting is extremely important to an understanding of how the merger was put over on the Congregational Christian Churches.

In order to go back more than thirty years, and tell the story as it really was, I have numerous very helpful sources of reliable information, in addition to some very vivid memories. I have the official minutes of that meeting and the copies of *Daily Advance* that were published while the meeting was in session. I have the personal letters I wrote home to my wife, day by day, before I knew what was going to happen. I have one six-page and one seven-page statement which I wrote immediately after the Council meeting: (1) "Sober Reflections on the Grinnell Council" of 5 July 1946; and (2) "Where Do the Issues Stand Now?" dated 12 July 1946. Just recently I received from Dr. Henry David Gray a letter corroborating in great detail something that happened with young people who were allowed to attend the Council meetings and who had been indoctrinated just prior to the meeting. I had personally witnessed a moment or two of this important gathering.

In addition to all of the above I have the rough draft of the history of merger procedures I wrote in the summer of 1955, but which I never finalized or published. To a large extent the rest of this chapter is something of a rewrite of that earlier effort.

I drove out to Grinnell, Iowa, with Rev. Alexander

Abbott of Norwich, Connecticut, and we left Connecticut in plenty of time for a leisurely trip with the idea of getting there early. We actually arrived about two days before the meeting began and had plenty of time to get settled in the dormitory at Grinnell College, to rest up and to look around. (Temperatures were above 100 degrees at first, but suddenly they dropped to 55 on the first day of the meeting.)

While wandering around the campus on the day before the Council sessions began, we passed through an open door, not realizing that people were in the room. There, seated in a sort of semicircle, were some young people. At the front of the room was Dr. Douglas Horton, leaning forward earnestly and speaking to these young people. The words which came from his lips as Alec and I entered were, "Now the ecumenical movement..." We backed out of the room a bit embarrassed and probably without having been observed.

I have always believed that these young people were being indoctrinated on the merger before the Council meeting. Afterward, as I know, they were permitted to sit, dispersed amongst the audience, during the nonvoting parts of the Council meeting. They formed a nucleus of emotionally aroused supporters of the merger who started clapping at every mention of the proposed union, from the start of the Council sessions.

Until May of 1977 I did not have any further details on what transpired at that meeting of young people. I did not know just who they were, nor what they were ostensibly there to accomplish. I do not know why I never thought to ask Dr. Henry David Gray whether he had been present and knew about that meeting. I knew that he had been the first national director of youth work and had organized the original Pilgrim Fellowship. I have known Dr. Gray very well for many years and served with him for four years on the Polity and Unity Committee of the General Council. But I never thought to ask him about that meeting of young people at Grinnell until thirty years later.

In his letter to me of 30 May 1977, Dr. Gray gives a much broader and more balanced view of what happened with the young people at Grinnell. But certainly the total impact was the same as what I had always suspected and believed. I have asked Dr. Gray for permission to use his letter in this book. In a note of 2 October 1977, he wrote, "You may use my May 30th letter as you see best . . . including its 'typos' if you are photocopying. The account is accurate." I have understood from other sources that some forty-seven young people were present. Here is Dr. Gray's letter of May 30 in full:

> Dear Malcolm:
> At the Grinnell Council in 1946 I arrived the evening before the Council began. The PF [Pilgrim Fellowship] was in session, that is, selected leaders. These YP [Young People] were given scholarships to come, ostensibly to act as pages, escorts for guests etc. I joined them in only part of one session, and most of the final briefing. So far as the PF leaders were concerned, they thought that their only job was to pass out papers, escort guests, run messages, etc. The afternoon you mention was the day before the Council began. I was already in the meeting at what appears to be the time when you and Alec entered, Doug began with a simple welcome to the YP, expressed appreciation of their willingness to help. Then he proceeded to "explain" how a General Council "worked," and followed with a discussion of what he thought were the important issues likely to come before the Grinnell meeting. This centered on the merger. But, it is necessary to realize that certain strong influences were then opposed, some of whom had considerable following among the PF (these were really post PF, most of whom had been PF officers . . . some were seminarians). Hugh Vernon White, and Will Frazier both opposed the proposed Basis of Union. Doug quite clearly hoped to indoctrinate the YP, to which I took exception, but certain of the leaders (at least one of whom today regrets his part in the whole merger business) were adamant . . . they felt they could influence the "course of history," and it may be that they did. There was much informal talk among the YP, not all of whom were in favor of merger, and some of whom did not know "what it was all about." As pictured by Doug the "merger" was the first step toward one GREAT CHURCH which would "fulfill our Lord's dream." I do not recall any discussion of the issues, organization, polity, or program. There were Questions asked, but I only recollect rather idealistic ones, with one exception, Will we have to give up our name "Pilgrim Fellowship." The answer was, that is the kind of question you and E & R YP would work out together but both of you would naturally expect to change some things, maybe even your name. Something was said by one of the Secretaries about the name being "recent" (it was then officially 10 years old), and a good deal was said about our being "Christian" be-

fore we were "Congregational." This latter point weighed heavily with youth, as you can readily understand.

Will Frazier was most upset by the briefing of the YP, but as you recall he had been moved out of the Executive V. P. to Treasurer. (of the Board of Home Missions)

The one person who did most to influence the YP was the same person who had most public impact on the Council, Ruth Isabel Seabury. She was idolized by many YP. Her platform appearance was heralded by most of the YP as if she were a gladiator going to battle against the "materialists" (Frazier, at that point), and the backward conservatives (that meant people like you . . . they didn't quite know what to do with Hugh Vernon White, Fred Meek, Keith and me. Can you imagine MB as a "conservative"?!)

I spent a lot of time with the YP during the Council, and with Frazier and White. The latter two were very despondent. Will of course was concerned about taking "missionary money to make E & R pensions the same as Congregational Christian," about "their men taking over vacant pulpits, especially in older, well-endowed Churches," etc.

I think that fills you in. It would take a book to fill out all the notes I made at Grinnell. I was involved in presenting the report of the team visit to survey bomb damage in the British Isles, and projected plans for the ICC." (International Congregational Council)

Best to you and Carol,
(s) Henry

It is well to note especially some of the points Dr. Gray makes. I previously had no way of knowing that different points of view were presented or that some of the older young people were not in favor of the merger. But Dr. Gray does not hesitate to say that "Doug quite clearly hoped to indoctrinate the YP," and that he, Dr. Gray, took exception to that. Also, under the guise of telling the young people the important things that were to come before the Council, it was the merger upon which Dr. Horton's talk centered. Actually many other important matters were before the Council, partly because this was the first meeting after the end of the Second World War and the first use of the atom bomb. It was also the 100th anniversary of the founding of the American Missionary Society. *Time* magazine had its representatives present for the sessions, and it was the observances of the founding of this missionary society (to help the slaves in the south) which received most of the write-up in *Time* magazine. So it is especially significant that Douglas Horton singled out the merger, especially since only routine votes regarding the plan of union were scheduled for action and when the churches had been asked *not* to express any opinions on it. The fact that Dr. Horton, in his presentation to the young people, singled out the merger as *the* important matter before the Council must be recognized as we appraise the events that took place and the responsibility for them. The inevitable question is whether the Council was manipulated by Douglas Horton and a relatively small group of his followers. Obviously the mass hysteria that was to play such a large part in the Council's consideration of the merger had already been created among the young people.

The delegates to the Council meeting began arriving about the time that the young people's meeting ended. For several days after that the average delegate continued to believe that nothing crucial was coming up regarding the merger. I have my letters that I wrote to my wife during the first few days. They record the fact that no one seemed particularly interested in the merger question, and I found it impossible to get into a discussion with anyone regarding its merits or demerits. Yet people were cordial to me, and some who had received my pamphlets commended me for the good work that I had been doing.

Starting on the first afternoon of the Council (Tuesday, June 18) little suggestions favoring the merger were introduced into the program. At first they had little effect.

The first "plug" for the merger came in the address of Dr. Horton, as minister of the Council. On Tuesday afternoon, right after the start of the meeting, he put in his adroit word supporting the merger and expressing the hope that it could be favorably acted upon. Later in the afternoon, Dr. Gordon Sisco, general secretary of the United Church of Canada, was presented to the Council as a fraternal delegate from that body. He reviewed the movements during the course of the century in which sixteen separate Presbyterian groups had achieved union in 1875, and eight separate groups of Methodists had formed a United Methodist Church in 1884, and then in 1925 Congregationalists had joined with Methodists and with about two-thirds of the Presbyterians to form the United Church of Canada. He cited "progress" since the consummation of their union and expressed the hope that similar movements of union might have as favorable an issue.

In the evening of the first day, Dr. Ronald Bridges, moderator, gave his address, and again the subject of the merger was introduced. Among other things Dr. Bridges urged "positive and constructive activities in making our heritage of Christian freedom effective, rather than negative and critical attitudes" (p. 14 of 1946 General Council minutes).

Each time that the merger was mentioned, the young people from the Pilgrim Fellowship, and probably the delegates from Indiana as well, started clapping. These individuals were scattered throughout the audience. At first this enthusiastic clapping by a relatively few people resulted in only desultory and half-hearted response from others. But from the beginning of the council meeting on Tuesday until Friday morning when a "hearing" on the merger was held, there were numerous other incidents when the merger was mentioned and a little "plug" given for it.

One astute individual, who sat with me on the bleachers at the side of the auditorium (the college gymnasium), commented to me on the small number of people who habitually started this clapping. A year later he became one of the leaders of the Evanston meeting, and I believe that his son may have been in the group of young people a few days before. His son, however, was opposed to the merger. This comment by an individual whom I was to know better in succeeding years, alerted me to what was going on. Up to that time I had not "put two and two together" in regard to the young people's meeting and the clapping. But from then on I studied the audience when clapping took place, and there was no doubt that the young people constituted the majority of those who clapped immediately and enthusiastically. Gradually, during the first several days of the Council, this enthusiastic clapping by a relatively small number of people "caught on," and others took it up, thereby preparing the stage for the Friday morning hearing on the merger.

At four o'clock on Wednesday afternoon a hearing on the proposed amendments to the constitution and bylaws was scheduled. Only about forty persons showed up at the hearing, and except for a further revelation of how Dr.

Horton reacted, the hearing had little bearing on the main events at Grinnell. This event will be discussed later.

In the evening of Wednesday, June 19, a skillfully prepared program for "A Service of Ecumenical Worship" gave further opportunity to push the merger in an indirect way. The program was six pages of printed type, some of which was quite condensed. The introductory statement began with the following:

> In this service of Ecumenical Worship, we seek to express and further the unity of the whole Church of Christ. At the World Conferences held at Oxford and Edinburgh in 1937, at Madras in 1938, and Amsterdam in 1939, a new experience of spiritual unity in worship was discovered. Instead of being an accidental accompaniment in the quest for unity, worship was realized as its highest climax, its central reality. To draw near to God through Christ is to draw near to one another. Through the act of corporate worship we would be lifted above the particular time and place to be united in the continuity of the worship of the Church throughout all ages, and we would deepen the consciousness that we belong to a world-wide Christian Community....

It takes little imagination to see the way that such a service would set the stage psychologically to do "big things" for the ecumenical movement. The fact that Dr. Horton had attended the World Conferences at Oxford and Edinburgh and possibly also those at Madras and Amsterdam, and that he had more to do than anyone else in setting up the program for the Grinnell meeting, leaves little room for doubt as to his part in arranging this program.

Presiding at the ecumenical worship was Rev. Paul G. Macy, director of the Midwest Region for the American Committee for the World Council of Churches. The intended speaker was Rev. G. Bromley Oxnam, Methodist bishop of the New York Area and president of the Federal Council of churches in America. (He failed to make train connections and Dr. Sidney Berry of Great Britain spoke in his place.) The service itself had numerous ancient litanies and an "act of penitence" in which we were to ask to be cleansed of various sins. All of this would have been quite proper and conventional under ordinary circumstances, but having us ask to be "cleansed" from "contentment with what is familiar" which may also have been something in which we strongly believe—was open to question. When we were asked also to say, in the Confession, that "we have broken the unity of Thy Holy Church," it was easy to suspect that ecumenical worhip was being used as a kind of propaganda medium. Certainly it was suspect at such a time as this, when an uninformed General Council was being skillfully conditioned to accept a surprise move on the merger. This was just one more step in building up a mass approval—or mob psychology—in favor of something that the churches and delegates had been led to believe would not even come up at this Council. Afterward, when it was all over, the results of this Council were hailed as proof of a "grass-roots groundswell" for the merger, when in all honesty it was the result of skillful manipulation. The entire future course of merger events was altered by the astute handling of events as they unfolded at this Council.

On Friday morning, when the time finally came for "discussion" on the merger, Dr. William F. Frazier, Dr. Frank Scribner, and Dr. Fred Field Goodsell were scheduled to speak. These were the three men who had turned the state superintendents against the merger at the midwinter meeting. Their being asked to speak could be viewed in two opposite ways. On the one hand it might be said that this was a "magnanimous gesture" that allowed the opposition to "have its say." But in the light of the prejudicial atmosphere that had been created before they were allowed to speak, it was like throwing down a challenge: "We dare you to say again what you said at the midwinter meeting!" They had no way of knowing ahead of time what the mood of Council would be. These were three able and dedicated men, and they tried openly and fairly to set forth their honest misgivings, but they were placed in the position of facing a thoroughly prejudiced and hostile audience. Soon after they had finished their presentations, Rev. Shirley Greene, whose letter in the April *Advance* we have already quoted, strode to the platform and demanded to know why these men had held back on their criticisms "until this late hour" and were now trying to wreck the merger. His caustic criticisms were greeted with cheers and loud applause. A resolution adopted by the Indiana Conference was read and was likewise greeted with sustained applause. Dr. Horton's activity in going out a few months earlier, "beating the bushes" and speaking for the merger in places like Indiana were now paying off.

Remember again that the delegates to this Council had been chosen at a time when everyone had been asked by the Executive Committee of the General Council *not* to take any straw votes on the merger because the plan was not ready yet. Most people, and especially those opposed to the merger, were not going out speaking on the subject. The only action that was supposed to come up at this Council was a routine action approving the drawing up of a "supplement to the Basis of Union" and of getting further information about what the merger would entail.

A number of leaders from the Evangelical and Reformed Church were paraded to the platform, accompanied by clapping. In my July fifth statement of 1946 (written just two weeks after the Council), I wrote in part as follows (in statement #14)

> Dr. Richards and Dr. Goebels of the Evangelical and Reformed Church ... spoke with great emotion for the merger and skillfully employed Congregational terminology to describe the proposed set-up. The subtlety of Dr. Richards' remark about having to find a *tertium quid*, or a third way (a polity which would be neither Congregational nor Presbyterian—if such is possible) was entirely lost on the audience, although it was probably the most important statement made. There was no leisurely back and forth discussion, no drawing forth of vital issues. So-called "concessions" only left confusion worse confounded.

This statement by Dr. Richards about seeking a *tertium quid* was the opposite of what he had written to me about a month earlier, and quoted in the previous chapter. In that letter he stated that the merger would have to be *"either-or* and not *both and,"* and he had seemingly ruled out "a third way." (Note: a *tertium quid* is defined as a "third way out of a seemingly hopeless dilemma.")

Another skillful change of position by the Evangelical and Reformed leaders came when Mr. Raymond Fiero, of our Executive Committee, asked a crucial question. Some months previously, when leaders of the two denominations had been together, Mr. Fiero had asked this hypothetical question: "In the event that a higher judicatory makes a decision contrary to a lower judicatory, which decision would be honored?" This was like asking whether an association could overrule a decision of a local church, or the General Synod overrule a conference. The answer that had immediately been given by Evangelical and Reformed leaders at the meeting in the early winter of 1946, was to this effect: "Well, of course, the higher judicatory would always prevail."

From the time of that meeting in the winter, Mr. Fiero had been confident that this one question and answer were enough to wreck the merger negotiations. Therefore, he asked the same question again at this session of the Grinnell Council. I remember vividly what happened, and I was able to follow up a month or two later on what Dr. Richards replied when I attended the Evangelical and Reformed Spiritual Conference at Allentown. Dr. Richards, in a seemingly very conciliatory way, said, "Well, now, we will yield to you on the matter of the higher judicatory if you will yield to us on the matter of installation."

Almost no one among the delegates had the slightest idea of what lay back of this question, or of what the previous answer had been. Neither did they get the import of what Dr. Richards meant by our yielding to them on the matter of installation. Nevertheless the Council broke out in loud applause, recognizing this as an attempt at compromise of some sort, even if they did not know what it was all about.

This was the nearest that the Council came to a discussion of the issues or a "grappling with the facts." When I was fortunate enough to go again to the Evangelical and Reformed Spiritual Conference at Allentown, I was able to find out for sure what Dr. Richards had meant. Actually his "concession" was a wholly inconsistent suggestion. It was like saying that "we will yield to you on the power of the higher judicatory in one regard, if you will yield to us on the power of the higher judicatory in another regard."

In reality, we simply could not yield to them on the matter of installation, in the way that they meant it, without recognizing authority to be exercised by the higher judicatories—in this case of associations or conferences over the local churches. This would mean the imposition of a recognized body of governing law (i.e., the overall constitution) and the end of the true principle of Congregational local autonomy. In other words, here was the whole issue of the merger in a nutshell. To pretend that a "concession" was being made was misleading and not straight thinking.

By the time that opportunity came for general discussion by the delegates themselves, only a half hour remained out of the advertised three hours. Over an hour had been taken the first thing in the morning by other, unrelated business. And by now the delegates had been whipped into a frenzy of excitement for the merger, partly by the attack made by Shirley Greene and the reading of the Indiana resolution. I had been sitting on one side of the auditorium where I could see Dr. Horton, who in turn was sitting behind the curtain on the stage on the opposite side of the room. He had looked very pleased with the goings-on. Certainly the broad smile on his face gave every evidence that things were going very much to his liking.

It was arbitrarily announced by the moderator at this point that everyone wishing to speak must come to the platform right away. This meant no chance for back-and-forth discussion from the audience in a logical sequence on any issues as they might come up. After fifteen or twenty people had come to the platform, Dr. Bridges, the moderator, walked down the line and took me by the arm, leading me to the rostrum to be the first speaker—knowing, of course, that I opposed the merger and that all the others could then speak after me. Just as I was ready to begin speaking, he reached out and restrained me while he asked the audience, "How long shall we give these fellows to speak?" Someone in a front row bawled out, "A minute and a half!" Immediately there was loud, prolonged, and ribald laughter. The moderator then ruled that all speakers would be limited to three minutes. Was this the way the most important proposal of the century—or of more than 300 years of American Congregationalism—was to be discussed? Where had there ever been opportunity for calm and objective appraisal of the very complicated issues at stake?

I can only give it as my personal testimony that I had never—before or since—faced such a "maniacal" sort of audience. I was later to address General Council meetings on this same subject of the merger in 1948, 1949, 1952, 1954, 1956, and 1958; but I never saw or felt such unbridled hostility and frenzied mob psychology as I did at this Grinnell meeting. There was deep bitterness at later meetings, and plenty of ostracism and caustic comments; never again was there anything to match what I can only describe as the mob psychology that had been whipped up at the Grinnell Council.

I can remember only two other speakers who were against the merger, and they were held over for an afternoon session which continued the abbreviated morning hearing. The issue of *Daily Advance* on Monday, however, mentioned one or two more. I remember Rev. Alexander Abbott of Norwich, and Rev. John F. C. Green of McKeesport, Pennsylvania. Most people had not come to the Grinnell meeting with any expectation that the merits of the merger would be discussed. Most of the speeches were little more than personal statements of support. One leader of the young people said, "I speak for the youth. They are for the merger." A minister's wife from New Hampshire said, "I speak for the women. The women are for the merger." Similarly others spoke, without authorization, for various groups. Rev. Roy Helfenstein, a minister from the former Christian denomination (as was Shirley Greene), had an article in *Daily Advance* saying that he favored a merger of all Protestant denominations immediately, and some speakers seemed to echo his view. There was simply no discussion of the specific implications of the Basis of Union or what its total impact upon the Congregational fellowship would be.

At the afternoon session the same fever pitch of emotional excitement prevailed. Alec Abbott tried to emphasize that the words used in the merger plan had different meanings to different people. He also told a story that ordinarily would have brought at least a chuckle. I guess that he was trying to loosen the delegates up a little. But he failed. His story was this: A Negro pastor in Norwich had said to Alec, "You know, Brother Abbott, my people are of three kinds. Some of my people are reasonable, and with them I can reason them into the kingdom of heaven. And some of my people are emotional, and with them I can emote them into the kingdom. But some of my folks are just plumb foolish, and if I am going to get them into the kingdom of heaven, I've got to fool them into the kingdom of heaven." Maybe the story was just too applicable to Grinnell to seem funny.

There had been mighty little reasoning done at this Council session, with its lack of any objective or factual approach by the delegates. (Dr. Frazier, Dr. Scribner, and Dr. Goodsell had tried to inject some facts, but with little success.) There had been plenty of emotional pressure evident. The address by Miss Ruth Isabel Seabury was one of the real "stem-winders," as Dr. Gray's letter indicated. But probably the least noticed method by which these delegates were being taken into the "merger kingdom" was the skillful way in which they had been fooled into believing that everyone else was for the merger and that it was time for them to get onto the bandwagon. What they did not suspect or reflect upon—even afterward—was the way in which the meeting had been manipulated from start to finish. There had been no strong merger sentiment at the beginning of the meeting, as I have mentioned before. But the buildup came through the way that the program was put together, the speakers chosen, the cheering section of previously indoctrinated young people, the way that three secretaries were put on the scaffold and pilloried, the tirade of the promerger "whip" from Indiana, the sweet talk and evasive answers from the Evangelical and Reformed leaders, and the total lack of any back-and-forth discussion of issues or genuinely factual information as to what the plan entailed.

The *Daily Advance* for Monday, June 24, reported on the afternoon session of discussion. This write-up includes the following report on Dr. Truman Douglass, which is well to keep in mind in regard to events that took place on Monday following:

> Truman Douglass, executive vice-president of the Board of Home Missions, gave the most forceful exposition of the mind of the Council. He announced that he had always favored the merger unreservedly and that he believed that it should be carried through to completion as speedily as possible. He added that he did not believe that those who had brought up the organizational and financial difficulties were obstructionists but were presenting problems which needed to be faced. He urged that the merger be pursued on the two levels

of broad issues and the detailed tasks involved in uniting agencies, and that neither level be allowed to interfere with the other.

Mention is made in this article of *Daily Advance* of several ministers and laymen who spoke (including John F. C. Green and Alexander Abbott) and of Ed Hawley, president of the national Pilgrim Fellowship who read a resolution that its national council had passed two years earlier. He also, as indicated previously, is reported as saying in his travels about the country "he found the young people overwhelmingly favorable to the merger." (*Daily Advance*, 24 June 1946)

Three officials of the Evangelical and Reformed Church "were invited to express themselves." They were F. A. Goetsch, secretary of International Missions, Silas P. Bitner, secretary of pensions and relief, and J. N. LeVan, secretary of promotion.

After the Friday hearing, there were no official meetings on the merger during the weekend. Group assemblies were held on Sunday afternoon that dealt with problems of the new atomic age. Two of these were "Christian Attitudes Toward Atomic War," chaired by Fred Buschmeyer; and "Individual Responsibility in the Atomic Age," led by Dr. Howard Conn.

Unofficially an informal group, partly from the Executive Committee, met me to discuss the implications of my "warning" pamphlet, *It Could Happen at Grinnell*. It was a significant and revealing session. The attitude of those meeting with me was still that of reproach for my having written the pamphlet, but the purpose of the meeting was to assure me that the Executive Committee and others had taken careful precautions to make sure that nothing of the sort that I had suggested—i.e., an attempt to vote the merger through at that meeting—would be allowed to happen. I was told that they had lined up nineteen or more persons to speak against any such attempt if it became necessary to stop such a move. The leading spokesman for the group was Ronald Bridges, the moderator. The only other person whom I remember specifically as being there was Rev. Philip Scott, then a pastor at New Haven and a member of the Executive Committee. As it later turned out, Dr. Bridges, as moderator, was able all by himself to deflect an effort that was made to vote a substitute motion intended to push aside the official recommendations of the Executive Committee and Commission on Interchurch Relations. For years afterward, when the battle for the merger was in full swing, one individual repeatedly reminded me, with a knowing look, "Remember: we could have voted the merger through at Grinnell!" And no doubt they could have, even if it would have been improper and very shocking to the fellowship.

The voting on motions having to do with the merger came at the 1:45 P.M. session of the council on Monday, June 24.

Dr. Blanchard, chairman of the Commission on Interchurch Relations, presented the official motion, calling for the postponement of sending out the Basis of Union for approval by the churches and setting forth the various steps that had been agreed upon as early as the January 29–31 meeting of the Executive Committee. These had all been published in the April issue of *Advance* (along with that letter from Rev. Shirley Greene). This motion, made by Dr. Blanchard, reads:

Recommended that the vote taken at the meeting of the General Council in June 1946 be not upon the matter of reference to the churches, etc., but upon the preparation of such a supplement to the present Basis of Union, which would include among other things:

(a) Definition of the relationships which are to exist between the missionary organizations of the denominations as to administration, finance and nomenclature.

(b) Definition of the relationship which is to exist between these organizations and the General Synod.

(c) Definition of the relationship between the Pension Boards of the two denominations and the relationship of those boards to the General Synod.

(d) Definition of the place and function of Conferences and Associations on the one hand and of Synods on the other, and the proposed relationship between them.

(e) Provision for suitable denominational headquarters and suitable branches of the same, and

(f) Provision for amendment.

(g) The preparation of such a supplement to be conducted by the organizations concerned (Boards, Annuity Fund, etc.) under the coordinating guidance of an able, practical committee to be selected by the Commission on Interchurch Relations and composed of persons of varying representative opinions among whom the members of that Commission may be named.

Probably the part which angered Shirley Greene the most was the provision to postpone any submission of the Basis of Union to the churches for a final approval at that time.

You will recall, as previously mentioned, that a "final edition" of the Basis of Union had been printed in September, 1945. It has each line numbered so that it could have been discussed line by line. This careful discussion was to have been done at a joint, three-day session of our General Council and of the Evangelical and Reformed General Synod. No such joint session was carried out. The Grinnell Council, meeting at the time when the joint session was supposed to have been held, spent absolutely no time examining the Basis of Union—line by line or otherwise.

Nevertheless the comments made by Dr. Truman Douglass on Friday afternoon, which we quoted above from *Daily Advance*, stated that Dr. Douglass favored going ahead "on both levels at once" and "that neither level be allowed to interfere with the other." This would mean submitting the Basis of Union to the churches immediately and working out the details of the "supplement" at the same time. At the time the supplement was still pictured as a document separate from the Basis of Union. Hence it might not be submitted to the churches for approval at all.

Before the motion from the Interchurch Relations Commission (Dr. Blanchard's motion) was put to a vote, Rev. Ned B. McKenney said that he wanted to make a *substitute* motion. This reads as follows:

> ...that this General Council expresses its satisfaction with the labors of the Commission on Interchurch Relations in exploring the possibilities of the union of the Evangelical and Reformed Church and the Congregational Christian Churches, and its sincere appreciation of the graciousness of the representatives of the Evangelical and Reformed Church who have been in attendance at our sessions; that we affirm our will to have the considerations looking toward union go forward without undue delay; and that we urge the appropriate officers of the Council, the Board of Home Missions, the American Board and the Ministerial Boards to proceed to consider the problems involved and seek their solutions with earnestness and despatch." (Minutes of the 1946 Council, p. 33)

It can be instantly seen that this motion, if passed as a substitute motion, would have eliminated the vote *not* to have the Basis of Union sent to the churches, associations, and conference at that time. Besides sidetracking the delay it would also tell the board officials to hurry up and get busy fixing up other details "with earnestness and despatch." It was thus directly in line with the recommendations Dr. Truman Douglass had made in his remarks on Friday, as printed above.

I have nothing else to prove what happened in this quick sequence of events, except an exceedingly clear and vivid recollection that was burned into my memory at the time by the drama of the situation. I watched and listened very carefully with keen interest, knowing that anything might happen. I remember Dr. Bridges saying to Ned McKenney, "Well isn't this a case of . . . ?" There followed two words that sounded to me like Latin and that I did not understand. Obviously Ned McKenney did not understand them either. He stammered out something to the effect of "I—I guess so." To which Dr. Bridges replied, "Well you just sit down here and I'll get to you in a minute." Then, without a moment's hesitation Dr. Bridges called for the vote on Dr. Blanchard's original motion, which carried by 474 to 4. This blocked any chance of a substitute motion intended to derail the original plans.

Following the vote on the official motion, Dr. Bridges then let the Council vote upon Ned McKenney's motion, as a *separate motion*, which is the way that it appears in the minutes.

My impressions of what happened, all so very quickly, were reinforced within minutes of the close of the session. Dr. Fred Fagley came to me and said that Rev. Shirley Greene had rushed up on the platform when business had adjourned and asked him, "Wha—, wha— happened?! We thought that we were voting the merger through!" This was enough, then and now, to settle any possible doubt in my mind as to the intent of Ned McKenney's motion.

Actually there would have been additional motions needed after McKenney's substitute motion even if it had been accepted as such. It would have been necessary to have a vote to send the Basis of Union out to the churches, etc., for approval. It would have been probable also that the pending amendments to the constitution would have been adopted—improper as they were. The Executive Committee had already voted to recommend that these amendments *not be adopted*. But a strong promerger majority could have easily voted to override such a recommendation. The proposed amendments were still a live option. They were not voted down until the next day, Tuesday, the twenty-fifth of June.

In the long perspective of history it probably made little difference that Ned McKenney's motion was passed only as an additional motion, and not as a substitute. The events at Grinnell furnished, as the officials chose to interpret them, a "mandate" to hurry up and rush things through without bothering with the kind of careful and decent procedures which had been originally outlined.

Dr. Blanchard presented a motion that could have made a careful discussion of the Basis of Union possible the following year:

> Resolved that this Council hereby authorizes the Executive Committee to call a special meeting of the Council in 1947, if negotiations with the Evangelical and Reformed Church warrant such action." (Approval voted; see Minutes of the 1946 Council, p. 34)

This resolution gave one last chance for a General Council to see and discuss in detail the provisions of the Basis of Union *before* it would be sent to the churches. As we shall see, however, a shortcut was adopted the following year, so that *no* General Council ever discussed the Basis of Union in any detail prior to its being sent out for voting by churches, associations, and conferences. The later mess which developed over the official "Comments" and the Oberlin interpretations could have been avoided by such a Council. The foolhardy attempt to patch the Basis of Union up with "interpretations" after it had been finalized and sent out was just one more scandal in the way that the whole merger procedure finally evolved. It would have been infinitely easier to get the wording clarified ahead of time than it was to try and patch it up afterward—and a great deal more honest and forthright, as later events will show.

Another action of the Grinnell Council added to the

pressure for union—including union on a far larger scale. This came with the presentation by Dr. Truman Douglass of the following motion:

46G 47. VOTED: Believing that the unity which now exists among Christians is deeper and more inclusive than has yet been expressed in the outward life and organization of our churches.

Confident that there is a holy impatience in the hearts of great numbers of Christian people that the Church, now set in a world threatened with annihilation for want of community, shall bear more convincing testimony to the reconciling power of God through Jesus Christ,

Mindful of the special urgency felt by returning chaplains and other veterans who have experienced in military service the liberty of ministering to and worshiping with Christians of all communions,

And assured that the agonies of our generation have quickened in the Church a new readiness to be obedient to the will of Christ,

We, the representatives of the Congregational Christian churches of the United States, assembled in General Council, respectfully memorialize the Federal Council of the Church of Christian America, asking it to convene a plenary session of representatives of American churches to consider the possibility of immediate closer unity of American denominations which already accord one another mutual recognition of ministries and sacraments. We ask that if favorable response is made to this request it shall be with the express understanding that such action shall in no way impair or interrupt negotiations looking toward unity which are now being conducted by any of the participating denominations. (Minutes of the 1946 Council, p. 34)

The Grinnell Council, already at fever pitch of excitement for church union, broke into tremendous applause and quickly adopted the motion.

One may ask what ever happened as a result of the Truman Douglass motion. It may be forgotten now, but the Federal Council of Churches did take up this project and a half dozen or so denominations did respond favorably. They sent representatives to work out a plan, which came to be known as the Greenwich Plan. This was something like the present COCU Plan. At least they got to the place where they agreed that there would be bishops and that they would appoint ministers to their churches. I do not recall ever hearing of the plan being abandoned or given up, but talk of it eventually stopped.

The Grinnell Council meeting as a whole, however, was unquestionably the one event that so thoroughly prejudiced the question of the merger that it could never again be successfully challenged within the *official* circles. It was different among the churches themselves, as the voting on the Basis of Union was to show. But for officials at every level—national and state—the merger became part of "the denominational program" and was promoted as such—except during the time when a court order prevented going ahead with the union.

As a kind of postscript to all these happenings at Grinnell, we should take one last look at the insights made possible at the open hearing on those proposed amendments to the constitution and bylaws. I refer specifically to the ones that would have permitted the General Council to pass an act that would affect churches, associations, conferences or all of them combined. This amendment would have fitted in perfectly with the merger scheme and particularly with the wording in the Basis of Union, as we previously pointed out. It also was in line with the original plan of procedures set forth at the Grand Rapids meeting in 1944. It would have let the Council act first in approving the Basis of Union, and then the churches, associations and conferences would have had twelve months in which to approve or disapprove the act with only a *majority of those voting* deciding whether the act would be approved or rejected.

When the hearing on this proposed amendment came on Wednesday afternoon, the first question asked was where did this proposed amendment come from? The minutes of the 1944 Council meeting show that a number of proposed amendments were made the first thing on the second day of the Council. The minutes show that the amendments were presented by Dr. Horton. Therefore Dr. Horton was called upon for information as to where these proposals originated. He professed to have no clear recollection as to their source, but haltingly suggested that he "thought" that some laymen in eastern Massachusetts, who had been concerned over some of the resolutions adopted on social action questions, had been responsible.

This explanation could hardly be the answer, however, because a resolution can not constitute an *act* that would affect churches, associations, or conferences. It had long been recognized, as we mentioned early in this book, that the General Council had the right to adopt resolutions, but that these carried no weight beyond that of the wisdom which lay in them, backed by the significance of the body that adopted them. Very little discussion followed, and the Executive Committee members seemed agreed that the amendments, both to the constitution and to the bylaws should not be adopted. Almost instantly Dr. Horton changed the subject and launched into a virtual tirade against something else that obviously disturbed him a great deal. This in itself was very revealing.

This hearing, it should be remembered, had been set up just for the purpose of getting reactions on the proposed amendments we have been discussing. The Executive Committee members were present, and only about forty other persons. What was disturbing Dr. Horton was the fact that a new *Manual of the Congregational Christian Churches* was about to be published without careful scrutiny by the Executive Committee before it went into print. Apparently Dr. Horton knew something of the content of the new manual being prepared by Dr. Oscar Maurer, and did not approve it. All of this raises some interesting questions on a matter about which I had considerable personal knowledge.

After our National Council had united with the General Convention of the Christian Church in 1931, a new manual was needed to reflect the customs and usages of both former groups. Therefore the Executive Committee had then asked my father, Charles Emerson Burton, to prepare a new manual. My father was the executive secretary at the time, and in 1936 his manual was published. I remember the great care which my father exercised in getting all his facts together. He sent for many constitutions and bylaws of local churches, local associations, and local conferences in both of the former denominations. He also used the last previous manual, which had been prepared by Dr. William E. Barton, the great authority on Congregational polity and organizations in his day. I can see my father yet with the many constitutions, etc., before him in his study in New Hampshire.

Just why a new manual was considered necessary so soon after Dr. Horton came into office is a mystery to me. Dr. Horton was elected in 1938, and in 1942 a committee was appointed to prepare a new manual. Its publication was delayed by wartime restrictions until 1947. This hearing at Grinnell was only shortly before the publication date.

Somewhere along the line I heard that there were still some two hundred copies of my father's manual, which had not yet been bound, at the Pilgrim Press. I was told through someone that inquiry was made of Dr. Horton as to what should be done with these—and possibly of the bound copies still available. His reply had been to "destroy them."

In the foreword to Maurer's manual is the statement that "The present issue is based on Burton's Manual, published in 1936," and the additional comment that there has been considerable revision and new material added. Also was the statement: "... the devotional section and the devotional orders of service, such as marriage, burial, etc., which appear in Burton's Manual, have been omitted as belonging more properly to the Book of Services or Ordinal, the formulation of which is in the hands of another committee of the General Council."

For years after the publication of the Maurer's Manual I received inquiries from ministers as to whether I knew any place where they could get one of my father's manuals. They missed especially the parts prepared for marriages and funerals.

Whose idea was this for a new manual, and for the separate Book of Services (which I, incidentally, cannot remember ever seeing and for which I never felt a need as a pastor)? What seemed to be transparently clear at the Grinnell hearing was that Maurer's manual was supposed to have "rewritten Congregationalism" and that Dr. Horton was not getting his opportunity for the kind of "input" that he wanted. That Dr. Horton tried on several occasions to "rewrite" Congregationalism is clear, as we can see.

At the 1940 General Council, which was his first as "Minister" of this body, Dr. Horton tried to have new state superintendents come forward to kneel and have a "laying on of hands" inducting them into their new offices. They refused when the plan was suggested, on the grounds that the General Council had no authority over them or the conferences which they served—which was true. Then in his address as "minister of the General Council" Dr. Horton objected to the word "Congregationalism," which he called a "monster." He said that he had recently, when helping to prepare some prayers for the fellowship, "crossed the Rubicon" and had written a prayer "for the Congregational and Christian *Church*" (emphasis his).

The distinction between *churches* and *church* is the difference between local autonomous churches and a national corporate church. It would deny the whole concept of the local body "as a complete church," which is a fundamental principle of Congregationalism. Dr. Rockwell Harmon Potter, former dean of Hartford Seminary, used to say that "he who is to the manner born never refers to the Congregational Churches as a Church."

Dr. Horton went on in the same address to urge that the Council adopt "legislation" to "take care of the matter of effective organization." The important word here was *legislation*, because historically it had been recognized that the Council was not a legislative body.

In 1950, four years after this Grinnell Council, Dr. Horton set forth two conflicting theories of Congregationalism. In "Congregationalism B" he gave a description unfamiliar to anyone but which had been a defense offered in the Cadman lawsuit and which he tried to promote. It would make the General Council free to ignore the wishes of the churches and to do as it pleased.

We have already set forth the evidence of how Dr. Horton's revision of *Adventure in Liberty* included, as though it were part of Dr. Atkins' writing, a section that did not appear in the booklet as Dr. Atkins wrote it. This material, which Dr. Horton presumably inserted, was along the lines of Dr. Horton's "Congregationalism B" and was an evident attempt to give an earlier origin to those ideas—a real attempt to rewrite Congregational history and theory.

Then, in 1954, at the General Council meeting, Dr.

Horton proposed that a committee be appointed "to write a Constitution for the fellowship." He claimed that the suggestion had come from several sources—as well it may have. The fact that Congregationalism had never been under an overall constitution had been one of the main issues in the Cadman lawsuit. It had been claimed that the merger would not involve an overall constitution. But in 1954 the lawsuit was behind him, because the courts had decided that they had no jurisdiction in the matter. But the testimony given in the courtroom had disturbed the Evangelical and Reformed leaders to the point where this issue of constitution remained a chief stumbling-block to the resumption of merger talks. To get our denomination to adopt an overall constitution right away would solve the problem, or so it might seem.

These various efforts of Dr. Horton's to rewrite Congregational theory and practice are all part of the same picture as the manipulation of the General Council meeting at Grinnell. We shall see that the same sort of operation continued for the ensuing years and especially for the next General Council meeting, at Oberlin in 1948.

9

Confronting the Ultimate Issues

THE LAST CHANCE TO PRODUCE HONEST DOCUMENTS

W E have seen in the last two chapters the methods that were used to force the merger through by mass psychology and emotional pressure. This came even before the Basis of Union was ready for a vote, and without the slightest opportunity for orderly discussion of what the plan really meant or any examination of its details. Yet this emotional commitment was openly acclaimed, by the editor of *Advance* and others, as "the decisive step" toward the merger (*Advance*, August 1946, p. 35).

The critical period of hammering out the final form of the Basis of Union, and how it was to be interpreted to the churches came during the years 1946–1948. This formative period represented the last opportunity for the leaders of the two denominations to work out a straightforward, unambiguous, and *honest* document. This they certainly failed to do, as was evident when they began almost immediately to give out "official comments," interpretations, explanations, and assurances in the vain effort to prove that the Basis of Union would guarantee the continuance of Congregational polity. This process of trying to shore up the faulty document with still more interpretations of the Interpretations, more claims of "guarantees," and even explanations to the courts, in sworn testimony of some of the highest officials in our Congregational Boards, was to continue for another nine years—with nothing ever really being settled. Such is the evidence of failure, during these crucial years, to produce an honest and forthright document. Most of this was quite inexcusable, as we shall readily see.

All of the issues had been out clearly in the open before the last three revisions of the Basis of Union were written. My own pamphlets and circular letters, numbering more than twenty before September of 1946, had crisscrossed back and forth over the issues time and again. These had been sent, as was mentioned before to all state superintendents, the Executive Committee and other important leaders. The pages of *Advance* attest even further to the complete way in which the basic questions had been aired before the whole fellowship. I was assured more than once that my pamphlets had been given thorough reading. The question that will persist as we pursue the events of these two years—and the nine years after that—is whether the leading officials sold Congregationalism short.

The truth of what I had written before the Basis of Union was finalized was underscored many times when the Evanston Meeting was held in November 1947. I had no part in calling that meeting; was not a part of the leadership for its sessions; was not asked to be a speaker there; and was not on its Findings Committee. Yet nearly 200 Congregationalists from all over the country came to the meeting and reached most of the same conclusions that I had. They were promptly told that they were wrong. But the issues kept arising.

In appraising the events of this period, we have the advantage now of seeing what has actually happened as a result of the documents drawn up in this crucial time. Thus we can judge more accurately whether statements made at the time were true, whether the persons responsible for this union were as straightforward as they could have been, and whether the churches ever had a decent and honest chance to comprehend what the merger would involve for them.

Books and documents have appeared in recent years that will be of great assistance to us in making our appraisal. First, of course, is the actual constitution of the United Church of Christ and its bylaws, which were supposed to be "based upon" the Basis of Union with interpretations. This constitution, adopted in 1961, dropped much of the language of the Basis of Union, especially in terms of the "fellowship" relations originally suggested. It has also had some important and far-reaching changes made in it. Two books published in 1977 under United Church auspices have likewise considerable importance to our inquiry. One is a kind of history of the United Church of Christ, written by a former Evangelical and Reformed minister who has served on various important commissions of the United Church and as assistant moderator of its General Synod. This is *The Shaping of the United Church of Christ* by Dr. Louis H. Gunnemann. The other book is *A Manual on the Ministry: Perspectives and Procedures for Authorizing Ministry in the United Church of Christ*. This was published by the Office of Church Life and Leadership of the United Church of Christ.

Another book of value to serious students of this period is a compilation I have recently put together, in which most of my earliest merger writings have been photographed and combined with some other writings in a volume entitled *Early Merger Pamphlets*. This includes the findings of the Evanston Meeting, pamphlets by Dr. Fred Meek and Mr. Joseph D. Fackenthal, and the Spring Valley Statement adopted shortly after the Oberlin Council by Congregationalists assembled in Illinois. *Early Merger Pamphlets* contains 262 pages with 46 separate items. These volumes are available, I am sure, in the Congregational Library, 14 Beacon Street, Boston.

When the time comes to quote from the above books, I shall simply refer to "Gunnemann" with page number; to *Manual on the Ministry*, with page number; and to *Early Merger Pamphlets* with page number.

For my own preparation of this chapter I have also a notebook I prepared years ago containing all, or most, of the articles, "Letters to the Editor," and "Forum on the Merger" that were published in our national magazine *Advance* from 1945 through 1948. These pages from *Advance* make a very sizable compendium of materials in themselves and give a clear picture of the way that the magazine manipulated its intake so as to emphasize points of view favorable to the merger as the time for the Oberlin Council meeting approached, while holding back "anti" materials that were submitted. One of the leaflets included in *Early Merger Pamphlets* was sent to Dr. Scotford for inclusion in the June 1948 issue of *Advance*, but was returned by him with the notation, "The time has gone by for this sort of thing" (pp. 201-4 of *Early Merger Pamphlets*). These pages from *Advance* bring back vividly the aura and the temper of those days.

In order to understand the significance of the events as they took place we need something of an overview of the situation and especially of the fundamental issues which should have been resolved.

The first and most obvious issue that faced the negotiators on this merger was the contradictory nature of the polities, or forms of organization, of the two denominations. I have already quoted in this book the letter of May 13, 1946 from Dr. George W. Richards, the first president of the Evangelical and Reformed Church and the chairman of their committee handling the merger negotiations. In that letter Dr. Richards said:

> Of course the polity of the Evangelical and Reformed Church directly contradicts that of the Congregational and Christian Churches. If either of the negotiating parties is ready to yield to the other, we can unite so far as polity is concerned. Personally I think the union must be *either-or* and not *both-and*. If one or the other method of polity is adopted with enthusiasm and voluntarily, union is possible; but union by compromise or surrender, I cannot endorse.

Here was "a moment of truth" such as rarely came in all the merger discussions. It is too bad that this was not followed up with serious inquiry. I gave publicity to this letter in my statement No. 15, but to no avail (p. 107 *Early Merger Pamphlets*).

The question on polity was that of authority and where it rested. The Congregational Christian Churches were made up of free and independent units. There was no instrument of authority, beyond that of the civil law, over any individual Congregational Church—none whatsoever. In like manner the associations were not bound by any rules or laws laid down by state conferences or our national General Council. They were free fellowships of churches, and each had its own constitution and bylaws. General usage throughout the country brought a certain amount of uniformity, but not authority; and there was always room for individual divergencies. All of this was true also for the state conferences. This became the subject of a very complete and exhaustive study by the Committee on Free Church Polity and Unity, appointed by the action of the General Council at Cleveland in 1950. Its report, submitted after four years' work, was based upon documents of state conferences and local associations, local church constitutions from all over the country, and many other official documents. Then the results of the study were sent to the state superintendents and up to 200 prominent Congregationalists for verification or criticism. No other study ever compared with this in its scope and thoroughness. We shall treat this subject further in another chapter. Unfortunately the Evangelical and Reformed people never seemed to get the picture straight, for the most part. Gunnemann in his book dismisses the Polity Committee's report as though the Congregationalists did not know what they were or why: "The content of the report was itself ambiguous and indefinite, failing to remove the uncertainties about free church polity that had opened so much debate" (p. 42).* As a member of that Polity Committee, I can say assuredly that there was nothing ambiguous or indefinite about the report so far as stating the nature of Congregationalism. The report was dubious, however, as to any proper way that the Congregational Christian Churches could, as a total fellowship, enter into union with a dissimilar denomination. Here again was a "moment of truth"—which was quickly brushed aside by the promerger forces.

In sharp and absolute contradiction to the Congregational setup was the fact that the Evangelical and Reformed Church had an overall constitution that declared in its first paragraph that:

... the Evangelical and Reformed Church, formed by the union of the Evangelical Synod of North America and the Reformed Church in the United States ordains this constitution to be its fundamental law and declares the same to have authority over all its ministers, members, congregations, and judicatories.

*Reprinted with permission from Louis H. Gunnemann, *The Shaping of the United Church of Christ: An Essay in the History of American Christianity.* Copyright © 1977 United Church Press.

This constitution went on to lay down the rules for all the bodies within the church and the creedal requirements for its members.

The problem confronting the negotiators for this union, therefore, was how on the one hand to combine a denomination in which there was no authority from the top down with a denomination of presbyterial order in which the authority of the church as a whole was set forth in a written constitution as its fundamental law.

As we go into discussion of the events that took place, we should keep clearly in mind this issue of contradictory polities or structures.

If the student of the merger procedures can find any point at which this fundamental problem was addressed in a forthright manner, or any time at which the official negotiators from both sides joined in a clear statement as to how these two contradictory systems were to be reconciled, he will be finding something this writer has never been able to discover. An evasive answer often given when the leaders were hard pressed was that "the Basis of Union speaks for itself." (See Dr. Blanchard on p. 34 of *Advance* for July 1947.)

Many people, as we shall often see, found very different answers to this question as they sought to interpret the Basis of Union for themselves. That is one reason why the Evanston Meeting was held just a few months after the Basis of Union was finalized. This ambiguous quality of the Basis of Union, as regards the question of the fundamental and underlying structure of the proposed union, also accounts for the adoption, in January 1948, of a whole set of official "Comments," which sought to assert that the union would be essentially congregational. These Comments, in turn, were the forerunner of the Oberlin Interpretations—which actually toned down some of the previous Comments—and which again sought to convince people that the union would be "congregational."

Nine years elapsed between Oberlin in 1948, before the convening General Synod of the United Church of Christ in 1957. During all the intervening years the subject of the true structure of the United Church of Christ was a matter of prolonged and bitter debate. From Congregational headquarters came a deluge of propaganda claiming that the Congregational Christian churches would suffer no

change in the merger. But never was there a *joint* statement, coming from the officials of *both* denominations,
either affirming or denying what the United Church would
have as its recognized and undisputed polity or structure.

The following options were open from the beginning.
The leaders could have agreed, in forthright manner:

1. that the new denomination would be congregational
   and that the Evangelical and Reformed Church was
   relinquishing its structure of "constitutionally established authority"—its presbyterian polity; or
2. that the United Church would be essentially presbyterial and that the Congregationalists would accept "constitutional authority for the church as a
   whole"; or
3. that the question of polity, or structure, was being
   left open, to be decided later; and that therefore no
   assurances were in order claiming that the union
   would be congregational or otherwise; or
4. that the union would be presbyterial—
   constitutionally ordered and controlled—down
   through the General Synod, Boards, state Conferences, and Associations; and congregational only in
   the limited sense that the local church was being
   promised its "autonomy."

None of these options were chosen openly and in
straightforward joint pronouncements. But we know now
the Evangelical and Reformed leaders had insisted on
number 3 above, that the question be left open; hence no
assurances were ever in order that the union would be
congregational in its polity—that is, in the polity of the
denomination as a whole.

It would also appear that the Congregational Christian leaders were accepting option number 4 above, that
the denomination as a whole would be constitutionally ordered down through the associations, and that only the
local church would be congregational—which of course it
could not be without a sustaining free fellowship. But
even this sort of interpretation was never set forth clearly
and in honest and forthright manner.

On 7 September 1946, I wrote to Dr. Blanchard:

> What you and Dr. Horton are proposing is that we accept
> a Presbyterian system down through the level of the Associa-

tions. This may look like only a half-way step to you; but with the Evangelical and Reformed ministers expecting a full system of authority, this proposition would only rest as a very temporary compromise. (See *Early Pamphlets*, pp. 119–121.)

Essentially the same thing appeared in *Advance* for October 1946, p. 39.

No acknowledgment that I was right, nor any denial of this charge that I made long before Oberlin, was ever received. No public statement confirming this point of view was ever given the Congregational Christian churches. These facts should be kept in mind as we appraise the later actions of General Councils, and the innumerable assurances sent out to the churches concerning the "guarantees" and the "congregational polity" of the proposed union.

As I also pointed out in the above mentioned letters, "autonomous" churches within a presbyterian system would *not* have the same freedom or right of self-determination they had in the former Congregational fellowship. It would be much like the ill-fated Plan of Union with the Presbyterians, 1801 to 1852.

Instead of facing frankly the fundamental problem of contradictory polities, the negotiators indulged merely in producing a patchwork of words. The one idea was to get a document that would "sound right" to the Evangelical and Reformed people on the one hand, and to the Congregationalists on the other. What they wanted was something that the people in both denominations would vote for and would think that they were getting what they wanted. Whenever we would point out portions that suggested uncongregational provisions, a few words would be changed. As Dr. Blanchard once wrote, "At every point where possible ambiguity has been pointed out, a forthright statement of the congregational principle has been introduced" (*Advance*, July 1947, p. 34).

The congregational phrases in the Basis of Union were like ornaments hung on a Christmas tree. The tree itself, however, was the basic framework of the Evangelical and Reformed Church: the concept of a single, national, unitary church with an overall constitution that could be amended by legislative assemblies on the national and state levels.

With Christmas trees it has been the custom to take off the ornaments and *save* them for the future, while the tree itself is *thrown away* and burned after a short while. In the case of the Basis of Union it was the tree that was to be saved for future and permanent use. The congregational ornaments, after serving their purpose of getting votes for the merger, have many of them been discarded already. The tree, representing the basic framework of the United Church of Christ, is the sure and lasting fact about the Church.

When we get into a more detailed study of what has happened; see the details of structure now set forth in the Constitution; begin to study Dr. Gunnemann's statement of the far-reaching changes wrought in the United Church during the sixties; and now get the picture of controls over the ministry from the new Manual, we shall learn how pertinent the above illustration of the tree with its temporary ornaments really is.

First, let us get back to a sequence of the events as they transpired after the Grinnell Council.

CONFRONTING THE ISSUES AT FIRST HAND

Almost immediately after the Grinnell meeting, I went for a second time to the Spiritual Conference of the Evangelical and Reformed ministers at Allentown, Pennsylvania. The frank and open way in which those ministers discussed the merger with me, and the fact that Dr. George Richards was there and took a leading part in setting forth their position, clinched the whole matter for me. From that time forward I tried to get the leaders of our own fellowship to face up to what I had learned. Their failure to come to grips with these insights left me permanently opposed to the merger.

To tell the story of those experiences at Allentown, both in 1945 and in 1946, I can do no better than to quote word for word from the letter I sent out on 9 September 1946. This letter was sent to all Congregational pastors in Connecticut and some other interested individuals throughout the country. It appears on pages 122–125 in *Early Merger Pamphlets*. I quote all but the opening portion, as follows:

It has been much more difficult than anyone believed to find the real heart and core of the issues. Last year Dr. David McKeith invited me to attend the Evangelical and Reformed "Spiritual Conference" at Allentown, Pennsylvania, for four days as one of the Congregational representatives. When I went to the 1945 Allentown Conference I had only a vague idea of what the issues were. I had the general feeling that the Basis of Union would carry us in the direction of a more authoritarian church, tied to a kind of middle-of-the-road orthodoxy. But it was hard to pin anything down in the Basis of Union.

At Allentown, however, I heard Evangelical and Reformed men asserting that the United Church was to have a system of Presbyterial standing for ministers. Like many Congregationalists, I did not have too clear an idea of what that meant. They seemed in perfect agreement on it, and I waited until I got home to find out more about it.

From that time, I went on the assumption that the Presbyterial set-up was agreed to by both parties. I started in October 1945, with the mimeographing of statements intended to show the significance of such a change. It was not until February that I learned that Dr. Blanchard was not willing to call the proposal "Presbyterial." Still, it seemed as though the confusion was mostly in the name for it. I kept on believing that agreement prevailed between top leaders of the two denominations on the essential points of the proposed set-up. Now it appears that among the leaders of our two denominations a genuine confusion has existed all along, and the same words have meant different things to the two parties.

Did We Agree To A Compromise at Grinnell?

At Grinnell a fine show of friendliness between the two denominations was made. But how much real progress in understanding of the crucial issues? There was no back and forth discussion. The Evangelical and Reformed men have worried all along about our lax standards for the ministry. And we have expressed concern about the authority of the higher judicatories over the lower. At Grinnell, therefore, Dr. Richards, chairman of their merger committee, offered a compromise. They would yield to us, he said, on the matter of the authority in the higher judicatories if we would yield to them on the question of ordination and installation.

"All that we ask of you," said Dr. Richards, "is that when your churches call ministers, they have them installed." This sounded Congregational enough, since we have always recognized installation as a very worthy practice. Dr. Richards' words were greeted by a round of applause. Did we accept the compromise? And if so, what did it mean? There was no question period to find out.

We Congregationalists have a great habit of agreeing to things in principle, and then doing little about it. Our General

Council can memorialize our churches, and it can tell our churches that it would be nice if every church would observe the custom of installation for its pastors. But that doesn't mean the churches must do it. A program of encouragement over a period of years might bring a measure of uniformity. But any church desiring to call a pastor without bothering the Association for its approval would still be free to do so.

It now appears that this is not what the Evangelical and Reformed men want. When Dr. Richards asked us to yield on the point of installation he meant that we must make it obligatory and universal. He wasn't asking us to say that it is a nice custom, worthy of recommendation to the churches. He was asking us to create the AUTHORITY which could IMPOSE a universal practice upon churches under the union. That is a very different matter. Neither the Evangelical and Reformed men, nor the majority of us, have stopped to think how much this proposition would entail, or the steps that would be necessary to achieve it.

Results of a Second Visit to Allentown

Proof of the Evangelical and Reformed position came with a second visit to the Evangelical and Reformed "Spiritual Conference" at Allentown, Pennsylvania, this year. When I returned from Grinnell, Iowa, I found an invitation from the president of this year's conference, asking me to attend again. I tried by phone to warn him that I was full of questions on the merger, but he insisted that he wasn't afraid of the truth.

This year I found myself in a better position to ask intelligent questions about the merger. I knew a little of what Presbyterians mean by the "Church" and their concept of democracy—on the strictly representative pattern. Before going to Allentown I prepared two statements especially for consideration there. One, No. 14, was "Sober Reflections on the Grinnell Council"; the other, No. 15, "Where do the Issues Stand Now?" In the latter, No. 15, I took up the question of what was meant by Dr. Richards' "compromise" at Grinnell. I began giving out copies of these statements on Monday, and continued doing so throughout my stay of 4 days. On Wednesday morning there was a paper on the merger by Rev. Clifford Simpson, of Manchester, Connecticut, emphasizing things we have in common with the Evangelical and Reformed Church. On that afternoon was held a three-hour discussion, with Dr. Richards, chairman of their committee, present.

At the Wednesday afternoon session opportunity came to give out more copies of my various statements. No. 15 was passed out first and emphasized in particular. It became the virtual basis of discussion for the entire afternoon. (Persons desiring this, or other statements, are welcome to write to me for them. I plan to have copies of them with me at the Connecticut State meetings this Fall.)

There was no question as to where the Evangelical and Reformed men stood. There was no division among them on this matter. Their whole conception of "The Church," and their general practice of the Presbyterial set-up, makes it unthinkable to them for a merger without uniformity of practice. When I asked Dr. Richards what he had meant at Grinnell, he tried at first to parry the question: "What is the better way? Should not the United Church have the best system?" But the issue was clear. We must accept authority over our churches in this matter of selecting pastors; the Associations must have a power of approval or rejection. And of course it would be necessary to have a general Constitution over all the churches to "sketch" their relationships to each other, the duties of church members, etc. Dr. Richards said: "If this matter is not clear and acceptable to Congregationalists, then we may as well drop the merger at the next meeting of the Joint Commission." This, remember, took place after our Council meeting at Grinnell. And all of the Evangelical and Reformed Ministers (some fifty of them) seemed in perfect agreement with Dr. Richards' summary of the case.

The question at Allentown, therefore, boiled down to this: "Will the Congregational Churches accept a Presbyterial system?" Six Congregational ministers were present as visitors. A majority of those present *assured the Evangelical and Reformed men that we will accept a Presbyterial system.* Rev. Clifford Simpson insisted that our churches are turning more and more to installation. He said that we recognize this as being the same as the Presbyterial set-up. He said that we'd be glad to make it a universal custom, and assured them that not a hundred Congregational churches throughout the country would refuse to go along. It is only their belief that we will accept the Presbyterial system that is keeping the merger alive in Evangelical and Reformed circles.

Where Do Our Leaders Stand?

Upon my return from Allentown, I found a letter awaiting me from Dr. Blanchard. I had sent him the same statement, No. 15, which had formed the basis of discussion with the Evangelical and Reformed men. His reactions were entirely contrary to those of the Evangelical and Reformed men, and contrary also to the assurances given them by Rev. Clifford Simpson. Since then I have had two more letters from Dr. Blanchard (one of which is to be published in October *Advance*), two from Dr. Horton, and one from Dr. Richards. All define the issue more clearly. It is evident that a serious disagreement exists among the leaders of the two denominations—at least if Dr. Richards is to have anything to say about it. All are promising to get a clear-cut statement at the next meeting of the Joint Commission in October.

The Evangelical and Reformed men, in all the conversations I had with them, made it plain that they will not enter a union which permits us to remain Congregational. As Dr. Richards says, this must be a "union," not a mere "merger." Merger, he says would give only a muddy result. They want a clear and uniform practice. They were told that we are tired of our system and consider it a failure. Our representatives have continually admitted that our system of ministerial standing is too lax and should be strengthened. We have agreed "in principle" to move in their direction. They have interpreted this as a willingness to become Presbyterial under the union. Dr. Blanchard and Dr. Horton, however, would draw the line short of the local church. They would evidently accept the Presbyterial system of a central authority for the over-all set-up of General Synod, Boards, State Conferences, and Associations. The local churches, however, they would leave "free" and "autonomous"—simply exerting pressure upon them to adopt more uniform practices.

This plan, as Dr. Blanchard outlines it, would not be acceptable to the rank and file of Evangelical and Reformed ministers today. It is also hard to see how such a set-up could last very long under a union. But Dr. Blanchard is probably aware that such a plan would be infinitely easier to "sell" to our churches. What is more, it could be largely accomplished by votes of the General Council, the State Conferences, and Associations. It would not require the tedious conquest of every single church; nor would it involve for the present any change in Constitution and By-laws for the individual church. These are strong bargaining points.

Dr. Blanchard continues very sure that the Joint Commission will accept his interpretation, even if it is contrary to the wishes of the Evangelical and Reformed men whom I met at Allentown. Dr. Richards has been side-tracked on previous occasions. The kind of frank and honest statement which the Evangelical and Reformed men gave me at Allentown may suffer eclipse at the Joint Commission meeting in a move of expediency. The issue is worth watching closely. Meanwhile, some further relevant facts:

Where Will the Evangelical and Reformed Leaders Stand?
Sometimes the most significant information comes in a very casual way. One of the Evangelical and Reformed men told me that their Church tried a few years ago to get a merger with a Presbyterian group.The Presbyterians looked them over and rejected them on these grounds: 1. Their pension fund was not adequately funded (they face a much worse situation than we did with our "Debt of Honor"); 2. Their Church-dependent colleges and schools had skimpy endowments; 3. Their missions and other Boards had few real assets. These liabilities mean a constant, heavy drain on benevolent giving (they are "assessed" over $5 a member for it); and so the Presbyterians turned them down. Yet all the Evangelical and Reformed men seemed agreed that their future lies

with Presbyterians. They are much more conscious of polity than we, and they constantly speak of Presbyterially-organized churches. They told me that there would be no point in their changing to a Congregational system, because there are no other congregationally-organized bodies with whom they would care to unite. But for the moment they seem blocked in possible mergers with Presbyterians because of lack of funds.

Their leaders have seemed awfully anxious for this merger with us. If they can carry through this union, they can count on two things: First, they will have greatly increased assets, which will make it easier to negotiate with Presbyterian bodies. Secondly, they can probably count on a majority of Presbyterially-minded ministers in the new United Church. (Their ministers will stand as a solid bloc, and enough of our ministers would accept a Presbyterial system to form that clear majority.) Furthermore, the "die-hard" Congregationalists will probably stay out of the union. After one or two more mergers (with Presbyterians) the residual elements of Congregationalism would be practically gone.

It may therefore seem expedient to the Evangelical and Reformed leaders to go along with Dr. Blanchard in his present interpretation of the Basis of Union. Then, after the union has gone through, a constant pressure can be exerted upon our churches to accept the rest of a Presbyterial authority. They can argue that we had "agreed to it in principle"; they can say that we are "morally bound" to go through with it; they can insist that a divided system is unworkable; they would already have control of our ministerial standing; and they would probably have a majority of ministers Presbyterially-minded. What then could stop them from putting the pressure on our churches, year after year, to re-write their individual Constitutions and By-laws so as to accept a fully Presbyterial system?

Are We Entitled to a Clear Statement of the Facts?

Many of my fellow ministers will feel great impatience with these details over polity, etc. But will they grant us the right to the truth? If this merger is "holy" and "god-inspired,"—as some have insisted—then it should come to us with clean hands. There must be a decent way of bringing a good thing to pass.

Some ministers would be willing to go Presbyterial, Methodist, Episcopal, or even Roman Catholic—if it was in the name of some "great cause." But others have strong convictions in matters of church polity. These convictions deserve the respect and consideration of others, even when not shared by them. As Christians we have no right to try and defraud each other. Let the truth be known. God will not prosper a merger that is built upon expediency and evasion. If we are to take a step that will ultimately liquidate Congregationalism, let us say so like men. If we believe the Presbyterian method is better, let us discuss the issue frankly and fully. We have the right to ask what Congregationalism is, and whether it has a right to live.

I have not tried to argue the merits of Congregationalism vs. Presbyterianism in this letter. I am begging simply that the facts be established. I am asking for a fresh start in our merger discussions, with facts now available laid openly before everyone. It isn't fair to take advantage of a state of confusion to rush a merger through. It is time that we had a passion for truth, regardless of whether we favor or oppose the merger. When we know the fundamental facts for a certainty, then we can begin to argue the merits of those facts.

One gets the impression that the merger has been "babied along." Nobody would think of saying anything that might hurt it. A great deal of time has gone into building up enthusiasm for it. But little time has been set aside for unhurried, reasoned discussion. After six years we find the central facts still uncertain.

If the Evangelical and Reformed leaders will state frankly what their men want, then the interpretation of Dr. Blanchard cannot stand. This might "hurt" the merger. It might lead to its immediate defeat. But it would not hurt the ultimate cause of friendship and understanding between our churches. We would part as friends with deepened understanding of each other, growing out of these contacts together. We would respect the Evangelical and Reformed leaders for sticking to their guns and for honestly reflecting the minds and hearts of their people.

On the other hand, if they accept a statement of the issues which is repugnant to the rank and file of Evangelical and Reformed ministers, they may employ a successful strategy so far as present negotiations are concerned. But in the end will come untold bitterness and strife. If our churches find that they have been misled, they may stubbornly oppose further efforts to make them knuckle under. There may also come years of litigation in the courts and unhappy legal battles over the possession of church funds. Certainly this would be no help to the "Ecumenical Church."

If this merger ultimately means a Presbyterial set-up for us, it is time that we knew all about it. Perhaps our churches will still go through with the union, just as Clifford Simpson intimated. But the only fair thing is to tell everyone frankly what the end-result will be. What I have seen and heard among the Evangelical and Reformed men these two years at Allentown cannot be lightly brushed aside. Our leaders can know these facts if they will go prodding after them. It is not enough to patch up agreements among the top leaders, just to carry the merger along. There can be no honor in a merger where fundamental truth has been neglected, and no creative union can be built upon false foundations.

Sincerely yours,

(s) Malcolm K. Burton

EVENTS HAVE ALREADY VERIFIED SOME ISSUES

I stated, before quoting the long letter above, that the experiences at Allentown convinced me of what the merger really meant and nothing after that time ever came to grips with what I had learned at those two conferences—nothing, that is, by way of official action trying to get to the real heart of the merger proposal.

What I stated in the letter above was repeated in other published pamphlets and in letters published in *Advance*. The replies made to these statements of fact were of a trifling nature, and not one of them ever came to honest grips with the question of the real constitutional structure of the proposed United Church of Christ.

I asserted at the beginning of this chapter that this was the crucial period in which the documents were hammered out in their final form. I mentioned that the issues were all brought out in the open during this period and that they had been crisscrossed over, back and forth, many times. One needs only to consider the above letter and the assertions made in it to get a good idea of the thoroughness with which these definite issues were set forth.

No one can possibly say that there was not ample opportunity for the leaders to see the issues and to know their importance even before the last three revisions of the Basis of Union were made.

The part played by the Evangelical and Reformed Church leaders in letting the rank and file of the Congregationalists believe that the union would have congregational polity, while at the same time they solemnly assured their own people that they would not accept congregational polity for the United Church, began before Oberlin but was of even greater import afterward.

Now, more than thirty years later, comes the book by Dr. Gunnemann giving us a vivid picture of the United Church of Christ as it has actually been shaped, and reshaped, by its General Synod through its use of "constitutionally established" authority and power. Dr. Gunnemann sets forth a picture of a very centralized power structure, consciously and purposefully sought and established. The General Synod has been made the "decision-making" body for the church as a whole, with direct control over all boards and agencies. In dizzying succession, agencies and committees have been formed and reformed, separated and then combined anew with different combinations.

In the midst of telling about the shaping and reshaping of the superstructure, Dr. Gunnemann states his perception of the place of the local church within the United Church of Christ. For anyone acquainted with the classic description of presbyterian polity his words should be instantly recognizable. They fall perfectly into accord with what I reported as the Evangelical and Reformed expectation of the structure of the United Church after each of my experiences at Allentown. The essence of presbyterianism, as I have pointed out, is that of representative bodies presuming to speak for the local churches. That is combined with the concept of "the Church" as the denomination, and the whole held together under a central constitution. On page 91 Dr. Gunnemann says:

> The establishment of a principle of authority beyond the local church *by a system of representation* while at the same time maintaining the freedom of autonomous units had an important consequence. Limited but creative use was made of the principle of representative government by giving greater control of the denominational or national level organization to representatives of local churches *without* turning that authority around to be exercised on the local churches. In doing so it lifted up a principle of Reformed ecclesiology that frequently is obscured; the autonomy of the local church has reality when its freedom is responsibly exercised on behalf of the whole church. To put it another way, the local church has its being in an expression of the lordship of Christ, which is a responsible relationship to those organizational structures that express the being of the whole church ... (The italics above are Dr. Gunnemann's.)*

*Reprinted with permission from Louis H. Gunnemann, *The Shaping of the United Church of Christ: An Essay in the History of American Christianity*. Copyright © 1977 United Church Press.

A footnote at the bottom of page 91 further emphasizes that this is Reformed church tradition and ends with an emphasis upon:

> ... an ordering of relationship between the units of organization in which binding constitutional requirements have not the force of legal constraint exercised by one unit on another but of assignment of responsibility (endorsed and voted by representatives of these units) to each unit. Thus, responsible freedom is dependent upon a voluntary assumption of responsibilities essential to the life of the church in all its component units.*

This is presbyterial polity and thought, pure and simple. Whether Dr. Blanchard or Dr. Horton would have maintained that such a system would be congregational in polity—just because "autonomy" is ascribed to the local church within a presbyterial framework—is impossible to say. But Dr. Gunnemann does not so interpret the United Church of Christ today. His description is typical of presbyterian rationale from start to finish. And Dr. Gunnemann, as we shall see, makes it plain in his book that the Evangelical and Reformed leaders repeatedly insisted that they would not go into the merger if it meant that their church would be swallowed up in Congregationalism. (See quotation from letter of Dr. L. W. Goebel, bottom p. 32 of Dr. Gunnemann's book).

As I said earlier, this description fits what I reported was the expectation of the men at Allentown. For any not well acquainted with Congregational theory and conviction, the above description is contrary to our historic principles in all of the following ways:

1. In congregationalism each local church is a "complete church" in itself. Dr. Gunnemann's use of "the church" to mean the total body of the denomination is contrary to our thought.
2. With us each local church considers itself under the direct headship of Christ—not through a General Synod or hierarchy.
3. With us an individual church is *in fellowship* with other churches but is not bound together with them

*Reprinted with permission from Louis H. Gunnemann, *The Shaping of the United Church of Christ: An Essay in the History of American Christianity.* Copyright © 1977 United Church Press.

through an overall constitution.

4. In Congregationalism it would not be true to say that "the autonomy of the local church has reality when its freedom is responsibly exercised in behalf of the whole church." Such a statement is typical of the attempt to hedge in, and limit, true autonomy. With us a local church can disagree with programs and objectives set by national or state bodies, and it is not obligated to cooperate.

5. The statement suggesting "binding constitutional requirements" in assignment of responsibility *endorsed by representatives of the units themselves* has no relevance in congregational polity. We do not recognize the power of "representatives" to endorse and vote for such assignments of responsibility. That concept is in the presbyterian pattern, not congregational.

Now see how thoroughly all this was covered in my letter to Dr. Blanchard, quoted below. Again remember that this was before the last three revisions of the Basis of Union were made. This was in response to a letter of August 7 from Dr. Blanchard, in which he wrote, "Please rephrase the sections as you think they should read."

New London, Conn.
Sept. 7, 1946

Dear Dr. Blanchard:

Herewith are the requested suggestions for changes in the Basis of Union, to make clear and undebatable the issue of ministerial standing as you have described it.

Section IX. Ministers, lines 182 to 188, should be re-written as follows: "Ministers and churches desiring to maintain a system of pastoral placement in which the Conference or Association shall have little or no part, shall be free to do so. No amendment to this Basis of Union, no article in the Constitution or By-laws, and no act of any body of the United Churches shall ever have power to take from Congregational Churches their freedom of selection in this matter or to impose penalties for failure to comply with church rules. But the recommended procedure shall be one in which minister, Congregation, and Conference or Association cooperate, the Conference or Association approving candidates, the Congregation extending and the minister accepting the call. Installation shall be optional, at the choice of minister and church, but is recommended."

This, I suppose, would constitute the kind of suggestion

for which you have been asking. It is utterly inadequate, however, to clear up the mental confusion surrounding the whole Basis of Union. To make even the above statement really clear and undebatable the following changes would also be necessary:

1. To clear up the confusion over name. It is all very well to speak of the "Church" in a loose, generic sense when talking of the "Holy Catholic Church" or the "Ecumenical Church." But in a legal instrument, or a formal document of organization, the distinction between "church" and "churches" must be closely guarded. "The Church" is part of the Presbyterian concept of a centrally ȯrganized authority, where elected representatives from all the churches have power to pass laws effective over every church. The Evangelical and Reformed ministers with whom I have talked constantly reflect this concept of "The Church," and to incorporate their term in our instrument of merger is deceiving to them unless we intend a Presbyterial set-up. It is senseless to speak of keeping inviolate the autonomy of our churches when we liquidate even the concept of separate churches. The name should be, "The United Churches."

2. Likewise the idea of "unit of organization." In the Presbyterian scheme the local "congregation" is just a branch office. Neither of these terms ("Congregation" or "unit of organization") is consistent with our understanding of autonomous churches. They should not be permitted to replace our concept of a "Congregational Church." Such words do not belong in the Basis if our churches are to retain their autonomy.

3. Elimination of words "Synod" and "Judicatory," in compliance with the Evangelical and Reformed offer at Grinnell. "Synod" and "judicatory" are terms recognized in the courts. They signify authority. If the Evangelical and Reformed men are willing to have the higher bodies "purely advisory," then other names must be found which are free from authoritative connotations. Otherwise the advisory character of these bodies will never become established, nor could it persist.

4. Prohibit legislative powers over local church. The concept of a central authority, as outlined in the Basis, should be clarified so as to enjoin it from any right to pass laws governing the local church. Lines 81, 82 should be amended to read, "These rights shall include the holding and operation of its own property and the right to act as the final arbiter in all matters relating to its own affairs." For the local church this is necessary to remain autonomous. For the Associations and Conferences this is necessary to guarantee that the power of the higher body shall be "purely advisory."

5. Limit the Fundamental law and coverage of the Constitution. Line 213–215 of the Basis must be amended to omit

the concept of a "fundamental law" and to limit the coverage
of the Constitution to the higher bodies alone. The concept of
a "fundamental law" is rather indefinite in the minds of Congregationalists. But the Evangelical and Reformed Church
has practiced a clear acceptance of it and has set it forth in
this fashion: "ordains this constitution to be its fundamental
law and declares the same to have authority over all its ministers, members, congregations, and judicatories." The inclusion
of this term, even in an inconspicuous place, is deceiving to us
and to the Evangelical and Reformed men alike if we intend to
preserve autonomy in our local churches.

All of the above changes would be necessary, I believe, if
the interpretation which you and Dr. Horton have given us is
to be made *clear* and *undebatable*. Otherwise the Basis of
Union will continue to testify against itself, and to be a false
and deceiving document to both sides. However, there are
even more changes that I feel essential to preserve what you
promised in the June *Advance*.

There was more to this letter, which is included in the
copy in *Early Merger Pamphlets*. I set forth, among other
things, the proposition that Dr. Blanchard and Dr. Horton
seemed to advocate a presbyterial system down through
the associations, and that the ministers would be "within
the authority of this unified top organization. It would
make them subject to provisions of the central constitution...." How true today! Here is where the new *Manual
on the Ministry* fills out the picture in dramatic fashion, as
we shall soon see.

The references in the above letter were, of course, not
to the final edition of the Basis of Union, but to the provisional draft of September 1945—the last one then printed.
The words *fundamental law* were dropped from later editions, but not the whole concept. By definition a constitution is the fundamental law of the body for which it is
adopted. The idea of the constitution for the whole
"church" remained.

In all discussions of the Basis of Union many people
were fooled by the single word *autonomy*. Probably this is
still true today. I endeavored to treat this subject in depth
in my pamphlet No. 22, *What Do We Mean By Autonomy?* I
discussed how the Evangelical and Reformed people used
it with very different understanding from what we did.
But people who favored the merger were impatient with

any such attempts at careful analysis of the meaning of even key words in the Basis of Union. Pamphlet No. 22 is in my book, *Early Merger Pamphlets*, page 159. It was printed 11 March 1947. It appears also in *Advance* for May 1947, pages 32 and 33.

Dr. Blanchard promised me that he would present my suggestions to the Joint Commission. If he did, then all of the Congregational members of the Joint Commission had the opportunity to know that these issues had been raised. Dr. Blanchard's later word to me was that he presented my suggestions and that the Joint Commission did not feel that they were necessary.

The ultimate issue of the autonomy of the local church is bound up with its freedom to get the kind of minister that it really wants, without interference or pressure from higher bodies. Even the Basis of Union was inconsistent on this point. The Oberlin Interpretations and the Constitution of the United Church added further complications when they spoke of "describing free and voluntary relations." Now the new *Manual on the Ministry* really puts the heat on, with plenty of Conference manpower behind it.

The Basis of Union, in its final sentence in the section on "Ministers and Congregations" (VI. C) stated:

> In all relationships between minister and local church or Congregation, the freedom of the minister and the autonomy of the church are presupposed.

Yet the sentence immediately preceding this stated:

> The new communion will appeal to all Congregations not to call or dismiss their ministers, and to all ministers not to respond to calls or resign, until the Association or Conference shall have given approval.

This last quotation embodies specifically what I reported—and Dr. Blanchard disputed—that the Evangelical and Reformed ministers were demanding. In the Basis of Union it was left on the level of merely "appealing" to the churches to conform. The new *Manual on the Ministry* leaves little suggestion of anything optional. It quotes chapter and verse from the United Church bylaws, just as though this is the way that it is going to be done—period!

VERIFYING THE ULTIMATE ISSUE

What is this *Manual for the Ministry*? Where did it come from, and what are the events that led up to the formation of the new agency which produced it? To answer these questions, and what lies behind them, we need to back up a little and retrace our steps concerning the "shaping of the United Church of Christ" and its organization as progressively designed by successive General Synods.

Dr. Gunnemann in his story of how the General Synod fashioned the present top structure speaks of the "quest for power and authority" and the problem of having to deal with a "conglomerate of autonomies."

On several occasions Dr. Gunnemann suggests that the social issues of the Sixties forced the United Church of Christ to shape its organization to deal with such social questions. Speaking of the organization as originally adopted in 1961, Dr. Gunnemann writes:

> ... it was experimental in its arrangement of autonomous administrative units with a supposed equality of power. The capability of such an arrangement was immediately tested by the critical events and circumstances of the Sixties. Gradual awareness that a "conglomerate of autonomies" would not suffice in such times led to the proposals which the Committee on Structure placed before the church and the General Synod. (pp. 88–89)*

While paying lip-service to autonomy and self-determination, Dr. Gunnemann comments:

> Acknowledging that the United Church polity formally affirms autonomy and self-determination, the committee saw this polity informally "described and practiced." "What the Church is to be and the relation of the parts to the whole are less well defined than the freedom of the parts." Expressing the hope that "the Church can formulate and achieve effective coordination while its several parts are truly free of central (authoritative) control," the committee made proposals for *coordination controlled by the objectives determined by the*

*Reprinted with permission from Louis H. Gunnemann, *The Shaping of the United Church of Christ: An Essay in the History of American Christianity*. Copyright © 1977 United Church Press.

General Synod. The key points in the recommendations were a clear affirmation of the General Synod as the *decision-making* body for national-level matters and the Executive Council as the *implementing* body for those decisions. They called for integrated and coordinated efforts authorized by the General Synod and managed by the Executive Council. (p. 89)*

This, you might say, was just the beginning. The following quotation shows how the power structure was strengthened and enlarged. It also shows how the conferences were now drawn into this top structure. (That is where things started getting closer to the churches.) Dr. Gunnemann goes on, immediately following the passage just quoted:

> To achieve this operational system the committees spelled out what would be required. Both the General Synod and the Executive Council would need to undergo change. To accomplish credible churchwide decision-making it was proposed that "where policy is made at a national level there should be present as active participants the most informed, competent and knowledgeable people our local churches, Conferences and Instrumentalities can provide." For implementation of General Synod decisions, it was proposed that the Executive Council be enlarged and reorganized. Of prime importance was the plan to broaden the representation on the Executive Council from the instrumentalities and conferences, thus "commanding the respect, adherence and cooperation of all parts of the church" in handling major issues.
> Delegates to the 1969 General Synod gave detailed attention to the amendments of the Constitution and Bylaws proposed by the Executive Council for implementation of the Structure Committee Report. Voting representation in the General Synod was enlarged to include the elected officers of the church, members of the Executive Council, and the moderators. To give continuity to the biennial General Synods the term of delegates from the conferences was changed from two to four years, with the possibility of one additional term. The Executive Council was nearly doubled in size and included six conference executives. . . .
> Detailed bylaw amendments about the organization and responsibility of the Executive Council underlined the crucial leadership role being assigned to that body as the General Synod ad interim. A major objective in this structural change was the kind of coordination of all aspects of the church's na-

*Reprinted with permission from Louis H. Gunnemann, *The Shaping of the United Church of Christ: An Essay in the History of American Christianity.* Copyright © 1977 United Church Press.

tional activities that could be accomplished through a sophisticated system of central administration. In this respect relocating the budget and finance operations from the General Synod to the Executive Council made this key responsibility less susceptible to the pressures of a large deliberative body. (pp. 89–90)*

All of this is part of the highly centralized power structure of which I spoke a few pages ago. Just think what the above means:

1. all officers and members of the Executive Council are members of the General Synod (which Dr. Gunnemann had tried to picture as the voice of the local church);
2. greatly enlarged Executive Council with heads of the instrumentalities and six conference executives included;
3. the terms of the delegates extended to four and possibly eight years.

Here is the picture of an entrenched leadership clique supported by delegates screened out at the conference level to get those most likely to support the leaders and programs already established. (We say, "screened out," because we have seen something in the past, even in Congregationalism, of the way that a state conference nominating committee, often dominated by the conference office, picks its slate.) To think that the delegates thus elected truly represent the sentiment and wishes of the average church members is either naive or a case of "straining at a gnat and swallowing a camel." But in Dr. Gunnemann's labored attempt to make the structure look like a preservation of the "freedom" of the local church it is probably the best that he could do and it is the stock argument of presbyterianism for "representative democracy."

But the end of centralization is not yet. Before we get to the later establishment of the Office of Church Life and Leadership, we need the following additional insights, which come in Dr. Gunnemann's book immediately following the last quotations above:

*Reprinted with permission from Louis H. Gunnemann, *The Shaping of the United Church of Christ: An Essay in the History of American Christianity.* Copyright © 1977 United Church Press.

Closely related to these provisions for the work of the Executive Council were those that assigned greater executive responsibility to the office of the president. As chief executive officer of the General Synod, under the new responsibilities assigned to the Executive Council, the president could no longer rely so heavily upon the "effectiveness of his personality and subjective powers of persuasion." Specific authority was now assigned. This included the elaboration of a staff of assistants as needs required, *i.e.*, p. 90.*

Much of the foregoing had to do with national level organization. We get closer to home with the local churches as the conferences get tied in more with the centralized top organization. This becomes the prelude for the Office of Church Life and Leadership, as we shall soon observe. We quote now from page 91 and 92 of Dr. Gunnemann.

... At the same time other centers of influence were appearing in conference structures as those bodies sought to minister to regional situations, which tended to reflect the diversity of the nation itself. Conferences enlarged their own staffs to meet these needs.... The conferences were in the strategic position of having the constitution assignment of providing the structured relationship of local churches to the denominational organization. This included participation in the General Synod's budget process and in the channelling of funds to the denominational treasury.

Some indication of the ever-increasing role of the conferences is given in the distribution of funds contributed by local churches for Our Christian World Mission. In 1962, the first year under the new unified treasurer's office, 67.2 percent of the total amount of $16,141,885 went to national level offices and agencies, while 32.8 percent was retained by the conferences. By 1969, the conference percentage had increased to 43.1 percent, and by 1974 to 47.7 percent, a figure approaching half of OCWM giving.*

Of course the increase in budgets reflects also an increase in staff personnel on the conference level, with presumably additional "area ministers" and other leaders in specific fields, all of them engaged to some extent in influencing local churches, trying to indoctrinate them on United Church programs and ideas, and "servicing" them

*Reprinted with permission from Louis H. Gunnemann, *The Shaping of the United Church of Christ: An Essay in the History of American Christianity.* Copyright © 1977 United Church Press.

in regard to finding ministers, and so forth. This budgetary increase must be added to the very great expendi-
tures, which Dr. Gunnemann mentions, for the Executive
Council and other top-level agencies. People in the United
Church who suppose that their Christian World Mission
contributions go to convert "heathens" in other lands
might be surprised to know how much of it is used in
bureaucratic administration of the United Church itself,
and in an endeavor to convert the churches and their
members to the social and political positions taken by the
General Synod on many key questions of our American
political and social life. On the national level of organizational expense, Dr. Gunnemann gives the following very
revealing figures:

> Another way to estimate the changing roles of confer-
> ences, instrumentalities, and the Executive Council that re-
> sulted from structural changes is to note the budget of the
> Executive Council. In 1962, the Council expended $576,654, or
> 5.3 percent of the total amount available to national level
> structures. This amount reached $1,000,000 in 1971, or 11.2
> percent. In 1974 the Executive Council had available $940,000,
> or 10.4 percent. Thus, the Executive Council's operating funds
> increased 73 percent from 1962 to 1974. The import of this is
> the changing role of the council—which is the General Synod
> ad interim—in relation to both instrumentalities and confer-
> ences. (p. 92)*

Along the way, although I do not see this mentioned
by Dr. Gunnemann, the Executive Council was incorporated, and its charter reads that it may do any and all of
the things which the General Synod may do. The matter of
whether the United Church should be incorporated, making it a national corporate church, was long a touchy point
with Congregationalists. We have always emphasized a
loose and free fellowship arrangement and have not
wanted to be part of a "corporate church." The Evangelical and Reformed Church was incorporated as a single national body. In congregationalism there was set up a Cor-
poration for the General Council, but the Council itself

*Reprinted with permission from Louis H. Gunnemann, *The Shaping of the
United Church of Christ: An Essay in the History of American Christianity.*
Copyright © 1977 United Church Press.

was kept a free association of individuals. I find no mention in the United Church Yearbook of this incorporation of the Executive Council, but I have seen a copy of the charter. Other United Church of Christ corporations are listed in the Yearbook. I do not pretend to know the legal implications of having the Executive Council incorporated, but it would certainly seem a halfway step, or possibly the full equivalent, of having the denomination as such incorporated.

Having followed the details of this high degree of centralization and authority, and the expanding budgets for bureaucratic oversight and control, we are more prepared to understand the creation of the Office for Church Life and Leadership. We should also realize that the growing power and personnel of the state conferences is part of the picture as the Office for Church Life and Leadership relates to the local churches.

We are ready now to examine the *Manual on the Ministry* and the new agency which prepared it. The Manual itself comprises seventy-four full size sheets, 8½ by 11 inches, and is a professional-looking and formidable book. It has four pages of appendices and Index, in double-column and small print, testifying to the large amount of contents and subjects covered.

The Office for Church Life and Ministry is not just another little committee or commission. Dr. Gunnemann explains:

> Major developments in organizational structure in the years following the 1971 General Synod provide examples of the new significance of the Executive Council in its denominational leadership role. The first was a response to the synod's action strengthening the local church, which called for a task force to "study and evaluate leadership development" in the United Church, with specific reference to the respective roles of the Council for Church and Ministry, and the Council for Lay Life and Work. From this assignment came a proposal to the 1973 General Synod to establish the Office for Church Life and Leadership, *accountable to the Executive Council* in its developmental phase (which was to extend to 1977) and subsuming in its overall design the functions of the Council for Church and Ministry, the Council for Lay Life and Work, the Committee on Theological Education, the Commission on Worship and the Theological Commission.
>
> The establishment of this new agency of the denomination

had the effect of implementing in part a concept proposed several years earlier by the Committee on Structure. At that time (1967) the committee had tentatively proposed the establishment of a third major program board to concern itself with "church ministries" as distinguished from "homeland" and "world" ministries. Although rejected then, the concept reappeared as a result of the growing concern for more intensive and extensive servicing of the local churches and the conferences. Institutional vulnerability, so glaringly demonstrated in church statistics throughout American religious bodies, became a cause for alarm as the Seventies unfolded. One clear need seemed to impress itself upon delegates and officials alike: better lay and professional leadership. The new agency, then, was designed to "combine in one nationwide office the policy-making, operational, and administrative function for leadership development in the United Church of Christ." (pp. 98–99)*

Probably the establishment of this new Office for Church Life and Leadership had as one of its purposes what Dr. Gunnemann refers to as the United Church finding its "identity." Dr. Gunnemann seems satisfied that the overhaul of the national organization had succeeded in establishing a kind of identity for the Church in its national aspects. But he laments the failure of this program of "finding its identity" in other areas. Thus, on page 103, Dr. Gunnemann states:

Nevertheless the question of identity was not resolved for large segments of the United Church. On the local level, in small and large communities, in urban and rural centers, churches drew their identity from quite different sources, most of them unaffected by a new style of life such as that experienced in national gatherings. In many cases local churches were still known in their communities by their former affiliation with either the Congregational Christian or Evangelical and Reformed traditions. But in style of church life even those traditional distinctions tended to be blurred by the pervading characteristics of mainline Protestant churches. For the average local church members the name United Church had little content. Some indeed felt it to be sharply lacking in the particularity of other church names that designated either polity or confessional distinctions.
If United Church of Christ identity is rooted in the free-

*Reprinted with permission from Louis H. Gunnemann, *The Shaping of the United Church of Christ: An Essay in the History of American Christianity*. Copyright © 1977 United Church Press.

dom and unity that Jesus Christ gives, making possible a faithful use of the tension between local church autonomy and mutual accountability, then the critical problems facing the denomination lie in the life of the local church. This was perceived in the decision of the General Synod to establish the Office for Church Life and Leadership, a national-level agency designed to work closely with conferences in the servicing of local churches. . . . (p. 103)*

When I first read about the extensive reorganization and centralizing of all the national bodies, and of the "quest for authority and power" combined with the feeling that the United Church of Christ had inherited from Congregationalism a "conglomerate of autonomies" that had to be dealt with, I could not help wondering: "When will they get around to turning their efforts toward the local churches with the possible intent of limiting or curtailing this ultimate autonomy—the last vestige of Congregationalism?"

This Office for Church Life and Leadership is one of the most recent reorganizations, combining as Dr. Gunnemann listed them five or six previous commissions and councils. The men's and women's lay work had already been combined in the Council for Lay Life and Work. So in reality there were six bodies merged into this new board. This certainly must be a formidable organization—a veritable powerhouse of constitutionally established authority and bureaucratic manpower. It has not had time yet to "show its stuff," but it will touch every aspect of the local church's life—its worship, the training of its ministers, its lay leadership, its theology, and the "servicing" of the churches.

Dr. Gunnemann manages to use some nice-sounding words to cover a few obvious intents. "Servicing the churches" sounds better than "telling the local churches how to run their own affairs" or "trying to persuade them to come across with more money" or "getting them to support the political and social pronouncements of the General Synod" or "making sure that they get only ministers

*Reprinted with permission from Louis H. Gunnemann, *The Shaping of the United Church of Christ: An Essay in the History of American Christianity.* Copyright © 1977 United Church Press.

who will support the national program of the United Church of Christ."

For those who consider bureaucratic institutions always benign and helpful, these characterizations would seem unkind. But who can honestly deny that here is the real meaning of "servicing" the local churches, even if it also be true that much conscientious work will go into trying to be genuinely helpful to the churches?

The problem of getting the local churches to accept the identity of the United Church of Christ, especially as exemplified in the pronouncements of the General Synod, runs counter to the expectations of most former Congregational Christian Churches. They were promised that they would remain just as they always had been, that they would still be Congregational Churches, and they would continue operating exactly as they had in the past.

Here in Massachusetts, where I have been living for the past nine years, the "identity crisis" for the United Church officials is probably acute, so far as local churches are concerned. Most of them have done just about what they had been promised they could do. If you want to get a local Congregationalist to flare up, all you have to do is to ask him why his church still goes by the name Congregational when it is supposed to be United Church of Christ. He will almost invariably insist that his church is still just Congregational and no different from what it has always been.

I understand that the New United Church Historical Council has been trying for several years, without success, to get the Congregational Christian Historical Society to merge and give up its separate identity, becoming just a part of the Historical Council for the United Church. Its members have been asked, "When are you fellows going to realize that you are now part of the United Church of Christ?" But so far the Historical Society has felt that when it comes to the matter of Congregational history, it needs to be kept at the grass-roots level, where it came from. To have some regional office of a United Church Historical Council presume to carry on the work of Congregational Christian historical interests would be just too much to hope. This is especially true when former Evangelical and Reformed Church people seem to be the ones who are the most disturbed about the Congregational Christian churches keeping their old identity.

In the *Manual on the Ministry* we find page after page of quotations from the Constitution and Bylaws of the United Church of Christ—quoted with the rather explicit suggestions that these are the rules of the church and that they are meant to be followed. What was formerly identified as Paragraph 21 is printed inconspicuously as Section 15. But nothing further is said about the local church being free to operate as it sees fit, and certainly nothing else in the *Manual* would suggest that a local church is free "to call or dismiss its pastor or pastors by such procedure as it shall determine"—as stated in that paragraph.

Some forty-one paragraphs from the Constitution and Bylaws deal specifically with ministers and how they shall be trained, licensed, ordained, called, and dismissed, and have their standing regulated. The paragraphs dealing most intimately with the way a church calls and dismisses its ministers, and related matters, are quoted on pages 9 and 10 of the *Manual*, as follows:

24. The Call of a minister to a pastorate establishes a covenant relationship between the minister and the local church. This relationship is also a concern of the Church at large as represented by an Association and a Conference.

121. It is the responsibility of a committee of the local church to seek a candidate for a vacancy in the office of pastor.

122. In filling a vacancy or in securing supply ministers during the period of a vacancy, the committee of the local church, through its Conference executive, seeks the counsel of the placement committee. This placement committee consists of the Conference executive and other officers elected or appointed by the Conference.

123. The committee of a local church requests the Conference executive to secure relevant information about any minister whom it wishes to consider for the vacancy.

124. Any minister may confer with the Conference executive concerning a pastoral vacancy. At the minister's request, his or her name shall be submitted by the Conference executive for consideration by the committee of any local church where there is a pastoral vacancy.

125. All vacancies within the Conference shall be reported promptly to the Secretary of the United Church of Christ by the Conference executive.

126. The committee of the local church presents to the church

the name of a candidate it recommends to fill the vacancy. The local church determines whether or not it wishes to call the person recommended.

127. In the call the terms of the pastoral relationship are stated, including the agreement of the local church to participate in the pension fund on the pastor's behalf. The minister, the local church, and the Conference executive should each receive a copy of the call. The Conference executive shall inform the Secretary of the United Church of Christ when the call has been accepted.

128. When a minister accepts a call to a local church, the minister and the church join in requesting the Association to arrange for a service of installation or recognition.

129. Report of the service of installation or recognition is signed by the proper officer of the Association and by the Conference executive.

130. When a pastor or a local church decide to terminate the pastoral relationship, notice of the decision is sent to the Conference executive and the Association. The Association takes action appropriate to the dissolution of the pastoral relationship. The Conference executive promptly informs the Secretary of the United Church of Christ of these actions.

Note that these provisions carry out, or provide for, the sort of relationships for which the Evangelical and Reformed men were arguing when I met with them in the summers of 1945 and 1946 at the Spiritual Conferences at Allentown. Bylaw 128, above, provides for the association to arrange for a service of installation or recognition. (*Recognition* has had different meanings in different times and places, but one interpretation is that it calls for the approval of a minister before he is accepted as pastor but does not require approval, at a later time, of his dismissal. *Installation*, on the other hand, requires that the association approve both his call and his resignation or dismissal.) Paragraph 130 provides definitely for the approval by the association of the dissolution of the pastoral relationship. Here is what we reported that the Evangelical and Reformed men were demanding.

One part of the above arrangement was not, however, in keeping with the wishes of the Evangelical and Reformed ministers whom I met. The role of state conference executives in acting as the channel through which ministers would be recommended to the churches was not part of Evangelical and Reformed Church practice, and their ministers were critical of the idea of State Superintendents, or state executive officers, and said so plainly to me. More on this a little later.

Taking the provisions above for what they say, sections 121 through 130, it is hard to see how local churches could be "free" in their own procedures. Only by defying the "recommended" procedures could the churches act in accordance with the promises made to them. And if they tried to "call or dismiss" their "pastors by such procedure" as they "shall determine," what ministers would dare to defy the rules laid down in the "recommended procedure" and accept calls that were issued in defiance of the rules clearly laid down in the bylaws?

It is hard to see how the average minister in the United Church of Christ can escape a feeling of subservience to the system outlined. Of coure the typical "organization man," looking for the ladder to sure success and promotion in the ministry, can see at one glance that he should follow the rules, and also curry favor from above. All this means that the churches are likely to get recommendations of those ministers who "follow the line" of the General Synod in its pronouncements and who are scrupulously careful to "obey" the Constitution and Bylaws of the United Church of Christ—including those parts which are supposed to be merely descriptive "of free and voluntary relationships" between ministers, churches and conferences.

Going back now to my comment that the present United Church of Christ practice is not in keeping with the wishes of the Evangelical and Reformed Churchmen whom I met at Allentown in 1945 and 1946, let me say that neither the Congregationalists nor the Evangelical and Reformed men have been permitted to keep the most democratic elements of their previous systems. And I did not get the full picture in my early pamphlets when I picked up the insistence of the Evangelical and Reformed men about the Presbyterian system being carried over into the United Church of Christ. The idea of constitutionally established authority has been carried over from the Evangelical and Reformed presbyterian system, but not the more local control of ministerial placement, which used to reside among the ministers themselves in their local synods. The new United Church of Christ setup is hierarchical in this respect, not presbyterial.

Let me return briefly to my conversations at Allentown in 1946 with the Evangelical and Reformed men. Possibly the most important revelation, and one that did not strike me so at the time, was the fact that the Evangelical and Reformed men felt great concern over the "power" exercised by our state superintendents. They asked Dr. Richards, in the Wednesday afternoon session whether the United Church would have such officers. They seemed displeased when Dr. Richards remarked that there would have to be some such full-time officers in the new conference setup.

As I got the picture, their own synod presidents were regular pastors elected temporarily to the additional office of local synod president. They emphasized that in their system it was the ministers themselves, in their local synods, who were the ones who decided whose names would be presented to churches for consideration in filling pastoral vacancies. As I have heard from men in Presbyterian churches, this is the Presbyterian way.

One personal illustration in this regard was given me by the late Rev. Frederick K. Stamm, pastor at the time of First Congregational Church in Chicago, but formerly pastor for many years of the Clinton Avenue Congregational Church in Brooklyn. I was surprised to find him at the Evangelical and Reformed ministers' conference. He was, however, a former Reformed Church minister and grew up with many of the men at the Spiritual Conference. He was present both years that I was there and was very much "one of the boys."

I asked Dr. Stamm why he had left his "buddies" and come over into the Congregational fold. His answer was blunt and direct. He said that the "boys" in his synod had him "boxed in" and would not let him move. That could refer to the requirement to have a resignation approved, or it could mean that they would not recommend him to a position such as he wanted. In either case it illustrated the way their system worked. Ministerial "placement" was in the hands of the ministers of the local synod.

Dr. Stamm went on to tell me that he simply could not believe it when he received a call from the Clinton Avenue

Congregational Church and found that the church, itself, without the approval of any higher authority, had the power to take him as its minister. It was an irony to me when Dr. Stamm later supported the merger and was one of the most strident voices in its favor at the Oberlin Council. One can understand, however, his sense of close affinity with his former classmates at college or seminary and the warm friendship he had with former colleagues.

The Evangelical and Reformed men seemed to feel that our superintendents represented a less democratic, and a more dangerously authoritarian trend, than their presbyterial controls. Thus, while I was expressing my fear of the constitutionally defined authority of their system, they were stating an equal—or possibly greater—distrust of having ministerial placement fall into the hands of professional conference officials. It is one of the ironies of the merger that the separate features the two groups distrusted most have, apparently, been combined in the stated practices of the United Church of Christ. From the standpoint of any genuine freedom, it would seem that the United Church of Christ has inherited the "worst of two worlds" by combining state conference hierarchies with the authority of a churchwide constitution, or fundamental law.

In respect to ministerial placement, therefore, I should amend what I was writing in 1945 and 1946 that the plan would create a presbyterian system. That was what I had been told by Evangelical and Reformed ministers on the local level. Not until 1948, however, did there surface a different attitude on the part of the top leaders of the Evangelical and Reformed Church. In 1948, right after the "Comments" had been approved by those attending the Congregational Christian midwinter meeting, Dr. Goebel and the executive group of the Evangelical and Reformed Church (its General Council) went on record to the effect that they would not be bound to any "traditional polity," for themselves or for the United Church of Christ. That would rule out any commitment to either Presbyterian or Congregational polity. Our leaders did everything they could to suppress that information at the time, and again when the same kind of statement surfaced after the adoption at Oberlin of the Interpretations. But the Evangelical and Reformed leaders were right. The United Church of Christ would not be like the Evangelical and Reformed Church, and it would not follow the lines of Congregationalism.

The United Church of Christ has incorporated the presbyterian concept of "representative democracy," as Dr. Gunnemann has emphasized. It has also carried over the presbyterian reliance upon constitutionally authorized authority. This includes the power of representative bodies to amend the constitution and even dramatically reshape the whole structure of the church, as Dr. Gunnemann's detailed account shows clearly. But these principles—of representative bodies and of constitutional, or canon law—would apply equally to Methodist or Episcopal churches. The system of ministerial placement in the United Church brings the denomination close to the episcopal polity, in which bishops have the power of appointing the ministers to their charges.

In some ways the United Church practice would give the ministers less security than in the Methodist or Episcopal churches. A Methodist bishop must give every minister in his conference a position somewhere. In the United Church of Christ a minister can be left out in the cold if he falls into disfavor with conference executives. Unless it has been changed in recent years, a minister's security is greater also in the Episcopal Church, where their practice would not permit either the bishop or the majority of the congregation to remove a minister. Only the Vestry could do it, as at the time of the famous Melish case.

Maybe the United Church of Christ has combined the worst features, from the standpoint of ministerial freedom and security, of not only the Congregational Christian and Evangelical and Reformed Church, but what we might call the "worst of all possible worlds" as compared to other leading denominations.

Some of what I have said above can be more accurately understood against a fuller picture of what prevailing practices were among our churches prior to the union. It is true that state superintendents did help churches to find ministers. Some of them may have wanted more authority in this regard, and this might account in part for the way that most superintendents supported the merger.

But our system was generously supplied with alternative methods of churches finding ministers, and of ministers getting new pastoral opportunities. These alternate practices were fully accepted and even supported financially, in the case of the Boards of Pastoral Supply, by the nearby state conferences.

There was a Pastoral Supply office in Chicago for the Midwest, and another at Boston—the New England Board of Pastoral Supply. As late as 1946, when the Basis of Union was in its 1945 edition, a motion was made and passed at the Grinnell Council meeting that additional Boards of Pastoral Supply be set up. That resolution was introduced by none other than Rev. James F. English, Superintendent of the Connecticut Conference and at that time president of the conference of superintendents.

That the boards of pastoral supply were at times giving suggestions to churches which were different from the recommendations of the state conference superintendents could go almost without saying. My twin brother, Myron S. Burton, was Treasurer of the Massachusetts State Conference during the late 1930s. He once remarked, somewhat facetiously, that Dr. Timberlake, the state Superintendent, spent most of his time trying to undo what Dr. Merrill, of the New England Board of Pastoral Supply, was doing; and that the same was true in reverse. At least it gave the ministers a break—as was true in my own case.

It was also a fairly common practice for churches to turn to some well-known preachers and ask them for suggestions. I know that Dr. S. Parkes Cadman used to recommend men whom he felt were promising. This happened to one of my predecessors in regard to a church where Dr. Cadman first asked the man to come and be his assistant. Then, a couple of years later, Dr. Cadman helped this young man get a very good position in a church in New Jersey.

To support some of this description of our practices, please forgive me if I give some personal experiences, involving as they did all three of the methods mentioned above. My first two pastorates, of four years each, were made possible by the recommendations of the New York state superintendent. Both of these situations were exceedingly difficult, nothing of the sort that a young man, starting at age twenty-four, should have been put into. But I managed, and I stayed on top. For the rest of my forty-two years of full-time active pastorates no superintendent had anything to do with my getting placed.

The Second Church at New London, Connecticut, which issued me a call just before Christmas in 1937, had already gone through a list of at least seven names from the state office. The members of the committee later told me that they had auditioned each of the men suggested. They gave me this sort of summary: these ministers seemed to them either "broken-down old war-horses" who needed one more church before retirement, or they were apparently men who had ardently supported the state conference program and to whom the superintendent seemed to owe a debt. There had also been some fifty ministers who had sent in their own applications for the position, some enclosing brochures about themselves.

The church at New London finally turned to the Board of Pastoral Supply at Boston. Dr. Charles C. Merrill sent a list of six names. He gave resumes of past ministerial experience and training; but he did not make any recommendation in regard to any of the six. My name was among them. The committee members of Second Church told me that they heard all six. Then they asked me to come and preach at Second Church as their recommended candidate. I served there for more than fourteen years, beginning before the effects of the Depression were over, continuing through the stringent years of the Second World War, and then six more years when the merger controversy was going through various critical stages.

My call to Pontiac, Michigan, fourteen years later, had some similarities. I did not know that the church at Pontiac was looking for a minister. It had spent many months in which its pulpit committee heard candidates recommended by the state superintendent and, I believe, a few suggested by the local Detroit area superintendent. Finally the members of the pulpit committee turned to an elderly retired minister in whom they had great confidence. He gave them my name. A very fruitful pastorate of more than nineteen years ensued, during which time the church was able to finish a fine Gothic church building which had stood, since the Depression, as an empty shell.

More than twenty-five years had gone by, and a whole generation of children had been born, grown up, and been married without ever seeing the "new" church anything but boarded up. During most of my time at Pontiac I served also, on a purely volunteer basis, as the director or Executive Vice-chairman of the Continuation Committee.

These are firsthand and intimate illustrations of what this matter of placement means in the life both of a minister and of a church.

To me it is a sad commentary upon the United Church of Christ that since its establishment the separate Boards of Pastoral Supply have been closed and that now there is a single standard of denominational procedure. The flexibility and freedom of the old ways are gone. After the publication of the new *Manual on the Ministry*, what sincerity or genuineness of meaning can be ascribed to those words in section 15 of the constitution that say that a church may "call or dismiss its pastor or pastors by such procedure as it shall determine?" And how far away the United Church of Christ has traveled from a Basis of Union which assured the Congregational Christian Churches that "ministers and churches desiring to maintain a system of pastoral placement in which the Conference or Association shall have little or no part, shall be free to do so ... "

In this chapter we have set forth the evidence first that the crucial issues of the merger were all set forth clearly and repeatedly prior to the time that the Basis of Union was put into final form. We pointed out that this was the last opportunity to produce an unambiguous, straightforward, honest document. Finally we have set forth the evidence of what the United Church of Christ actually is, confirming many of the predictions made by Congregationalists who opposed the merger. We have referred to the many assurances given by Congregational leaders that the United Church of Christ would be "congregational in polity." But the details of those assurances, and the long story of methods used to put the merger through, during the ten years from 1947 to 1957, remain to be told, at least briefly.

—— 10 ——

Deep Religious Conviction as the Basis of Opposition

Protestantism was bound by the very genius of it, when the right time came, to try the experiment of the liberty of the Christian man with all its implications and issues, completely and at all costs. . . . historically the American Congregational Christian churches have made the congregational way of exercising the liberty of the Christian more consistently central than any other of the denominations whose polity is Congregational. The Polity itself, as one sees it in its entirety has always been a means to an end. . . . Congregationalism believes this to be necessary to the liberty of a Christian man, and whatever else is built must be upon this foundation.
—Gaius Glenn Atkins, in *An Adventure in Liberty*

CONGREGATIONALISTS who opposed the Basis of Union did so, for the most part, because they were convinced that the Congregational Way had a priceless and eternal value that should never be lost. As Dr. Atkins said, "Whatever else is built must be upon this foundation."

Dr. Gunnemann, in tracing the formation of the United Church of Christ, seems to have failed utterly to sense this deep motivation on the part of convinced Congregationalists or to give them any credit for their honest convictions.

In many ways Dr. Gunnemann ascribes idealistic or religious motivation to those who tried to force the merger onto others. For him these proponents of the union were "seeking the mind of Christ" or were deeply committed to His Lordship.

Dr. Gunnemann portrays the sense of disillusion that set in when Congregationalists adopted the Oberlin Interpretations, and before that the Comments of the mid-winter meeting in 1948. "What had begun," he says, "as a high venture in Christian idealism was now floundering on the rocks of organizational and political realities."

What Dr. Gunnemann did not recognize—or did not admit—was that the union was foundering because it had been promoted with a lack of forthrightness and because the leaders were withholding the real truth. On this same page Dr. Gunnemann reveals in a footnote something which the leaders were keeping just to themselves. While Congregationalists were being encouraged to accept the Comments of January 1948, as proof that the union would be "congregational," Dr. Goebel was protesting to Dr. Horton personally that such interpretations would "wreck the union." This sort of information was withheld from the Congregational Christian fellowship during all the critical voting period:

> On February 2, 1948, when apprised by Douglas Horton that some "interpretations" had been devised to meet anti-union objections to the Basis of Union, Dr. Goebel wrote a very strong letter of protest that such procedure would "wreck the union." Nevertheless, Congregational Christian leaders felt bound to prevent a schism by attaching "assurances" of Congregational polity to the union agreement.*

Ironically this same date, February 2, 1948, appears on the letter sent out by the Congregational Christian headquarters to our ministers stating that these same interpretations "give assurance that our essential Congregational Christian polity and freedom would be protected and preserved." Copies of the Comments were sent out with this letter. But no information was subsequently sent to the ministers or churches informing them of Dr. Goebel's letter to Dr. Horton.

Now, thirty years too late, is evidence of double-dealing of which the Congregationalists as a whole had no knowledge at the time. Here is stark evidence that Evangelical and Reformed leaders were content to continue their plan to put the merger through even after

---

*Reprinted with permission from Louis H. Gunnemann, *The Shaping of the United Church of Christ: An Essay in the History of American Christianity*. Copyright © 1977 United Church Press.

making their protest and after they knew that the interpretations *"had been devised to meet anti-union objections to the Basis of Union."* What clearer evidence could one ask for proof of downright conniving on the part of leaders on both sides?

Yet on this same page 32, in pious tone, Dr. Gunnemann tells us:

> As the General Council (E&R) considered the *Interpretations* at a September 1948 meeting, an effort was made to reintroduce the idealist spirit by proposing the insertion of a sentence into paragraph (b) (4) as follows: We hope that the Constitution of the United Church may, through the guidance of the Holy Spirit and the experience of the new church, not merely develop a compromise of the two former polities but may bring a new polity and plan of organization to the United Church."*

What sense, and what possible honesty, can then be attributed to this same action by the Evangelical and Reformed General Council when it voted to send the *interpretations to their local Synods for "approval?"* The Evangelical and Reformed General Council had already voted on two days that neither the Evangelical and Reformed Church nor the United Church of Christ would be bound by these interpretations—although they were willing that congregationalists interpret the Basis of Union in such fashion as indicated!

For anyone like myself who believes that piety without honesty is a sham, and for whom the guidance of the Holy Spirit must always be, as St. John intimated, "even the Spirit of Truth," the above passages are lacking the genuine qualities all true Christians should seek.

One can almost sense that the pious hope that "through the guidance of the Holy Spirit . . . the new church . . . may bring a new polity and plan of organization to the United Church" was in reality aimed at eliminating Congregational polity. Dr. Gunnemann, again on this same page, had restated his argument for a governing constitution:

> Traditional Evangelical and Reformed practice saw the constitution as the guarantor of orderliness, justice, and freedom

---

*Reprinted with permission from Louis H. Gunnemann, *The Shaping of the United Church of Christ: An Essay in the History of American Christianity*. Copyright © 1977 United Church Press.

in all organizational relationships, and therefore binding for all. (p. 32)*

Thus, having put in his "plug" for the Evangelical and Reformed setup of constitutional authority, Dr. Gunnemann quoted, as we have above, the action of the Evangelical and Reformed General Council hoping for a "new polity."

For myself, and for many other Congregational people such pretenses of piety are downright offensive. I remember a story told by Dr. Donald J. Cowling, president at Carleton College, of how he was sent out with another man as a money-raising team for denominational schools. The other man kept favoring his own institution, and always with the argument that "I am convinced that it is God's will that we do this my way." After a while Dr. Cowling asked his companion, "Did it ever occur to you that I might be just as convinced that it is God's will to do it some other way?"

The freedom of which Congregationalists have always spoken is that of being able to seek the truth directly for themselves. This is not idle talk. Perhaps such an ideal, as Dr. Atkins sets forth in his *Adventure in Liberty*, represents something so pure, so rarified, and seemingly ethereal as to escape Dr. Gunnemann's notice. But it was for this that Congregationalists were fighting when they opposed the Basis of Union, and therefore the merger.

Dr. Gunnemann's portrayal of the "idealist" spirit, and the hope for the future guidance of the Holy Spirit, on the part of a General Council that was contriving to keep the merger alive at a time when forthrightnes and truth-speaking would have killed it, will continue to be offensive to clear-thinking men of God.

Offensive also is the whole picture of the "shaping up" of the United Church of Christ by a power-wielding General Synod, as Dr. Gunnemann describes it in his book and which we discussed in our last chapter.

Not for one moment can I conceive of the Master Teacher from Galilee wanting the kind of centralized and nearly totalitarian setup Dr. Gunnemann has seemed to

*Reprinted with permission from Louis H. Gunnemann, *The Shaping of the United Church of Christ: An Essay in the History of American Christianity*. Copyright © 1977 United Church Press.

describe as the structure of the United Church of Christ. For Dr. Gunnemann to keep saying that these changes took place because the delegates to General Synods were so committed to the Lordship of Christ is to me almost blasphemous. Here were secular and materialistic details being settled according to personal whims and desires.

At this point, however, I must admit that differences of theological interpretation as to the meaning of Jesus and of "the Christ" make room for widely divergent or contradictory viewpoints.

If Dr. Gunnemann happens to be one of those who hold to the ideas of Karl Barth, and if he believes that the historical Jesus was really not too important but that the "pre-existent Christ" is all that really matters, then I could understand Dr. Gunnemann's apparent enthusiasm for the new structure of the United Church. This concept of Christ coming as an earthly King might suggest a theocratic dictatorship that would indeed go far beyond the present setup of the United Church of Christ, or even of that proposed for COCU.

You may recall that I mentioned earlier the differences in viewpoint regarding Jesus and the "pre-existent Christ" as reflected in the writings of Karl Barth. See the passage quoted from Dr. Vallon in chapter four of this book.

When it comes to such extreme differences of conviction regarding the person of Christ, the only gentlemanly thing that we can do is to grant the other fellow the right to his own beliefs, and to hope that he will do the same in return. In a way this is exactly what I am asking. In everything that I have read in Dr. Gunnemann's book, I fail to find the slightest awareness, appreciation, or generosity toward the religious viewpoints of Congregationalists who want to preserve the Congregational way. It is understandable that he may not comprehend what was the heart and soul of the Congregational thought. He certainly does not reflect anything beyond parroting a few phrases taken out of context.

For Dr. Gunnemann to take the attitude that those who opposed the merger did so on "secular" grounds (see footnote 29 on page 234 of his book) while those who favored the merger—and especially the Evangelical and Reformed Church people—were moved by their commitment "to the mind of Christ" is to show a failure to grant the kind of tolerant recognition of the other man's right to his own convictions.

The glory of Congregationalism has been the great minds that it has produced. This has been possible because there were not the strictures within its framework that would bar truly great and original minds. Dr. Horace Bushnell would not have had a chance in a highly structured church in his day. At the time that he began his great new interpretation of the love of God, the Congregational circles were dominated far and near by men of Jonathan Edwards's extreme Calvinistic persuasion. With its tremendous emphasis on our being "children of the devil" and damned in sin until we are "saved," there would have been no room for Bushnell's newer insights. The insistence that we are born "the children of God," as set forth in Bushnell's teachings, was heresy to the followers of Edwards. Washington Gladden was one of Horace Bushnell's early followers, and according to a story that I have heard from old residents of Springfield—where Dr. Gladden was a pastor one hundred years ago—he was himself "thrown out" of a meeting at Old First Church in Springfield. Presumably that was at a meeting of an association or a church council of some sort. Dr. Gladden was a representative not only of what is now called "social action" or "social concerns," but even before that he was an advocate of new religious thought. His books on the Bible and on Christian doctrine place him squarely within the fold of the "higher criticism" of his day and part of the best tradition of the critical and historical approach to the Bible. Few people, perhaps, know this side of Dr. Gladden.

The list could go on almost endlessly, and always the story is the same. Men came into Congregationalism just to escape the confines of the ecclesiastical and theological barriers of other denominations. S. Parkes Cadman, pastor of what became our largest church, was a Methodist and held his Methodist standing until his death. Henry Ward Beecher left the Presbyterian Church. I believe that Dr. Charles E. Jefferson was a former Methodist.

In my own case every fiber of my being would oppose the kind of rules, regulations and strictures which the United Church is setting up, or those which the Evangelical and Reformed Church previously had. I could never belong to a denomination that told me that I could choose between the Heidelberg Catechism, Luther's Catechism, or the Augsburg Confession. I could not be honest with myself pretending to accept one or another of those creeds.

I had no intention of going into the ministry. I felt at college that many of the prominent clergymen coming to college chapel from various denominations were just telling us what they were supposed to say, rather than anything which they really believed. I had the very strong feeling that religious concepts had been evasive of the truth for centuries past and that a person could hardly accept the conventional doctrines and be an honest and intelligent man. I remember a very dramatic moment in one of our evening chapel services, with 800 students present, when Dr. Albert Parker Fitch, former president of Andover Theological Seminary, suddenly shouted out from the audience, in a booming voice, "No! No! No!" Then, blushing deep red, he buried his head in his hands. But Dr. Fitch, in that one embarrassing moment, expressed some of the deepest feelings of the student body toward much that passes as conventional and organized Christianity.

My final decision to enter the ministry came as a result of courses in psychology. One professor kept hammering away on the need of the human being for "integration of personality." Fundamentally this meant being honest with oneself and of facing all of the problems of life with an absolute integrity. Finally, this hammering away on this theme got to me. Suddenly, as in a flash, I realized that of all the people who ever lived, Jesus probably represented the epitome of an integrated personality; not only that but his teachings were directed toward helping others to "be made whole." The first sermon that I preached, while still a student at college, was on this theme of the integration of personality. Friends in the National Association may recall that I was asked to give the communion meditation at the second annual meeting of the National Association in 1956. My talk was on this theme of integrity, and the fact that Jesus represented in my mind the epitome of an integrated personality.

In the light of this it is easy to see why the doctrines of Barth were fundamentally abhorrent to me. Far from being profound, as some have tried to make out, they represent to me a denial of truth and of basic things in our faith.

In all my ministry this emphasis upon integrity and the integration of personality has been of utmost value and help. Many of the "personality disorders" with which a minister has to deal stem from the absence of a well integrated personality and the inability to develop one. The modern emphasis on mental health is based upon the same essential facts of human nature as those with which Jesus had to deal. "What think ye?" he would ask, and then tell a parable to make people face the realities which they were seeking to evade. This basic principle of honesty belongs, if anything does, to the Divine Will for our lives.

In the light of this it should be easy to comprehend why I was so disturbed with merger negotiations that failed to come to grips with the truth. The situation became worse, beyond the possibility of dispute, when the negotiators for this merger were willing to go forward, even when they knew that Congregational leaders were telling their people one set of interpretations while Evangelical and Reformed leaders were saying that they would not be bound by these same interpretations. In like manner I hold the leaders of the Evangelical and Reformed Church morally responsible for willingly going ahead with a merger which they had every reason to know could not be put through except as Congregational leaders kept pressuring their people with promises and assurances which the Evangelical and Reformed leaders had already rejected as unacceptable to their church. I cannot believe that a merger was in obedience to the "mind of Christ" when it had to be accomplished, as I see it, by connivance shared by the leaders of both denominations. It is not enough for the Evangelical and Reformed Church people to have taken the attitude that they could wash their hands of what was going on within the Congregational Christian ranks when they apparently knew what was going on. They were implicated. This became absolutely clear in the meeting of the joint commissions on 10 November 1948, when they had a virtual knockdown, drag-out fight over the Oberlin Interpretations. Then the Evangelical and Reformed people agreed, under duress, to have their synods "approve" the Oberlin Interpretations. The Congregational leaders had insisted that "we cannot get the vote for the merger unless you approve these Interpretations." The Evangelical and Reformed leaders had voted in September that they would not be bound by those interpretations. They had voted the same thing again at the time of this November meeting. But then they went along—with tongue in cheek. Years later Dr. James E. Wagner was to say that the Oberlin Interpretations had always been "repugnant" to the Evangelical and Reformed Church:

> The composite resolutions adopted by the ER General Council in September-November, 1948, really echo the reluctance and the reservations with which we voted to approve the Interpretations. It must not be forgotten that we voted this approval only because at that time the merger proceedings had gone so far that it seemed worth paying any price, worth making any further concessions, rather than assume responsibility for bringing those proceedings to an abrupt halt. It is not inaccurate to observe, however, that the substance of the Interpretations was essentially repugnant to the Evangelical and Reformed Church in the light of the full organic union to which it had committed itself from the beginning. (Dr. James E. Wagner, president of the Evangelical and Reformed Church, in his opening statement at the October 12-13 joint meeting of the two executive groups in the fall of 1954)

The Oberlin Interpretations were supposed to convey to Congregationalists the promise and assurance that the union would be congregational. It was part of the sales pitch to get the denomination to "buy" the merger. This the Evangelical and Reformed leaders knew full well. For all of this I can find no justification from a religious standpoint. To claim or to imply that the call of the ecumenical movement was a "higher loyalty" than telling the truth is an awful reflection upon that movement and its supporters.

In like manner after the Congregational leaders had gone into the courts, and under solemn oath had given certain explanations of the Basis of Union, the Evangelical and Reformed leaders later said that these were "troubling" to them. They insisted that such explanations be brushed aside if they were to go on with the merger. The same question of integrity was involved.

Again, the fateful hours of the meeting of the joint executive groups on 12-13 October 1954, when for a day and a half the honest differences were laid bare and when it was made plain that the Evangelical and Reformed Church leaders were insisting upon things contrary to the assurances upon which Congregationalists had voted, the same kind of capitulation took place. This time it was the Congregationalists who abandoned their solemn promises to their own people. It has been admitted by those who were at these sessions that everything seemed impossible, and that the merger would have to be dropped. Then it was suggested that they have a period of prayer. Meanwhile a small committee, ignoring the general discussion and its stark facing of the real issues, had been at work on a pious statement that "Christ calls us to Mission and to Unity." After the "religious exercises" with a little prayer together, members of the two executive groups reassembled. Dr. Ben Herbster—who was later described as having helped "pin-point" the Evangelical and Reformed concerns—asked, "Why should we let little things stand in our way?" (or so he was reported to have asked in newspapers afterward.) The "little things" in this case were such things as the assurances that had been solemly given to the Congregational Christian people for more than ten years—the things which had been used to "sell" the merger and which were now being repudiated and ignored.

Dr. Gunnemann repeatedly portrays the Evangelical and Reformed people as being motivated by a religious impulse, standing by patiently through the troubled times of uncertainty, and showing their loyalty to the "will of Christ" in regard to the merger. But he never mentions the material considerations, such as the large amounts of money in the Congregational Christian national boards, or the higher salaries paid in Congregational Christian churches.

The way that the constitution of the United Church of Christ dropped the language and assurances in the Basis of Union and interpretations bears out my illustration that they were like ornaments on a Christmas tree. Gone immediately were all suggestions that this would be a kind of union in which churches were merely bound together "in fellowship" (Basis of Union III, B., C.).

The Basis of Union had said that decisions of the higher bodies would be advisory, not mandatory. The first two provisional drafts of the constitution of the United Church contained such a phrase. But at the 1960 General Synod meeting, when the constitution was finally revised, that provision about "advisory and not mandatory" was stricken out. Mrs. Burton and I were present at the time and were almost dumbstruck by the way that this was allowed to be stricken out without even serious protest or debate.

In like manner the Basis of Union had said that "in all relationships between minister and local church or Congregation, the freedom of the minister and the autonomy of the church are presupposed." Nothing appeared in the Constitution about the freedom of the minister.

As we have already mentioned, the Basis of Union provided that "ministers and churches desiring to maintain a system of pastoral placement in which the Conference or Association shall have little or no part, shall be free to do so. . . . " Yet we have seen the way that the United Church has fixed up its recommended procedures in such a way that neither ministers nor churches could possibly "maintain a system of pastoral placement" in which the conference or association would play little or no part except by defying United Church officials and the strongly emphasized "recommended procedures."

Congregationalists were assured that the constitution "must be" based upon the principles set forth in the Basis of Union and Interpretations. But, once established, the United Church of Christ has apparently seen fit to do as it pleases. Whatever the General Synod decides now becomes the "decision of the church as a whole."

To the foregoing I could add a few personal notes and one of them is very important to my way of thinking.

The present generation is too far past the time of Mussolini's rise to power to know the meaning of his fascist regime. My generation went through that period. Not only so, but in 1926 the subject of whether Mussolini had been a benefit or a detriment to Italy became the assigned topic for intercollegiate debate. Carleton College then ranked number one or number two in the country for its debating and forensic achievements. Being on the debate squad there meant that for two or three afternoons a week you took part in a debate session lasting about three hours, all of it dealing with the subject that would later become the one which the college team would have to defend. Our team was assigned the side of defending Mussolini. In practice we had been required to debate both sides of the issue. In our preparation we had read practically every article that had appeared for years back on the subject of Mussolini, together with books. We knew the issues backwards and forwards. The arguments of efficiency, and that Mussolini had made the trains run on time and had chased the beggars out of St. Peter's Square, all had an appealing ring to some people. That he had smashed ballot boxes in his youth and had taken power in Italy by marching on Rome with his black-shirted legions, were necessarily downplayed—along with his treatment of his adversaries.

People today may not realize that the word *fascist* meant the "do something" party. Italy had been torn by a hundred different political parties, none of them able to work up a managing majority.

In reading Dr. Gunnemann's euphoric account of the "shaping up" of the United Church of Christ I could not but feel a kind of glorification, and the same sort of a "do something" policy with which I had been previously familiar. The idea that the structure of the United Church of Christ had to be torn out of shape because James Forman had read a "manifesto" in Riverside Church, or because there were student riots and unrest in the colleges, or because of the war in Vietnam, could only mean that there was no loyalty to any previous basic plan. All promises made in the Basis of Union or otherwise were thus meaningless.

In like manner, if the meeting of such social issues is to be the chief "mission" of the United Church, it is hard to distinguish between this "mission" and the issues raised by our major political parties. But where in the United Church is there room for the dissent that the two-party system in our country's body politic affords? Congregationalism, as we have emphasized, recognized the right of private judgment. But the United Church would appear to present a one-party system. When its leaders cancel hotel appointments in cities where the state legislatures have "failed" to ratify the E. R. A. amendment, what happens to the many members of the Church who cannot conscientiously support that amendment and believe it to be deeply flawed? The whole gamut of social issues, on many of which the United Church of Christ General Synod has made pronouncements, is fraught with the same liability.

In Congregationalism we put the reins on our Council for Social Action at the New Haven General Council meeting in 1954—when it presumed to speak or act for our members at large.

Dr. Gunnemann seemed thoroughly pleased with what was undoubtedly intended as an exceedingly efficient and thoroughly organized structure. The arguments for it and their implications could not but bring back the memory of those debating years when we "defended" Mussolini. Again I say that I cannot picture Jesus as being the leader of that kind of a "do something" party, or of being committed to a "sophisticated" and streamlined, highly structured church. Perhaps some people still think in terms of medieval kingship for the Christ, as an absolute monarch who would expect his church to be a monolithic autocracy. But can we visualize Jesus as leaving no place for the personal convictions of his honest followers?

The United Church of Christ says in its constitution, section 16, that "actions by, or decisions or advice emanating from the General Synod, a Conference or an Association, should be held in the highest regard by every local church." In sharp contrast to this is the time-honored statement that appeared in the preamble of the consititution of the General Council of the Congregational Christian Churches as quoted previously:

We hold sacred the freedom of the individual soul and the right of private judgment. We stand for the autonomy of the local church and its independence of ecclesiastical control.

I have seen nothing in either the constitution of the United Church or in the Basis of Union that says anything about the right of private judgment or the freedom of the individual soul. In fact section 16 of the United Church of Christ Constitution would seem to say just the opposite.

The very heart of Congregational belief and practice resides in this right to individual conviction and belief, absolutely untrammeled by edicts from Bishops, Conferences, or General Synods. The concept of Christ being the head of *each local church* is in sharp contrast to the "headship of Christ" ascribed to the General Synod. As Dr. Gunnemann indicated in regard to some other matters, it is a question of where the authority lies. In Congregationalism it abides in the local church.

Dr. Gunnemann's apparent failure to sense the religious basis of Congregationalism, and his characterizations of the Evangelical and Reformed people as trying to inject an idealistic or religious motivation into their actions on the Oberlin interpretations is unfortunate. Here were Congregationalists trying to preserve something which they hold permanently valid. Then the Evangelical and Reformed leaders try to "upstage" them by injecting an "idealist" emphasis in their rejection of those interpretations.

When the Evangelical and Reformed leaders insisted that the United Church of Christ must not be bound to any "traditional polity" this might seem as though they were saying that the Evangelical and Reformed Church leaders did not see anything permanently valid or uniquely worth keeping in their own polity. But such was clearly not the case. They had from the beginning insisted upon a over-all constitution and upon installation of ministers by a higher body. They also wanted the General Synod to be a "representative body" with power to act for the denomination as a whole. These were all features of their own presbyterian system. Upon these issues the Evangelical and Reformed leaders continued to press their demands even after saying the United Church must not be bound to any "traditional polity."

Promerger leaders in both denominations seemed to look upon opponents of the union as merely intransigent and narrow-minded obstructionists, when in reality they were trying to hold fast to the pearl of great price, the freedom wherewith Christ would make us free.

As I commented in some of my early pamphlets, I liked most of the Evangelical and Reformed men whom I met personally. They were frank and honest in stating their differences of opinion, in gentlemanly and courteous fashion. But I remember one Evangelical and Reformed man at the Allentown Conference for whom I could not make the above remark. With a tactlessness hard to comprehend he said to me, "You know I think that this merger is a good thing. You have the money. We have the religion." The reading of Dr. Gunnemann's book has made me think of that remark several times. But this man at least recognized that there were material advantages for the Evangelical and Reformed Church in this merger.

It was Clement DeChant who told me of the Presbyterians having looked over the Evangelical and Reformed institutions and deciding that their financial situation was not too good. But part of this was cleared up before the merger finally took place. They had a heavy indebtedness on their office building in Philadelphia at the time that negotiations started, but I understand that the heavy mortgage on that was later paid off.

The real discrepancy in funds came with our national boards, but even this did not directly affect the churches as much as one might first think. At the time of the Cadman trial the national assets of the Congregational Christian boards was in the neighborhood of $60,000,000. By the time of the merger it had increased to around $90,000,000. The largest part of this was in the Annuity Fund and that really belonged to the individual members for their future annuities. Another $12,000,000, or so, as I remember it at the time of the Cadman trial, was in endowment of funds for southern colleges. Only the approximate $9,000,000 in Church Building Society funds and the original $6,000,000 in the Pilgrim Memorial Fund were of direct and personal interest to our churches and ministers. But even these, we, of the opposition, would have gladly shared with the Evangelical and Reformed Church if the union had been one that would really preserve the things precious to us.

What really bothered the opposition regarding the national funds was the scheme to take everything into the merger and dispossess those who stayed out—beyond that of the life of current annuities and church mortgages. In

Canada an act of Parliament required the United Church of Canada to divide assets on a prorated basis. In our country the courts merely looked the other way and washed their hands of every case brought before them—with the exception of Judge Steinbrink in the original Cadman decision, and later the Michigan Supreme Court in its hearing on *res judicata*. (See also 1980 Groton case, Appendix 33.)

In like manner we of the opposition had no objection to the Evangelical and Reformed Church uniting its past traditions with those of the Congregational Christian Churches—provided only that they genuinely wanted what Congregationalism stood for and would permit us to keep our most precious gifts of freedom. But Dr. Goebels is reported as saying that they were not willing to be "swallowed up in Congregationalism." And Dr. Wagner insisted that they wanted complete "organic union"—one body and not just "one top."

My first visit to Allentown was only a few months after V.E. Day, which marked the end of fighting in Europe for World War II. Evangelical and Reformed men told me that in the two world wars some people looked upon them as enemy aliens because of their German ancestry. Yet their people had been here since before the Revolution, had fought valiantly in that war, and had always been loyal Americans. They showed me their church in Allentown where the Liberty Bell was hidden when the British took Philadelphia. I had full sympathy with them and would have welcomed them into a union if it would really let us stay congregational.

———— 11 ————

Setting the Stage for Oberlin

How the Basis of Union Was Sent to the Churches

B RIEFLY, the techniques used for Oberlin were similar
to those used for the General Council meetings in 1944 and
1946—but this was a far more fateful and important event.
In both of the earlier cases all indications given out prior
to the meetings were to the effect that only routine motions on procedure would be taken up as official business
on the merger. In both instances, however, the meetings
were so conducted as to turn them into enthusiastic pep
rallies for the merger. The manipulations for the Oberlin
Council followed the same general pattern, only to a more
extreme degree and with far more at stake. In none of the
three Council meetings, covering a span of six years, was
there ever a dispassionate, objective discussion of the
Basis of Union. In fact that document was never "before
the house" for discussion, and the order of the day was
always arranged in such a way that a person would have
been out or order in trying to get the issue before the
meeting.

In retrospect one can see that emotional commitments
overrode all commonly accepted rules of decent and fair
procedure. An individual church may not, under its own
bylaws, and frequently under state law, consider extremely important matters at an annual meeting unless
the members are properly warned in the call to the meeting. For instance, a local church cannot vote to sell or
mortgage its building, nor vote to dismiss its minister,
without due notice being given in the official call to the
meeting. This was stipulated by state law as well as
church bylaws for the churches I served. Likewise the
town meetings of New England require, or did require, a
public "warning" or notice of any important meeting, stat-

ing the purpose for such meeting. Surprise actions were unlawful in both church and town meetings.

Then how could the Oberlin Council suddenly, and without previous warning to the churches, vote approval of a Basis of Union which virtually meant "selling" the denomination as such? And why were there no great leaders, whose voice and wisdom would be heeded, who could call the Council to order and demand respect for decent and orderly procedures? Part of the answer can be found in the steamroller tactics employed where no voice could have been heard, and where the overriding "will of the majority" would have shouted down any man, no matter how great. But of course the real responsibility rested with the official leaders—and those with whom they were plainly in league.

Part of the scandal of Oberlin was that word went out before the meeting that the Executive Committee was of one mind that it would be best if "no definitive action" were taken on the merger at that meeting—and no official word to the contrary was ever given to the churches and delegates, in advance of the meeting. Another part of the scandal is that this recommendation from the Executive Committee went out over the signature of Douglas Horton; yet we have proof now from a private file of letters that he, himself, ignored that recommendation and worked steadily to see that something definite did happen—and he did not tell the churches what he was doing. Likewise a Promerger Committee had been set up at the midwinter meeting, and this committee did not reveal what it had up its sleeve for the meeting. And to make the scandal more complete, the churches had been led to believe, by the printed "procedures" recommended in the Basis of Union, that the merger should be approved only if seventy-five percent of all churches voting, and seventy-five percent of all individual members voting, had approved the Basis of Union. The voting of churches and members had fallen far short—yet Oberlin, without advance warning, voted the approval anyway. (Conferences and associations were also included in the voting procedures, and these approvals had been easily obtained. But in Congregationalism it is the local churches and their members who are supposed to count.)

Such then is the nature of the issues at stake in our discussion of the Oberlin Council. We shall try, therefore, to give an understandable and reliable account of how this quite astounding event took place.

The Basis of Union went through three revisions in the fall of 1946. Yet nothing was done to meet the problem that Dr. Fagley had set forth, more than a year earlier, on "constitutional provisions." Dr. Fagley had pointed out that the General Council simply did not have power or authority to do what the Basis of Union proposed for it to do. Belatedly, just as the Oberlin Council approached, the promerger spokesmen began saying that "the General Council is competent to approve the Basis of Union solely for itself." This became part of the same motion in which the Oberlin Council approved the Basis of Union. Yet here was a Basis of Union that provided, in articles VI and VII, that "the ministers of the two communions shall be enrolled as ministers of the United Church," and that "all persons who are members of either communion at the time of the union shall be members of the United Church." Did they say the Council was competent to approve the Basis of Union *solely for itself?* Then what authority did the council have to approve a document containing such provisions?

In like manner the interpretations, which were all adopted as part of the same motion as that approving the Basis, stated that "the Basis of Union calls for a union of the Boards of Home Missions, the Boards of Foreign Missions, the Annuity Boards, the Councils for Social Action, and similarly all related Boards, commissions, agencies, and instrumentalities of the two denominations." The council was approving the Basis of Union *solely for itself*—or was it really approving it for the whole denomination? Where was there any basic sense of honesty or integrity in pretenses and actions of this sort?

And as Dr. Fagley had so clearly pointed out, with documentation from the Council's own Constitution and that of its predecessors, the General Council had no power or authority to act as a legislative or judicial body. Yet, here, it was implicitly trying to do both.

As we mentioned above, the Basis of Union went through three revisions in the fall of 1946. Many of its inconsistencies, weaknesses, and presbyterial features had been clearly pointed out before this. With each new revision those responsible for the changes assured everyone that the document "was now all fixed up to meet the previous objections." None of this appeared true to those of us who had criticized the Basis of Union in detail. Dr. William F. Frazier wrote to me that they had eliminated "every weasel word." He went on to say that, even if I had not won many individual battles, I had "won the war." I wrote him a long and detailed letter telling him why I could not see that they had accomplished anything of the sort that he mentioned.

Dr. Blanchard, you will recall, had stated that wherever there was any question, they had added a sentence stating the Congregational principle. We heard also that the Evangelical and Reformed leaders claimed that they had "yielded, and yielded and yielded, and that the Basis of Union was 'Congregational.'" This seemed to us at the time as so much "eye-wash" and tongue-in-cheek propaganda. But recently I came across an address delivered by Dr. George W. Richards to the Evangelical and Reformed special General Synod in 1949 in which he, in most scholarly and thorough fashion, pointed out how the Basis of Union and interpretations represented a denial of the whole structure of the constitution of the Evangelical and Reformed Church. Yet he gave an eloquent appeal for going ahead with the union and said that if it was consummated, he would consider himself a member of the "Congregational Christian Church under the name of The United Church of Christ." So apparently there were Evangelical and Reformed leaders saying that the union would be congregational.

The one thing lacking, however, from Dr. Richards' careful analysis was that the Basis of Union still called for an overall constitution that could be amended by action of just the General Synod, with ratification by the state conferences. And, to borrow a phrase from Thomas Carlyle, this overall constitution is what would "creatively determine all the rest." Eight years were to intervene between the 1948 (and 1949) approvals of the Basis of Union by the two denominations and the convening of the first General

Synod. In the meantime there came a change of leadership in both denominations, and with Dr. James E. Wagner as president, and Dr. Ben Herbster to back him up, this overall constitution became the central issue. Now, as Dr. Gunnemann has so clearly shown, the Constitution has been the instrument of shaping a United Church quite different from what Dr. Blanchard and Dr. Palmer were talking about.

As we pointed out in our second chapter, the overall constitution and the fact that it could be amended by the General Synod and conferences was the whole issue in a nutshell.

At no time, however, was I able to detect that either Dr. Blanchard or Dr. Palmer had the slightest comprehension of what an overall constitution meant as a legally binding instrument. Both of them categorically declared that the merger would be congregational. Both took the attitude that people who said anything to the contrary were not stating "the facts." Both men seemed exceedingly brittle on this point. Yet I am inclined to doubt that there was any intended deception or dishonesty on their part.

I must credit Rev. Alexander Abbott with having alerted me and indoctrinated me on this matter of the overall constitution. I can remember plainly the morning that a number of our Congregational ministers of New London county were meeting at our home in New London, for a group called the Reading Associates. The merger question came up through Dr. Theodore Shipherd, who was on the national Executive Committee and knew something about it. Alec, whom I did not know well at the time, stood up, quite agitated, and started pacing the floor a little as he started emphasizing that a "constitution is the *fundamental law* of the organization to which it applied." Frankly, his comments seemed to me at the time as somewhat mechanical and academic. But gradually I could see what he meant. Months later he worked out a comparison between the Evangelical and Reformed constitution and the Basis of Union, which I mimeographed and sent out as my pamphlet No. 10. Then in two more pamphlets he and I analyzed what this comparison showed.

His comparison, incidentally, paralleled to some extent the comparison later made by Dr. Richards, and mentioned above. but Alec drew opposite conclusions. Dr. Richards pointed out how individual provisions differed whereas Alec Abbott pointed out that the basic structure was much the same. Alec's comparison stressed as its first main section "The Fundamental Law and the Constitution." From then on the matter of the constitution was frequently mentioned in my pamphlets as one of the main things wrong with the Basis of Union.

When I said previously that I am inclined to doubt that there was any deliberate deception on the part of either Dr. Blanchard or Dr. Palmer, and that neither of them seemed to me to have the slightest comprehension of what an overall constitution really meant, I was quite mindful that there are people who simply cannot visualize "structural relationships." Men who are civil engineers, and are called upon to design bridges and other buildings, must have the aptitude of structural visualization. In our case the constitution for the United Church needed to be visualized and understood in terms of what it could and would be in the future. The inevitable result of giving the General Synod and conferences the power to amend this document simply meant that the General Synod and conferences would use that power as they saw fit—which is precisely what has happened. Not once have I been able to detect from the writings and letters of Dr. Blanchard and Dr. Palmer that they were able to comprehend what I have just said. The same, I am sure, would go for most Congregationalists throughout the country. We had had no experience with an overall constitution.

The final wording of the Basis of Union was approved by the Executive Committee of the General Council at the time of the midwinter meeting in January, 1947. The plan for its submission to the churches again circumvented any opportunity for a meeting of the General Council to discuss the Basis of Union, or to make any recommendations as to whether it should be altered before it was submitted. Instead, and with the plea that it would "save money," the delegates to the Grinnell General Council were called together in state groups. Each group by itself was to approve or disapprove the idea of sending the Basis of Union, as then prepared, to the churches for a vote. Each conference then sent one delegate to report what the majority of its delegates had decided. This meant that there was no national discussion of the Basis of Union nor even of submitting it as then prepared. The state groups of delegates were asked simply to "take it or leave it." Remember that these were the *same delegates who had been worked on at Grinnell* and who had voted by a large majority in support of proceeding with the merger plan as rapidly as possible. This group did not represent a new sampling of opinion from the churches, and most of them, as usual, were ministers and their wives. The results were easily predictable.

The Basis of Union was sent out sometime after the end of April 1947. It contained, inside its cover but not as an official part of the Basis of Union, a statement as to the "recommended procedures." These stated that if seventy-five percent of all the conferences voting, seventy-five percent of all the churches voting, seventy-five percent of all the individual members voting and seventy-five percent of all the associations voting, had responded in favor of the plan of union, then the General Council should proceed with the merger. The date of 1 April 1948 was set as the time when all the votes by the churches should be completed and sent in.

Shortly after the Basis of Union appeared in its final form, I prepared, in cooperation with Rev. Alexander Abbott, *An Independent Analysis of the Basis of Union*. This was sent to all of the churches, including both pastors and clerks. It was accompanied by a letter signed by many prominent Congregationalists, urging a careful reading of the document. Among the signatures to that letter were those of Gaius Glenn Atkins, Dr. Rockwell Harmon Potter, and Donald Adams, former head of our national Laymen's Fellowship and former president of Rotary International.

The analysis also appeared in our national magazine, *Advance*, partly in the June 1947 issue, and partly in the August 1947 issue. Shortly after the first portion appeared, Dr. Blanchard was given opportunity to reply in the July 1947 issue of *Advance*. In each section of the analysis I had raised a specific question. Dr. Blanchard, in his presumed reply, followed something of the same format, but with the question first and his answer second. However, he did not use my questions as I had asked them, and he made up some that were not mine. Instead of using my questions, which I had carefully worded, Dr. Blanchard reworded things to suit himself. In no instance, as I recall, did he quote exactly what I had asked, nor did he give an answer that was a direct and forthright reply to my inquiry. This sort of thing was typical of the way that we could never join with the other side in meeting an issue head-on, or in getting straight answers to straight questions. The same evasive techniques were to be followed in all the years that followed during which whole leaflets were published "answering" our questions. Only they were not answers to *our* questions and they evaded the issues we wanted clarified.

Early in November, 1947 was held the Evanston Meeting—the first national meeting called together to explore the meanings of the Basis of Union and to take a stand on it. As I indicated in an earlier chapter, I was not one of those who called the meeting, had nothing to do with its planning, and took no part in writing its findings. I did, however, cooperate with Dr. Niel Hansen—who was one of the three who called the Evanston Meeting—and gave to him the mailing list I had gradually built up of persons who were evidently opposed to the merger. I attended the Evanston meeting, and I estimated, in looking over the crowd that roughly two-thirds of the people present had already been on my list.

At the close of the sessions I was made a member of the Continuing Committee of the Evanston Meeting; but I did not write any of the materials which went out under the name of that committee. (See appendix of this book for Findings of the Evanston Meeting.)

As I have already indicated, as soon as the findings of the Evanston Meeting were published and sent to the churches, Dr. Blanchard prepared a "Letter Missive" in which he went through the findings, point by point, and categorically denied everything in them. Yet here were the carefully considered conclusions of nearly 200 very competent and informed Congregationalists. They had come to opinions absolutely contrary to those of the chairman of the commission responsible for giving out the Basis of the Union.

A few months later the midwinter meeting of 1948 was

held. By that time there was widespread concern over the misunderstandings that had already arisen over the Basis of Union.

On 30 December 1947, a Brooklyn attorney, Oscar S. Blinn, had written to me as follows:

"About a week ago I learned from Dr. Walton, who is a member of our denominational committee on Interchurch Relations (which consists of our representatives on the joint merger committee) that during the first week in December the committee in question met here in New York and deliberately concluded and resolved that the difficulties arising out of the proposed merger come, not from the Basis of Union itself, but from the widely differing and sometimes diametrically opposite interpretations which equally honest and able clergymen and laymen have placed on many of its important clauses. This is letting the cat out of the bag with a vengeance; and the only thing that surprises me is that it took that committee so long to discover what nearly everybody else who has studied the Basis of Union has known for a long time. This clear admission that the Basis of Union contains numerous ambiguities is significant. During 36 years of active practice of law I have been involved in numerous cases in which parties entered into contracts in the mistaken belief that the provisions were clear and definite; but this is the first instance that has ever come to my attention, in which the two parties deliberately proposed to enter into a contract with the full knowledge of the fact, in advance, that there were various ambiguities and differences of interpretation as between the parties themselves.

This letter gives a double insight. It not only sums up the situation as it was, but it also shows that Dr. Walton had a deep concern about it. This concern led Dr. Walton to repeated efforts to "patch up" the faulty document by seeking through interpretations to clarify it—at least from the Congregational standpoint. As I emphasized in previous chapters, the officials had plenty of time to have produced an honest and straightforward document. But instead of facing the central issue of the main framework of the plan, as it is related to the two contradictory polities involved, they fiddled around with a patchwork of words. Apparently the leading men on our committee did not themselves know the significance of the real issues with which they were trying to deal.

PERSONAL DEBATES WITH DR. DOUGLAS HORTON

Going back now a little in time, I would like to describe a few debates which I had with Dr. Horton. I do not recall ever hearing that anyone else met him as many as four times, as I did.

Actually, I had, through these thirty years since, more or less forgotten the details about two of those debates. If I had been asked a year ago to name the places where each took place, I could probably have mentioned only the last two. But fortunately I wrote letters to various people almost immediately after these events took place. I came across a letter some months ago dated 17 October 1947, which I had written to Dr. Neil Hansen about two weeks before the Evanston Meeting was held. This letter was written after the first two debates with Dr. Horton and gave details in regard to both.

The first debate was at the Frankfurt Congregational Church in Philadelphia. This was later to have very special significance because Mr. S. T. Roberts was a member of that church and he was later chosen as chairman of the Continuing Committee of the Evanston Meeting.

The second debate was at an association meeting at Plymouth, Pennsylvania. The letter to Dr. Hansen made a casual reference to something that Dr. Scribner had said, but that might have been in a debate that I had with him at South Church in Concord, New Hampshire, a short time previously. Recently I have found, in a file of Dr. Palmer's letters, one I wrote to him regarding my debate at the Frankfurt Church, giving even more details on that encounter.

My letter to Dr. Hansen was three pages of single-spaced typing, and therefore I shall limit my quotation, even though there is much more that might be of interest. Quoting now from my letter of 17 October 1947:

> We did cover a lot of ground and Dr. Horton was pressed to making far-reaching admissions. At Philadelphia he insisted that he would vote against the merger if he felt that it would endanger our Congregational Way. At both places he was most emphatic in wanting to "associate himself with Malcolm Burton" in everything that had been said about the importance of Congregationalism.

Then he went on to quote passages from the Basis of Union favorable to the Congregational viewpoint (quite ignoring all the passages to the contrary which I had carefully pointed out). He insisted that no one could vote for the Basis of Union without voting for the Congregational principle. He and Scribner and Blanchard all use the same language: "Wherever there was any doubt about the polity of the proposed United Church they added a sentence stating the Congregational principle." No reply is ever made to the charge that the Evangelical and Reformed men read the opposite interpretation into the Basis of Union by selecting only those parts which seem favorable to their system.

Dr. Horton was most lavish in urging churches to write their own reservations to the Basis of Union, although he made no explanation as to what difference these would make in the ultimate nature of the United Church. Most of his reasoning seemed very loose and wishy-washy. But he became exceedingly definite when men asked what would happen to their standing in the Annuity Fund if they did not go along with the merger: "The money they have paid in would be theirs, but they would no longer be permitted to stay in the plan." Likewise any church that votes against the merger is out of the denomination and the ministers not going along lose their standing in the United Church. You are right that Dr. Horton can be "hard" when he wants to be.

I am quite sure that an air of incredulity prevailed among the laity as well as the ministers at both meetings. Dr. Scribner seemed far more convincing than Dr. Horton, but he made much wider concessions as to dangers inherent in the plan and changes that it might involve.

The one clear recollection that I have of this meeting was in reference to the ministers' annuities. I had been asked by a person in the audience as to whether we would lose our annuities in the merger if we did not go along. I explained, as I had been told, that our relationship with the Annuity Plan was a contract binding on the Fund regardless of the provisions of the Basis of Union. I explained that they couldn't take our annuities away from us, and that we were perfectly safe in taking our own stand on the merger. I recall very definitely how Dr. Horton practically leaped to his feet after I had spoken, and stated that he wanted to make one "correction." He said that the money would remain in the account of a man who did not go along with the merger, but that he could no longer be an "active member of the plan," which is a little more specific than my letter above would indicate. Being an active member means that one can continue to pay into the fund and keep adding to the amount that he would draw when his annuity comes due. What happens if a man leaves the ministry, or if he leaves the Congregational ministry, is that his membership in the fund continues to be on an inactive basis and the money already accumulated to his credit continues to build up interest and increase to that extent. But, by not being an active member, he could no longer add to it or have his church add additional amounts for his benefit. This is probably what Dr. Horton meant.

In later meetings of the General Council and of the Annuity Fund actions were taken that nullified the possibility of the sort of thing that Dr. Horton jumped up for at this time. (Actions were taken in 1948 and again in 1958 safeguarding the rights of ministers not going along with the merger. I remained an "active" member throughout my ministry and am now drawing my annuity, just as those do who went along with the merger.)

There are two other portions of this letter to Dr. Hansen that were significant. In one Dr. Horton explained that they "haven't tried to answer the question of Congregational versus Presbyterian because Presbyterianism is so complicated and so varied that it is hard to say anything definite about it."

I realize that bylaws and so forth can be different from place to place in different Presbyterian bodies, but the things which I had emphasized from the beginning are universal. With Presbyterians the denomination as a whole is "the church." The principle of representative bodies having power to legislate for the denomination is a definite Presbyterian attribute. The concept of an overall constitution is, I believe, universal with Presbyterians.

Dr. Horton was pastor of a federated Presbyterian-Congregational Church at Hyde Park in Chicago, Illinois, just before coming to his position in the General Council. He had been accepted by the Chicago Presbytery, I understand, as an associate member and was even elected as a delegate to the General Assembly of the Presbyterian Church, U.S.A. He had also attended Princeton seminary which had been traditionally a Presbyterian institution. Certainly he was aware of the fundamentals of Presbyterianism and there was no excuse for trying to evade a straightforward answer to my charges.

Another statement I had made in my letter to Dr. Hansen, reporting on something which Dr. Horton had said, appears in substance also in a letter to Dr. Palmer. The latter is among many from Dr. Palmer's file which have been copied and placed in the archives of the Congregational Library in Boston. The version which appears in the letter to Dr. Hansen is that Dr. Horton had said:

> With leaders like himself and others who are so strongly committed to Congregationalism and with over a million Congregationalists behind him, how could a smaller group endanger us? Besides he believes ideas will win and all we have to do is stick to our principles.

My third debate with Dr. Horton was at Second Church, New London, on 19 November 1947. I felt that since I was so much opposed to the merger, I should let the people of the church I was serving hear the other side. (Very few promerger ministers ever granted that privilege to anyone of the opposition: Many of them put the vote through in a very quiet way, as though there was nothing to it, just a good idea that would not make any difference to the local church.)

I do not have too clear a recollection of precisely what Dr. Horton said—partly because there was nothing very precise. There was a sense of frustration in not being able to get anything pinned down. One incident during the questioning period typifies what went on. Rev. Gurdon Bailey (the father of Harold Bailey, who was later secretary of the League to Uphold Congregational Principles) stood up and asked Dr. Horton a question. Mr. Bailey was wearing a long black overcoat and he remained standing after asking his question. Dr. Horton gave some interesting comments on various and sundry matters but never came close to answering Mr. Bailey, whereupon, after five minutes or so, Mr. Bailey said, "Dr. Horton, you haven't answered my question."

Dr. Horton went on again. His performance seemed like "tripping the light fantastic" all around the issue. Again, after a second five minutes, Mr. Bailey said, "Dr. Horton, you haven't answered my question." Somewhat embarrassed, Dr. Horton, without apologizing, again went on discussing all sorts of little things about the merger but again evading the issue that Mr. Bailey had raised. After another embarrassing five minutes, Mr. Bailey stated again, "Dr. Horton, you still have not answered my question," and then sat down.

The meeting had been attended by approximately 350 people from all over the state, including a good number from Second Church. At the close of the meeting, Dr. James F. English, our state superintendent, was in a dither about the whole affair. He was fretting and fuming, muttering things under his breath. It was reported that he said, "About two more debates like this and we shall lose the state."

Perhaps it is no wonder that soon after this the General Council Executive Committee voted that there should be no more "debates" in which any of the officials would take part.

My final debate with Dr. Horton came at Hope Church in Worcester on 8 January 1948. Because of my frustration in previous debates at getting anything settled, I wrote out a careful speech entitled "What Are The Facts?" (*Early Merger Pamphlets*, p. 175). Dr. Horton had ended his remarks at New London with "I agree with Malcolm Burton on everything except the facts."

Dr. Horton began his talk at Worcester with very gracious words as to how greatly he had enjoyed his appearances with Mr. Burton and that his one regret that night was that these pleasant encounters would now be ending.

The auditorium was not large, and the people were not far from the speakers. The platform was small, and when I was speaking, Dr. Horton's seat was only eight or ten feet away. After his very gracious introduction, it was a little surprising to hear him muttering under his breath before I had talked more than five minutes. I glanced over and saw him gripping the seat with both hands and gritting his teeth, muttering something that I couldn't get. He was in full view of the congregation, and this was the one time that I saw Dr. Horton "lose his cool."

My talk cited one instance after another of thinking people stating their impressions of the Basis of Union and then immediately receiving categorical denials. The first instance mentioned was the one when the New London Association had sent in its original resolution on May 1944, stating that the General Synod would be a smaller body than our Council, less representative but with more power; that the conferences would take over from the local associations their present power of electing delegates; and that the General Synod would have power to establish standards and methods of ordination to the ministry and to draw up the constitution and even change any parts of the present proposed Basis of Union. To that, as you may recall from Chapter 5, Dr. Horton had written that none of these statements was true. Yet all of them were in accord with the plain provisions of the Basis of Union. I suggested that the members of the audience read the Basis of Union for themselves on these points. Again, "what are the facts?"

Next we used the illustration of the Evanston Meeting with its twelve pages of findings and the way in which Dr. Ferdinand Blanchard had sent out a high sounding "Letter Missive" declaring, "This brochure contains certain statements that call for correction." Again the question, "What are the facts?"

Something is wrong, it seemed, when honest and sincere Christians cannot agree on even the facts of an important proposal on which they have been urged to vote. I mentioned the prominent attorneys on both sides, some claiming that the merger was perfectly legal and others of equally high standing insisting that it was not. I quoted Judge Maltbie's letter in which he had said, "There is, I am sure, nothing in the proposed Basis of Union which in any way runs counter to the accepted concepts of Congregational polity or the usages of Congregationalism." Also from Maltbie; "The union goes no farther than to admit into one fellowship Congregational, Christian and Evangelical and Reformed Churches." Then I mentioned that if Judge Maltbie had sat with me on the memorable Wednesday afternoon at Allentown when the Evangelical and Reformed ministers, including the chairman of their committee, Dr. George W. Richards, had expressed themselves, I doubted if he could have written those sentences. Again, "What are the facts?"

About an hour's discussion followed the addresses, and then the church took its official vote on the merger question. The result was approximately four to one against the merger.

In the discussion period that followed the main addresses, I brought up in greater detail facts I had learned in Allentown. Dr. Horton came back at me by saying, "You know, there were five other Congregationalists at Allentown besides Mr. Burton. None of them returned with the impression that he did." This was a way of attacking my reliability, but I was able to tell the audience that a letter printed in the *Advance*, in August 1946, had included my report on Allentown in much the same detail as given that night. Also the letter had been mailed to various Evangelical and Reformed ministers who had been present, including Dr. Richards, and that these men had responded that there was no question but that I had understood their point of view and their attitude.

At this point a very dramatic event took place. To understand it, one must remember that this debate took place less than three years after the first atomic bombs had been exploded in Japan, and people everywhere were jittery at the prospect of an atomic holocaust. Dr. Horton jumped to his feet and, throwing out his arms full length on both sides, shouted, "With the whole world on fire, this is no time to be fastidious about polity!"

Rev. Alexander Abbott and Rev. S. Read Chatterton had driven up with me to Worcester that night. Driving home on a cold January night, through the snow covered countryside, one of these companions said, "Malcolm, I never thought that I would ever hear you called a fastidious so-and-so." The three of us laughed, and then I protested, "But that is not what he said." Whereupon the other companion replied emphatically, "No, but that is what he meant!"

We could laugh about this one incident, but it is certainly no laughing matter when a great fellowship like the Congregationalists, with a wonderful history and heritage, is on the brink of making its most fateful decision in history and cannot obtain the clear and certain facts needed to make the right decision, and when the leader most responsible for the plan is evasive.

THE MIDWINTER MEETING, JANUARY 1948

When the various officials of the General Council and Boards met early in 1948, they found that Dr. Alfred Grant Walton had prepared a set of "interpretations" of the Basis of Union. They were circulated among members of the joint commission that had prepared that document. Practically all of the members of the Joint commission then signed a statement that these comments by Dr. Walton were now being presented as the "understanding" of those members of the joint commission. Two were unavailable, and hence did not sign. Dr. Douglas Horton and Dr. Truman Douglass had previously been members of the joint commission but did not sign. Probably no one had more to do with its preparation, from the Congregational Christian side, than Dr. Horton, but at critical times it would seem that Dr. Horton managed to keep in the background and let others "carry the ball."

These interpretations were mimeographed under the heading, *"Comments on the Basis of Union by the members of the Joint Committee which prepared it."* Tremendous pressure was put on all present to accept these interpretations. In a letter of 12 February 1948, Rev. William A. Keith wrote to Dr. Albert W. Palmer, the moderator of the General Council:

> ... I was one of the five who met the Ex. Comm. Roberts, (layman from Philadelphia) who is the mouthpiece of Hansen and McGiffert, read a lengthy document asking withdrawal of the Basis of Union and replacing it with a document proceeding on the Federative Principle. They also reported the growing schism in our churches and denomination. My word was to the effect I doubted if Michigan would carry fifty percent for the Merger and that my own church would probably vote ninety percent against it. I must say the reception we got was icy, contemptuous and unbelieving. The next day (Tuesday) at noon they announced an open hearing on the merger. It was all staged to bring pressure and a showdown. McGiffert had gone to Chicago. Hansen was put on the spot and slipped out. Walton made a statement of interpretation of what many people seemed to want. Then Horton brought in copies of the Interpretation. I asked if it could be officially adopted by the Ex. Comm. and if churches could attach it to their vote as their interpretation. I further said that this cleared a big area for me. I had not known of this document before. It, by the

way, was written, first seven points by Walton and last two through Roberts, at a meeting held of the Joint Committee earlier in January. In the Grand Rapids meeting there was an earnest desire, I think, for understanding. You will realize, however, there were not more than a half dozen of us present known to be opposed. Some silent lay people were there too. Then another steam roller tactic was tried to take a straw vote which many more moderates saw was unfair, at least in the use made of it. Of course the whole officialdom is either for it or going along. At the end, Howard Conn said he had been opposed but couldn't we have a resolution showing a desire to reach understanding and accepting the Interpretation. While I was out of the room getting my belongings to go home, I was placed on the committee to write the resolution. Conn caught me just as I was leaving. I told him I agreed with his motion and to go ahead and sign my name. I have no quarrel with the resolution. But my name, Conn's and Walton's were used at the Chicago Area meeting and in Chicago churches and interpreted as though we were now out crusading for the merger." (Albert W. Palmer file of letters, Part III, in Congregational Library, Boston, p. C 13.)

The resolution to which William Keith's name was affixed, appeared afterward as follows:

A STATEMENT

adopted by those assembled for the mid-winter Meeting of the Missions Council (American Board, Board of Home Missions, Council for Social Action, Superintendents, Women State Presidents, Executive Committee of General Council, etc.) 26-29 January, 1948

The ministers and lay people assembled at the Mid-Winter Meeting of the Missions Council of our Congregational Christian Churches entered into a discussion of the proposed union of our churches with the Evangelical and Reformed Church. Both proponents and opponents were represented in the discussion and the atmosphere was one of earnest enquiry and tolerant understanding. The entire group was heartened by the further intepetation of the Basis of Union as approved by members of the Joint Committee and recognized this interpretation as a clear-cut statement of intent to preserve the traditional polity of the autonomy of the local church. The hope of the overwhelming majority of those present was that we may continue to move toward the consummation of the proposed union as a vital contribution to the ecumenical movement.

Howard Conn
Katherine Schroeder (Mrs. John C.)
William A. Keith

As we read the above statement with its claim that the interpretations in these Comments are recognized "as a clear-cut statement of intent to preserve that traditional polity of the autonomy of the local church," remember that the Basis of Union did not have any clear-cut statement of this sort! And when you look at them, you see that these interpretations did not contain any such statement either. In other words, here was an interpretation of interpretations—of a document that could have contained an outright provision that Congregational polity would be preserved, but avoided doing so.

Bill Keith, who was in seminary with me, did not have long to wait before some disillusionment came to him.

A "promerger committee" was organized at the Grand Rapids midwinter Meeting, with Rev. Albert Penner as chairman. It sent out, almost immediately, a leaflet *For the Merger*. The signatures of some 127 persons at the midwinter meeting were on this leaflet. But the leaflet ignored the Comments, and furthermore it contained no statement about preserving Congregational polity in the union.

On 5 March, 1948, Bill Keith wrote to Dr. Palmer:

> You must have received this week a copy of a statement signed by many at the Grand Rapids Meeting indicating support for the merger. I assume that this is the committee for the Merger with Penner as Chairman. Obviously this letter came after the Interpretation was adopted. I am alarmed they make no mention of it, however, but only say they are for the Merger on the Basis of Union. This is certainly poor strategy. It will only confirm the contention that the Interpretation is being ignored. . . . (Palmer file, part I., p. 7)

A few days later Bill Keith received a letter from Dr. Douglas Horton, dated 12 March 1948, with this:

> As for the "Comments" the Evanston Group are dead right in saying that they do not have the standing of the Basis of Union. The latter is the only document that is officially before us. . . . (Palmer File, Part III., p. C28.)

On April 26 Keith wrote about this to Dr. Palmer:

> I had intended writing you these recent weeks but had little further to say. Horton telephoned me after receiving my

letter you forwarded to him and then wrote a confirming letter. Among other things he said, the interpretations could not
be regarded as official though we were all standing by them.
Then the Evangelical and Reformed declared them as not official or to be presented to their churches. So I was left out on a
limb on the interpretations. (Palmer file Part III., p. C 54)

Already set forth in a previous chapter is the quotation from Dr. Gunneman's book in which he revealed the
letter of Dr. Goebel to Dr. Horton, which said that the
adoption of any such interpretations "would wreck the
merger" (See p. 32 of Gunnemann.)

So far as I am aware, neither the substance of what
Dr. Horton received in the letter of Dr. Goebel's dated 2
February 1948, nor such information as Dr. Horton gave
to William Keith in his letter of March 12, ever became
common knowledge in the denomination.

By coincidence, the letter from Goebel to Horton had
the same date on it as the letter of Dr. Fred Buschmeyer
sending out these Comments to the Congregational Christian churches, and which contained the following:

The *Comments on the Basis of Union* were drawn largely
by Dr. Alfred Grant Walton as a series of interpretations
which, if agreed to by responsible leaders of both the Evangelical and Reformed and the Congregational Christian churches,
would clarify important points of issue regarding the Basis of
Union, and give assurance that our essential Congregational
Christian polity and freedom would be protected and preserved. (Palmer file, p. C 6)

Thus we find a situation in which Dr. Horton was
being informed that the Evangelical and Reformed Church
leaders were not approving any idea of interpretations of
the Basis of Union, at the very time that the Congregational Christian churches were being assured that these
Comments would protect and preserve our freedom and
polity.

Months went by in which these Comments were being
pressed upon the churches as reliable, right when the
main part of the voting on the Basis of Union was taking
place. Our churches never were told, during this voting
period, what Dr. Horton already knew—presuming, of
course that Dr. Gunnemann is correct in his information

about the brutally frank letter from Dr. Goebel, the president of the Evangelical and Reformed Church.

THE FINAL COUNTDOWN BEFORE OBERLIN

The file of Dr. Albert W. Palmer's letters given to me before I retired seven years ago, shed tremendous light on the events just before Oberlin. They show a general mood in the country quite contrary to the spirit later exhibited at Oberlin, and they also trace the step by step development of the strategies to be used by different leaders— including Dr. Palmer and Dr. Horton—in regard to Oberlin.

One of the most interesting revelations is the way that Dr. Palmer at first cooperated to the full with Dr. Horton. Then suddenly, in May, there seemed to come a parting of the ways between the two. From then on Dr. Palmer was "his own man." Why? The reader can certainly read between the lines to see where Dr. Palmer's attitude may have changed.

Undoubtedly the most important revelation, which has already been mentioned, is the way that Dr. Horton kept pressuring for action at Oberlin, even after having sent out, over his own name, the recommendation of the Executive Committee that no definitive action be taken at Oberlin. We shall quote from a number of his letters that show clearly this attitude after Dr. Palmer was taking a different attitude.

The letters in the Palmer file (as copied and sent to the Congregational Library in Boston) have been arranged and bound in three parts. These are letters only from the pre-Oberlin period. Additional letters from the two or three years following Oberlin are yet to be copied and added to the collection.

Part I of the letters are principally between Dr. Palmer and Dr. Horton and give a dramatic sense of the interplay between the two. Coming into the picture are also letters from Dr. A. C. McGiffert, Jr., and others. In a limited sense this first section gives an outline of developments for which Parts II and III furnish more detail.

The Part II letters deal almost entirely with the affair

created after Mr. S. T. Roberts, chairman of the Continuing Committee of the Evanston Meeting, sent a letter to all Evangelical and Reformed ministers telling them what the Congregational Christian people were being told by their leaders. He asked the Evangelical and Reformed ministers to say whether this was their understanding.

Dr. Palmer, apparently encouraged by Dr. Horton, then wrote a letter to the Evangelical and Reformed ministers deploring the Roberts letter. Unfortunately for Dr. Palmer he did the very things of which the anti-merger people were constantly accused: he failed to verify some of his information; he stated half-truths; and he indulged in very unkind innuendos. Dr. Palmer sent his letter to Dr. Wm. Frazier and Dr. Horton with permission to edit it, as is stated plainly in a letter from Horton to Palmer on March 24. Later it turned out that some of the worst things in the letter were innuendos about "anonymous" things in the Roberts letter. Roberts, without naming Horton or Scotford, had just quoted precisely what Dr. Horton and Dr. Scotford had been telling Congregationalists. This was the moment in which Dr. Horton should have "come clean" with Dr. Palmer. He should have told him immediately, "I'm sorry, but I am the one who has been saying those things." Instead he processed the letter, with some changes in other places, but let stand the following very damaging statement:

> 2. The unkind attitudes toward you which he cites, you will note, are entirely anonymous. In behalf of all right thinking members of our churches, I disclaim them. If we enter into this union it will be squarely on the Basis, honestly, lovingly, and without reservations.

What a surprise for Dr. Palmer it must have been when letters from all over the country, from prominent men, wrote to Dr. Palmer telling him that they, personally, had heard Dr. Horton say the very things that Mr. Roberts had stated. Dr. McGiffert wrote to Dr. Palmer correcting him on many things in his letter and telling him that the reason why the Evanston group had not mentioned the names of Horton and Scotford was because they did not wish to deal in personalities (Letter of March 24, pages 15, 16, 17 of Part I).

But all correcting information came too late to prevent a second blunder on Dr. Palmer's part, this time obviously at the prompting of Dr. Horton.

Mr. Roberts' letter to the Evangelical and Reformed ministers was dated February 27. Dr. Palmer's reply was dated March 3 but was not mailed out with Dr. Goebel's accompanying letter until March 11. By March 8 Dr. Horton wrote Dr. Palmer:

> Your letter has gone to Dr. Goebel with a few slight editorial changes. I am now standing by for your letter to our Congregational Christian ministers, church clerks, and delegates to the General Council—for it seems to us on this end that all of these groups should hear from you. We shall have your letter printed by photo-offset process as soon as it arrives. Your telegram tells of its coming.

Thus Dr. Horton was pushing Palmer to get a second letter out, replying to the Roberts letter, before the feedback began coming in on the first one. Apparently Dr. McGiffert's letter of March 9, written before he had seen Palmer's letter, gave the first hint that Palmer had jumped to wrong conclusions. Palmer had called three people whose names were on the back of the Evanston letterhead and asked them if they had authorized Roberts to write his letter. McGiffert heard of these inquiries and wrote, among other things:

> While the detailed wording of the statement was left to Mr. Roberts, and as in all such cases wording can be improved, the decision to send out such a letter was made after a group discussion that brought in a number of people from various states, both here and in the East.

This, however, was just the beginning of Dr. Palmer's enlightenment. The Roberts letter had stated:

> We have been told that, if we accept merger, it will be possible for us to make the United Church thoroughly Congregational by reason of our greater numerical strength. We believe it would be most unfair and really dishonest to enter into merger with such reservations. . . .

Roberts had already quoted Judge Maltbie's statement saying that "the union goes no further than to admit into one fellowship Congregational, Christian and Evangelical and Reformed Churches." At the close of his letter Roberts wrote:

> We would appreciate an expression of opinion from you in this matter. Do you understand the basis of Union to mean that the fellowship of the Congregational Christian Churches will be merely broadened, without change, to include your churches? Do you understand that, in the event of merger, your churches will be, to all intents and purposes, Congregational Churches? We have been told that this is just what you want. Is it? (Palmer File, Part I, p. 3)

In the right-hand margin, side of this last paragraph, Dr. Palmer wrote, "Unfair! Who told him?" It was just such statements as Mr. Roberts reported here that Dr. Horton had been making all over the country.

Dr. Palmer received many letters of praise and adulation from committed promerger enthusiasts, praising him for his "courage," etc., in answering Roberts. But in some eighteen letters many significant leaders in the country began to enlighten Dr. Palmer on the source of Mr. Roberts' allegations. How silly Dr. Palmer must have felt at having written, regarding the "entirely anonymous" attitudes that later proved to come from Dr. Horton: "In behalf of all right thinking members of our churches, I disclaim them. If we enter into this union it will be squarely on the Basis, honestly, lovingly, and without reservations." This after Horton had repeatedly urged churches to write their own reservations into their votes!

Is it too much to guess that this experience with Dr. Horton changed Dr. Palmer's attitude toward the Minister of the General Council? Since Dr. Horton saw Dr. Palmer's letters in advance, and admittedly edited them, just where did it leave him in Palmer's eyes after Dr. Palmer learned the truth of what Dr. Horton had been saying around the country? To my way of thinking, if Dr. Horton had been any sort of forthright individual he would have set Dr. Palmer straight before he let any such letters go out.

This file of Dr. Palmer's correspondence covers many other subjects which came up during the period. At first, as we indicated in the previous section, there was the discussion of the midwinter meeting and the Comments adopted there. In a sense these Comments carry through, in one form or another, until and during the Oberlin Council. Dr. Walton, originally responsible for the Comments, came out on March 3 with a different and far more limiting proposal—wherein the Evangelical and Reformed bodies would continue in their own ways and the Congregational Christian in theirs, with only the top bodies uniting.

When it became obvious that the vote for the merger was falling short of the 75 percent required, a Connecticut group sent to the Executive Committee a proposal that the Basis of Union be recommitted to the joint committee and also that other denominations be invited to join the discussions. This recommendation, appearing as Appendix E of the Executive Committee meeting of April 20, carried signatures of leading promerger men: Russell J. Clinchy (at that time strongly in favor of the union), James F. English, Theodore A. Greene, Harold C. King, Elden H. Mills, and Rockwell Harmon Potter. (See Appendix, Document 10.)

A month later, on May 18, Dr. Palmer sent out his own proposal that the Basis of Union be pushed aside and the whole proposition be approached *de novo*. He set forth a whole new "Bill of Rights," to replace perhaps the Comments, as the grounds upon which future discussions might take place.

It was this proposal of putting the Basis of Union aside, and starting *de novo* that brought the new relationship with Dr. Horton. As soon as he heard about it, Dr. Horton sent first a telegram, then two letters at once, and about five more protests prior to the Oberlin meeting. But here is where Dr. Palmer showed that he was now "his own man." He persisted and set forth his alternative proposals in his Moderator's address at Oberlin. Dr. Truman Douglass also came down hard on Dr. Palmer's suggestion, sending him an urgent five-page, single-spaced typewritten letter against any such proposal. (See Appendix, Documents 18–22, for these letters.)

We shall quote from several of these letters shortly, especially those which show how Dr. Horton ignored the recommendation of the Executive Committee that no definitive action be taken at Oberlin.

Dr. Henry David Gray has written to me recently that the idea of a Bill of Rights was something which he worked out for the Los Angeles Association shortly before Dr. Palmer made up his own. (See Appendix Document 33.)

Dr. Palmer sent out his suggestions to twelve men, six promerger men teamed up with six antimerger people. Although less than a month before Oberlin, the replies to these letters, from promerger and antimerger people alike, were warmly in favor of Dr. Palmer's suggestions. In a sense these various suggestions for a new approach carried along in the spirit of the midwinter Comments in seeking a clarification of our status before proceeding any further.

At this point I would like to digress briefly to describe some of the close personal relationships that existed among some of those who played important roles in the pre-Oberlin drama of events. I shall mention also the special roles that several persons tried to play by way of a kind of healing ministry within the fellowship.

Dr. Palmer was chairman, I believe, of the Inter-Church Relations Commission during the first two years that the Basis of Union was being written. As indicated earlier in this book, Dr. Horton acted as secretary for the Joint Commission and typed out the passages of the Basis of Union on a typewriter in his lap. (It was Dr. Hugh Vernon White, a member of our commission, who gave me this account.) So Dr. Palmer had worked with Dr. Horton almost at the beginning of the merger plan.

Dr. Blanchard was Moderator of the General Council while Dr. Palmer headed the Commission. By the time of the Oberlin Council the offices of the two men had been reversed, with Blanchard as head of the Commission and Dr. Palmer as Moderator. Even so, it was Dr. Palmer, as head of the Commission, who chaired the session on the merger at the 1944 General Council meeting, with Blanchard's help.

Dr. Arthur Cushman McGiffert, Jr., was the immediate successor to Dr. Palmer as president of Chicago Theological Seminary. In many ways the two men were on very cordial terms with each other and obviously respected each other highly. But on the merger issue they were on opposite sides, at least prior to the Oberlin meeting. However, the two corresponded freely with each other and each tried to explain his point of view. After the voting on the Basis of Union had failed, before April, to come even close to the recommended percentages of approval, the two had a meeting together. In his letter of May 18, when he sent out his suggested Bill of Rights, Dr. Palmer made this acknowledgement:

> It may interest you to know that this letter, but not its wording, are the result of a three-day conference President McGiffert and I have just had (at my request) here in Altadena. We are deeply concerned that a positive liberating note be struck at Oberlin to move us out of current antagonisms and frustrations, and we crave your cooperation. (Palmer File, Part I p. 25) (See Appendix, Document 17.)

This cooperation between Palmer and McGiffert disturbed Dr. Horton greatly, as several of his letters show.

Dr. McGiffert in one letter reminded Dr. Palmer that they were both of them "minority" presidents at Chicago Theological Seminary. Dr. Palmer, an ardent pacifist, had led the pacifist opposition to the Second World War at the 1942 General Council. He was as determined in his opposition then as any of us were later in our opposition to the merger. But his faculty and his Board of Trustees were not with Dr. Palmer on the pacifist issue. So likewise with Dr. McGiffert on the merger. I understood at the time that all but one of the faculty favored the merger, and so did the majority of the trustees.

Dr. Palmer was not a well man. His physician required him to take three-hour rest periods during the day. Many doubted the wisdom of his trying to preside at Oberlin. Frankly, although some things he said irritated me greatly, I am amazed at how dedicated Dr. Palmer was to his task, the almost countless letters he acknowledged (including some of mine) and the stubborn way that he resisted pressure from Dr. Horton.

A few further words about Dr. McGiffert seem to me in order. He was considered "the brains" of the Evanston Meeting's pamphleteering efforts. An article he wrote for the Chicago Seminary *Register* (March 1947) was one of the best summaries I have ever seen on what "one big church" would mean. On the other hand he was, I believe, the one who insisted, more than anyone else, that the

Evanston Meeting disband at Oberlin. This was not on the grounds that we were all to agree to go along with the merger (as it was soon interpreted by the promerger people) but for the simple reason that Evanston had been formed to fight against the adoption of the Basis of Union. Now that the Basis of Union had been approved by the Council, we should not hold members of the Evanston group to new phases of the struggle.

For me there have always been additional factors involved for Dr. McGiffert. I have what seems to me very strong recollections on an incident which took place at Grinnell in June 1946. The meetings there took place in the college gymnasium. On the sides of the large room were wooden bleachers, with plain wooden planks. I recall sitting there alongside Dr. McGiffert, whom I did not know too well at the time. Incidents connected with the merger came up while just the two of us sat there looking on. It was Dr. McGiffert who first called my attention to the fact that the vigorous clapping that broke out any time the merger or church union was mentioned came from a small number of young people, scattered throughout the audience. After a while Dr. McGiffert shook his head, and, with grim face and both hands clenched to the wooden plank on which we sat, he said, "This is the wave of the future." That phrase, used by Anne Morrow Lindbergh, and expressing the defeatist attitude that the great Lone Eagle, Charles A. Lindbergh, felt after he had toured the airplane factories of Nazi Germany and worried that America could never catch up or win a war, has always seemed to me significant of a certain inner feeling Dr. McGiffert felt all along. Yet this was before the Evanston Meeting. He put up a valiant fight. But with the situation he had to face at the Seminary, who can blame him for his stand after Oberlin? This much is clear from his later letters to Dr. Palmer (not included in the three parts already in the Boston Congregational Library). He never came to speak and act like most of the promerger people. He raised the question of whether the minority was being treated rightly. He suggested that, in all fairness, there should be a division of denominational assets. He reported with objectivity and, I feel, fairness on meetings he attended where antimerger action was taken.

Dr. Walton, as we mentioned, came up with a new

proposal in March. Nothing seemed to come of that. But his original comments were to show up at Oberlin in slightly revised form. At first they were part of the Minority Report from the Commission on Interchurch Relations, known also as the Walton Report. Later, agreement was reached between members of the Commission, and these interpretations became part of the final motion from the Commission—the consideration of which took up all the attention and time and thus protected the Basis of Union itself from even coming to the fore as an item for frank discussion or debate. Dr. Walton tried to be a mediator. But in the end he was disillusioned with the results. He, like Howard Conn, wound up not going into the United Church.

Wendell Fifield was another who tried to wield a moderating influence and who was greatly concerned for the fellowship. Both he and Henry David Gray believed that nothing decisive was coming up at Oberlin, just as indicated in the Executive Committee recommendation, and did not plan to attend the Oberlin sessions. How many other influential leaders stayed away we shall never know, but by "playing dead" the promerger leaders helped make Oberlin a one-way proposition.

Other men who played roles in this pre-Oberlin drama were Rev. Albert Penner, Rev. Joseph King, and Dr. John Scotford. We are limited in our knowledge of the full part which each of these played. We do know from letters in the Palmer file a little of the part played by each.

Albert Penner was made chairman of a promerger committee at the midwinter meeting in January 1948. On February 2 he wrote to Dr. Palmer:

> Many of us at the Midwinter Meeting last week expressed a very great concern that those who favor the Merger are not articulate. A great amount of negative material is being sent to our churches by the Evanston Group, and by individuals such as Fred Meek which goes to ministers and clerks. Especially in our smaller churches this appeal may be quite effective.
>
> As a result of our discussion a NATIONAL COMMITTEE FOR THE MERGER was formed, and I was asked to serve as chairman. The treasurer is Emerson G. Hangen of Meriden, Conn. We hope to prepare two or three things of a popular appeal type for the Merger, and to send these to all our churches and ministers. The first is a short letter signed by 126 who were at the Midwinter Meeting. Frazier and Scribner were

asked to prepare a second; and a small group of men around New York a third. It was thought that these latter should be sent out over the signatures of a Steering Committee, Ronald Bridges, Helen Kenyon, Vere Loper, M. R. Boynton are some of those who very willingly consented to have their names used in this way. Because of the shortness of time it would not be possible, probably, to get everyone's consent in every instance. It would mean a very great deal to have your name included, not as Moderator, but as an individual.... (Palmer File, Part I, p. 0)

That first circular sent to the churches was the one which Rev. William Keith criticized. The statement said "we are for the merger," etc., but never mentioned the Comments that had just been adopted, and said nothing about any intent to make the union congregational. A second letter from Penner to Palmer on February 26, written in longhand, reported:

We are trying to push propaganda on Conference levels. Here in New England, for instance, we have set up State Committees to prepare and distribute material. Our Mass. Com. has already sent out a letter and the enclosed statement which is an answer to Meek. The enclosed legal opinion signed by Mr. Lucius Thayer who happens to be an Ex-Moderator of the Mass. State Conf. is being mailed to all the Ministers in the country. We are meeting in New York Monday to consider further steps. I haven't yet seen the latest "Evanston" pronunciamento, but I understand they are listing all the churches voting against, which is a poor list really, but by itself looks very impressive. I am anxious that we should get out as large a favorable vote as possible. We shall, on Monday, also consider what wider use might be made of your statements. I think they would do a very great deal of good.
Ever sincerely yours
Albert J. Penner
(Palmer File, Part I, p. 1c)

This is the last in the Palmer file from Al Penner until the telegram of June 11 addressed to Rev. Joseph King, Jr., Oberlin, Ohio:

Is Finney Chapel available for large meeting at 10 P.M. Thursday. Otherwise James Brand House. Please wire collect. Albert J. Penner.

Rev. Joseph King was pastor of First Congregational Church of Oberlin, and hence the host pastor in charge of some arrangements. He was also the son-in-law of Dr.

Palmer. He made his church available for the mass meetings.

The full story of the countdown before Oberlin would be more complete, of course, if there were access to all the personal files of this promerger Committee. Undoubtedly we could get from them a better picture of just how the blitz for the Oberlin Council was planned and executed.

But even these two letters from Albert Penner tell us something. Just how Dr. Palmer could be a member of the committee "not as moderator, but as an individual" is hard to conceive. Everyone could identify him as the moderator. Included in the committee were national secretaries Frazier and Scribner, former moderator Ronald Bridges, assistant Moderator Helen Kenyon and members of the Executive Committee. Then in Dr. Horton's letters to Palmer in May, and the very long letter from Dr. Truman Douglass, both speak of their very many contacts with "leading men" throughout the country, with whom they had talked in their official travels about the country. Horton mentioned especially leaders in Vermont. At Oberlin the first crucial step, that of moving to lay the Executive Committee's recommendation on the table, was suggested by a Vermont man. It is not hard to see how plans were shaped up.

We can hardly estimate the far-reaching effects of Dr. Scotford as editor of *Advance,* our national denominational paper. At this juncture he beat Al Penner to the punch when it came to printing a list of people favoring the merger. The January 1948 issue of *Advance* contained three pages of names, three columns on a page, of people in states throughout the union. The statement which these people presumably signed reads as follows:

WE BELIEVE

That union with the Evangelical and Reformed Church will demonstrate the sincerity of our faith in the spiritual unity of Christians.

That the *Basis of Union* safeguards the cherished liberties of the Congregational Christian fellowship.

That the questions of finance and administration have been examined, and that there is nothing in these fields to present an obstacle to union.

That a large part of our laity and especially our youth would be gravely disappointed by failure to effect the union.

That after five and a half years of discussion of the union, and after its favorable reception by the Evangelical and Reformed Church, further postponement is uncalled for and the time for decision is now.

WE EARNESTLY HOPE

That the Union will be accepted by Congregational Christian churches by a vote so nearly unanimous as to promise a church united not only in organization but by unity of the Spirit in the bond of peace.

Dr. Scotford had started as early as the June issue of 1942, before the initial negotiations were authorized at Durham, supporting the merger by printing a long article by Douglas Horton about the similarities of our two denominations. Through all the merger considerations, he had outspoken, even brash, editorials supporting the union, ridiculing criticisms of the plan and seeming to pose as the self-appointed authority on all aspects of the merger. In addition, he printed many signed articles in support of the merger. Whenever any of us objected to the free-wheeling tactics of Dr. Scotford, we were waved off with "Oh, you know how Scotford is." Or we were told that he was guaranteed his freedom as an editor, and nobody had any control over him. But in these letters in Dr. Palmer's files are cross-references between Horton and Scotford, and two letters—one from Horton and one from Scotford—which say so nearly the identical things, that in retrospect we may have good reason to believe that Scotford had always been Horton's mouthpiece. The payoff comes when we read the full-page, unsigned article which appeared on page 3 of the June 1948 issue—just weeks before Oberlin met. In this editorial Scotford called the shots perfectly on what the Council was going to do. The editorial was in Dr. Palmer's file because Henry David Gray had torn it out of his copy and sent it to Palmer with the comment: "This all seems rather disconcerting." Dr. Gray sensed that it was an attempt to force a vote at Oberlin on the Basis of Union. He told Dr. Palmer that his plan for a Bill of Rights, and starting *de novo*, "is much more positive, stronger, and more likely to yield permanently valuable results in a solid, united, future union." (Palmer File, Part I, p. 41)

I feel that we have the right to the conjecture that Scotford's June editorial revealed Horton's plan.

Editorial from June 1948 Issue of Advance
with Dr. Gray's Handwritten Comments

Henry you & ____) is much more positive, stronger, and more likely
enclosed ____ (to yield permanent ____ ____ ____ ____ ____ ____
with a letter

The Council Faces Church Union

WHEN IT ASSEMBLES IN OBERLIN ON JUNE 17 the General Council must decide what to do about the merger with the Evangelical and Reformed Church.

The responsibility for a decision will be upon the Council. The Executive Committee and the Commission on Interchurch Relations and Christian Unity are instrumentalities created by the Council. Although their recommendations will be the result of careful deliberation, it is not bound to accept them. The votes taken by the churches, associations, and conferences on the merger are advisory to the Council and not mandatory upon it. On the other hand, the Council cannot legislate for the churches, associations, and conferences; it can merely suggest possible actions. Positively it can do two things. It has the power to merge itself with the General Synod of the Evangelical and Reformed Church. It can recommend the union of the boards of the two denominations, and, as the Council constitutes the majority of the voting membership of these boards, its recommendation would be followed. The responsibility for taking, or not taking, these steps rests upon the Council alone.

In making its decisions the Council will be confronted by a number of facts.

Much emphasis is being placed upon the fact that approximately 37 per cent of the churches voting and somewhat more of the popular votes were negative. By the time the Council meets a careful analysis of this vote will be available for study.

Another fact is that over 63 per cent of our churches have voted favorably. Granted that there are conscientious people in the minority; can it not also be assumed that the majority is also guided by conscience? Must the majority yield to the minority just because that minority is insistent? This is a nice question.

But there are other facts to be faced. These same churches have voted upon the merger in the district associations and the state conferences, and in both instances the results have been overwhelmingly favorable to the proposed union. What is the reason for this seeming contradiction? Might it not be argued that the churches which take an active part in the affairs of the associations and conferences and the members which they send as delegates are likely to have a broader and more informed attitude than those whose activities are limited to the local church?

Another inescapable fact is that the synods of the Evangelical and Reformed Church have voted in favor of union by a large majority, although the *Basis of Union* involves more concessions on their part than on ours. If the merger is turned down, the responsibility will be upon us.

We must also consider the implications of a negative decision. We have prided ourselves upon being the most broad-minded, liberal, and progressive of the American denominations. A proposition has been put before us which has been accepted by the other party and by a majority of our churches and people. If we cannot unite with a church as reasonable, as gracious, and as Christian as the Evangelical and Reformed, what chances are there of reducing the divisions which plague Protestantism? The eyes of the world will be upon us at Oberlin; the hope of future unions depends upon our decisions.

The opposition claims that there will be numerical losses if the merger is consummated; over against this must be put the deterioration in morale, particularly among our young people, our seminary students, and in many of our churches, which may be anticipated if the proposed union is dropped. One must be balanced against the other.

Repeated and strenuous efforts have been made by our leaders to conciliate the minority and to find a middle way upon which we can agree. These have failed. Our traditions put much store by the wisdom of the larger group. We believe in the democratic process. This issue must be decided by the General Council. It will need wisdom, ingenuity, imagination, courage, and the prayers of our people.

*Palmer's Letter of 18 May 1948
and Douglas Horton's Telegram in Reply*

THE GENERAL COUNCIL
OF
CONGREGATIONAL CHRISTIAN CHURCHES
OF THE UNITED STATES OF AMERICA
287 FOURTH AVENUE :: NEW YORK 10, NEW YORK

ALBERT W. PALMER, *Moderator*
Residence: 1185 East Foothill Blvd.
Altadena, California

May 18, 1948

Dear Dr.

You are "co-opted"! I need your help right away as a "consultant to the moderator". Please look over the enclosed "Bill of Rights for Free Churches" and talk it over with your team-mate in the list given below, and with any others you two may invite in.

Then write me a letter of comment and constructive suggestion. I plan to make some such proposal as this "Bill of Rights" in my moderator's address at the opening of the General Council at Oberlin, June 17. But I am holding final proofs on that address open until June 12. Please write so as to reach me here in Altadena before June 2 or in Oberlin (271 Forest Street) before June 12. Be brief, be frank, be constructive, be conciliatory!

It is my hope that some such proposal as this may heal some wounds, allay many fears, and provide a track upon which we can go forward safely, unitedly and effectively toward an acceptable and inspiring ultimate union with the E. and R. and any other free churches which may be willing to unite with us on such a platform of progressive churchmanship. "Not frustration, not retreat, but progress", should be our motto at Oberlin.

This letter is being sent out to six pairs of consultants across the country as follows:

1. Rev. Stuart L. Anderson and Rev. Henry David Gray.
2. Rev. Raymond A. McConnell and Rev. Fred Hoskins.
3. Rev. Arthur D. Gray and Rev. Harvey Young.
4. Rev. William A. Keith and Rev. Howard A. Blanning.
5. Rev. Alex. J. MacKenzie and Rev. L. Wendell Fifield.
6. Rev. Frederick M. Meek and Rev. George H. Gibson.

It may interest you to know that this list and this letter, but not its wording, are the result of a three-day conference President McGiffert and I have just had (at my request) here in Altadena. We are deeply concerned that a positive liberating note be struck at Oberlin to move us out of current antagonisms and frustrations, and we crave your cooperation.

-2-

We are moved to take this step also because it is in line with a suggestion (No. 8) which was made at Buck Hill Falls by the Evanston group to the Executive Committee, namely that, if the Basis of Union does not secure a sufficient mandate to authorize action at Oberlin, further plans should at once be undertaken to prepare alternatives. This proposed "Bill of Rights" we conceive of as the first step in such alternative plans. It would clear the way for the appointment by the Oberlin Council of a Committee or Commission to take up the whole matter of union afresh.

You will note that what I am suggesting is not a mere revision or commentary on the Basis of Union but an approach to the whole problem de novo. Of course the experience gained in the negotiation of the Basis of Union will be helpful and the Bill of Rights as an accepted background will prevent fears from arising which have unfortunately clouded the interpretation of that document.

I feel that the adoption of such a "Bill of Rights" will save a lot of abortive, premature and even acrimonious discussion at Oberlin, especially since both opponents and proponents of the Basis of Union have been consulted about its formulation. This fact, in itself, should be taken as symbolic of a reunion of our denominational spirit.

I hope these considerations will move you to help vigorously to this end both now in advance and later on at the General Council.

Fraternally yours,

Albert W. Palmer

AWP:ec

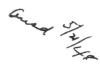

WESTERN UNION

TA713

T=CDU740 NL PD=CD NEWYORK NY 20   1940 MAY 20 PM 7 30

DR ALBERT W PALMER=

1185 EAST FOOTHILL BLVD ALTADENA CALIF=

TO BEGIN DENOVO OUTSIDE FRAMEWORK OF BASIS WILL SIDETRACK UNION FOR GENERATION. E & R CHURCH CANNOT VOTE AGAIN= NO IDEA MORE INCENDIARY FOR OBERLIN= BEG YOU NOT TO INTRODUCE IT=

DOUGLAS HORTON=

Horton's Letter of 22 May 1948
in Reply to Palmer's Letter of 18 May 1948

THE GENERAL COUNCIL OF THE CONGREGATIONAL CHRISTIAN CHURCHES

TWO EIGHTY SEVEN FOURTH AVENUE NEW YORK

Saturday 22 May 1948

Dear Albert,

Since this is Saturday morning, I am all alone in the office, but the matter of your letter which enclosed the 'Bill of Rights' is of such importance that I must expose you to the idiosyncrasies of my own typing.

I wonder if you know that this is the second 'Bill of Rights' which has been spoken of in connection with the proposed union. Massachusetts appointed a committee to draw up a 'Bill of Rights' about two years ago, and the requests made by that committee were incorporated into the Basis of Union.

The issue which will come before the Oberlin Council is now being clearly drawn. We shall either (a) proceed with our negotiations, probably after appropriate delay, within the framework of the Basis of Union or (b) reject, table, or ignore the Basis and give up any hope of union for a generation at least.

Any 'approach to the problem de novo' will meet with opposition you cannot overcome. (a) It will meet with Congregational Christian opposition. Only two of our fifty conferences are apparently voting against the Basis: that is a 96% affirmative vote. The associations will be overwhelmingly 'pro'. In spite of the Evanston pressure-group (of a type which, as every political scientist knows, can make terrific inroads on a loose democracy), the churches are 2-1 in the affirmative—a really immense majority. Vermont is only one of several conferences that are going to push for some sort of affirmative action: the Vermont committee writes me, 'Ninety percent of the Vermont Congregationalists would rather see our denomination split into schisms than retreat on the issue of Church union' (and by that they mean this union). (b) The approach de novo would lose us the E. and R. Church. The successive editions of the Basis of Union have been progressively Congregational. The 'comments' to which we asked their leaders to agree were even outré Congregationalism. If now we should ask them to begin again so that we could make an instrument even more Congregational than this, they would rightly resent being drawn into association with so denominationally minded a group. We have this in writing from their leaders.

Albert, what I am now about to say is said in confidence, and I shall ask you not to repeat it. The plain fact is, however, that Evanston knows that these are the issues. They have talked to the E. and R. leaders. They are too intelligent, in my judgment, to have misunderstood them. They know that a call for a union de novo is really a call to bury the idea of union ten fathoms deep. But what an adroit move to get you, our Moderator, to stand for this kind of procedure! What a front for their attack you would make! (Now may the Lord forgive me if I am wrong about this. I shall repent in dust and ashes—but I have had too many dealings with them to think otherwise of them. Remember: they are the ones that wrote to the E. and R. ministers.)

In a word, I hope you will make no appeal to Oberlin, using your immense prestige for the purpose, to proceed outside of the frame of reference of the Basis of Union.

Ever affectionately

Douglas Horton

Dr. Albert W. Palmer

1948 BUCK HILL FALLS MEETING OF EXECUTIVE COMMITTEE

On the preceding four pages we have printed some of the documents we have just been discussing, which will have even greater significance as we consider the events which took place at Buck Hill Falls, Pennsylvania, April 20–22.

Other very important documents which we have mentioned previously, such as the Comments adopted at the midwinter meeting in January, together with the Evanston Meeting statement and many letters from the Palmer file, appear in the Appendix. There is far more in all of these documents than mere piecemeal quotations would ever reveal.

As we come to the Buck Hill Falls meeting it is well to remember that all of the voting by the churches was supposed to be completed by April 1, according to the procedures set forth with the Basis of Union. And furthermore it was provided that 75 percent of both churches and individual members were supposed to approve the union if it was to be approved by the General Council. These were the ground rules laid down in advance by the commission that prepared the Basis of Union, and these were considered by the churches as having been set forth in good faith. Any charge that these were "weasel-worded" provisions, or that they would not be honored by the leaders of the denomination, would have brought forth shrieks of indignation from near and far. Those of us who lived through those days know how the promerger ministers and their friends reacted to any suspicion of duplicity or bad faith.

As of 1 April 1948, only a small proportion of the total number of our churches had voted favorably. Out of some 1,444 churches reporting, 714 had voted favorably and 531 negatively. Of those *voting*, only 56 percent of the members had voted in favor and 57 percent of the churches. If these figures had been taken as final, the Basis of Union had been clearly defeated according to the terms set forth when it was distributed.

Allowing for dilatory practices, and tardiness of making reports, we can look also at the report by Frank F.

Moore, assistant secretary of the General Council, for May
25—almost two months after the voting by churches was
supposed to have been completed. It is well to remember,
however, that promerger efforts were redoubled after the
Buck Hill Falls meeting, and state superintendents had
been urgently requested to get the votes in.

The official report by Frank Moore showed a total of
5,487 churches with a total membership of 1,012,022. Of
these only 3,872 churches had voted, with the promerger
count 2,514 and 1,334 churches against. The percentage for
those voting favorably was then 65.3 of the churches and
63.7 of the members voting. But only approximately 30
percent of the total membership voted at all. (See page 254
of *Early Merger Pamphlets*.)

Considering that the merger had been pushed by the
top leadership for six years, and by most of the Superintendents since the Grinnell Council of 1946, these results
are far from impressive. Yet men like Dr. Horton, Dr.
Douglass and Dr. Scotford were claiming, as we can see by
their letters, that an "overwhelming majority" of our
people were for the merger.

The Buck Hill Falls meeting of the Executive Committee sent out the following in its mimeographed minutes,
which I have before me. (No minutes of this meeting appear in the *Advance Reports* for the Oberlin meeting, presumably because copy had to go to the printer at an earlier date.)

An open meeting of the Executive Committee was called to
order at 2:30 P.M. by Mr. Buschmeyer.
Those present were: Messrs. Buschmeyer, Callahan, Edwards,
Fiero, Folwell, Houser, Merrill, Nethercut, Phillips, Rowell,
Scott, Shipherd; and Mesdames Beach, Read, Swartz, Williams.
Secretaries Horton, Fagley, and Timmons.
Corresponding members: Messrs. Blanchard, English, Good-
sell, Gray, Moore, Scribner, Tuttle and Mrs. Medlicott.
Guests: Messrs. Burton, Hansen, McGiffert and Roberts repre-
senting the Evanston group.
A general discussion was held on the present status of the
Basis of Union now before our churches. Mr. Horton gave an
opening statement, and this was followed by written state-
ments from Dr. McGiffert, Moderator Palmer, Mr. Meek, Dr.
Blanchard and the Connecticut group, which are included
herewith as Appendices A, B, C, D, E.

No votes were taken by the Executive Committee at the opening sessions, at which we were present. But in the evening session, Rev. Boynton Merrill read a proposed resolution. This suggested statement was discussed at length in both morning and afternoon sessions on the following day—after we had left. At no point in the recorded discussion is there any suggestion that the General Council ought to ignore the failure to secure a seventy-five percent approval of the churches voting, or to "barge ahead" with the merger in violation of the distinct understanding which the churches had in regard to the procedures.

The vote, after the acceptance of numerous changes, came later on April 21 (page 7 of mimeographed minutes) and was printed in Appendix G of these minutes, and again in Appendix D, page 41, of the 1948 General Council minutes. This was the resolution recommending that no definitive action on the Basis of Union be taken at Oberlin in the absence of a 75 percent vote of approval by the churches. (See Document 14 in the Appendix to this book.)

Dr. McGiffert gave a six-page statement, carefully setting forth the issues and calling attention to the fact that only about 30 percent of members in the churches voting had expressed themselves, and that of these only a little over 17 percent had voted favorably. He suggested that "we quit talking about the majority and minority position." He also stated:

> In considering the size of this negative vote, it should be remembered that, with few exceptions, employed denominational officers, national and local, as well as denominational funds and denominational channels of promotion have had their weight and influence ardently behind the support of the present Basis of Union.

Dr. McGiffert went on to enumerate various suggestions being made at the time, including one that would have us "discover a technicality by which the Basis of Union may be theoretically accepted but immediately on acceptance rendered a dead letter." He mentioned that at least three different statements looking to such a solution had been made. (Appendix to the 1948 General Council Minutes, Document 31)

In closing, Dr. McGiffert presented eight propositions

(see the conclusion of Document 12 in the Appendix). Among these were the recognition that the basis of Union had been rejected by the votes of churches and members voting, according to the recommended terms of procedure, and the Executive Committee take the necessary steps to prevent merger on the Basis of Union. Dr. McGiffert asked the Executive Committee to examine what powers, if any, the General Council had in trying to effect a merger and to inform the churches on this. He spoke of the possibility of federative union, suggested also by Dr. Frederick Meek. He suggested possibility of other alternatives to the Basis of Union, and stated, "Unless some such constructive alternatives to the Basis of Union can be worked out in principle, if not in detail in time for presentation at Oberlin, it is hard to see how the now impending spiritual calamity can be avoided."

Dr. Palmer was not able to be present because of his health, but his paper was read. It dealt mainly with an attempt to explain the reasons for the opposition, "the fears" and the "resentments" of opponents. Not once did he try to meet head-on the issues actually raised by the many opponents. His moderator's address at Oberlin included this same approach of trying to "psychoanalyze" the opposition.

Dr. Meek, like Dr. McGiffert, gave a splendid and careful presentation. It is printed in my *Early Merger Pamphlets*, pages 251–253. It stressed the thought of federative union rather than "organic." This had been the suggestion also of the original Evanston Meeting statement (see Document 3 in the Appendix). It is hard to see how anyone could expect to unite a fellowship of free churches, where there was no authority from the top down with a unitary church in which authority at the top is the first and distinguishing characteristic and then to claim that it would not change either group. The suggestion of a federative approach was only a very realistic alternative.

Dr. Meek's paper at Buck Hill Falls really echoed his earlier pamphlet, *The Critical Conflict between Ideals and Reality*, which is also printed in *Early Merger Pamphlets* (pages 241–250).

I recall nothing of Dr. Blanchard's presentation, nor can I find a copy of it. But we shall come later to a letter of his, dated April 29, which was only a few days afterward, and to a letter of mine to my sister-in-law, which reflect his sentiments.

I have some vivid recollections of the meeting. I remember Mr. Edwards, a layman from Rhode Island, jumping up and down in his chair and saying, "All I know is that the laymen are sick and tired of all the divisions in Protestantism and want unity."

The most striking and emphatic statement made by any member of the Executive Committee was from Dr. John M. Phillips of Duluth. In no uncertain terms he laid it on the line that the churches had been consistently led to believe that 75 percent approval by the churches voting would be required, and that the churches would consider it a shocking breach of faith to try to effect the merger without that vote having been obtained. I had the feeling that all the members of the Executive Committee were with him solidly as he spoke.

But I remember vividly how Dr. Horton sat at the end of the long table where the Executive Committee was assembled, and, sitting sidewise with head somewhat down, said in a kind of sulking manner, "Well, there is nothing to prevent somebody from making a motion from the floor to go ahead." That should have been a tip-off to everyone present.

I have tried many times to figure out how Dr. Horton, Executive Secretary of the General Council as well as "Minister," could feel that he was free to ignore, or to work against, the important recommendation made by the Executive Committee at Buck Hill Falls. Presumably it was his duty to carry out the vote of the Executive Committee—which was also said to be the General Council "ad interim."

Perhaps I have found an answer of sorts to this question. On page 30 of *Advance Reports* for the Oberlin Council of 1948 is the "Report of the Minister of the General Council." The following brief paragraph is all that it contains on the merger:

> Since the responsibilities in connection with the proposed union with the Evangelical and Reformed Church derive from the Commission on Interchurch Relations and Christian Unity, which I serve as Executive Secretary, rather than directly

from the General Council, I shall not here make report of my work in that field.

This evasive statement led me to another thought: What kind of an address did Douglas Horton make to the Oberlin Council as it faced the most crucial issue of the century?

By insisting, when he took office, that he have title of Minister, as well as Executive Secretary, I can understand how Dr. Horton may have wanted to broaden his field beyond that of merely carrying out responsibilities connected with votes of the Council itself. But as Minister, did he not assume wider responsibilities also for the overall well-being and spiritual health of the Council and the fellowship?

In 1948 the General Council faced the most serious division our fellowship had known since the council was established. As it turns out, Dr. Horton had intimate and inside information on how the Evangelical and Reformed leaders felt, which our people should have been told. Yet at this critical juncture the Minister of the General Council made no endeavor to come cleanly before that body and give it wisdom and mature judgement on what ought to be done, nor did he pass on to its members some secrets he had known since February. Later in the meeting, after the Council had been engineered through many proposed motions and revisions of motions, and finally carried off its feet in ecstasy and joy in the mistaken belief that it had found a magic formula to solve all its problems and to heal the wounds of the fellowship, he called on Dr. Goebel to tell the Council what he, Dr. Horton, should have revealed either months before or at the least at the beginning of the Council session, namely that any interpretations would wreck the merger. (See the third paragraph from the end of Document 29.)

None of the addresses by Dr. Horton at the General Councils are printed in the Minutes for 1942, 1944, 1946, or 1948—the years when the merger was initiated and promoted. (They are in the Minutes for 1940, 1950, 1952, and 1954.) But *Daily Advance* at Oberlin printed his long address in two sections, the first on June 18 and the second on Monday, June 21. It dealt with stewardship and roamed far and wide, all over the world, and was headed, "Dr.

Horton Appeals for Implementation of Spiritual Emphasis." It avoided the merger issue. Dr. Horton, the person most responsible for the merger, did not come out front at this critical moment to do anything that would set the record straight.

From the Buck Hill Falls meeting on, we find Dr. Palmer pursuing a course in line with the Executive Committee's recommendation. He came out with his proposed Bill of Rights as an alternative plan, and a *de novo* approach. Dr. Horton deplored this and tried hard to stop him. (See Horton's telegram and his letter reproduced just a few pages back; also see Documents 18, 19, 20, and 21 in the Appendix.)

Dr. Horton's letters also attest to his having been closely in touch with promerger people everywhere who were insistent upon going ahead at Oberlin. There is not the slightest hint that Dr. Horton was trying to dissuade them. Rather he presents many arguments as to why the Basis of Union must *not* be sidetracked at Oberlin.

Dr. Palmer, despite his characterizations of the opposition, was nevertheless genuinely concerned about a split in the fellowship. Dr. Horton shows little or no concern over this. Dr. Palmer in his opening address at Oberlin strongly endorsed the Executive Committee's recommendation that no definitive action be taken. He also set forth in detail his Bill of Rights and his plea for a *de novo* approach. Horton said nothing openly and in straightforward fashion to the whole Council. He had been talking privately to individuals, and in the months just previous to the meeting it would appear that careful plans had been laid. Others would carry the ball and Horton, the chief architect, would keep out of the act—except for the one "emergency" when he called on Dr. Goebel to tell the Council the truth.

Returning to the Buck Hill Falls meeting for a few additional details, I have a personal letter which I wrote on April 2, 1948—just three days after we met with the Executive Committee. It is five pages, single spaced on the typewriter, and was written to my sister-in-law in Chicago, Mrs. Mary Berkemeier Quinn. I had promised to tell her about the meeting. I did not yet know that the Executive Committee had voted as it did.

The letter details many of the things mentioned above, but it also includes some very important items I had forgotten in these thirty years since. I quote from the opening part:

> The meeting was in session from 2:30 until after five in the afternoon and then from 7:30 until 10 in the evening with no other subject up for discussion. Dr. Horton began the meeting by trying every way he could to suggest that something must be done to find a solution that would not lose all the wonderful things that had been built up in the merger negotiations. To him it would be a pefectly terrible tragedy if this merger should fail and nothing must happen which could possibly make the Evangelical and Reformed people cut off negotiation at once. Every time that we suggested giving up the Basis of Union and starting *de novo* he would go up in the air and insist that meant the end of everything and that it would put us back 25 or 50 years in all efforts towards union of any kind.

This claim by Dr. Horton is reiterated in letters to Dr. Palmer, i.e., in the one reproduced above and in Documents 18–21 in the Appendix, in which he also makes other dire predictions.

Another portion of my letter deals partly with Dr. F. Buschmeyer's handling of things as chairman of the Executive Committee:

> One of the most disturbing things to me was the way that Dr. Buschmeyer ran interference for Horton all the way along. I had been told that Dr. Buschmeyer was a man of considerable independence and integrity. If that were ever true he has been thoroughly Hortonized by now. Dr. Horton's trick was to try and make it appear that we were guilty and that we should be expected to bring forth a constructive solution. After spending all day with the Executive Committee, carefully explaining our position, when the moment came for our departure Dr. Buschmeyer tried to leave as the parting impression the very thing that Horton was trying to pin on us. He said as we got up to go, "Then you people have nothing constructive to suggest at this time, is that true?"

From our standpoint the federative plan of union urged by both Dr. Meek and Dr. McGiffert, was the only realistic, constructive plan—that and dropping the Basis of Union.

I had forgotten everything I might have said at the

meeting, but the following passage clears up two things: first, Dr. McGiffert's reference to some plan to adopt the Basis of Union and then make it a dead letter; and second the claim that Dr. Horton later made in a letter that even Malcolm Burton favored the writing of a constitution. The following passage clears up both matters:

> One suggestion which I made along the way was that we start with the writing of the kind of Constitution which Dr. Horton promised us the future constitution would be. He had set before us a plan suggested by Dr. Goebel. This plan is typical of the Evangelical and Reformed mind. Dr. Goebel suggested that we vote the merger through on the present Basis of Union with the understanding that as soon as we elect the future General Synod the first act of that body would be to repeal all provisions of the Basis of Union except the one looking toward the setting up of a committee to write the constitution. In other words we would vote to consummate the merger with no details agreed upon in advance. Then he was generous enough (?) to suggest that the Evanston Committee be represented on the Constitution writing committee and that we proceed from there to iron out all difficulties. My answer to that was that our objections had centered very largely around the fact that the Basis of Union is too much of a "pig in a poke" as it is and also against the whole principle of a constitution as such. I emphasized that if our churches ever accept the idea of a central constitution which can be amended by General Synod and Conferences they have already accepted the principle which shall creatively determine all the rest. Dr. Horton then tried to emphasize that the constitution would relate only to the national bodies and it would be descriptive only (as the interpretations have suggested.) My rejoinder to that was that if that is the idea and if this constitution is to be just like the constitution of the present General Council, as he also promised, then the thing to do is to junk the Basis of Union entirely and appoint a committee to draw up such a constitution and present it to our churches.... But Dr. Horton reverted then to his steadfast claim that if we so much as reject the Basis of Union even technically, that the merger is off and that the Evangelical and Reformed will have nothing further to do with us.

My letter then took up the matter of a proposed motion for the General Council which we of the Evanston Meeting had already seen and had evaluated just a few days previously. This is printed as Document 9 of the Appendix. In substance it was the Comments of the Midwinter meeting and it also is the forerunner of the Oberlin interpretations, which are also in the Appendix. The following is very pertinent to both documents:

> Along this same line of suggestions offered by Dr. Horton was the matter of the proposal which we were told at our Evanston meeting had been drawn up by Dr. Frank Scribner. That proposal was the three pages of mimeographed material headed, "A Motion to be presented at the Oberlin Council." As regards that, the position of our group at the Executive Committee was that these suggestions were simply the incorporation of the interpretations which had been given out as the official "comments." If the Basis of Union had been accepted by our churches after those "comments" had been received, then, according to our understanding of it, such a motion as Dr. Scribner had suggested would be in order. But according to our understanding of it the churches have already rejected not only the Basis of Union but also these "comments" or official interpretations. So that means that the motion suggested by Dr. Scribner has already been rejected by the same churches that have rejected the Basis of Union. Dr. Blanchard, however, made a rather fiery speech in which he insisted that as chairman of his Commission he was going to make whatever report he saw fit regardless of the Executive Committee or anybody else and he promised us that he was going to make that motion.

I interrupt my narrative for a moment just to say that at Oberlin Dr. Blanchard did just about as is indicated here, but at the time of writing the above letter I did not suppose that he would. My letter continued as follows, right after the above quote:

> There was considerable discussion after that time, however, and I would not be surprised if Dr. Blanchard gave considerable afterthought to his statement of intended purpose. At the close of our discussion with the Executive Committee, four of us went to take a 10:30 P.M. train. They were, Dr. McGiffert, Dr. Hansen, Dr. Blanchard and myself and we rode together as far as Scranton and had opportunity, the three of us from the Evanston meeting, to discuss further with Dr. Blanchard. Our discussion was thoroughly amicable and it may be that Dr. Blanchard will think twice before he tries to follow up along that line.

Of course we had no way of knowing whether we had made any progress with Dr. Blanchard. Quite obviously, from a letter we now have, we made no progress whatever.

Writing to Dr. Palmer on 29 April 1948—just nine days
after our meeting with him—he said:

> The opponents persist in emphasizing certain things
> which simply do not exist anywhere. I have thought that you
> might like to have a brief statement of the situation as I see it
> to date.
> The effect of the voting in the churches, with a result of
> obtaining less than seventy-five percent approval, has been,
> unfortunately, enough to convince a great many of the sup-
> porters of the plan that it has been defeated. In a recent meet-
> ing of the Executive Committee at Buck Hill Falls several of
> these individuals gave expression to their feeling in what was
> virtually a surrender of their hope and the belief that nothing
> could fairly be done at Oberlin. In the line of this conclusion
> the Executive Committee decided to recommend putting off
> decision at Oberlin without any clear indication of what
> should next be done. (See Document 15 in the Appendix.)

Dr. Blanchard then went on to write of a letter to Dr.
Goebel—which we do not have—and wondered whether Dr.
Goebel would feel inclined to accept the proposal therein
or to say the Evangelical and Reformed Church would
quit.

Most significant, perhaps, in this letter are Dr. Blanchard's total inability to grasp the real issues involved in
the plan he was promoting, and also the fact that he
seems to show not the slightest sense of concern over the
issue of breaking faith with the churches in regard to the
75 percent recommendations set forth in the procedures
which his commission had prepared and had caused to be
printed with the Basis of Union.

I said earlier in this book that it seemed to me that
neither Dr. Blanchard nor Dr. Palmer had the type of
minds which could visualize and understand the structural implications of the Basis of Union. When he said, as
above, that "the opponents persist in emphasizing things
which simply do not exist anywhere," he demonstrated
what I meant. The United Church today is living proof
that we were right all along.

As for his seeming indifference to the question of good
faith on the voting procedures, I find this nothing short of
shocking. It is ample grounds for a claim that the whole
proposition was promoted by a misrepresentation so seri-

ous as to make invalid all claims of the churches having approved the Basis of Union, or the plan which it envisioned.

As for the many dire predictions as to what would happen to Congregationalism if the Basis of Union were sidetracked at Oberlin, as set forth in letters of Dr. Horton, Dr. Truman Douglass, and Dr. Scotford—which the reader is urged to read in the appendix—no other documents or letters of the time seem to reflect this near hysteria.

One of the papers before the Executive Committee at Buck Hill Falls was one referred to as the "Connecticut Group" and listed as Appendix E to the Executive Committee minutes. (See document 10 in the appendix.) Far from being alarmed at holding back on the Basis of Union, this group of six promerger ministers urged not only that the Basis of Union be resubmitted to a joint committee of the Evangelical and Reformed and Congregational Christian churches but that other denominations be invited to "send official representatives to participate in the discussions." Those signing the statement were Russell J. Clinchy (then ardently promerger), James F. English (State Superintendent), Theodore Greene (who at Oberlin shortly afterward was one of the most extreme promerger speakers), Harold G. King, Elden H. Mills, and Rockwell Harmon Potter (former pastor of Center Church, and former Dean of Hartford Seminary; also a former moderator of the National Council.)

Space does not here permit the printing of the letters received by Dr. Palmer in response to his suggestion of a Bill of Rights and of starting *de novo* by holding back on the Basis of Union and seeking a new approach. These replies are in the Palmer file of letters in the Congregational Library. None of them took the attitude of alarm as expressed by Dr. Horton and Dr. Truman Douglass, and without exception they seemed generally favorable to Dr. Palmer's idea of a bill of rights.

Douglas Horton's insistence that nothing be done at Oberlin to side-track the Basis of Union was certainly not shared widely in the denomination. Dr. Horton, however, may have known that the whole merger proposal was shaky. He may, in his heart of hearts, have recognized the

Basis of Union as a lot of double-talk, meaning one set of propositions to the Evangelical and Reformed people and something quite contrary to most of the Congregational Christian constituency. He, and possibly the top leaders of the Evangelical and Reformed Church as well, may have realized that any plan to hold back, or to resubmit the plan, or to seek a new plan would merely "let the cat out of the bag." People sure of their ground, and confident that they have nothing to fear from the truth can always afford to wait until all aspects of the proposals have been genuinely and fully explored. The touchiness of the Evangelical and Reformed leaders over the January comments, their refusal to let the General Council make them a condition to its vote, and the spectacle of Congregationalists being swept off their feet by these same comments as though they banished all misunderstandings, was certainly enough to show that something was wrong.

Such then is the setting for the Oberlin Council.

——— 12 ———

The Oberlin Council of 1948

Wᴇ have mentioned before that no clear announcement was ever made to the churches that certain actions of great import to them either would happen or even that they could happen. Unlike annual meetings of local churches, the Oberlin Council did not limit itself to matters specifically mentioned in the call to the meeting. In fact the churches had been given precisely the wrong impression by the announcement of the Executive Committee's recommendation that no definitive action be taken. (See Documents 13 and 14, in the Appendix.)

As at Grinnell, when everyone was led to believe that only routine matters on writing a "supplement" to the Basis of Union were scheduled for action, the delegates were taken by surprise after they arrived and subjected to well-planned propaganda and pressure tactics to sweep them off their feet.

Secrecy and surprise were deliberate and intentional. On May 7 Douglas Horton wrote to Dr. Palmer: "In great confidence may I say that the Commission is now proposing to lay the enclosed motion before the Council . . . " (Appendix Document 26) And Dr. Blanchard, in a long letter on June 1 to Dr. Palmer, said first: "May I suggest that you do not speak to anybody about this plan." Later in the same letter: "It is however, at this time exceedingly important not to give to those who are so violently in opposition an outline of what we shall propose." No matter that the plans then were far less harmful than what was finally put through at Oberlin, the spirit and the method followed by the leaders is significant. Since the Oberlin action, as finally rammed through, meant "selling the denomination" to a new, different body, transferring over $60,000,000 in assets, the procedure of secrecy was contrary to legal practice in business, church, or the body politic. Yet at Oberlin many claimed that the "Holy Spirit" had descended on them and made them do it!

As late as 8 June 1948, Dr. Arthur Cushman McGiffert, Jr., wrote to other members of the Evanston group:

> At the present writing we have reason to believe that plans are being made by the pros to secure certain action on the floor. We have no information to date as to what these plans may be. *Any information you can secure to help us estimate the situation will be appreciated.*

The Council meeting itself started out harmlessly. The minutes, after recording routine opening business, state: "The Moderator called the General Council into session and the Rev. Douglas Horton, Minister and Secretary of the General Council, gave an address on the subject, 'The Next Emphasis.'" Despite its topic, and the imminent actions on the merger, nothing was included that would indicate what was coming. Dr. Scotford, in Daily Advance, summarized the address thus:

> Dr. Horton made a powerful appeal to the people and churches of the Congregational Christian Fellowship for a strengthening of Christian stewardship and the implementation of the spiritual emphasis through the next Biennium.... (No tip-off there!)

Following immediately after Dr. Horton's address, Rev. William E. McCormack spoke on "The Call to our Christian World Mission." Again came routine business. But then, on page 13, is this:

> The Rev. Ferdinand Q. Blanchard, Chairman of the Commission on Interchurch Relations and Christian Unity, read a message of greeting from the Mercersburg Synod of the Evangelical and Reformed Church, as follows: "The Mercersburg Synod of the Evangelical and Reformed Church, the last but not the least of the Synods to vote in favor of the merger, closing its sessions at Mercersburg, Pennsylvania, today sends greetings to the Congregational Christian Churches opening their Council tomorrow."

There followed an historical note about where they were meeting, and then this:

> ...in our favoring church union we are but echoing the spirit of such early leaders of the Reformed Church as Doctors

Schaff, Nevin, and Rauch, who did for theology and religion among the people of the Middle Atlantic States what the great theologians of the same era in the New England States did for your forebears. May the spirit of the Christ who is Lord of all direct your deliberations and decisions. . . .

Nothing wrong, we say, about fraternal greetings, but the timing could have been part of the "warming up" on the merger issue.

At 4 P.M. the moderator announced that the business sessions would be in recess until the following morning. At 5 P.M. came the first of the Council lectures on the theme "The Ecumenical Movement Crosses Jordan," by Walter Horton, never to be confused with Douglas. He was always just calm and philosophical. But still the lectures for the Council were on the ecumenical theme.

In the evening came the address of the moderator, Dr. Palmer, on "World Peace, Church Efficiency and Christian Unity." (1948 General Council Minutes, p. 80.)

Dr. Palmer had some strong words to say about peace, not only in the world but among ourselves: "If," he said, "we are resorting to coercion, political sharp practices, corrosive recriminations, any kind of dishonesty or lack of sportsmanship, now is the time to stop!"

Dr. Palmer spoke warmly for church unity, and stated his faith in the proposed union and in the leadership of both denominations, but he also insisted that the Council must allay all fears, including the:

> ... fears that this Council may disregard the seventy-five per-cent recommendation made by its Executive Committee and try to force the merger through regardless. This fear I think will soon be allayed when the Executive Committee presents its admirably conceived and worded resolution that no action either accepting or rejecting the Basis of Union be taken at this meeting. That resolution I hope will be overwhelmingly approved. (1948 General Council Minutes, p. 84)

Dr. Palmer also presented his plan for a new approach and for his Bill of Rights, in which he had this paragraph:

> 4. All organizations through which this fellowship is expressed and implemented, such as associations, conferences, councils, boards or synods must be voluntary and autonomous—subject only to the churches which create them

as vehicles of their cooperative desires and necessities. That is to say, they are to be controlled democratically from below, not by any centralized organization from above. (1948 General Council Minutes, p. 85)

If Dr. Palmer thought that this was what the Basis of Union was intended to create he should see the United Church of Christ today. As suggested before, neither he nor Dr. Blanchard seemed to have the slightest idea of what an overall constitution would make possible.

He was wrong, too, in his expectation that the Council would approve the Executive Committee recommendation of no decisive action being taken. But he probably had no knowledge of the scheming and planning which had been going on behind the scenes. Anyone reading merely the minutes of the General Council would see nothing to suggest what really happened.

Even the original motions from the Commission on Interchurch Relations were against taking definitive action at Oberlin. The Commission made both majority and minority reports. The majority report had this in it: (1948 General Council Minutes, p. 43)

> 1. MOVED, that this Council believes that the unity and peace of our fellowship is best maintained if no definitive action on the Basis of Union is taken at this meeting in Oberlin in 1948.

The majority report did, however, provide for adjourning the Oberlin Council for one year and then acting upon a whole series of suggested resolutions. This, of course, would have given the churches a chance to know what was proposed. This would meet the very serious objection that we have previously raised—namely, that the Oberlin action was taken without the slightest official warning. But the minority report went even further. It expressed the feeling that the interpretations, included in both reports, should be gone over with the Evangelical and Reformed people and also submitted with the Basis of Union for a second vote by the churches, with the provision that two years be taken before definitive action (1948 General Council Minutes, pp. 44–46).

How, then, did it happen that precipitously a vote was taken on Saturday to lay on the table the Executive

Committee's resolution, urging that no definitive action be taken? Such a motion cannot be debated, thus preventing even a discussion on this overriding question of "good faith" on the 75 percent recommendation. To get the answer one must have sources other than the official minutes of the General Council. Helpful are the issues of *Daily Advance* for the Oberlin Council, where the editor told—at times quite brashly or even boastfully—of the way that things were really done. Letters in the Palmer file are also quite revealing. We shall draw from these sources and also from vivid personal recollections as well as the report I made shortly after the meeting in my leaflet, "What Really Happened at Oberlin," and then from the Final Report of the Evanston Meeting group.

In an earlier chapter mention was made that Rev. Al Penner was made chairman of a promerger committee, at the time of the midwinter Meeting. A telegram from him to Rev. Joseph King, on June 11, asked if Finney Chapel was "AVAILABLE FOR LARGE MEETING AT 10 P.M. THURSDAY OTHERWISE JAMES BRAND HOUSE ... " Joe King, host pastor, made his church available instead. *Daily Advance* made this report on Monday, June 21:

> PROS, ANTIS HOLD NOCTURNAL MEETINGS
> The most unusual features of this Council have been the nocturnal unofficial meetings on the merger of both those who favor it and those who have opposed it (Notice the tense!) The hours have been from 9:30 on ...
> The proponents of the Merger began with a chaotic meeting on Wednesday night out of which emerged a Committee of Twelve charged with producing a workable procedure for consummating the Merger.
> On Thursday they met again with the floor of First Church full and the balcony well filled. Judge C. B. Adams of Vermont gave the group some coaching on parliamentary procedure, the first fruit of which was the speedy way in which the recommendation of the Executive Committee was laid on the table Saturday morning.

Before quoting more from this article, a few comments are in order. One, it was Ronald Bridges, a member of the Executive Committee who was not present at Buck Hill Falls, who made the motion to table the Executive Committee's recommendation. Some thought this very clever—having an Executive Committee member do the job. Others felt that it was a double-cross and an act of infamy. For me, thinking back to the trick that Ronald Bridges pulled at Grinnell to prevent the merger from being "voted then and there," it seemed as though Ronald Bridges felt that he owed it to the pros to keep them from being frustrated further.

Far more significant, however, is the callous way that Judge Adams suggested, and the "pros" accepted, the idea of brushing aside the moral issue. Congregationalists all over the country had accepted this representation of 75 percent approval as being made in good faith, by honest men who would be true to their word. The overriding consideration of good faith was firmly fixed on this matter of 75 percent approval. It was to most Congregationalists an absolute necessity that this recommendation be satisfied before the Basis of Union could be adopted. To this the "pros," after their mass meetings, showed not the slightest concern.

Two additional revelations are pertinent at this point.

Earlier we have printed Dr. Horton's letter to Dr. Palmer of May 22, just a month prior to the actions at Oberlin. Note that he said the following:

> ... Vermont is only one of several conferences that are going to push for some sort of affirmative action: the Vermont committee writes me, "ninety percent of Vermont Congregationalists would rather see our denomination split into schisms than retreat on the issue of church union" (and by that they mean *this* union).

This letter, if it does not show that Dr. Horton was collaborating with persons planning to force action at Oberlin, does at least show that he was informed of such intentions and *he shows not the slightest disapproval* of such plans—even though his signature was on the letter telling the churches of the Executive Committee's recommendation not to go ahead. If Congregationalists throughout the country had known of this type of correspondence at the time, I am sure that they would have felt that they were being double-crossed at the top level. And they might have been able to make better preparation to meet the maneuvers carried out at Oberlin. But the trick of "playing dead" just before an important meeting was an old one in certain quarters, as we have already seen.

A second revelation at this point is something I found in the notebook I prepared just before the Cadman trial in the fall of 1949. I do not remember it or when I received it. But it is significant and attests to the spirit and rationale of the Oberlin leaders (I copy from the sheet exactly, with heading):

PROPOSED MOTION

(Of the Pro-Merger Committee—June 20, 1948, presented to Inter-Church Committee by Dr. Liston Pope and Rev. Al Penner.)

Whereas the Congregational Christian Churches, the ecumenical Church and posterity should know the basis for our actions at this Council;

Whereas the Commission on Inter-Church Relations in presenting the Basis of Union recommended that the General Council vote approval of the Union if 75 percent of the Conferences, Associations, Churches and members voting had already approved the Basis of Union, but made no recommendations to the Council as to what it should do in case such a percentage was not obtained in all categories;

Whereas such recommendation is not a part of the Basis of Union and has never been approved by the General Council, but is a recommendation on procedure by the Commission, which is a body subordinate to the General Council; and

Whereas the Basis of Union contemplates no change in the status of the local churches; and

Whereas this Council recognizes its obligation to keep faith with the Commission which, under Council authority, has been negotiating with the Evangelical and Reformed Church; to keep faith with our historical traditions; to keep faith with the Evangelical and Reformed Church which has approved the Union; to keep faith with our belief in the unity of the body of Christ;

Now therefore be it resolved that this General Council is in no sense obligated by the 75 percent recommendation of the Commission on Inter-Church Relations; and

Be it resolved that this Council considers that the recommendation was unwise; and that, if adopted, it would tend to do essential violence to our obligation to keep faith, but that if rejected by this Council it would in no wise injure any Congregational Christian Church or violate any other of the Council's obligations; and

Be it further resolved that this Council therefore rejects this recommendation and that it is free to proceed in accordance with its best wisdom to act upon the Basis of Union.

I do not know of any official record of this motion, nor do I remember the source from which I got it. But I am sure that I would not have kept it, or put it in my notebook, if I had not known at the time (which is thirty years ago) where I got it and had more than reasonable assurance that it was authentic.

Whatever its authenticity, nothing could more perfectly express the overall rationale upon which the promerger majority went forward with the merger. Action speaks louder than words.

It is shocking that the idea of "keeping faith" could have been so completely subverted. The one all-pervasive question of keeping faith had to do with honoring the representations given to the churches when they voted. The above suggested resolution sounds like a whole series of rationalizations and alibis of someone who desperately wants to do something which he knows is wrong. Imagine suggesting that they should keep faith with the Commission on Interchurch Relations by repudiating the solemn representation that Commission had made!

As for the truth of such statements as the one claiming that the basis of Union "contemplates no change in the status of the local chuches," there was certainly no general agreement. In fact this is where the action was in the opposition to merger.

Let us return now to another portion of the article in *Daily Advance* about the promerger "nocturnal meetings":

> ... The majority and minority reports were read and analyzed. On Saturday night both groups met again, with Liston Pope making a remarkable speech to the pros which was distinguished by both its wit and meaning.
> Sunday was a day of mellowing discussion, with Boynton Merrill's sermon as a distinct influence towards drawing the two groups together. By afternoon it seemed desirable to call together the Commission on Interchurch Relations and Christian Unity for a try at a new and unanimous report to the Council. At the first session three representatives were invited in from the Evanston Meeting and the group which had been burning midnight electricity in First Church. The Commission itself found that it was possible for it to achieve unanimity within itself. ...

The real story in all that this article says lay in the growing mass psychology, the mob spirit, and the tremendous pressure being put on everyone to yield.

The promerger people approached the anti-group as

though this were a management-labor union dispute over a new contract. They took the attitude that we must come to an agreement sooner or later, and frequently they suggested, "This is our last offer." Some from the Evanston group fell for this line of reasoning and "settled for the best that we can get."

Dr. Boynton Merrill, who was a past master in "the art of worship," gave indeed a moving sermon on Joseph's admonition to his brothers in Egypt, "Except your brother be with you, ye shall not even see my face" (Gen. 43:3). It was a plea for the end of divisiveness, and a "finding of our brothers." But it was unmistakably a promerger sermon:

> The church is divided and distraught. These sad things are so because we are seeking to save our small life. We seem afraid to lay it down. We seem to be afraid that God is not able to lift it up again in greater strength, a unified church.

We who believed in Congregationalism, and its great creative power of intellectual freedom and honesty of thought, had grown used to the characterization of our not being willing to give up our "small things." *Above All Selfish Cares and Fears* was the title of one widely circulated promerger leaflet.

The nighttime meetings of the promerger people were essentially pep rallies at which they were told what they wanted to hear. They were also in the nature of a political caucus where strategy was planned.

By scheming to table the Executive Committee's recommendation, this caucus had prevented any discussion of the single most important issue before the Council. The issue of the 75 percent vote not having been attained was an issue that involved the honor and integrity of the leaders and of the whole Council.

A motion to table is undebatable. Usually it is made only *after* a deliberative assembly has debated an issue for a long time and has reached a stalemate. In decent parliamentary practice a motion to table is not intended to establish gag-rule. Once this matter was tabled, no one could address himself to that issue without being "out of order." Conversely, since the issue of *not* taking definitive action had been settled, it virtually meant that the Council had already decided—without debate—that it *would* take definitive action. How clever, indeed, and how expeditious were the means chosen!

I stepped in the side door of First Church for a while one night and sensed the raucous excitement, the laughter of those who "knew they had the power" to do as they pleased (in a body that was not supposed to have any such power!). I came just in time to hear Dr. Theodore Greene, of New Britain, Connecticut, tell a story:

> A flotilla of Union gunboats sailing up the Mississippi during the Civil War came around a bend in the river and found a number of Confederate boats. The Captain or Admiral in charge of the Union boats signalled for the Confederates to surrender. They did. Then someone asked, "Suppose they had not surrendered; what would you have done?" With great gusto Dr. Greene shouted the reply that was given: "I'd have blown them out of the water!"

This story fairly brought the house down in laughter and applause. Its application to our situation was obvious. I left that meeting with a chill going up my spine that I shall never forget. In some ways what I had witnessed made me think of the pep rallies that we used to have at Phillips Academy, Andover, before our final football game. I thought also of those huge crowds who shouted, "Heil Hitler," as he gave them frenzied speeches in an outdoor square. I also contemplated a lynch mob, and the way that decent citizens were sometimes carried off their feet and excited into abandoning their reason and human decency. Yet this was a church gathering, with ministers of the gospel in the majority!

I can well imagine the effectiveness of Dr. Liston Pope's address. In the brief three months that I was in the army in 1945, Dr. Pope was supply preacher for us at Second Church, New London. As good fortune would have it, I was permitted weekend leaves to return from Fort Devons for every Sunday but one. It kept me in touch with my congregation, and I could make the announcements for the week. It also gave me opportunity to hear Dr. Pope. He was always the master of gentle understatement, with its wit and sarcasm. These he used on the most serious questions. The method was especially effective in dismissing controversial questions very lightly, and often with a joke.

After the pressure from these pep rallies, and the

"deeply spiritual" impact of Dr. Merrill's sermon, it is no wonder that the Commission on Interchurch Relations was willing to meet again and to come up with a unanimous report. And—more important—the unanimous report left out both the recommendation of the earlier majority report that the action on the Basis of Union be put off for a year, and also the minority report's urging that the Council wait two years.

One small part of my leaflet *What Really Happened at Oberlin* might be compared to the article already quoted from *Daily Advance*. It describes much of the same story, but tells it as I saw it:

GOVERNING FACTORS

The theme-song of the Oberlin Council was "the will of the majority." From the moment that the Council convened, that is all we heard. How this so-called majority was obtained, what its proper place might be in a fellowship of free and independent churches, and what limitations exist in the nature of our General Council were never mentioned. The only consideration was how the "will of the majority" could get its way.

Even this was something of a relief to us who had been nauseated at Grinnell by the ever reiterated claim that this union was The Will of God. We'd much rather the blame for it fell upon a wilful majority.

The strategy through which this will for action developed was a series of evening meetings, where the pro-merger forces met nightly to plan their attack. The beautiful and convenient edifice of First Church had been reserved for this purpose, and a series of rousing speakers were presented to tell the pro-merger forces what they wanted to hear. No magnanimity toward the opposition was shown, no desire to get down to fundamentals or discuss the real issues at stake, no Christian effort at a genuine meeting of minds; only a succession of "hireling prophets" who tried to convince this majority that it had a right to do what, in its heart of hearts, it knew to be a breach of faith.

We are supposed to believe that these meetings came about through the mere action of individuals, expressing their individual initiative in true Congregational spirit. No questions were asked as to the planning for these meetings, or the possible collaboration of Dr. Horton or other administration leaders. That here a political machinery, foreign to Congregationalism, was proving its power is certainly suggested by John Scotford's frank label for it—"the pro-merger caucus."

This leaflet was written about two months after the

events at Oberlin, and actually represented a second attempt. My first draft I decided as "too hot to handle." I had a grandfather who, I was told, insisted that he never lost his temper. His was only "righteous indignation." In this case the same could be said for me!

JUST WHAT DID OBERLIN DELEGATES TRY TO ACCOMPLISH?

The first thing which the Oberlin delegates tried to do was to incorporate the interpretations, pretty much as they had been adopted by the midwinter meeting, into an "official" action of the Council. This is evident by the fact that the interpretations were included from the start as part of both majority and minority reports.

The Evanston Committee had attacked the Comments as not being official, but only the opinion of individuals at the midwinter meeting. The delegates had *not* been told that the Evangelical and Reformed leaders had objected as early as February to the adoption of *any* interpretations on the grounds that the Basis of Union was the *only* official document before both groups. Nor had the delegates been warned—as Dr. Horton had warned some of his friends in letters—that the Evangelical and Reformed Church would refuse to vote again and would drop the union if asked to make any more concessions, or to resubmit the plan to their synods.

The major part of the debate at Oberlin was over the wording of the resolution intended to make the interpretations "official" and also over the timing for adopting the Basis of Union. As we noted, the majority report advocated waiting one year, with the idea of adopting the Interpretations and giving the churches one more year to bring the vote up to 75 percent. The minority report, however, suggested adoption of the interpretations and then of waiting two years, during which the Evangelical and Reformed and the Congregational Christian churches would vote again on basis of Union with Interpretations. (This latter, as we know from his letters, is something that Dr. Horton was dead set against, since he was sure that the Evangelical and Reformed would refuse to go along and would just drop the merger.)

As far as some in the opposition were concerned, the

whole procedure was a case of "tweedle-dum and tweedle-dee," because the interpretations did not get down to the basics, and they did not change the fundamental character of the Basis of Union. As we have indicated frequently in earlier chapters, the Basis of Union itself never came before the Council for discussion. Procedural matters preempted the floor at all times. Adoption of the Basis of Union was finally slipped into the middle of a very long resolution, and was preceded by the Interpretations, a number of "whereases" that sought to justify the Council "voting for itself"; and then after the paragraph adopting the Basis of Union came a whole set of provisions for future steps to be taken.

But before the vote could be taken, the promerger caucus, the pep rallies, and a lot of individual persuasion had to be exerted to get the steamroller going with sufficient ruthlessness to create a truly impressive stampede. After that nothing would matter—not even a traumatic setback that would have brought an average Council session to its senses.

There was an unbelievable amount of pressure being exerted upon individual antis to get them to change their minds. During those hectic days, "committees" came down to the pool room to which the Evanston meeting had been assigned, trying to get agreement to a late revision of official plans. Sometimes a few from the Evanston meeting were invited in on the sessions of the Commission in Interchurch Relations. Rumors spread thick and fast about this person or that having been "won over."

An amusing incident will help to illustrate the point. One noon, for what reason I cannot recall, Rev. Eugene Bushong invited me to come over with him for lunch. He was on the Board of Home Missions, and its members had a meeting place together for lunch. I protested that I would be out of place there and that people might resent my being there. But he said that it would be perfectly all right and no one would think anything of it. So I went. Immediately I was aware that furtive glances were being made continually in my direction. Gene and I had some personal matter to discuss that was not connected with the merger. But after lunch, and through the afternoon, I was accosted with the question, "Is it true that you have changed over?"

After the pep rallies had done their work, the Commission found, as Dr. Scotford wrote, that it could come in with a unanimous report. As we noted, it left out the previous conditions that would have delayed for either one or two years the actual approving of the Basis of Union. Instead it provided that approval would be voted but that implementation of the provisions of the Basis of Union would be put off until after 1 January 1949. Meanwhile a renewed effort would be made to get nonassenting churches to vote yes and a Committee of Fifteen would be appointed to "get the vote." In case of failure, another Council would meet.

Putting the above "compromise" together was hailed as a great achievement, and the claim that many antis had been won over was added "proof" that the Holy Spirit was at work and that the Council's vote would be a truly blest event.

There was one more hurdle, however, that the Council did not anticipate. The whole idea of the interpretations was that they would be some kind of "condition" to the adoption of the Basis of Union, and that the Basis of Union would have to be interpreted in the way officially voted by the Council. This was necessary if they were to be convincing to the churches.

Page 19 of the 1948 minutes records seven votes of the Council as it ploddingly approved separate paragraphs of the new unanimous report of the Commission, which was now labeled the Walton Report. Dr. Walton had headed the minority report previously, but using his name for the new report was like saying that the antis now favored it. (Significantly, Dr. Walton later stayed out of the United Church of Christ.)

Suddenly something quite dramatic happened. The minutes obviously have a mistake in the wording of the paragraph in question, because nothing would make sense the way it stands and *Daily Advance* published the entire text and has it correct. The paragraph in question read (as printed in *Daily Advance*, June 21):

BE IT RESOLVED THAT THE GENERAL COUNCIL APPROVE THE BASIS OF UNION and makes the following provisions for its future implementation: (Note: the minutes had this paragraph start, "Whereas the Basis of Union provides . . . "—this could not fit with the next two entries in the minutes.)

At this point Judge Adams moved to put a period after "Basis of Union" and strike out the rest of the paragraph, speaking of "implementation."

Then Dr. Fred Meek moved to amend Judge Adams' amendment by adding the words "with the foregoing interpretations" after the words "approves the Basis of Union" (this is taken exactly from the 1948 General Council Minutes, p. 20).

The minutes then record that Dr. Meek's amendment to Judge Adams' motion was voted, and finally Judge Adams' amended resolution was also voted—with three dissenting votes recorded.

Then, according to the minutes, the moderator called on Dr. Louis W. Goebel, president of the Evangelical and Reformed Church who:

> . . . brought words of greeting. Dr. Goebel explained, however, that in his judgment the Council's action in passing the above amendment would make it necessary for the General Synod and the local synods of the Evangelical and Reformed Church to act again on the Basis of Union and the included interpretations, thus postponing formal action for some years.

A motion was then made to recommit the report to the Commission for further revision and action at a later time. This motion, however, was withdrawn, although its purpose was soon carried out.

Judge Adams then asked the Council to reconsider its motion (which he had made but which had been amended by Dr. Meek's motion). This was done. Then Judge Adams moved to strike out the words that Dr. Meek had added. But since time was running out, it was agreed to recess and make consideration of the Walton Report the first business of the day on the following morning. Much transpired before the following day. And far more was involved in what we have already recorded than the cold minutes and recitation of votes taken could possibly indicate.

The promerger majority had been lifted up to "seventh heaven" when the vote approving the Basis of Union was taken. Then suddenly they were dashed to the ground and left bewildered, confused and apprehensive that everything was lost. Dr. Max Strang refers in his memorandum (Document 29 in the Appendix) to the reporter for the *Cleveland Plain Dealer* having said that the delegates were "stunned" by Dr. Goebel's words.

In order to get a clear picture of the power politics being employed and the "wheeler-dealer approach" being used, let me go back one day and quote from the Final Report of the Evanston Meeting, prepared June 24, 1948— one day after the Council meeting. This report validates my previous claim that the promerger caucus was responsible for eliminating from the report of the Interchurch Commission any thought of postponing action for a year or of respecting the 75 percent recommendation about voting. It also would indicate that the proposed "motion," from Dr. Pope and Dr. Penner was authentic, and that it was presented to the Interchurch Commission on Sunday—the day before the Commission came in with its first unanimous report.

Members of the Evanston Meeting learned on Sunday that the Interchurch Commission was at work making the effort to agree on a unanimous report to present to the Council on Monday. Several Evanston Meeting members were asked by several members of the proponents' Steering Committee to go with them to the Interchurch Commission late in the afternoon when these proponents would tell the Commission of their plans for action on Monday. The representatives of the proponents said they had the power, because of the many delegates they represented, to secure the action they desired at the Council...

We interrupt the quotation to emphasize that here was a virtual ultimatum from the "caucus" that its members and leaders were prepared to take matters into their own hands. Note what follows—from that motion we quoted earlier. Only the last half of the motion was included in the Evanston Meeting report:

They read a statement of which the following is a part: "Whereas this Council recognizes its obligation to keep faith with the Commission which, under Council authority, has been negotiating with the Evangelical and Reformed Church;..." Then follows all the rest of the resolution, down through: "now therefore be it resolved that this General Council is in no sense obligated by the 75 percent recommendation of the

Commission on Interchurch Relations, and be it resolved that
this Council considers that the recommendation was unwise
and that, if adopted, it would tend to do essential violence to
our obligation to keep faith, but if rejected by this Council it
would in no wise injure any Congregational Christian Church
or violate any other of the Council's obligations; and be it
further resolved that this Council therefore rejects this recommendation and that it is free to proceed in accordance
with its best wisdom to act upon the Basis of Union." The
Evanston Meeting representatives indicated they would resist
this, knowing that this action, if adopted by the Council, would
divide our fellowship of churches.

At this point it might be appropriate to mention that
all through the merger discussion we had been told that
"we must trust our leaders." Just how much, in the light
of the above, can church people, at large, really trust their
leaders and the representations they solemnly make?

The Evanston Meeting Final Report goes on to report
further negotiations Sunday night, leading to the agreement on the unanimous report to be presented on Monday
morning. It also recounts what we reported above about
the Commission's Report being amended until it read, "Be
it resolved that the General Council approves the Basis of
Union with the foregoing interpretations." The report tells
also of Dr. Goebel being called upon to speak, and then
this: "The Council, after hearing his statement, voted to
reconsider its action and adjourned."

I was not one of the representatives of the Evanston
Meeting who met with any of the negotiators, and so my
account must fall back again on the Final Report of the
Evanston Meeting, from which we have just been quoting.
Continuing right after the above quotation:

> The Evanston Meeting members met for five hours on
> Monday night. The Interchurch Commission was meeting up-
> stairs in the same building. The Evanston Meeting and the
> Commission were laboring to see if there was some satisfac-
> tory way of meeting the difficulty pointed out by Dr. Goebel to
> the Council at its morning session. Apparently a phrase to the
> effect that the interpretations of the Basis of Union in the re-
> solution before the Council would in no way alter the Basis of
> Union was satisfactory to Dr. Goebel and his advisors, one of
> whom was a lawyer. The Evanston Meeting recognized that
> now the Commission had squarely before it the responsibility
> of adhering to the requirements of the Evangelical and Re-
> formed representatives and dividing our fellowship of

churches, or of finding a way whereby our fellowship could be restrained from schism. . . .

We pause to comment that here, again, was the method of trying to find a patchwork of words that could "get by" with both groups, even though it should have been plain that there was an irreconcilable difficulty. The only point of trying to pass the Interpretations was so that Congregationalists would think that they really mattered, and that in places where there was doubt as to the meaning of the Basis of Union the Interpretations *would* alter the Basis of Union. Also, as we have noted before, the Evangelical and Reformed people were "cracking the whip" and telling the Congregationalists what they could, and could not, do. Going on now from the Evanston Meeting report:

Dr. Palmer, the Moderator, visited the Evanston Meeting in its pool room meeting place twice and Dr. Horton also undertook to consult the Evanston meeting. The Evanston Meeting members were firm in their requirement that satisfactory phrasing must be secured so that the Basis of Union would be adopted with official interpretations of the Oberlin Council. Almost at mid-night the Commission decided upon this statement: "Whereas, this General Council accepts the above interpretations as the basis on which our future action shall be taken, these interpretations being in harmony with the spirit and purpose of the Basis of Union; Be it resolved, that the General Council approves the Basis of Union." The report was sent to the printer so that copies could be available for distribution at the Council meeting Tuesday morning. The Evanston Meeting decided it would only accept this phraseology if the "Whereas" was changed to "Be it resolved"—so that the official interpretations would have the same standing as the approval of the Basis of Union.

The Council met on Tuesday at eight-thirty, and after devotions proceeded to act upon the newly revised report of the Commission, referred to as the New Walton Report. Then the Council proceeded to pick over the new report paragraph by paragraph, making little changes here and there—something that was never done with the far more important Basis of Union. I count thirteen votes on paragraphs and changes made on this New Walton Report. Finally came the vote of approval, which was estimated at 1,000 delegates in favor, to 12 opposed.

I made the last, or nearly the last speech, before the vote, in which I stressed that I did not believe the interpretations to be consistent with the Basis of Union and suggesting that, since it was so important, we postpone action to a later meeting so that the issues could be clarified. I got shouted down for that suggestion. Incidentally, I have a recording of that impromptu speech. I was lucky enough that night, sometime after midnight when almost no one was around, to run into the young person who had made the official wire recording of the proceedings. He obligingly made a copy—a wire recording—for me. He worked for the Board of Home Missions. My address, made at that time, is included in my book *Early Merger Pamphlets*, p. 199.

Again I must say that the printed reports cannot possibly convey the atmosphere, the terrific pressure, the nerved-out condition of the delegates, or the pious humbug with which the very wilful majority kidded itself into thinking that a genuine understanding had been worked out, and that the "Holy Spirit" had descended upon the Council to bring about a near miracle.

Daily Advance, for Monday, June 21, in reporting on the three hours of debate when both majority and minority reports were before the Council on Saturday, reported that "Max Strang of First Church, Dubuque, Iowa, stated that the representatives of the Evanston Meeting with whom he had been in contact were prepared to support the Walton Report." (This was when the report still called for a two-year delay, but the item shows how the delegates were led to believe that the opposition was being won over.)

I can remember how, in the final stages of consideration, Rev. Harry Butman sat on one of the high stools in the pool room (the only chairs we had) dangling his feet, looking thoughtfully at the cement floor and saying, "I think that I can live with it." That referred to the final action at Oberlin. But three months later, shocked by the action of the Evangelical and Reformed leaders in repudiating the Oberlin Interpretations, Harry Butman became one of the strong leaders of the Continuation Committee, and Max Strang was its first executive Director. (See Appendix p. 72)

The unreality of the Oberlin episode is further revealed in the fact that Dr. Goebel was called to the platform a second time—in this instance after the final vote was taken. Asked what he thought of the Oberlin action, he tried in a sort of bluffing way to pass it off lightly. He referred to the interpretations as "self-evident" and told us that he was sure that the General Council, when it met in September, would approve them. (Their General Council was to them what our Executive Committee stood for.) How wrong he was! But one must remember that he, too, had been under terrific pressure. If one wants to know how he really felt, read the memorandum that is Document 29 in the Appendix. Here, frankly recorded is the story of a chance meeting that Dr. Max Strang had with Dr. Goebel on June 23 in the Harvey Restaurant at Union Station in Chicago. This was just the day after the final action at Oberlin.

At the time of the Oberlin Council, there was less than a two-thirds' vote of approval from the churches *voting*, and less than one-half of the total number of our churches. Evanston Final Report said:

> The Basis of Union had no place at Oberlin. Nothing of its contents was discussed. The churches back home were not mentioned. No one spoke for the people. The fact of significance was that 144,221 of the 1,012,022 members had voted favorably on the Basis of Union and this 14 percent was estimated to be a "majority." The other important fact was that most of the delegates were proponents of the merger, many of them ministers, and they had the power.

The associations and conferences had voted above ninety percent for the merger, and they were the ones who, in most instances, elected the delegates. A small majority favoring the merger within an association or Conference could elect—and often did—a batch of delegates heavily stacked in favor of the merger. Thus the Los Angeles Association, the largest in the fellowship, was almost evenly divided in its vote on the merger—only about a six-vote margin, according to Henry David Gray. But the delegation elected to Oberlin was heavily promerger.

Both Dr. Horton and Dr. Scotford had begun stressing the heavy approval of conferences and associations as though this offset the failure to reach the 75 percent among the churches. Both stressed, in some of their letters, that the people who attended conferences and associations were the "best informed" and the ones who "supported the denomination." (See Dr. Horton's letter of May 24, Document 18 in the Appendix, and John Scotford's letter of April 29, Document 27 in the Appendix.)

In the Presbyterian order the presbyteries and General Assembly are looked upon as places where the local churches "vote"—*through their representatives.* But in Congregationalism the churches do not "vote" unless each has called its own meeting for that purpose. The Oberlin Council and the denominational leaders were acting as though they were Presbyterians. Their action was "outside of the law." There was no law to stop them, and no legal right to do what they did.

And so, "The approval of the Basis of Union was achieved by an impatient Council after something more than 24 hours which might be described as trying if not exasperating," said *Daily Advance* on June 23.

Also, in the words of *Daily Advance,* "Drama marked the moment of acceptance with the delegates rising to sing the Doxology . . . " What an event!

13

From Oberlin Through the 1949 Special Council

W HEN the Oberlin delegates went home, they had the feeling that everything would be easy from that point on. They were sure that most opposition was overcome, that the Oberlin Interpretations would make it easy to bring the vote of churches well up above the 75 percent mark. But just to be sure, the Oberlin Council had left the way open—in case the 75 percent approval was not reached—to go ahead with the merger anyway.

Provision was included in the Oberlin vote for a special Council to convene and to determine whether the approval by the churches warranted going ahead with the merger. Since the same delegates would comprise this new Council as had already been thoroughly committed to union at Oberlin, the results would surely be favorable for the merger.

The euphoria of the Oberlin Council did not last long before there were rude awakenings. In fact, try as they would, the Oberlin delegates never were able to get the churches to accept the rosy picture which they tried to sell.

Immediately after Oberlin the Evanston Committee sent out its "no comment," factual account. This was written partly by one who agreed to go along with the vote at Oberlin, and partly by another member of the Evanston Meeting who was still opposed. We have already quoted some of the facts which were reported in this carefully balanced report. They left room for plenty of misgivings.

By mid-August we received the first communication from the Committee of Fifteen, which tried to make the most of the Oberlin action and to paint a good picture of the whole affair, urging churches that had voted no, or had not voted, to vote yes. We quote now from "A STATEMENT ON THE UNION in the light of the Action taken at Oberlin" (pp. 4 and 5):

> There have been in the past, genuine doubts among certain of our Congregational Christian Churches as to whether significant Congregational beliefs, methods and practices would be preserved if we went forward with this Union. Therefore, the General Council has taken the progressive step of debating at length, and adopting certain "Interpretations" of the Basis of Union, which now represent its official explanation to all of our churches, of what the Basis of Union accomplishes. These are set forth in the inset paragraphs Nos. (a) through (h) of the attached "Report of the Commission," and we earnestly suggest that you read and consider them. They are in harmony with the Basis of Union, in our opinion, and leave our individual churches in a position to maintain their work and their standing in the same manner in the proposed new United Church of Christ, as is their status at present.

Note the ever-recurring claim that the local churches would be left in a position to maintain their work in the same manner as "is their status at present."

This statement from the Committee of Fifteen went on to say that the General Council came to its approval of the Basis of Union with remarkable unanimity and also to suggest that there was now almost no opposition to the merger. We quote again:

> In other words, the membership of the Council, which had its diverse opinions on this subject when it convened, by the time of adjournment had reached a place of splendid and substantial unity of feeling that we have it within our power to make a great forward step for the denomination. The largest group which had opposed the union voted formally to disband and to terminate its efforts, feeling that in the adoption of the "Interpretations," it had fairly safeguarded the principles for which it stood.

This last statement was hardly an accurate account of the vote by the Evanston Meeting to disband. The group as a body certainly did not feel that it "had fairly safeguarded the principles for which it stood." The argument used by those who favored disbanding was that "we organized for the purpose of preventing the adoption of the Basis of Union. Now that the Basis of Union had been adopted, it is not fair to hold any of our members to carry on further objectives." This paraphrase of the argument is a far cry from the claim that the Evanston Meeting as a whole felt that its objectives had been attained. As indicated in plain language in the Final Report of the Evanston Meeting, we recognized that each person was to act as an individual in true Congregational fashion, and was not bound by any action of the group.

The statement of the Committee of Fifteen went on to declare that:

> This Committee knows of no further organized opposition to the basis of Union, in existence at this time.

This statement reached me while vacationing in New Hampshire. It was highly disturbing, so much so that we packed up and went home immediately. It was then that I wrote, *What Really Happened at Oberlin* and a companion leaflet. Organized or not, there was plenty of opposition left to the Basis of Union and the way in which it had been handled.

My leaflets were mailed out early in September. Almost at once I had reactions. Dr. James W. Fifield, Jr., phoned me from Los Angeles and asked that I have my leaflets reprinted and send him six thousand of each. Immediately he set about calling persons in many states to serve on a national Anti-Merger committee. Three publications called "Anti-Merger" were published before the meeting in February of the special meeting of the General Council. In January "Anti-Merger" changed its name to the Committee for the Continuation of the Congregational Christian Churches in the United States.

In the years which followed many people forgot that the Evanston Meeting group had "disbanded," for, as Dr. Neil Hansen used to say to me, "We are still the same group." There were new faces, to be sure, and some of the former ones were missing. But on the whole the opposition never accepted the forced solution attempted at Oberlin.

Meanwhile the Evangelical and Reformed Church leaders took action that made a mockery of what Oberlin had claimed to accomplish. This action taken at the meeting of the Evangelical and Reformed General Council (its executive committee) on September 28–29 brought an instant request from the Congregational Christian Executive Committee that the action be kept secret until the two executive committees could get together and try to thrash things out.

I received an anonymous phone call, which went like this:

"Have you heard what the Evangelical and Reformed General Council did recently?"
"No," I said. "Dr. Goebel said at Oberlin that they would undoubtedly approve the Interpretations."
"Well, they have done just the opposite. Do you have a pencil?"

My caller then dictated to me very carefully the following:

The General Council of the Evangelical and Reformed Church recognizes the right and privilege of the General Council of the Congregational Christian Churches to interpret the Basis of Union according to its own understanding. The Evangelical and Reformed Church, however, interprets the adoption of these interpretations as not binding it or the United Church to any traditional polity for the present or for the future.

I asked my caller if he was Mr. Fiero (of our Executive Committee). He laughed and gave me a facetious reply. I felt confident the information was reliable, as was later proved to be true. The following day I received in the mail a small slip of paper with the same wording typed on it.

As soon as possible, I went to the post office and purchased 5,000 postcards. I asked my printer to do a rush job for me. Then we found twenty ladies in our church who would do addressing in a hurry. We cut the names and addresses of the ministers out of the back of the Year Book and divided the sheets among our volunteers. Within twenty-four hours after I purchased the one-cent postcards, we had mailed out a "Newsflash" to all the Congregational Christian ministers giving them the text of what I had learned over the phone.

This proved to be the most effective single piece of printed material we ever sent out. Ministers began calling their state conference offices and the leaders of the General Council. They were not able to get either confirmation or outright denial of the truth of what we had sent out. But voting to approve the Basis of Union with Interpretations came to a virtual standstill.

Probably many state conference officers did not know anything about the Evangelical and Reformed action, because the Executive Committee of the General Council, upon learning of the action, asked the Evangelical and Reformed General Council to suppress news of its action and wait until the two groups could get together to go over everything once more. Executive Committee members were likewise asked to observe secrecy. Here was the effort for a complete cover-up. By this time the Executive Committee had become "stacked" with more and more promerger members. But one member saw no reason why he should suppress truth of this sort.

Adding to the nationwide confusion, a letter had gone from General Council offices containing an outright falsehood. Under a date of 7 October 1948, a letter from the Committee of Fifteen went out with this paragraph:

> 2. Do the Interpretations actually have no significance because they have not been accepted by the other contracting party? Answer: The Evangelical and Reformed Church voted on the Basis of Union before the Interpretations were before our fellowship. They have since had notice of our action. Their leaders have asserted that they find nothing in the Interpretations contrary to their understanding of the Basis of Union. They have indicated no need for re-reference and we do not anticipate such action. We believe their view coincides with ours that, in the language of the Council, the Interpretations are "in harmony with the spirit and purpose of the Basis of Union."

The letter was signed by David K. Ford as chairman, and Arthur S. Wheelock as Executive Dirctor of the Committee of Fifteen.

During the Cadman Church trial, a little more than a year later, Arthur Wheelock was on the witness stand testifying in regard to this letter. At first he claimed that he did not know about this action of the Evangelical and Reformed Church before the letter of October 7 went out. But after the minutes for the Congregational Christian Executive Committee meeting of October 5 were introduced into evidence, showing that Mr. Wheelock was present when the Evangelical and Reformed action was discussed, he admitted that he knew but "it wasn't 'official' yet." Justice Steinbrink asked Mr. Wheelock if he could not have stopped the mailing of the letter. But the answer was that the Evangelical and Reformed action wasn't "official" yet because they had agreed to a reconsideration of it in a joint meeting with the Congregational Christian committee. The judge was furious!

All through the merger discussions we had been confronted by "official" answers to almost every allegation that we made. Dr. Bradshaw was wont to quote a certain Scandinavian bishop as saying, "Nothing, nothing, nothing is so absolutely repugnant in the sight of Almighty God as everything that is 'official'!"

Needless to say, confusion was worse confounded when the ministers and church people received our "Newsflash" postcard, following almost immediately the letter from the Committee of Fifteen saying that there was such mutual feeling and understanding. Persons writing to Dr. Horton were likely to receive, as I did, a reply saying, "Let's wait until after November 10," which was the date for the joint meeting.

When it came, the joint meeting was something of a rerun of previous attempts to patch up a statement that would gloss over the difficulties without ever getting down to specific details as to who meant what in regard to any parts of the Basis of Union or the Interpretations. Meeting first by themselves, the Evangelical and Reformed leaders voted to reaffirm their previous action. Then came the hassle with the Congregational Christian leaders and the final agreement of the Evangelical and Reformed people to rescind their previous statement and to agree to submit the interpretations to their synods and General Synod—but only *after* the Congregational Christian people voted to go on. As Dr. Goebel put it, "You get your 75 percent vote and then bring it to us on a platter; or your vote of the General Council. Then we will submit the interpretations to our Synods for approval."

THE NOVEMBER TENTH JOINT MEETING AT
CLEVELAND

Fortunately, an informal record of the joint meeting

was kept, and it later showed up at the Cadman trial, was accepted into evidence, and is printed in the Record on pages 2708 through 2727. Dr. Frederick L. Fagley had been taking minutes for our Executive Committee for some time. He was not officially appointed to be scribe for the Joint Session, but he took copious notes for himself, as he told me later.

Actually Dr. Fagley did not anticipate these notes becoming public. He said to me that he did not expect anyone to see them for possibly twenty-five years. But Mr. Fiero told me that he asked for a copy and was told that he would have to ask Dr. Horton. On the witness stand in the Cadman trial Mr. Fiero testified that he wrote to Dr. Horton asking for a copy of these notes and that they were then sent to him from our denominational headquarters. I have often wondered just what happened. Did a secretary send them when Horton was out of town? Or could Dr. Horton have thought that they were not important, or that Mr. Fiero would keep them secret? We shall probably never know. Dr. Fagley, himself, was surprised that Mr. Fiero got them.

At any rate they are very revealing, and their authenticity was attested to in court by Mr. Fiero and, begrudgingly, by Arthur Wheelock, at least in part. In January, I printed about half of this document in a leaflet entitled *Facts Our Members Ought to Know*. It was probably sent to ministers and church clerks.

When the leaders of the two denominations met, nobody got down to "brass tacks" or tried to pinpoint just what the interpretations meant or where they differed from the Basis of Union. Only generalizations were made, or statements summarizing individual reactions.

The real point of the meeting was to put pressure on the Evangelical and Reformed General Council to rescind its September motion so that the Committee of Fifteen could "get the vote" among Congregationalists, to bring it up to the "necessary" 75 percent approval.

The person to lead off the discussion, as reported now by Dr. Fagley, was Douglas Horton (p. 2708):

> Mr. Horton presented a brief review of the Oberlin action, appointment of the Committee of Fifteen and its work. He read a postcard circulated by the Reverend Malcolm K. Burton and also a letter of October 20 signed by Mr. S. D. [T.]

Roberts, as evidence of the spirit and method of the opposition in the Congregational Churches. He said ... that the interpretations adopted at Oberlin were not amendments but are, as stated, interpretations in harmony with the spirit and purpose of the Basis of Union.

Dr. Goebel, president of the Evangelical and Reformed Church, was the next scheduled to speak:

Mr. Goebel stated that he desired greatly this union and that he was persuaded that the Congregational Christian Churches are as ecumenically minded as are the Evangelical and Reformed. In his judgment the interpretations are for the purpose of clarification and if that view prevailed, then the road was clear, but that it was becoming evident that the interpretations were being considered as more than explanatory. If that view prevailed, then the Evangelical and Reformed Church said "no."

He himself thought that the interpretations were validated in the Basis of Union, but that others did not so think. It has become evident that some Congregational Christians considered the interpretations not as clarification but as amendments. If the interpretations are considered only as a means of clarification, the way would be clear but if not then the matter must be resubmitted to the Evangelical and Reformed Church. Mr. Goebel believed that if the United Church of Christ is to be, it must have a polity so flexible as to permit the inclusion of elements of church government of the Reformed, the Presbyterian, the Episcopal or the Congregational. If for any reason this union fails, there will be serious effects on the Evangelical and Reformed Church.

We pause to comment that Dr. Goebel's statement about the United Church's being flexible enough to combine all sorts of church government was in direct conflict with the impression being conveyed to the Congregationalists, who were being assured that the interpretations were one more proof that the union would be congregational. Several times later Dr. Goebel was quoted as saying that they would not be "swallowed up in Congregationalism." Yet the joint meeting went on without apparent protest from Congregationalists, who had been promising the very thing which Dr. Goebel so clearly renounced; and who had denied the specific suggestions of Presbyterian elements that Dr. Goebel affirmed as a necessary free choice. Apparently nobody insisted on knowing the *fundamental* polity.

Dr. George W. Richards was next to speak and reemphasized the main points that Dr. Goebel had made:

> Mr. Richards thought that there ought to be a way found to avoid sending the interpretations to the Synods. The Congregational Christian Churches had gone a long way towards making this necessary, but that perhaps a way yet could be found.
> The Evangelical and Reformed Church does not want to bind either side so that the United Church of Christ would be free to plan its future. The backgrounds of the two bodies should be studied.

It would seem rather late to be suggesting that the backgrounds of the two denominations should be studied. Later Dr. Richards said, "It should be made perfectly clear that the Evangelical and Reformed Church is not to be bound" (p. 2712).

And Dr. Goebel reiterated, "We do not intend to be swallowed up in Congregationalism" (p. 2715).

When Wendell Fifield said, "Our people think that the Evangelical and Reformed Church in repudiating the interpretations have repudiated the meaning of the Basis of Union," Dr. Goebel replied, "Do you want the Evangelical and Reformed Church to come into the Congregational Christian Churches?" To this Dr. Fifield replied, "We do not want the Evangelical and Reformed Church to say one thing and we another."

It seems that after a break for lunch, the two groups met separately and then came back with prepared statements which we do not have (listed as D and E).

Dr. Goebel, however, summarized the Congregational statement thus:

> The statement presented by the Congregational group simply sets forth what action was taken at Oberlin. It says the Congregational Christian Churches enter through one door, the Basis of Union plus the interpretations; the Evangelical and Reformed Church enters through another door, the Basis of Union only . . .

This is where Dr. Goebel suggested:

> . . . go ahead and get your 75 percent on the Basis of Union plus the interpretations and then take a platter. Put the Basis

of Union on it and the interpretations and the statement that
you have your 75 percent approval and present it to us. Then
we will go to our churches and ask them if they are willing to
go in on that basis. We will take no move until you get your 75
percent.

At this point Dr. James E. Wagner protested that "we
are trying to . . . live by a double standard of morals."

But apparently Dr. Richards saw something else in
the Congregational statement:

I like the honesty of this report from the Congregational
Christian Churches. Now we know what you want. We never
knew before. Now we are able to proceed. We must submit the
new statement to the General Synod. All we can do today is to
say that when you have your offer ready, we will submit it to
the Synod as soon as possible.

There was still—and the same was true throughout—
no statement on just what differences there were between
the interpretations and the Basis of Union. But a little
later Dr. Horton protested: "But the interpretations do
not present any fundamental differences." (p. 2720)

To this Dr. Richards replied: "That is where we differ
with you, and it will not do to minimize the differences of
opinion for now we know where we stand."

A little earlier Dr. Wagner had said (p. 2713):

The crux of the whole matter is: can we bring these two
groups, so widely separated in tradition, together? We are
traditionally Presbyterian, yet both churches and ministers
enjoy full freedom. The troubles we now face are due to the
fact that our leaders have so much zeal for union that the difficulties in the way were minimized. In my judgment the interpretations do make a difference.

I believe that every element of Congregationalism is present in the Basis of Union and that the Basis of Union is 95
percent Congregational. Yet each side protests. The Basis of
Union is a masterpiece not of ambiguity but of straight thinking. Now, if to the Basis of Union, weighted so heavily in behalf of Congregational principles, the interpretations are added, this throws an additional weight in favor of Congregationalism. This is a serious situation.

May I interject here that I cannot see how anyone in
his right mind could have said that the Basis of Union was
95 percent Congregational when it called for an overall

constitution, a national unitary church instead of our "churches," and its system of judicatories. Nor can I believe that Dr. Fagley failed to comprehend correctly the import of Dr. Wagner's words.

One of the purposes of this book has been to show how uniformly the Congregational Christian people were assured that the union would be congregational. We were told on other occasions that the Evangelical and Reformed leaders were insisting that it would be 95 percent Congregational. This means that they, too, were implicated in that representation. To me it always seemed a grievous misrepresentation. But the above passages certainly help to sustain my main contention that the Congregational Churches were led into the union on the assurance that the merger would be congregational.

Would it be improper at this point to mention how, eight years later, this same Dr. Wagner, then president of the Evangelical and Reformed Church, addressed our 1956 General Council in the following words:

> To my own people I have recently been saying, "It cannot inaccurately be said that the United Church of Christ will have a presbyterian structure depending on the congregational spirit of free and voluntary co-operation for its implementation?

Returning now to the joint meeting on 10 November 1948, mention should be made of numerous other people and their comments.

Rev. Wendell Fifield "stated ... the condition that is in the Congregational Christian Churches at present. He said that the problem is very much more serious than many of us realize." He further indicated that because of the interpretations the argument is being made "that something has been added or changed." (pp. 2711 and 2712)

Rev. Gerhard W. Grauer of Evangelical and Reformed Church said that "the Evangelical and Reformed Church is for union on the Basis of Union without reservations, but that he would like to ask this question. How can we write a constitution if we cannot write a Basis of Union?" (pp. 2712–13)

Rev. Edward A. Thompson of the Congregational Christian Churches mentioned that "the Oberlin Council approved the interpretations on an understanding that they have been approved by Dr. Goebel and his attorney, acting on behalf of the Evangelical and Reformed Church. The action of the Committee of Fifteen was worked out on that basis, but now the Evangelical and Reformed Church representatives tell us they do not approve."

Later Rev. A. C. McGiffert, Jr., raised the same question. Dr. Goebel in reply said that he had put forth the proposition at Oberlin "that the Evangelical and Reformed group would agree to any interpretations 'that did not add to or subtract from, that is do not alter the Basis of Union' " (p. 2719).

Miss Helen Kenyon, now the Congregational Christian moderator, said: "Yes, we voted for the Basis of Union and interpretations, and we now are on the verge of losing the union, yet we want the union. There are 1,000 delegates who want this union." To which Dr. Goebel replied, "I feel as you do. I was elated by the spirit at Oberlin" (p. 2722).

Dr. Alfred Grant Walton, who initiated the comments and the Oberlin interpretations said:

> I helped form the interpretations and also advocated their adoption. Since then in spite of the interpretations a tremendous amount of confusion has developed, far more serious than anyone would have expected.
>
> Congregational Christian Churches are hopelessly divided. The denomination is too weak to join with anyone. We hold the destiny of the 300 year old Congregational Christian Churches in our hands. If necessary, we should resubmit, even if it takes three years. (pp. 2714 and 2715)

Dr. Ronald Bridges, a former Congregational Christian moderator, said:

> There are three alternatives—One, decline further negotiations between the two denominations until we of the Congregational Christian Churches have gained solidarity. Second, go forward with the Committee of Fifteen and the Evangelical and Reformed Church wait for further consideration of the situation until we get the 75 percent. Third, start all over again.

Rev. Paul Schroeder, pastor of the largest Evangelical and Reformed church and a member of the committee which drew up the Basis of Union, spoke out forcefully at least six times. He viewed the interpretations as making the union congregational and predicted the Evangelical and Reformed synods would not approve. At one point he urged:

> I again advocate laying aside of the Basis of Union and all documents thereto and turn the whole matter back either to the present Joint Committee or a new Committee to be constituted. (pp. 2724-5)

Dr. Palmer then "suggested that we accept the Evangelical and Reformed proposal and we proceed on that basis with the Evangelical and Reformed Church resubmitting the Basis of Union with the interpretations to the Synod." (p. 2725)

And Dr. Goebel came in with the excuse for rescinding the September resolution:

> As the whole matter is to be submitted to the General Synod, then the Evangelical and Reformed statement of September 29 could be rescinded for it would be unnecessary as the General Synod itself would have the opportunity to pass on the interpretations. (p. 2725)

Dr. Schroeder again protested that "the slower way is the safer way."—to which Dr. Horton interjected, "The matter must not lag."

This was certainly one of the times (and there were others) when the merger should have been either dropped or postponed for more careful consideration.

Few people would know that history was almost repeating itself. In 1907 a Tri-Church Union plan had been prepared over several years and came before the National Council. Belatedly some Congregationalists had begun to question it. A committee was appointed, which included Dr. Washington Gladden, to work out some interpretations. Late at night this large committee put together some wording which it presented the next morning as an explanation of the Plan of Union. The Council joyously adopted it, and then spontaneously rose and sang the Doxology. Representatives were present from the other two denominations—both of which churches had already approved the plan. But when these representatives went back to their respective bodies they reported the attitudes the Congregationalists had set forth in their National Council. Both of the other denominations dropped the whole idea. Their honesty and sense of integrity made it impossible to go on.

With the Evangelical and Reformed Church it was different. For one thing the ecumenical fever was strongly in the air, as we must admit. But it is also true that Congregational Christian Churches were a prize well worth angling for, even if it meant patience and playing out the line a little.

The real pressures at the joint session came from the Committee of Fifteen and from the pleas for ecumenicity.

Mr. David Ford, chairman of the Committee of Fifteen had said:

> We can't get the 75 percent approval if you do not approve the interpretations. If we do not get a common statement approved by both denominations, then the Committee of Fifteen has an impossible task. (p. 2722)

And Rev. Arthur Wheelock, executive director for the Committee of Fifteen added:

> At the time of the Oberlin Council we had 65.25 percent and as of the last of September we had 67.33 percent. The sentence which has been widely quoted from your action of September 29 played right into the hands of the opposition. The opposition had been active, but when your statement was made public then it boomed and left us with a most difficult job. (p. 2722)

A committee had been at work getting a joint statement together.

Rev. Fred Buschmeyer of the Congregational Christian Churches reminded the group of a recent World Council of Churches action:

> He called attention to the Amsterdam meeting and stated that the American churches to have more effective influence must be united and furthermore that we stand under the condemnation of God for our divisions. (p. 2727)

To this Dr. Goebel added: "Amsterdam pronounced division a sin."

Then, "Mr. Goebel announced a recess for dinner and stated that the two denominational group would meet separately to discuss the statement to be prepared by the Committee of Four and would reassemble for joint meeting after the denominational meetings."

Dr. Fagley's account goes on to say that this program was carried out and, after separate meetings, there was a joint meeting at which the final draft of the statement was unanimously adopted and the meeting adjourned. The joint statement was mainly a restatement of events that had taken place at Oberlin, a summary of the situation it created, the promise that the Evangelical and Reformed Church would submit the Interpretations to their synods, and the statement that "we trust that the United Church under the guidance of the Holy Spirit may ... develop a polity which, while preserving cherished traditions, will be free to adjust itself to the needs of the times."

The Evangelical and Reformed leaders had agreed to rescind their previous motion, but here in the joint statement was reaffirmed their dogged insistence that the United Church must not be "bound" as to polity. As usual the joint statement gave the impression that everything had been smoothed over and harmony reached.

In the years just following, Mrs. Burton and I came to know Dr. Paul Schroeder very well. We visited him several times at Rochester, New York, where he was pastor. One time, when I was traveling alone, I called him from the New York Thruway. He insisted that I come on over. His church was having a large church supper, as part of the Every Member Canvass. Nothing would do but that I sit at the head table with him. When he introduced me, probably no one knew anything about me—except, probably, his young assistant who looked up in consternation.

Dr. Schroeder told us, more than once, that all his interest and enthusiasm for the merger was lost when the Oberlin Council adopted the Oberlin interpretations. He saw them for what they were, and for the first time realized that the Congregationalists wanted and intended the union to be congregational.

Incidentally, my wife's grandfather was a German Reformed minister and her father and several uncles were Lutheran ministers. To her Dr. Schroeder represented the finest of the "Herr Pastor" tradition, and there was a close bond of feeling, which I readily shared.

The joint meeting, as mentioned before, did not pinpoint anything new or different in the Oberlin Interpretations. This should not have been difficult. Dr. Schroeder sensed a change—one making the document more clearly congregational.

Anyone comparing the two documents could see that the Basis of Union did not contain the statement:

(b) The constitution for the United Church of Christ ... (4) will define and regulate as regards the General Synod but describe the free and voluntary relationships which the churches, associations, and conferences shall sustain with the General Synod and with each other.

Congregationalists of the time may have rationalized that this was all implied in the statement that each of these bodies would have "autonomy in its own sphere." But almost thirty years later, Dr. Gunnemann takes up this question in his book, *The Shaping of the United Church of Christ.* After quoting the above paragraph, he writes:

Traditional Evangelical and Reformed practice saw the constitution as the guarantor of orderliness, justice, and freedom in all organizational relationships, and therefore binding for all. The concept of a descriptive constitution had not been considered in that group.

A time of disillusionment set in. What had begun as a high venture in Christian idealism was now floundering on the rocks of organizational and political realities. (p. 32)*

Thus Dr. Gunnemann, in 1977, points to a specific provision in the Interpretations that did alter or amend the Basis of Union. Many important provisions of the Basis of Union were not carried over into the United Church of Christ Constitution. (As for instance the provision that the decisions of higher bodies would be "advisory, not mandatory"; and the statement that the freedom of the ministers is "presupposed.") But this new stipulation that the relationships of churches, associations and conferences would merely be "described" as "free and voluntary relationships" did get into the final draft of the constitution.

Thus we see that in the joint meeting of 10 November 1948, many sincere misgivings were expressed: urgent

*Reprinted with permission from Louis H. Gunnemann, *The Shaping of the United Church of Christ: An Essay in the History of American Christianity.* Copyright © 1977 United Church Press.

suggestions that delay and new approaches be sought were made. But in the end we find another patchwork of nice sounding words and phrases that avoided the realities and truth of the situation. Those who speak easily of the guidance of the Holy Spirit do not always remember that "God is a Spirit, and they that worship Him must worship him in spirit and in *truth.*"

Early in this book mention was made that those of us who went through this period in our church life could not feel that the Watergate scandal was so bad. We suffered cover-ups, the withholding of pertinent information, the releases of false propaganda, and most of the indignities suffered in Watergate. But as one of my friends put it, Watergate was like child's play. It was as though some Boy Scouts had been caught in a naughty prank. But, said my friend, ours was more like Hitler's subversion of the mind, the conscience, and the will of the German people. In our case it was the subversion of a church people with a glorious history of 350 years of developing and refining freedom in church life and thought.

The November 10 joint meeting was just one episode in what my friend referred to as the "subversion of a people." His comments are worth pondering.

FROM THE NOVEMBER 10 MEETING THROUGH THE 1949 COUNCIL

The period of November 10 to 5 February 1949 was full of activity for people on both sides of the merger controversy. But with the delegates already stacked in favor of the merger, and with a "tails-we-win, heads-you-lose" proposition where the Council could vote the merger anyway, there could be no real doubt of the outcome.

Antimerger meetings sprang up in many parts of the country. The Hallowell Meeting on November 15, at Hallowell, Maine, issued a long and thought-provoking statement. So did the Galesburg Meeting on September 30, in Galesburg, Illinois. There were other meetings in Iowa, Minnesota, Michigan, Connecticut, and elsewhere throughout the country.

It was a time of publishing many leaflets and pamphlets. Dr. Max Strang addressed an *Open Letter to the*

Committee of Fifteen, and so did Dr. Marion J. Bradshaw. On the back of Dr. Strang's Open Letter was printed the memorandum of his conversation with Dr. Goebel on the morning of June 23, which is printed in our Appendix as Document 29.

I had personally been rather inactive in pamphleteering during the time that the Evanston group was carrying on its work. But now I issued periodic releases covering new developments. Sometime Dr. Bradshaw and I would combine our mailings, with a statement from each of us in one envelope. Most of these various publications, including many I have not mentioned, may be found bound together in a book *Later Merger Pamphlets,* Volume II, in the Congregational Library in Boston. Most of them should also be there separately as they were originally printed.

Armed with its new "unanimous" report from the Joint Committee, and the fact that the Evangelical and Reformed leaders had "rescinded" their September 29 statement, the Committee of Fifteen was hard at work to "get the vote." So were the denominational officials.

Bitterness and personal animosities were increasing daily. The Oberlin delegates who still favored their action were particularly provoked with opposition people who had not accepted the Oberlin claim of all difficulties having been resolved. Even the saintly, revered Dr. Warren Seymour Archibald, pastor of South Church, Hartford, was openly called a "liar" in a meeting of Connecticut delegates to Oberlin. His accuser had been one of the speakers at the promerger rallies in First Church, Oberlin. By the time of the February 5 meeting of the Council, attitudes had hardened so that no rational, gentlemanly discussion of issues was possible.

The attempt was made, however, to provide equal time for both sides at the meeting. Pros and Antis were allotted twenty minutes for a main, first speaker. After that speakers were to alternate.

The Continuation Committee designated me to lead off with the twenty-minute speech. This was the first time, actually, that anyone could address the whole question of the merger, or present an analysis of the Basis of Union. The opportunity was welcomed, but the time for calm, rational presentation being attentively received or courteously considered was long since gone. My address was a careful analysis of the Evangelical and Reformed Church structure, compared with an equally careful analysis of the genius of Congregational structures. Then came a point-by-point comparison of the Basis of Union with the polities in question. The complete address is included in *Early Merger Pamphlets* on pages 259 through 262.

I do not recall the promerger speakers as attempting any calm, rational, and reasoned approach. My recollection is that of the derision, personal attacks upon the opposition, and the assumed superiority of the promerger cause. It was not a pleasant meeting, nor one marked by too much genuine Christian spirit or tolerance. There were two exceptions.

The Chaplain of the meeting was Rev. Raymond Waser, who did a sincere and genuine piece of devotional leadership. And at the close of the meeting Dr. L. Wendell Fifield did address both pros and antis with what was hoped could be a healing word. Both men did rise to the difficult occasion in the best Congregational tradition. Other than that, many scars were added to the already grievous split in our fellowship.

Mr. Palmer D. Edmunds, one of the judges of voting, had been designated to make the report for the committee when the other two members could not attend. But the ushers refused for a long time to let him into the meeting because he did not have delegate's credentials. Even when he tried repeatedly to tell his position, he was treated with distrust and less than courtesy. The report of the Judges of Voting showed 72.28 percent in favor by 1 January 1949; and was raised to 72.77 percent of the churches voting by 1 February—which was beyond the official date for voting.

Actually the judges of voting had not themselves had any opportunity to see or to check the original reports from the churches. They met in New York and simply accepted the figure handed out at headquarters. No list was published showing how individual churches were recorded.

There were forty-five-minute presentations by pros and antis in the morning, with four speakers on each side. In the afternoon there were one-hour presentations on each side. Dr. Liston Pope was the first promerger speaker at this time, and I was the first for the antis. Altogether six speakers were heard on the pro side, and nine on the anti, including an extra fifteen minutes for a summary by

Rev. James W. Fifield, Jr. An extra fifteen minutes was then given to Dr. Ronald Bridges for summary for the pros.

In the evening there were eighteen five-minute speeches alternating between pros and antis, with two "mediating" speeches sandwiched in. Then followed nine two-minute speeches, again alternating.

On Saturday the time was taken up with parliamentary motions and some votes of appreciation, etc. There were 929 registered delegates. The key motion, of some six paragraphs contained the following:

> That the General Council makes a finding and determination that the percentage of Congregational Christian Churches approving the Basis of Union with its Interpretations warrants the consummation of the Union in accordance with the Basis of Union and the Interpretations.

The vote for this consummation was 757 in favor and 172 against. This, of course, represented a dramatic drop from the estimated 1,000 in favor at Oberlin to only 12 or 14 against. And it was still contrary to the representation made when the Basis of Union was sent to the churches.

According to its own terms (or the terms included with the Basis of Union) the Basis of Union had been defeated on 1 April 1948. It was still defeated at Oberlin on June 22. It was defeated on 1 January 1949, the time extended from Oberlin. It was still short of the 75 percent that all ordinary, everyday members of local churches had assumed would be honored by men of the cloth and denominational officials at all levels. These facts can never be gainsaid, or lived down. It was naturally assumed by all who read the "procedures" printed with the Basis of Union that failure to reach the 75 percent (of the churches voting) meant that it had *not* been approved and that therefore it would *not* be consummated. The action taken on 5 February 1949 must forever be judged in this light.

The minutes of the 1949 Council list the names of those who spoke, pro and anti. For the longer speeches brief summaries are given. James, W. Fifield, Jr., Dr. Max Strang, Mr. J. D. Fackenthal, Judge Brown, Dr. Palmer D. Edmunds, Dr. Archibald, and H. D. Gray are some of the anti speakers listed.

——— 14 ———

The Proposals of 1705 in Retrospect

I REMEMBER hearing one time that Congregationalists had considered, or been engaged in union talks, twenty or more times—most of which fell through.

More important is the fact that Congregationalists have often been unable to appreciate the values of the true Congregational Way and have therefore been easily drawn into union talks on vague notions that they would "strengthen" Congregationalism or promote "the Kingdom of God."

Not always have union talks been responsible for attempts to improve on Congregationalism.

In 1705, before Congregational principles had been so fully explored, the clergymen around Boston came up with fifteen "Proposals" for "the better ordering of our church life."

At the heart of these proposals was the plan for "standing" associations, permanent in nature, which would have the power to decide whether certain ministers should be accepted by individual churches, and also the power to intervene in cases of scandal or impurities in the faith.

The lay people in Massachusetts, and particularly the General Court (the legislature), did not go along with these proposals, and they were not put into effect in the Bay Colony.

But in nearby Connecticut, a synod was ordered by the legislature, to be made up of delegates elected by the churches of each county. Remember that the Congregational churches were the "state church," supported by taxes. This Synod, meeting in Saybrook, where the new Yale College was then located, adopted the Saybrook Platform, which was essentially the same as the proposals of 1705 suggested by the Boston "divines."

Promptly the Saybrook Platform of 1708 was declared the law of the Colony by the legislature. It remained such until after the Revolution, but continued more or less in use until the late eighteen hundreds.

The platform was semipresbyterian and has always been recognized as such. The central idea was the control over the ministry and the power of the Consociation to decide whether a minister could, or could not, serve a particular church. It also provided the right of the Consociation to step into the affairs of a local church and try its minister for heresy if even a few members requested it. It has often been said that Horace Bushnell would have been tried for heresy if the other ministers in Hartford could have found two members of his church to bring charges against him. But they could not. Horace Bushnell was a leader against the strict Calvinism of the times that had been preached by Jonathan Edwards.

Other ministers were not as fortunate. Rev. John A. Harrer, longtime librarian of the Congregational Library in Boston, has recently published a biography entitled *Rev. Abiel Abbot of Peterborough, N.H.* In it he gives three vivid illustrations of the way that Consociations, under the Saybrook Platform, intervened in the affairs of local churches against the will of the local congregations. One was that of Rev. John Bass of Ashford in 1751; a second was Rev. John Sherman of Windham County in 1806; and the third was Abiel Abbot in 1811 (see Chapter VI, p. 39, of the Abbot biography).

The Proposals of 1705 and the Saybrook Platform had been vigorously attacked by Rev. John Wise, of Ipswich, Massachusetts, in two pamphlets: *The Churches' Quarrel Espoused, Etc.* and *A Vindication of the Government of the New England Churches, Etc.*

Actually John Wise carried the Congregational concept farther toward democracy than its original. At first a gathered Church was supposed immediately to "elect some choice men to rule over it." Wise insisted that ordinary people—farmers, carpenters, butchers, tailors, or whatever—can be led of the spirit and are capable of governing themselves. Wise's pamphlets were republished after his death, and in 1772 became part of the literature of the American Revolution.

Soon after its adoption the Saybrook Platform had led to a split in the Congregational Churches. Dr. S. L. Blake, in his book *The Separates or Strict Congregationalists of New England*, tells of the withdrawals, or establishment of new dissenting churches, to the number of approximately 100. These churches had to raise their own money, and their members still had to pay taxes to support the established churches.

Next came what Dunning called "the disastrous plan of union" with the Presbyterians (Albert E. Dunning in *Congregationalists in America*, p. 318).

In 1801 the Connecticut Congregationalists entered into agreement with the Presbyterians for cooperation in establishing churches on the western frontier. They considered Congregational polity too weak to survive in sparsely settled areas. The plan would permit individual churches to be either Congregational or Presbyterian and to be connected with either Presbyteries or Congregational Associations. The plan worked to the advantage of the Presbyterians, and it caused a split among the Presbyterians around 1838.

In 1852, at the Albany Convention, the Plan of Union was renounced by Congregationalists. This came after the Iowa Band, and the Illinois Band had gone out from Yale determined to start Congregational Churches free of the Plan of Union.

The little Tercentenary booklet, *Pilgrim Deeds and Duties*, discusses all of the above episodes of our history and then speaks of "a curious modesty":

Congregationalists were so determined not to be guilty of sectarian zeal nor to put on any ecclesiastical airs, that they fell into a way of excessive deference to other forms of church organization, and a corresponding lack of aggressiveness in extending their own influence and developing their own life.

The same mistakes were the reason for the fiasco of church union talks in years to come, including the Tri-Church Union plan of 1907 and those with the Episcopalians in the early 1920s.

In retrospect, the merger with the Evangelical and

Reformed Church had similarities with earlier events. As with the Proposals of 1705 and the Saybrook Platform, the key was installation of pastors. Presbyterian principles were involved in each. The Plan of Union was renounced after fifty years of disillusionment. What will the future bring for Congregationalists who know the value of our heritage of freedom after they experience what the United Church of Christ is really like?

Appendix

Documents Relating to the Merger

Document 1.
Christus Victor Poster (1942)

CHRISTUS VICTOR

A fellowship of those who are appalled by the lack of incisiveness about Christian Faith as expressed in the Churches of our denomination and who unite in a desire to do something about it.

In the world today there is tremendous confusion and uncertainty. This is natural. But within our church there is also tremendous confusion and uncertainty. This is unnatural. Multitudes of Christians both lay and clergy are groping for the sure and unshakable rock on which they can live their lives, and by which they can die. Frequently they do not find it in our churches, for the voices of our churches are confused. They do not "speak all the same thing". This situation is tragically true of the churches of our denomination.

We believe that this vagueness is a luxury no longer tolerable. If our churches are to remain truly a part of the Body of Christ, it must end. We believe that the time has come to reassert in unequivocal terms that Jesus Christ, the Revelation of God and the Redeemer of Men, who has already "overcome the world" has been, is now, and always must be the eternal rock of our faith whereby men find Life even in the midst of Death and Destruction. We believe that this faith must also result in social action and the most rigorous criticism of the injustices of our society. However, we believe that no system of ethics, no program of social action, no matter how nobly conceived can be a substitute for this faith. Rather we believe that an ethic and social action consciously and militantly rooted in a fellowship of those in Christ can provide a vitality yet unknown.

We believe in the traditional freedom of our church. We do not desire to pass resolutions or laws, nor compel others to agree with us. But we believe there are many in our denomination who share our concern and our faith.

We invite all who are like-minded to a meeting where we can discuss what can be done about it.

Arlan Baillie	Robert James
W Burnet Easton, Jr.	Charles Jones
Ray Gibbons	Roy Pearson
Emerson Hangen	Winthrop Richardson
	Amos Wilder

Friday, June 19 - 9:00 P.M.
Room 16, New Hampshire Hall

Document 2.
Fagley's Statement of Constitutional Issues (1945)
Brief Statement on Constitutional Provisions

The National Council held its first meeting in Oberlin in 1871 in response to a call issued by the Pilgrim Memorial Convention which had met in Chicago, April 27, 1870 to celebrate the 250th anniversary of the founding of Plymouth. This convention passed the following resolution:

"Resolved: That this Pilgrim Memorial Convention recommend to the Congrega- tional state conferences and associations and to other local bodies, to unite in measures for instituting on the principle of fellowship, excluding ecclesias- tical authority, a permanent national conference".

There had been discussion throughout the churches of the advantages of having regular meetings of a Council; but there was considerable opposition lest such a Council would attempt control of the churches. The debates as reported in the papers at that time ranged over a wide list of topics, the Congregational Review saying:

"The positive exclusion of all idea of authority or jurisdiction over individuals or churches from the ___ ____ence by express provision, effectually secures the churches in their Divine liberties."

and Pastor Robinson was quoted:

"May not the officers of one or many churches meet together to discuss and con- sider matters for the good of the church or churches? I deny it not, so they infringe no order of Christ or the liberty of the churches."

The Call for the Council stated on the positive side:

"That a declaration be made of the two cardinal principles of Congregationalism, viz., the exclusive right and power of the individual churches to self-government; and the fellowship of the churches one with another, with the duties growing out of that fellowship and especially the duty of general consultation in all matters of common concern to the whole body of churches."

"That the objects of the organization be to express and foster the substantial unity of our churches in doctrine, polity, and work, and to consult upon the common interests of all our churches, their resources....and their relations to all parts of the kingdom of Christ."

On the other hand, it set limits:

"That the churches withhold from the National Council all legislative or judicial power over churches or individuals, and all right to act as a council of reference.
"To provide as simple an organization, with as few officers, and with as limited duties as may be consistent with the efficiency of the Council in advancing the principles and securing the objects of the proposed organization."

When the Council met, in response to this call, at Oberlin, two days were given to the discussion of the porposed constitution, which when adopted contained the following paragraph:

"The churches, therefore, while establishing this National Council for the furtherance of the common interests and work of all the churches, do maintain the Scriptural and inalienable right of each church to self-government and administration; and this National Council shall never exercise legislative or judicial authority, nor consent to act as a council of reference."

Under the constitution of 1871 with minor amendments, the Councils were held until 1913.

2.

In the Council of 1913, when it was proposed to reorganize the missionary work and strengthen the Council, the question naturally arose - was there any encroachmen on the fundamental principle of complete autonomy of the local church - and the discussion of this question was summed up by Dr. Nehemiah Boynton, moderator:

"The autonomy of the local church is, and will always be, the slogan of our American Congregationalism. Every local church, free and independent in its pulpit and in its pew."

The revised constitution of 1913 included the following preamble and section on polity:

"The Congregational Churches of the United States, by delegates in National Council assembled, reserving all the rights and cherished memories belonging to this organization under its former constitution....and affirming our loyalty to the basic principles of our representative democracy, hereby set forth the things most surely believed among us concerning faith, polity, and fellowship

"POLITY. We believe in the freedom and responsibility of the individual soul, and the right of private judgment. We hold to the autonomy of the local church and its independence of all ecclesiastical control. We cherish the fellowship of the churches, united in district, state, and national bodies, for council and cooperation in matters of common concern."

Under this revised constitution the Council carried forward its work until 1931 when the proposal was made for the Council to unite with the Christian Church. It was then explained that in the Christian Church the principle of church government, resting completely with the local church which was absolute in its range no portion of which had been delegated to any other body in that fellowship, was identical to that of the Congregational churches. Therefore, while the question was raised as to whether or not the delegates elected by the Congregational churches to the Council of 1931 possessed the right to vote on the question of merger with the Christian churches, the question was not pressed because the churches were not being asked to surrender any of their authority nor to confer upon the Council any rights beyond those possessed by the National Council under its previous constitution.

The new constitution as adopted in 1931 contained the following paragraph:

"The Congregational Christian Churches of the United States by delegates assembled, reserving all the rights and cherished memories of their historic past and affirming loyalty to the basic principles of unity and democracy in church polity, hereby set forth the principles of Christian fellowship immemorially held by these churches.
"We hold sacred the freedom of the individual soul and the right of private judgment. We stand for the autonomy of the local church and its independence of ecclesiastical control...."

The opinions of Dr. Barton and Dr. Burton on the powers of the Council may be noted. Dr. Barton stated:

"The national Council is not an ecclesiastical court, and has no jurisdiction in matters of discipline, or ecclesiastical standing. It has no authority over any local church, association or conference..."

and Dr. Burton:

"The General Council is not a legislative body with ecclesiastical authority over the churches, the conferences, the associations, or the denominational societies.

3.

It does, however, pass recommendations addressed to any of these. It also bears testimony to its faith through approved statements or resolutions on various topics at its own will. These expressions carry with them no authority beyond the weight of their own wisdom, backed by the significance of the delegation from which they issue...."

Among the several constitutional questions suggested from a study of the Basis of Union, two may be cited:

I. The Basis of Union provided under Article 2 - Practice - that:

"The government of the United Church shall be exercised through Congregations (Associations if desired), Conferences, and the General Synod in such wise that the autonomy of each shall be respected in its own sphere, each having its own rights and responsibilities:

This section proposes that the delegates to the General Council shall establish a Synod which will have autonomy and authority, and the question arises - Do the delegates elected under our present constitution have any authority themselves which they can pass on and lodge with the agency they are asked to create?

II. In Article 4, Section 5, it is provided that:

"The General Synod shall have power to receive overtures and petitions; to give counsel in regard to cases referred to it; and to maintain correspondence with other denominations."

But the original constitution specifically states that:

" this National Council shall never exercise legislative or judicial authority, nor consent to act as a council of reference".

This provision was reaffirmed, in general statements, in the constitution of 1913 and 1931.

It would appear therefore, that to enable the delegates to the General Council to vote on the several proposals in the Plan of Union, the first step might be to seek a revision of the present constitution by which the churches would confer upon the General Council the necessary authority, clothing it with the rights and duties it would be expected to transfer to the proposed Synod. For if the free churches of our fellowship are to unite with a church, with a centralized authoritative nature, that these independent churches should first become a church themselves with corresponding authority, rights and duties comparable to the body with which they seek to unite. Then the Congregational Christian Church thus created could transfer to the new body, the General Synod, the autonomy in its own sphere and the authority over the boards and agencies of the fellowship which are implied in the Basis of Union.

Respectfully submitted,

Frederick L. Fagley

Document 3.
Statement of the Evanston Meeting (4–5 November 1947)

THE EVANSTON MEETING

We reject the present Basis of Union

It is a defective instrument for accomplishing its purposes of organic union

We believe the kind of union it proposes is short-sighted and ill-timed

We hold that the genius of Congregationalism calls for a federative rather than an organic union of churches

(Detailed Findings—Pages 3—15)

190 members of our Congregational Christian Churches from twenty-seven states, having grave questions concerning the proposed merger of the Congregational Christian Churches and the Evangelical and Reformed Church, met at the First Congregational Church of Evanston, Illinois, November 4 and 5, 1947.

Their deliberations are presented in the following findings which were unanimously adopted at this meeting.

The Evanston Meeting voted that there should be a Continuing Committee of ministers and laymen. This committee will continue the work of the Evanston Meeting as long as the proposed merger on the present Basis of Union is before our churches for decision. This committee will provide leadership and counsel, and act in behalf of those who in the name of Christ oppose the merger in its present form.

The Continuing Committee may be addressed as follows: The Evanston Meeting, Room 1302, 19 South LaSalle Street, Chicago 3, Illinois.

The Evanston Meeting elected a Budget Committee consisting of Mr. Allen T. Burns, Mr. Horatio Ford, Rev. Niel E. Hansen—to receive contributions from individuals and churches with which to carry forward the work of the Evanston Meeting.

FINDINGS COMMITTEE: Mr. S. T. Roberts, Chairman, Rev. Hugh Elmer Brown, Mr. Raymond H. Fiero, Mr. Horatio Ford, Mr. Stanley S. Gillam, Rev. Niel E. Hansen, Rev. Charles F. Jacobs, Rev. William A. Keith, Rev. A. C. McGiffert, Jr., Rev. George W. Shepherd, Rev. Max Strang. (For addresses, see page 16)

The Prayer At the Evanston Meeting
— HUGH ELMER BROWN —

Our Great Companion, Who art with us in all the chances and changes of this mortal life, in the incessant flow of our days, in the moral momentum of great causes, and in the everlasting march of thought,

Here in this Church may we feel afresh our divine kinship with Thee and with all men. Here may we rededicate ourselves to the building of an honest and friendly world. Here may we rise above the perspectives of class, church, nation and generation and catch something of the view from Galilee.

Send down Thy light and truth and let them guide us. If our meeting is unworthy, bring it to naught. If our meeting is worthy, give power to its decisions. Correct us where we are wrong. Inspire us where we are right.

Save us from living on a small scale in a great age. Save us from dealing on a small scale with great things. Save us from seriousness over trivial things and from triviality over serious things.

Deliver us from all pettiness, all pride of opinion, all prejudice, all intemperance of statement. Give us the spirit of restraint and judgement, of humility and patience. And may no unbrotherly moods or words mar our deliberations.

Give valor to our dreams of good. Lay across our lives the magnificent imperatives of Jesus. Let none of us forget the giant agony of the world. Help us to play a Christian part in the dreadful drama of our generation.

Amen.

Statement of the Evanston Meeting

(This is a summary. Numbers at the end of sentences refer to longer statements on the following pages.)

WE ARE UNITED in the Evanston Meeting in the conviction that, in view of the fact that the Basis of Union proposes a change from the congregational to the presbyterial polity, organic union with the Evangelical and Reformed Church according to this Basis of Union is undesirable and should not be consummated.

WE BELIEVE the Basis of Union must be accepted or rejected according to its printed word, without reliance upon the oral or written interpretation of anyone. (1)

WE ARE CONVINCED that the Basis of Union, if accepted with its ambiguities, contradictions and omissions, will, among other things, take away the autonomy of the local church. (1, 2, 3)

WE BELIEVE the Executive Committee of the General Council adopted uncongregational procedure for which it had no justification when it agreed to receive the Basis of Union from the Joint Committee; and that it assumed authority it did not possess when it sent the Basis of Union to the churches and set a date on or before which the churches must vote. (4)

WE POINT OUT serious defects concerning the Basis of Union such as the following:

It includes two contradictory methods of calling and accepting resignations of ministers. (5)

Though our time in history demands the largest possible expenditure for Christian work at home and abroad, a large amount of the missionary giving will be used annually for thirty years to fund ministerial annuities. (6)

Though the uniting of the Home and Foreign Mission Societies of the two groups may be legally effected, the legal question remains whether this could be done if some of our churches do not vote or vote "No". (7)

The uniting of the societies of the two groups will not increase Christian service or giving. It will bring heavy, time-consuming tasks in this grave hour in the world when the present vital force of all our national societies should be used to the utmost in Christian service rather than in organizational rearrangements. (8)

There will be very little consolidation of local churches of the two groups in any given community because of cultural, geographical and other differences. (9)

Legal difficulties exist in the proposed merger which need to be explored professionally by all churches inclined to vote favorably. (10)

A comparative financial statement of assets and liabilities of the two groups has never been published. (11)

WE BELIEVE it essential that a constitution and by-laws and a statement of faith, if we are in favor of either or both, be presented to our churches *before* a final vote is taken on the Basis of Union, if the proposed United Church and General Synod need anything more than the minimum constitution of our General Council. (12)

WE RECOMMEND the following to churches before they vote on the Basis of Union:

That they postpone voting until adequate opportunities have been given their members to study the reasons for and the reasons against the merger. (13)

That full recognition be given the right of Christian people to differ or dissent without penalty. (13)

That ministers and laymen, before voting, consider with wisdom the wider interests and possibilities under our present fellowship. (14)

That the Executive Committee of the General Council arrange for adequate education concerning the proposed merger for the members of our churches, and take responsibility for eliminating one-sided official propaganda for and promotion of the merger. (15)

That churches in voting on the proposed merger use the secret ballot. (16)

WE BELIEVE a person who opposes the merger as proposed in this Basis of Union cannot justly be understood to be opposing church unity. (16)

WE REPORT without prejudice a proposal acceptable to many in the Evanston Meeting that churches voting "No" on the proposed merger and those which refrain from voting should indicate their right and purpose to continue as Congregational Christian Churches and to seek fellowship with like-minded

Congregational Christian Churches if the United Church of Christ is formed according to the Basis of Union. (17)

WE ASK our young people to realize that the proposed merger, if voted, will take from them their inheritance of a place among the free churches, and deprive them of a position of leadership in bringing about and working out in their generation a new formation of American Protestantism—the federative union of many denominations. (18)

WE BELIEVE a "No" vote on the proposed merger will maintain for our churches the opportunity to help bring into existence a new pattern of federative union among many denominations. We believe this pattern to be of vastly greater importance for American Protestantism and the life of the World Council of Churches than the organic union of the Congregational Christian Churches and the Evangelical and Reformed Church. (19)

WE ARE UNITED in the Evanston Meeting in the hope and prayer that our fellowship of churches, beginning with the meeting of the General Council at Oberlin in 1948, will seek the guidance of Almighty God to lead us in ways wherein we may help bring into existence the federative union of many denominations. This is the time in church history when American Protestantism should form new bonds of fellowship for more cooperative Christian work to advance the Christian life of our country and forward the Kingdom of God in all the world.

Complete Statement of the Evanston Meeting

1. Interpretations of the Basis of Union

We have noted many different oral and written interpretations of the Basis of Union. Dr. Frank M. Sheldon, Chairman of the Commission on Inter-Church Relations and Christian Unity when the merger was first considered, and who has been a member of the Committee which developed the Basis of Union, attended the Evanston Meeting at our invitation. He gave an address and was accorded full privileges of speaking throughout the Evanston Meeting, as were others who wished to speak in behalf of the merger.

We also had available the answers to eighty-four questions given in writing by Dr. Douglas Horton. As we listened to their statements, we concluded that we can accept personal clarifications and interpretations only when they have been incorporated into a revised Basis of Union.

The various interpretations are sincerely given. We know that those who in an official capacity have helped to write the Basis of Union have certain individual insights and understandings that may be important. However, we see ambiguities, contradictions and omissions in the Basis of Union, and the personal interpretation of any Congregational Christian official cannot be accepted without the express approval of the Evangelical and Reformed officials.

We believe the Basis of Union constitutes a threat to the autonomous way of our Congregational Christian Churches. In our deliberations we have had to do exactly as churches must do. We have ignored all private and personal interpretations and have based our conclusions, so far as possible, on the printed words of the Basis of Union.

We believe that a vote in favor of the Basis of Union according to oral or written interpretation could result in our yielding the autonomous formation of our Congregational Christian Churches and in a short time finding that our churches have been moved from their place as a fellowship of churches into a centrally organized denomination. If this should happen, the only recourse of our churches after the merger is voted would be to create a minority group of churches using the congregational way within the United Church, or to seek fellowship outside the United Church. We know there is the thought in the minds of some that, if the merger is voted, those of the former Congregational Christian Churches will strive to make the United Church congregational. It is reported that some Evangelical and Reformed people, if the Basis of Union is voted, will strive to make the United Church centrally organized and presbyterial. We are convinced that the Congregational Christian people have certain concepts in mind when they consider the Basis of Union and the Evangelical and Reformed people have different concepts. We believe that to the people of the two groups the language of the Basis of Union means different things.

Personal interpretations of the Basis of Union; the dangers that are within it because of its ambiguities; the opportunities that are afforded those of either group to develop the United Church into a presbyterial or congregational form with consequent tension and strife; and the widely different opinions of many as to what the United Church will be like, all bring us solidly to the conclusion that the Basis of Union must be considered inadequate and must be rejected by those who rely on its printed and official word.

2. Ambiguities, Etc., in the Basis of Union

We point out that the Basis of Union contains many ambiguities, contradictions and omissions. Some of these matters have to do with fundamental differences in the theory and practice of church life as differently conceived by the Congregational Christian Churches and the Evangelical and Reformed Church. The final interpretations of these differences will not depend upon the words themselves but upon the habits of thought and the presuppositions that color the minds of the two groups. In due time interpretative decisions will have to come out of the silent background of the thought and experience of the two groups. Particularly will these conflicts arise in building a constitution. We foresee untold difficulties in reaching common agreements. Unless and until such common agreements are reached, the United Church would become a handicap to itself, to the cause of cooperative Protestantism, and to the world we are called upon to serve.

3. The Basis of Union if Accepted Will Take Away the Autonomy of the Local Church

We call attention to the fact that the provision in the Basis of Union for the autonomy of the local church (Article III, F, H, I) is actually rendered meaningless by other provisions of the document.

How can it be said that the freedom and autonomy of the local church are maintained when a Congregational Christian Church which does not vote on this merger or which votes negatively is cut off from the fellowship of which it has been a part, and with which it has cooperated according to the usage of the Congregational Christian Churches? Its autonomy is interfered with when it is deprived of any of its present rights as a local church and its present relationships with its association, conference, the General Council and the various Societies of our churches which it has helped create. How can it be said that the freedom and autonomy of the local church are preserved when some other body assumes authority to determine its ecclesiastical relationships? How can it be said that the freedom and autonomy of the local church are maintained when the Basis of Union proposes to change the character of the local church by incorporating it into an organic, centrally organized denomination? How can it be said that the autonomy of the local church is to be preserved when the local church, according to the Basis of Union, is to be subjected to the terms of a superior constitution; when it must secure approval in the calling, settling and resignation of its ministers or bear the onus of seeming to be abnormal, irregular and uncooperative, and actually treated as a minority group?

We find additional specific ground for urging a negative vote on the present Basis of Union in that it includes Article III-G, setting up a judicial system foreign to our congregational way.

We suggest that churches deciding to vote "Yes" on the Basis of Union attach to their vote an explicit statement as to how they understand their autonomy. According to the Basis of Union their autonomy includes the right without prejudice to make use of the alternate way of calling and ordaining ministers. It includes the right of declining to vote on ratification of the constitution or on approval of the statement of faith. They should further declare that they understand that churches declining to vote on constitution or creed will nevertheless retain full standing in the United Church.

4. Centralizing Tendencies

We view with dismay and alarm the tendency on the part of Congregational leaders (perhaps quite unconsciously) to take to themselves the kind of power that rightly belongs only to officials in a presbyterial system. We foresee in a merger with the Evangelical and Reformed Church, where such procedures are normal, that this tendency toward centralization of control will be disastrously increased, to the detriment of our congregational freedoms.

By way of illustration, the Joint Committee which was appointed by the General Council did not report directly to the General Council but to the Executive Committee. While such procedure may be legal, according to the constitution of the General Council, we hold that in a case of such grave import as the proposed merger, the Executive Committee should have declined to take the responsibility of receiving the report and sending it to the churches for voting, but should have referred it to the General Council. If this had been done, there would have been no need for such a gathering as the Evanston Meeting .

We believe that the Basis of Union should have been first submitted to the General Council which ordered it, so that a representative assembly gathered from all parts of the country could consider the document in full detail, make any desired changes in it and only then, if satisfied with it, submit it to the churches for a vote.

5. Ministers in the United Church and the Autonomy of the Local Church

We call attention to the fact that the Basis of Union provides two alternative ways of ordaining, calling and placing ministers (Article VI A, C). We believe two ways had to be proposed because it proved impossible to effect a compromise between contradictions. One of these ways is that commonly used by Congregationlists. The other is the presbyterial way of the Evangelical and Reformed Church. The Basis of Union declares that in the United Church the standard way shall be the presbyterial way of the Evangelical and Reformed Church. The Congregational way is permitted, but the United Church will appeal to congregations and ministers to adopt the presbyterial way. Such an appeal seems to imply the use of a subtle kind of pressure upon churches and ministers who do not conform to the preferred presbyterial system.

This provision of the Basis of Union threatens to destroy the Congregational conception of the minister as a layman elected by the churches to the office of minister. The standard way recommended in the Basis of Union of calling a minister nullifies the place of a local church as a completely autonomous part of a fellowship of churches.

6. Funding Ministerial Annuities from Missionary Giving

We call attention to the provision in the Basis of Union according to which money will be set aside from missionary giving to fund ministerial annuities (Article VIII-G 6, 7). This sum has been estimated at various times as from $132,000 to $500,000 annually. This amount will be withdrawn annually for about thirty years from the missionary money of the two denominations. We strongly support ministerial annuities. We recognize that in the long run the proposed plan will save money. But we believe the critical issues and urgent problems confronting the world and the churches in the immediate present are too grave to justify our subtracting this sum yearly from the apportionment. We dare not weaken the work of missions at home and abroad, and the work of education and social action, by decreasing their shares in the missionary giving of our people.

7. Merger of Home and Foreign Missionary Boards and Other Agencies of the Two Groups

We question whether any benefits are to be secured from the organic union of the respective Foreign Missionary Boards, Home Boards and other national agencies, as proposed in the Basis of Union, even though legal and other difficulties of adjustment may not make such organic merger impossible (Article VIII). We see no reason to believe that such merger will make for progress in programs, service and the securing of increased giving. We understand that the uncompleted mergers of certain Evangelical Boards and Reformed Boards present difficulties and doubtful financial pictures which have not been revealed to our members.

8. An Ill Timed Move

If the Merger goes through, we shall have to divert much of our energy and leadership to the task of working at the multiple adjustments necessary to crown the merger with success. Hitherto the merger negotiations have withdrawn from the main tasks of Christian service a relatively small number of our people; mostly, until very recently, the members of the Joint Commission. But, if the Merger should be consummated, every individual Church, Association, State Conference, and the General Council, as well as our several Boards, will have to spend a vast amount of time and energy working out the big and little problems involved in integrating the new denomination into a functioning unity, intermeshing of denominational machinery, preparing an acceptable constitution and creed, etc. This time and energy will have to be taken away at a crucial time from the main tasks which confront our churches in these critical days,—namely to present the Christian faith and way to those who know not Christ, to steady the nerve of faith in those who call themselves Christian, and to increase the cooperative action of American Protestantism at home and abroad. Congregationalism's strategic leadership lies in the wider, not the narrow, horizon.

9. Voting For the Merger Will Not Mean Fewer Local Churches

The proposed merger of the Congregational Christian Churches and the Evangelical and Reformed Church will not result, except in a few isolated instances, in the merger of local churches of the two orders, since the patterns of distribution of the two groups are diverse. Then too, there are cultural differences in some communities where there is now a local Congregational Christian and a local Evangelical and Reformed Church, making their merger difficult. Therefore there will be no appreciable gain through the uniting of two weak local churches to form a strong unit, nor any material decrease in the total number of churches in a community.

10. Legal Considerations To Be Examined Before Voting

We call upon individual churches and conferences, before voting, to examine their charters to determine whether, as in some instances appears to be the case, there may be legal obstacles to an affirmative vote; and to make sure that an affirmative vote will not jeopardize trust funds and property interests, and even the retention of the charter itself.

We point out that a vote in favor of the merger is a consent to a contract which may give up essential rights long held by individual Congregational Christian Churches and cause legal reversions of titles. The extent of this loss of rights is a question dependent upon varying interpretations of ambiguous phrases in the Basis of Union. We strongly recommend that, before waiving its rights, each church safeguard itself with competent legal advice.

As an example, a church voting favorably on the Basis of Union might be interpreted as accepting an invitation to leave the fellowship of Congregational Christian Churches and join with another and different body of churches, thereby ceasing to be an independent Congregational Christian Church. The members of such a church who voted favorably on the Basis of Union might be declared to have seceded from the membership of that Congregational Christian Church and joined with another body. It is a question also as to whether any number of Congregational Christian Churches voting favorably on the merger can in any way decide that Congregational Christian Churches which vote "No" on the Basis of Union shall become other than what they are now.

11. The Need of a Comparative Financial Statement of the Two Groups

We call upon the Finance Committee of the General Council to provide a condensed comparative statement of the assets and projected annual commitments of the Evangelical and Reformed Church and the Congregational Christian Churches, according to the instructions given it at the meeting of the Executive Committee at Cleveland in January, 1947. Large corporate interests are involved in the proposed merger. Our constituency should have at its disposal this basic information before being required to pass judgment upon the merger.

12. We Ask for a Constitution and By-Laws and the Statement of Faith Before Voting

We observe that many provisions of the Basis of Union can be given widely different interpretations. There are several important questions with which the Basis of Union does not deal at all. Thus there is no way for us to know what actually will be the principles and procedures of the United Church.

We call, therefore, upon a Church that desires a constitution which will settle these matters, to insist that a specific constitution and major by-laws be worked out before it votes favorably on the merger. This constitution should include definite statements upon procedures and practices on fundamental issues about which the Basis of Union is either ambiguous or silent (Article IV, A).

We also call for a statement from the Joint Committee to explain why any over-all constitution is actually needed. Congregational Churches have managed for well over three hundred years to get along without an over-all constitution. Such constitutions as we have are limited to specific bodies and agencies within our fellowship. That is why Congregationalism has had singularly little appeal to the legalistic mind, which finds a happy hunting ground in constitutionally minded denominations. We call for the maintenance of our freedom from the standardizations, authoritarianism, and rigidities which a constitution tends to impose.

We make the same request for a Statement of Faith as this time, which the churches may have before them prior to a vote on the Basis of Union.

13. Adequate Study Should Be a Requirement for Voting On the Basis of Union

We call upon every Church, Association and Conference not to vote until it has examined both sides of the merger. The subject matter of this study should be, first of all, a historical study of Congregationalism, and upon that background, the Basis of Union itself, so that it may be intelligently understood. The second subject should be a consideration of the fundamental issues involved in the proposed shift from a Congregational fellowship of churches to a more centrally orangized and controlled church, such as the Basis of Union proposes. Attention should also be given to the meaning and function of Congregationalism as it now exists and its importance for the future. (We recommend "An Adventure in Liberty", Pilgrim Press, 10 cents.)

These study meetings should not be testimonial meetings in general glorification of Christian unity. We all take Christian unity for granted. They should be meetings devoted to the analysis of the document and to an understanding of the alternative and mutually exclusive theories of the church on which we must cast our vote. If we propose to move over toward a presbyterial theory of the church, we should do so understanding fully what we are doing.

Full recognition should be given to the right of Christians to differ, which is part of the genius of the Congregational Christian fellowship.

14. The Wider Interests and Possibilities of the Congregational Christian Churches

We call upon each minister and layman to consider before voting not only his particular interest and geographical situation, but also the long Congregational heritage of which he is a part by birth or adoption, and the importance of a fellowship of autonomous churches in the wider interests of the Kingdom of Jesus Christ.

15. Education Instead of Propaganda and Promotion

We call upon the Executive Committee and the various Boards and agencies, including publications, of our fellowship to recognize that their function is not to promote the merger but to inform the constituency, both adult and youth, about the nature of the fundamental issues involved and what can be said on both sides. We believe their task should be that of education, not propaganda.

16. Recommend Use of the Secret Ballot, Etc.

We recommend that every vote be taken by secret ballot.

We recommend a vote of "No" against the merger by those churches which believe our considerations in the Evanston Meeting regarding the Basis of Union and the values of Congregationalism for our Protestant faith are valid.

We recommend a vote of "No" against the merger unless a person feels confident the merger will not destroy or weaken vital services Congregationalism can render to the Christian cause and to American democracy at this time.

We recommend a vote of "No" against the merger unless a person believes we are justified in the present world crisis, in spending the time and energy on the innumerable problems of mutual adjustment which the merger will lay heavily upon us all.

We point out that a vote of "No" against the merger in its present form is not a vote against church unity, nor even against merger with the Evangelical and Reformed Church on terms that more adequately safeguard the service Congregationalism can render to the Protestant faith and way in these tragic times and in the long years ahead.

17. For Attention of Churches Not Voting or Voting "No" On the Basis of Union

We call attention to a proposal made on the floor of the Evanston Meeting, that churches, in voting, use another ballot than that submitted by the Executive Committee, as follows:

1) Resolved that the . . . . . Church (Association, Conference) finds the Basis of Union unsatisfactory in its present form and, therefore, rejects the merger proposed in said Basis of Union.

2) Resolved that the . . . . . Church (Association, Conference) having voted to reject the merger, proposes to continue as a Congregational Church (Association, Conference) in fellowship with all like-minded Congregational Christian Churches, Associations and Conferences, to the end that the historic General Council of the Congregational Christian Churches and the Boards and agencies which have been created by the Congregational Christian Churches, may be maintained and continued.

18. Our Youth and the Merger

We express our concern for the youth of our churches to whom the leadership of our fellowship will pass in a few years. We believe this proposed merger is contrary to the trend of the creative Christian life of our time. Our fellowship of Congregational Christian Churches as now constituted has the great opportunity of effective leadership to bring into existence the federative union of many denominations. We believe such federative union can transform the life of our nation and the world if vigorously sought under able leadership. We pray that the young people of our churches in the years to come may be a part of that leadership in cooperative Protestantism that will develop stronger local churches, a united American Protestantism and full cooperation with the World Council of Churches.

19. We Desire Federative Union With Many Denominations

We call for strong leadership on the part of the Congregational Christian Churches, in which we hope the Evangelical and Reformed Church will share, to explore and vigorosuly promote ways and means of bringing about a federative union of Protestantism. Congregationalists can appropriately take the lead here for our Congregational Christian fellowship is in itself a federation of churches.

We heartily approve the revolutionary move the General Council has already made along this line by inviting other denominations which accord one another mutual recognition of ministries and sacraments to participate in a plenary conference to consider the possibilities of closer unity.

We call upon our churches to put their strength behind this movement, in even greater force and vigor than has been devoted to the merger. We urge that our leaders in this enterprise be instructed to accept as their task the achievement of unity according to the federative rather than the organic principle.

We call upon our churches to lift their eyes away from secondary matters and see this wide and hopeful horizon: a federative union in which many denominations will have a part. Its federative structure will express the fellowship and catholic unity of Protestantism and conserve the rich and diverse treasures of the bodies constituting it. Such unity can become a more adequate instrument in the Hand of God for the bringing in of His Kingdom.

Such a federative union will indeed deserve the magnificent name of the United Churches of Christ in America.

Findings Committee of the Evanston Meeting

Mr. S. T. Roberts, Chairman, 4916 Cottage Street, Philadelphia 24, Pa.
Rev. Hugh Elmer Brown, 1820 Asbury Avenue, Evanston, Ill.
Mr. Raymond H. Fiero, 32 Court Street, Brooklyn 2, N. Y.
Mr. Horatio Ford, The Williamson Building, Cleveland 14, Ohio
Mr. Stanley S. Gillam, 632-636 Builders Exchange Building,
Minneapolis 2, Minn.
Rev. Niel E. Hansen, 19 South LaSalle Street, Chicago 3, Ill.
Rev. Charles F. Jacobs, 312 Home Park Boulevard, Waterloo, Iowa
Rev. William A. Keith, 709 Edgemoor Avenue, Kalmazoo, Mich.
Rev. A. C. McGiffert, Jr., 5757 University Avenue, Chicago 37, Ill.
Rev. George W. Shepherd, 85 Grand Avenue, W., Highland Park, Mich.
Rev. Max Strang, 74 S. Grandview Avenue, Dubuque, Iowa

Document 4.
Letter Missive from Blanchard on the Evanston Meeting

COPY.....   LETTER MISSIVE

Cleveland, Ohio
18 December 1947

The Commission on Interchurch Relations and Christian Unity

To the Congregational Christian Churches of the United States

Sends greeting:

This Commission, acting for the past five and one-half years under instructions given by the General Council and recorded in the Council Minutes of 1942, 1944, and 1946, has submitted the Basis of Union with the Evangelical and Reformed Church which it was ordered to prepare.

Eleven of our honored friends, acting for a group of individuals opposed to the Basis of Union, who met last month at Evanston, Illinois, have sent to the churches a brochure entitled 'The Evanston Meeting'.

This brochure contains certain statements that call for correction. The Commission has thought it fitting to bring to your attention the most important of these:

1. The brochure states in bold letters (page 7): 'The Basis of Union if accepted will take away the autonomy of the local church.'

The truth is stated in Article III Section H of the Basis of Union:

'Each Congregation...has the right of retaining or adopting its own charter, constitution, by-laws, and other regulations which it deems essential and proper to its welfare. This right includes the holding and operation of its own property.' Nothing else in the Basis denies or qualifies this statement.

Note also that the vote which the churches are asked to take in approving or disapproving the Basis of Union assures the continuance of autonomy:

'In the event of the consummation of the union, this body undertakes to continue the same relations with the United Church of Christ that it now holds with the fellowship of the Congregational Christian Churches.'

2. The brochure states (page 3, line 21): '....the Basis of Union includes two contradictory methods of calling and accepting resignations of ministers.'

The methods are different but not contradictory. Both can be employed.

3. The brochure states (page 3, line 26): '....a large amount of the missionary giving will be used annually for thirty years to fund minister-ial annuities.'

Any one who has a question at this point may learn the facts by writing to The Pension Boards, Room 902, 287 Fourth Avenue, New York 10, N. Y.

4. The brochure states (page 3, line 29): 'Though the uniting of the Home and Foreign Mission Societies of the two groups may be legally effected, the legal question remains whether this could be done if some of our churches do not vote or vote 'No'.'

There is no legal question about this whatever. The Societies are legally independent and can choose the relationships they desire.

-2-

5. The brochure states (page 4, Line 4): 'Legal difficulties exist in the proposed merger....'

We do not know of any. <u>Legal counsel has been had</u> at every step of the negotiations. The opinion of Chief Justice Maltbie of Connecticut, declaring that there are no such legal difficulties, is available.

6. The brochure states (page 7, bottom): '....a Congregational Christian Church which does not vote on this merger or which votes negatively is cut off from the fellowship....'

The truth is as stated in the 'Information on Voting' which has been sent through the Conference offices to the churches:

'If the union is consummated, all....local churches....of the present Congregational Christian fellowship will be regarded as belonging to the fellowship of the United Church of Christ, <u>whether they have voted approval or disapproval</u>....' (This applies to both resolutions to be voted upon.) '....Local churches....desiring not to be regarded as belonging to the fellowship of the United Church should take action of a positive nature to that end.'

7. The brochure states (page 8, line 19): '....the Basis of Union.... includes....setting up a judicial system foreign to our congregational way.'

The Basis of Union should be read. <u>The proposed procedure is advisory</u>, not mandatory; and we believe that it creates possibilities for just action beyond that which is now obtainable.

8. The brochure states (page 9, line 14): '....the Basis of Union provides two alternative ways of ordaining, calling and placing ministers....The Congregational way is permitted, but the United Church will appeal to congregations and ministers to adopt the presbyterial way. Such an appeal seems to imply the use of a subtle kind of pressure.'

Actually the proposed way is <u>not presbyterial</u>—and there is no more pressure in it than for instance in the appeal to churches and ministers today to enter the pension plan.

9. The brochure states (page 14, line 15): '....a vote of 'No' against the merger in its present form is not a vote against church unity....'

It is, however, a vote against the <u>one practical step</u> in the direction of church unity available to us today.

    Wishing you grace, mercy, and peace, we are

               The Commission on Interchurch Relations and
                     Christian Unity

               Ferdinand Q. Blanchard, Chairman

Document 5.
Buschmeyer's Letter on the "Comments"

(C O P Y)   THE CONGREGATIONAL CHRISTIAN CHURCHES

                OF THE UNITED STATES OF AMERICA

287 Fourth Ave
New York 10, N.Y.

                                    2 February 1948

    Dear Fellow Ministers:

                As Chairman of the Education Committee ap-
    pointed by the Executive Committee of the General Council of the
    Congregational Christian Churches I have been requested by the
    Executive Committee to pass on to you the two documents enclosed
    herewith.

                The Comments on the Basis of Union were
    drawn largely by Dr. Alfred Grant Walton as a series of inter-
    pretations which, if agreed to by responsible leaders of both the
    Evangelical and Reformed Church and the Congregational Christian
    Churches, would clarify important points of issue regarding the
    Basis of Union, and give assurance that our essential Congre-
    gational Christian polity and freedom would be protected and pre-
    served.

                The members of the Joint Commission on Union
    whose names appear here have agreed upon the accuracy of these
    comments and interpretations. The members of the Executive Com-
    mittee of the General Council likewise concur in believing that
    these comments are a true interpretation of the essential articles
    of the Basis of Union.

                In the open meeting out of which the second
    statement came, these comments were similarly approved for their
    accuracy and helpfulness in clarifying points that had seemed un-
    certain to some people. A number of persons present at that meet-
    ing said frankly and openly that this clarification changed their
    own position from questioning or opposition to approval of the
    Basis of Union. It was the request of this meeting that the Exe-
    cutive Committee take the appropriate steps to submit these two
    documents to the ministers and people of our churches for their
    information also.

                It is the sincere hope of the Education Com-
    mittee that these documents may prove helpful to you and your
    people in their study of the Basis of Union and in their voting.

                        Respectfully submitted,

                        Fred S. Buschmeyer
                        Fred S. Bschmeyer

Document 6.

"Comments" from the Midwinter Meeting (January 1948)

Comments on the Basis of Union
by the members of the Joint Committee which prepared it

Inasmuch as questions have been raised regarding the meaning of the Basis of Union at certain points, the following comments are submitted as the understanding of the undersigned members of the Evangelical and Reformed Church and the Congregational Christian Churches.

E. & R.: George W. Richards, Roberts R. Appel, L. W. Goebel, G. W. Grauer, John R. C. Haas, Nevin C. Harner, John Lentz, John W. Mueller, S. D. Press, Paul M. Schroeder

C. C.: Ferdinand Q. Blanchard, Simon A. Bennett, Mrs. Henry B. Davis, Noble Strong Elderkin, David K. Ford, Harold B. Frame, David McKeith, Jr., Charles C. Merrill, J. Chester Molyneux, Wilhelm Pauck, Herman F. Ressig, Frank Milton Sheldon, Russell Henry Stafford, Alfred Grant Walton.

1. The United Church of Christ will be a union of churches joined in fellowship and cooperation without involving any invasion of the rights now enjoyed by local churches.

2. Congregations, Associations, Conferences, and the General Synod, being voluntary fellowships, possess autonomy in their own spheres, which autonomy is acknowledged and and will be respected.

3. The American Board of Commissioners for Foreign Missions and the Board for Home Missions are agencies and instrumentalities of the United Church of Christ and while the members of the Boards will be nominated and elected by the General Synod, the Boards will have authority in their own sphere of activity, and the General Synod, except for its right to allocate undesignated denominational benevolent moneys, shall have only advisory powers in relation to them.

4. The Constitution of the United Church of Christ will also be the constitution of the General Synod, and no other constitution for the General Synod is contemplated (a) It will be functional and definitive in relation to the General Synod but descriptive in relation to the Boards, Conferences, Associations, and churches. (b) It will not contemplate any legal control over the local churches, Associations, and Conferences by the General Synod. (c) It will describe the relation of the various Boards, commissions, agencies, and instrumentalities to the United Church and also the relations of Conferences, Associations, and congregations to the United Church. The present Congregational Christian churches may ratify this Constitution, but there is no mandate upon them to ratify it if they do not desire to do so. See the Basis of Union, IV A.

5. No member of the Congregational Christian Annuity Fund shall be penalized in any way by his refusal to accept ministerial standing in the United Church or by reason of the failure of the church he serves to accept fellowship in the United Church.

6. In the event that the apportionment giving in any year falls below the $ 3,3000,000 mentioned in Art. VIII G 7 of the Basis of Union, the prior claim of the Merged Fund will be reduced sufficiently so that there will be no disproportionate losses to the missionary work of the denomination, except that the prior claim shall in no case be less than the amount sufficient to meet the requirements of the year in question for the unfunded portion of the annuities under the 'original plans' plus the necessary expenses of promotion and administration.

7. It is fully expected that churches and ministers preferring to maintain a system of pastoral placement in which the Conference or Association shall have little or no part may do so without prejudice, since the Basis of Union provides that 'in all relationships between minister and the local church or Congregation, the freedom of the minister and the autonomy of the church are presupposed.'

8. The vote of any Congregational Christian church on the proposed union, even though negative, will not in itself or in any way in the event of union impair the fellowship of that church with Association, Conference, or General Synod. It is not the intention of the Basis of Union or of the provisions for voting thereon in the event of merger to withdraw fellowship from any Congregational Christian church now of the fellowship. The relation of a church to its Association will not be affected by its vote on the union, provided that the church continues to abide by the rules and regulations of its own Association.

9. Appeals, complaints, and references shall be dealt with by Associations and Conferences in accordance with their own rules.

- -

A STATEMENT

adopted by those assembled for the Mid-Winter Meeting of the
Missions Council (American Board, Board of Home Missions,
Council for Social Action, Superintendents, Woman State Presidents, Executive Committee of General Council, etc.)
26-29 January, 1948

The ministers and lay people assembled at the Mid-Winter Meeting of the Missions Council of our Congregational Christian Churches entered into a discussion of the proposed union of our churches with the Evangelical and Reformed Church. Both proponents and opponents were represented in the discussion and the atmosphere was one of earnest enquiry and tolerant understanding. The entire group was heartened by the further interpretation of the Basis of Union as approved by members of the Joint Committee and recognized this interpretation as a clear-cut statement of intent to preserve the traditional polity of the autonomy of the local church. The hope of the overwhelming majority of those present was that we may continue to move toward the consummation of the proposed union as a vital contribution to the ecumenical movement.

Howard Conn
Katherine Schroeder (Mrs. John C.)
William A. Keith

(Note: above is exact copy of the mimeographed copies of the "Comments" which were sent to the churches when they were voting. The "Statement" which appears immediately above was reprinted in "ADVANCE" for March, 1948, but the comments themselves were not so published.)

Document 7.
Conn's Letter on the "Comments"

COPY///   PLYMOUTH CONGREGATIONAL CHURCH
            1900 Nicollet Ave.   Minneapolis 4, Minnesota
Howard Conn/David J. Julius/Arthur B. Jennings/Ruth E. Bailey/Ruth J. Easterday
                                                Hazel Fraker
TO THE CONGREGATIONAL MINISTERS OF MINNESOTA:

I owe an apology and explanation to each one of you. In the February issue of
CONGREGATIONAL MINNESOTA you will find an article by me in opposition to the
Merger. This article was written in early December. I have just returned from
the Mid-Winter meetings of our Missions Council, where the question was thoroughly discussed. I return home "converted" - convinced that Christian state-
manship requires that we do all we can to consummate this merger.

In a single paragraph let me try to summarize the evidence that led to my changed
viewpoint. (1) I learned from Dr. Frazier some historical data concerning the
E & R Church which indicates that they are a people who have a record for liberty
which is as impressive as ours. (2) At the Mid-Winter meeting Dr. Horton presented
a statement of interpretation which clearly secures the Congregational polity of
autonomy of the local church as being at the heart of the Basis of Union. This
statement was drawn up by Dr. Walton, an opponent of the Merger, and submitted to
the Joint Committee of the two denominations to see if they truly intended their
instrument to be Congregational in polity. The E & R members as well as our own
agreed completely. This new development undercuts all opposition on the ground
that Congregationalism will be lost in the Basis of Union or the new church.
(3) Written legal opinions of the lawyers of all our Boards were presented to
indicate that the Basis of Union would not expose said Boards to effective or
successful adverse litigation. (4) We will not lose our name, but rather strengthen historic Congregationalism as the guiding spirit in the new and growing
United Church of Christ in America. Our local parishes will still be "The First
Reformed Church of Lancaster", "The First Church of Christ in New Haven", or
"Plymouth Congregational Church"; but we will be knit together in the larger
fellowship of "The United Church of Christ". (5) If the Merger should be defeated, the cause of Christian unity would be set back many years, for such defeat would demonstrate that practical partisan concerns are stronger than the
passion for unity; if, on the other hand, the Merger is consummated, several
other groups will take prompt steps to come in with us on the same Basis of
Union. The Free Church bodies which are Congregational in polity will have a
strong inclination to do so. (6) It became quite apparent to me in the discussion at the Mid-Winter meeting that the motives of many vocal opponents are not
truly worthy. Hitting at the Basis of Union has been a cover-up for (a) pride
that does not want to lose the name of our denomination, (b) Anglo-Saxon superiority that looks down on German origin groups even though many of these people
have been on our soil since the days of William Penn; (c) the human psychological
reaction of the-man-on-the-outside-against-the-man-on-the-inside which in this
case is resentment against the leadership of our denominational officials; (d)
fear lest in certain areas the E. & R. strength may deprive our group of control.
Frankly, I think some of these unworthy motives influenced me in my earlier
judgment. Yet, when I heard the incontrovertible Congregational interpretation
of the Basis of Union, and when I saw the sincere and passionate interest of
our national leaders in the cause of church unity, I could not help but feel
that Christ's Kingdom and His Church can best be served by consummating this
merger.

This letter is not written to influence you to think as I think but as a frank
confession of my own changed viewpoint. I owe it to you in the light of the
public statement written earlier for our state paper.

                                        HOWARD CONN

January 31, 1948

Document 8.
Horton's Letter to Conn

COPY/// 　　　The General Council of Congregational Christian Churches
　　　　　　Two Eighty Seven Fourth Ave., New York 10, N. Y.
　　　　　　　　　　　　　　　　　　　　　　　9 February 1948
Dear Howard,

　　　Entirely apart from the issue of the proposed union itself, it took no end of both courage and conviction to do what you have recently done. I believe that you have come to a true view of the situation, but whether or not that had been the case, I could not but have respected you for your action. You have done our fellowship a service which will pay dividends to our children and our children's children.

　　　Now to answer the question of Stanley Gillam. In a word, the Basis of Union cannot be changed at this stage in the proceedings. The General Synod of the Evangelical and Reformed Church has already voted upon it in its present form, and many of our own churches have done the same; to attempt to alter it in any way just now would be to cause endless confusion and delay the consummation of the union by at least three years -- since the General Synod is not due to meet again 'til 1950. I should not be perturbed by the delay, but this would mean a prolongation of discussion--and that I believe would be spiritually devastating. Possibly the E. and R. people could be induced to call a special meeting of their General Synod in a year, but for the following reasons I do not believe that the matter is of sufficient importance to ask them to do so. Furthermore, even a year's continuation of the debate would have harmful effects, I believe.

　　　I would personally do anything I could to meet Stanley Gillam's objections, but I wonder if he has considered the following:

1. We have had good legal advice at every turn of the road. Loren Wood, senior partner of the firm Wood, Molloy, and France, of New York, who has been our chief counselor, believes the Basis to be thoroughly Congregational.

2. The Chief Justice of the Supreme Court of Connecticut also believes it to be Congregational. This is not a snap judgment; it is his considered opinion after studying it, the charters of all our organizations, and innumerable related documents, for many days.

3. The only carefully written opinion of a practicing lawyer to the contrary which I know about is that of Harold S. Davis of Boston. Mr. Davis, however, starts from a definition of Congregationalism which no student of American or British Congregationalism can accept, viz, that Congregationalism is the polity of churches joined in a fellowship of such a type that the fellowship itself cannot act. His own words are: '...the Congregational "denomination" is not an entity capable of taking action of any kind.' One might as well say that the United States cannot take action of any kind--but actually it can act, through Congress, etc. So our fellowship can act, through the Association to ordain ministers or recognize them through the General Council to set the percentage of undesignated gifts to go to the Boards, etc. It is from this same angle that Mr. Fackenthal, a Brooklyn business man who studied law in his youth, approaches the matter. The briefest reference to any of our standard treatises such as Barton's The Law of Congregational Usage must convince any enquirer that Congregationalism has never stood for Freedom without Fellowship but always for both Freedom and Fellowship.

4. Mr. Davis' position would have no standing whatever in any court of law. It has been completely demolished by an exhaustive review by Lucius E. Thayer, another Boston attorney retained by The Massachusetts Conference. Stanley S. Gillam might secure a copy of this by writing to the Conference; it is 36 pages in length.

5. The United Church of Christ will not have that type of polity which I have defined above as Freedom without Fellowship--the kind that Mr. Davis believes we

[315]

-2-

have now. It will, however, have the same kind of polity that we enjoy today;
Freedom with Fellowship. We cannot keep people from suing us on this score if they
want to (though I know of no one who intends to do so) but we are so sure of our
ground that we have not the slightest apprehension regarding the result of such a
suit.

6. If Stanley Gillam himself as a lawyer will sit down with the Basis of Union,
and set aside all that has been written by fearful and suspicious people about
the Basis of Union, I am sure that he will come out where Judge Maltbie and all
the other grade-A lawyers have come out -- with the opinion that no one can accept
that Basis without accepting the Congregational idea.

But now, what of the future? We cannot amend the Basis just now, but there
is no reason in the world, so far as I can see, why some of us Congregationalists
could not guarantee that so far as in us lies these interpretations in substance
would be written into the Constitution. Such a pledge would be a most powerful
instrument not only because we Congregationalists would be in a majority in the
new denomination but because we should be joined in it by the overwhelming number
of the E. and R. people.

Just one word of warning. We Congregationalists cannot in decency say, "The
new denomination is going to be completely Congregational" - period. The way to
put the matter inoffensively to the E. and R. people and yet fairly from the point
of view of truth is to say that both of us are going to make contributions to the
new denomination, the E. and R. people contributing their own values, we contributing the idea of the self-governing church in fellowship with other similar
churches.

Ever yours,

Douglas Horton

The Rev. Howard Conn,
Minneapolis, Minn.

(The above letter was not published or circulated generally, but copies of
it caused considerable discussion in limited circles. Eventually Dr. Horton,
upon being pressed on the matter, acknowledged in a letter to Mr. Fackenthal
that the latter does rate as an attorney of standing.

This letter is important, however, in showing Dr. Horton's reasoning
and some of the personal persuasion which he used. Dr. Howard Conn had originally opposed the union, but was won over at the Mid-Winter meeting of 1948
by Dr. Horton's reading of the "Comments", which Dr. Conn accepted as proof
that the union would be "Congregational" in polity.

Dr. Conn, after changing his mind in January of 1948, sent out a
letter explaining his change of view. This went originally to thechurches
in Minnesota, but it was later used extensively in other states. Dr. Horton's
statements in the first paragraph of his letter refer, no doubt, to the statements made by Dr. Conn in his published letter of January 31, 1948.)

Document 9.
Proposed Motion for General Council

PROPOSED MOTION FOR GENERAL COUNCIL

Revision of April 12, 1948

WHEREAS the Congregational Christian Churches have been traditionally in favor of church union and favor at this time union with the Evangelical and Reformed Church, and

WHEREAS the Council has now before it the Basis of Union prepared under instruction of the Councils of 1942, 1944 and 1946, and

WHEREAS the following paragraphs express the meaning of the Basis of Union and the interpretation of certain terms used in the Basis of Union, upon which the following votes of the General Council relative to the union are based:

a) <u>United Church of Christ</u>. "United Church of Christ" is the name of the national Christian Fellowship, formed by this union, and its use in the singular does not express or imply any theory regarding the nature of the church.

b) <u>Congregation</u>. Wherever the word "Congregation" is used in the Basis of Union, it is equivalent to "local church".

c) <u>Former Congregational Christian Churches</u>. The expression "former Congregational Christian Churches" contained in Article IV, Section A of the Basis of Union, is defined as, Congregational Christian Churches existing at the time the union of the two communions is effected. It does not imply that such Congregational Christian Churches either go out of existence at the time of the union of the two communions, or suffer any impairment or diminution of their historic freedom and continuity of relationship through their Associations to the Congregational Christian fellowship. In consummating this union Congregational Christian and Evangelical and Reformed churches are uniting in one fellowship without break in their respective historic continuities. The Congregational Christian Churches will continue to be Congregational Christian Churches, and it is assumed that Evangelical and Reformed Congregations will continue to be such though both communions are united in the United Church of Christ.

d) <u>Government</u>. The word "government" in Article III, Section F, is defined as church polity, and does not express or imply any theory regarding the nature of the church.

e. <u>Members</u>. The expression "members of the United Church" in Article VII signifies persons who are in full fellowship in the united communion through their membership in one of the churches which comprise it.

f. <u>Successor</u>. In Article X, Section B, in the clause reading "The General Synod of the United Church of Christ being the successor to the General Council of the Congregational Christian Churches, etc.", the word "successor" is understood as applying to the spiritual and churchly functions of the General Council only. The General Council remains in existence for legal reasons.

g) The United Church of Christ will be a union of churches joined in fellowship and cooperation without involving any invasion of the rights now enjoyed by local churches.

h) Congregations, Associations, Conferences, and the General Synod, being voluntary fellowships, possess autonomy in their own spheres, which autonomy is acknowledged and will be respected.

i) The American Board of Commissioners for Foreign Missions and the Board of Home Missions are agencies and instrumentalities of the churches that unite to form the union, and while the members of the Boards will be nominated and elected by the General Synod, the Boards will have authority in their own sphere of activity, and the General Synod, except for its right to allocate undesignated denominational benevolent moneys, shall have only advisory powers in relation to them.

j) The Constitution of the United Church of Christ will also be the constitution of the General Synod, and no other constitution for the General Synod is contemplated. (a) It will be functional and definitive in relation to the General Synod but descriptive in relation to the Boards, Conferences, Associations, and churches. (b) It will not contemplate any legal control over the local churches, Associations, and Conferences by the General Synod. (c) It will describe the relation of the various Boards, commissions, agencies, and instrumentalities to the United Church and also the relations of Conferences, Associations, and congregations to the United Church. The present Congregational Christian churches may ratify this Constitution, but there is no mandate upon them to ratify it if they do not desire to do so. See the Basis of Union, IV A.

k) No member of the Congregational Christian Annuity Fund shall be penalized in any way by his refusal to accept ministerial standing in the United Church or by reason of the failure of the church he serves to accept fellowship in the United Church.

l) In the event that the apportionment giving in any year falls below the $3,300,000 mentioned in Art. VIII G 7 of the Basis of Union, the prior claim of the Merged Fund will be reduced sufficiently so that there will be no disproportionate losses to the missionary work of the denomination, except that the prior claim shall in no case be less than the amount sufficient to meet the requirements of the year in question for the unfunded portion of the annuities under the 'original plans' plus the necessary expenses of promotion and administration.

m) It is fully expected that churches and ministers preferring to maintain a system of pastoral placement in which the Conference or Association have little or no part may do so without prejudice, since the Basis of Union provides that 'in all relationships between minister and the local church or Congregation, the freedom of the minister and the autonomy of the church are presupposed.'

n) The vote of any Congregational Christian Church on the proposed union, even though negative, will not in itself or in any way in the event of union impair the fellowship of that church with Association, Conference, or General Synod. It is not the intention of the Basis of Union or of the provisions for voting thereon in the event of union to withdraw fellowship from any Congregational Christian church now of the fellowship. The relation of a church to its Association will not be affected by its vote on the union, provided that the church continues to abide by the rules and regulations of its own Association.

o) Appeals, complaints, and references shall be dealt with by Associations and Conferences in accordance with their own rules.

and WHEREAS the Basis of Union provides under Article X that said Basis shall be approved by the General Council of the Congregational Christian Churches proceeding according to their own polity and

WHEREAS according to this polity the General Council is legally competent to approve the Basis of Union solely for itself and is not legally competent to commit conferences, associations or churches by any act on its part.

RESOLVED that the General Council approves the Basis of Union.

RESOLVED that the General Council recommends to the national boards, agencies and instrumentalities of the Congregational Christian Churches that each take such steps as fall within its respective proper and lawful sphere to implement Article VIII of the Basis of Union.

RESOLVED that the General Council instruct its Nominating Committee to prepare a ballot by means of which approximately 300 of its members be designated to represent it at a joint meeting which shall constitute the first meeting of the General Synod of the United Church of Christ.

RESOLVED that when at the joint meeting of the General Synod of the United Church of Christ, the actions of the two uniting communions being duly reported as having each been taken according to its own polity, and a joint resolution having been adopted declaring the union of the two communions to be effected, the General Council of the Congregational Christian Churches hereby entrusts to the General Synod of the United Church of Christ all those spiritual and churchly purposes which the General Council has hitherto possessed and which have been described in Article II of the Constitution of the General Council, and the General Council constitutes the General Synod in this spiritual and churchly sense its successor.

RESOLVED that the General Council expressly recognize that certain provisions of the Basis of Union can be carried out only by the voluntary action of autonomous local churches, associations and conferences.

Document 10.
Suggestions from the Connecticut Group

Connecticut Group   Appendix E

                                                April 16, 1948

Some Suggestions relative to the Basis of Union:

1. That we notify the Evangelical and Reformed group of the present
    status of the vote in the Congregational Christian churches and
    give the opportunity of suggesting that the matter of the Union
    be recommitted to a joint committee for further discussion.

2. That the Executive Committee of the General Council recommend to
    the Council meeting at Oberlin that inasmuch as other national
    bodies have expressed an interest in union, we recommit our Basis
    of Union to a joint committee and invite other denominations to
    consult and advise with us toward the formation of a greater body
    of uniting churches.

3. That at the meeting of the Connecticut Conference to be held on
    May 24th we are prepared to submit the following motions:

    That the vote submitted by the Executive Committee of the
    General Council be laid on the table and the following
    resolution be adopted.

    Whereas other national church bodies have signified an
    interest in a larger union of Protestantism, and

    Whereas the present Basis of Union between the Evangelical
    and Reformed and the Congregational Christian Churches has
    brought forth divergent interpretations,

    We recommend to the General Council that this Basis of Union
    be resubmitted to a joint committee of the Evangelical and
    Reformed and the Congregational Christian Churches for further
    study and revision, and that other church bodies interested in
    union be invited to send official representatives to partici-
    pate in the discussions.

                Present: Russell J. Clinchy
                            James F. English
                            Theodore A. Greene
                            Harold G. King
                            Elden H. Mills
                            Rockwell Harmon Potter

Document 11.
Report of Moderator Palmer (20 April 1948)

Appendix B

REPORT of the MODERATOR
to the
Executive Committee meeting at Buck Hill Halls
April 20, 1948

Dear Friends:

I am glad to report encouraging gains in my own personal physical strength since your last meeting at Grand Rapids; but not sufficient to make it expedient for me to come east at this time. I am conserving my strength and laying plans to be with you at Oberlin in June.

You all know of my letter to the E. and R. churches dated March 3rd, and to our own churches dated March 10th. These letters were called forth by a letter of February 27th sent by Mr. S. T. Roberts to the E. and R. churches. My letters were sent entirely on my own motion and responsibility. The initiative came from a young Congregational minister in the middle west who phoned me by long-distance of his distress over the reaction of the E. and R. ministers in his vicinity to the Roberts letter. As soon as I read the Roberts letter (which he sent me air-mail, following his phone call), I felt that someone ought to speak out promptly in behalf of the denomination; and, as moderator, I accordingly did so. I trust that you think I acted wisely, and I hope that history ten years from now will justify my action.

My letters have brought me both brick-bats and bouquets. The bouquets have been much more numerous, but the brick-bats hurt more. The whole experience has been rather disillusioning. I had expected more dispassionate judgments from a fellowship like ours.

But, when people are emotionally disturbed, you learn some things about what is really on their minds which might not otherwise have been revealed. And so I have tried to analyze this very disturbing and, to me, completely unexpected denominational brain-storm about the Basis of Union.

As I size up the situation, the emotions which have been aroused and, in some instances, rather astutely played upon in this unfortunate, and one year ago quite unforeseen, debacle in our denominational life can be classified under four fears and four resentments, as follows:

A THE FEARS

1. The general fear of change, the inertia which is always present.

2. The fear of regimentation. "We don't want to lose our freedom". This fear (to my mind completely unwarranted) is partly a carry-over from the fears and tensions of current secular life--fascism, communism, stateism, etc.

3. The fear of losing our name, Congregational, and our distinctive conception of church polity. Here a student of semantics would say that the magic word over-rode the realities of the situation, and led to a championing of our historic polity in its most primitive and even anarchic form regardless of our actual current practices and problems.

4. The fear, largely sub-conscious no doubt, on the part of individuals of losing present power, prestige or security.

B THE RESENTMENTS

1. The perfectly natural resentment against those in official position. "This is not a grass-roots proposal". "The powers that be are trying to put something over on us". This, I feel, has been a very influential factor. All who have had any grievance against any kind of authority, any smouldering hostility against "287", have naturally and quite unconsciously been stampeded by cries of "Presbyterianism" and "top-level dictation". This seems almost unbelievable when one considers the remarkably modest, unselfish and devoted quality of our paid staff and professional leadership. Nevertheless it happens even in the best of organizations.

2. The resentment against the unhappy memories of yesterday. One man wrote me a long letter complaining of his treatment by the Presbyterians 50 years ago. He had been told the Basis of Union was Presbyterian----therefore!

3. There is also a more or less unconscious resentment against amalgamation with a non-New-England-origin group. A distinguished retired minister said to me: "If we are going to have a merger, why don't we unite with some out-standing denomination like the Presbyterians?"

4. And, in some instances, purely personal resentments have entered in. One letter to me revealed that what the writer really hated was my plea for tolerance for the pacifist position at the Durham General Council in 1942.

This analysis is doubtless crude and incomplete. Each of you will add other important items. But the most important thing of all is that we should not fear these fears nor resent these resentments, but learn what they have to teach. Then, humbly and constructively, with true Christian patience, let us try to devise a program from here on which shall avoid these pit-falls, and make possible a union with the E. and R. and other Christian bodies which shall both preserve our own historic witness for freedom and also strengthen the whole cause of Christianity in this critical but possibly creative age.

Your friend and moderator,

Albert W. Palmer

April 17, 1948

Document 12.
Statement of the Evanston Group (20 April 1948)

<u>A statement presented to the Executive Committee on April 20, 1948
by representatives of The Evanston Meeting.</u>

We are glad to be here as guests of the Executive Committee and as representatives of the "Evanston Meeting". The Evanston Meeting includes some 2,000 people scattered across American Congregationalism, who have discovered their common conviction and concern that the present Basis of Union must be rejected as a wholly inadequate instrument for effecting a merger with the E&R Church.

This is our third official contact with the Executive Committee.

The first occurred at Grand Rapids at our request. At that time we presented a document to you containing several suggestions and recommendations.

The second meeting was the Committee of Ten, which you set up. At that meeting agreement was reached that the so-called "Comments" had no official standing, a position subsequently taken by the E&R Church. The Executive Committee, which forwarded the "Comments" to our churches, has not as far as we know sent a follow-up to the churches informing them of the unofficial standing of the "Comments".

The Committee of Ten failed, however, to accomplish what appears to have been its main purpose, which was to see if there could be worked out an alternative to the Basis of Union. Its efforts proved to be abortive, despite good-will on both sides, because the proponents at that time did not take seriously the possibility that the Basis of Union would be voted unsatisfactory by the churches. Hence they had no heart for participating in joint efforts with the opponents to work out a substitute for the Basis of Union. And the opponents were unwilling by themselves alone to assume responsibility for undertaking what they felt was the responsibility of both proponents and opponents together. So the Basis of Union remained sacrosanct.

I.

In accepting your invitation, we understand that the Executive Committee has adopted a new premise. It now recognizes that the Basis of Union has failed to receive adequate support from the denomination as a whole and that, consequently, the merger cannot or should not be consummated at Oberlin on the present Basis of Union.

We understand that the Executive Committee, as a Committee, is neither pro nor con with respect to the Basis of Union and has taken no official position with regard to the merger, whatever may be the attitudes of individual members of the Executive Committee.

The Executive Committee is elected by the delegates from some 5,000 Congregational Christian Churches. It represents the whole of the fellowship, a fellowship which includes within it churches and individuals who favor as well as those who oppose merger on the present Basis of Union.

Within the fellowship the discussions and voting now going on to determine the will of that fellowship with regard to the proposed merger have reached a fairly conclusive point, according to the latest statistics.

[323]

The figures most recently available at "287" indicate that 1252 churches which have voted in 14 conferences, show as follows:

Yes: 714   No: 531

(Parenthetically, it may be added that the Evanston Meeting has received informal reports from 820 churches, indicating they have voted "No". These No-voting churches are located in 35 states and vary in size as follows:

Under 100 members	295
100-299	313
300-499	96
500-999	84
1,000 and over	32 (includes 12 with over 1,500 members)).

The "287" statistics indicate further that approximately 57% of the churches voting have voted pro; and 56% of the members voting have voted pro.

In considering the size of this negative vote, it should be remembered that, with few exceptions, employed denominational officers, national and local, as well as denominational funds and denominational channels of promotion have had their weight and influence ardently behind the support of the present Basis of Union.

It also appears that about 30% of the members of the churches have voted. In other words, a little less than 17% of the membership are opposed to the merger and a little more than 17% favor it.

(In view of these statistics, it may be appropriate to suggest that we quit talking about the majority and the minority position with respect to the Basis of Union and confine ourselves to referring to the proponents and the opponents or to those who favor and those who do not favor the merger on the present Basis of Union.

These figures from "287" appear to be based on the returns of the voting up to April 1, the date set in the Statement of Procedures, Page 3 of the Basis of Union for churches and members. This leads us to enquire whether the Executive Committee is responsible for the unsigned announcement in April Advance, page 39, to the effect that the vote of churches and members after that date will be counted. To permit this seems to us to come close to a case of changing the rules of the game after the game has started. We therefore raise the question whether the Executive Committee has instructed the Committee of Judges on Voting to disregard votes made after the polls were closed. Unless this is done, it will be necessary for opponents of the merger on the present Basis of Union to continue their efforts to enlighten our constituency about the document. Furthermore, we all need to have some firm knowledge about the way the voting has gone. Otherwise, a conference like this will take on the unreality of our former meetings. And the denomination, as a whole, will not have a chance, before Oberlin, to take stock of the situation that confronts it and take steps to meet it.

II.

As the Executive Committee, responsible to the total fellowship, you trans- cent certain lines of argument which proponents and opponents respectively are taking.

Proponents say to opponents:

"we have proposed a Basis of Union which you opponents, by your votes, have declared to be unsatisfactory. All right! Now it's up to you to propose a substitute way."

On the other hand, opponents say to proponents:

"The rejection of the Basis of Union by so large a number of churches and members is a clear indication that you proponents erred in judgment when you concluded that the present Basis of Union would serve as an adequate and acceptable instrument for effecting a merger. It's up to you to try again to work out another kind or form of Basis of Union which will serve as an adequate and acceptable instrument."

The Executive Committee transcends this kind of argument. Your concern and responsibility seem to be to provide ways and means by which the denomination as a whole may make another try at merger. The denomination as a whole includes proponents, opponents and the large number of churches and members who have taken no stand one way or the other.

The purpose of this meeting, so we understand, is to explore the possibility of finding ways to compose the differences within the denomination, while at the same time conserving the integrity of the denomination as well as its vital interest in church unity.

III.

What precisely is the problem before us?

Certain proponents of the Basis of Union define the problem as follows:

Granted that the present Basis of Union is unsatisfactory, the problem is to discover a "middle way". This is not our definition of the problem. We consider the Basis of Union is itself a "middle way" between two different and incompatible theories of the church, and attempts to restate the middle of an already unsatisfactory middle way get nowhere, however valiant the attempts to do so.

Other proponents of the merger on the present Basis of Union define the problem somewhat differently. They say:

"We must discover a technicality by which the Basis of Union may be theoretically accepted but immediately on acceptance rendered a dead letter. The 'mechanical' means by which it is proposed to carry out this plan are the attachment to the Basis of Union of a series of interpretations, definitions, modifications, and restrictions."

At least three different statements looking to such a solution have been prepared, into each of which much earnest effort has been put.

None of them actually offers a satisfactory solution, however. And this for a simple reason. All these "interpretations" refer to the Basis of Union itself for reference and control. So in the end the Basis of Union still has its authority and power. Even if the Basis of Union were declared to be a dead letter, it would retain a permanent thread of resurrection.

In a word, the scheme to render the Basis of Union a dead letter, while still voting for it, cannot be equivalent to rejection of it.

Furthermore, these Congregational Christian interpretations are ex parte and ex post facto interpretations. In order to become official, they will need to be accepted by the E&R Church. That will require the E&R Church to engage again in the process of voting. If the E&R Church is thus willing to study and circulate for voting a modified form of the Basis of Union, then there is some justification for hoping that they will be willing to entertain a quite different document to vote on.

And that brings us to the premise which seems to underlie all these proposals. What is that premise? It is that unless we accept the Basis of Union, the E&R Church will have nothing further to do with us. It is alleged that the E&R's do not care how many modifications are made, so long as technically the Basis of Union is accepted by us. But they are unwilling to rehearse again the business of having another instrument approved by the General Synod and the various local Synods. To ask the E&R Church to do this, it is claimed, would be equivalent to breaking off all hope of union with them. Hence the various attempts to retain the Basis of Union, subject to unilateral interpretations.

If this premise is a correct analysis of the mind and mood of the E&R Church, then it would appear to the opponents of the merger that nothing further can be done. A merger of any kind is out of the question since the present Basis of Union is unsatisfactory., and no new plan would appeal to the E&R's.

IV.

It may be, however, that the premise is incorrect. It may be instead, as some of the E&R leaders say, that, though rejection of the present Basis of Union by us would be a serious obstacle to their continuing negotiations, such rejection would not be an insuperable obstacle. For them to start again, if we reject the present Basis of Union, would be difficult, but not impossible. For that matter, it would be difficult for us, too.

Either of these two premises is, of course, an assumption and a guess about a future attitude of the E&R Church. There may be stronger grounds for the first guess than for the second guess. No possibility of forward action, however, can come if the first premise be accepted. Until the second premise is proved to be invalid, it should at least be given a try.

Let us, then, assume that the E&R Church will prefer to undertake the exertion of working out and voting on another plan of union rather than to abandon altogether the hopes raised between us by our efforts thus far jointly engaged in. Let us frankly and completely reject the Basis of Union and invite them to work out a new form of union with us.

Perhaps before beginning this undertaking we should make further enquiry of the E&R Church about our new proposal; if we may assume, what cannot be assumed within the CC fellowship, that their leaders can deliver the vote of their Church. To be sure, the Evanston Meeting was not too successful in its unofficial attempts to communicate with the E&R pastors. But the passions aflame and inflamed by that effort might not be stirred by further attempts to get in touch with them.

But whether or not the E&R Church will be willing to make another try
with us, the CC fellowship will certainly not stop working for church unity. An
adequate plan for increased unity and cooperation among the denominations we must
work out, a plan which will be applicable not just to two denominations, but to
many denominations, a plan that will provide for such cooperative life and action
as are consistent with the recognition and maintenance of the valid diversities of
the participating denominations. To devise such a plan may well be Congregationalism's contribution to universal organized Protestantism.

In conclusion and summary we present the following propositions:

1. We of the Evanston group reaffirm our rejection of the merger on the present
Basis of Union.

2. It is the sense of our group that the Basis of Union has been rejected by
churches and the members of the churches according to the recommended terms
of procedure of the Joint Committee and that therefore the merger has failed
to secure denominational approval.

3. Because of the rejection of the Basis of Union by Congregational Christian
Churches and members, we urge the Executive Committee of the General Council
to take the necessary steps to prevent the proposed merger on the present Basis
of Union from coming before the General Council at Oberlin for a vote.

4. We submit the above proposition in the interest of stating the considered
opinion of the Evanston Meeting: first as reiteration of the original position
of the Evanston Meeting; second in view of the great disruption that the voting has caused in our fellowship of churches; and third in the interest of
the preservation of our fellowship for its vital present life and in the interest of our fellowship being able to go forward to work immediately with other
denominations for a plan of federative unity.

5. We further request the Executive Committee to advise the churches of the powers,
if any, of the General Council itself to enter into a merger of any kind, without a practically unanimous vote of all the Congregational Christian Churches
of the United States, this advice to be secured from legal counsel, and to be
received by the churches on or before June 1, 1948. The Evanston Meeting requests that an attorney it designates be one of those from whom legal counsel
is secured.

6. The Evanston Meeting has consistently maintained that it   is unwilling
to submit a plan of federative unity. We have taken this position because we
believe any such plan should be developed by Congregational Christian members
in fellowship with one another and not by a group of our fellowship that
favors or does not favor the present Basis of Union.

7. We have considered a proposal made by Dr. Frederick Meek dated April 15, 1948. The statement in part reaffirms points already made above, and in part deals with new matters not thus far considered. We believe Dr. Meek has proposed a hopeful plan for the beginning of a federative or functional union. We request you to have him present it.

8. If the Executive Committee, having determined to make plans to prevent the Basis of Union from coming to vote at Oberlin, should decide to undertake further plans to prepare alternatives to the present Basis of Union, we have a further suggestion to make: We suggest that the Executive Committee authorize the appointment of a committee of Interchurch Cooperative Union, one-half of the committee to be appointed by the Executive Committee from among the proponents of the present merger, and one-half to be appointed or nominated by the Evanston Meeting.

To this committee should be assigned consideration of Dr. Meek's proposal and of any others which do not presuppose the present Basis of Union. This committee should become a joint committee with representatives of the E&R Church and of other denominations.

9. Unless some such constructive alternative to the Basis of Union can be worked out in principle if not in detail in time for presentation at Oberlin, it is hard to see how the now impending spiritual calamity can be avoided. If the General Council should, in spite of the vote of the churches, accept the Basis of Union and consummate a merger, a part of the "No" voting churches may decide to remain the Congregational Christian Churches, allowing the "Yes" voting churches whose delegates consummate the merger to withdraw and become component parts of the United Church. If the Basis of Union is rejected without constructive alternatives, the proponents may suffer a profound sense of frustration and resentment.

We hope that it will become clear to the Executive Committee that the way to avoid either of these twin catastrophies is to have available at least in outline one or more alternative procedures for merger to present to Oberlin.

The Executive Committee's invitation to have representatives of the Evanston Meeting present here today we take to be a happy augury of the kind of statesmanlike decision you are called upon to make. That decision will be of critical significance for the denomination.

Document 13.

Horton's Report on the April 1948 Executive Committee Meeting

Please return to Albert W Palmer

THE GENERAL COUNCIL OF THE CONGREGATIONAL AND CHRISTIAN CHURCHES

TWO EIGHTY SEVEN FOURTH AVENUE NEW YORK

Dear Superintendents:

The Executive Committee in session at Buck Hill Falls, Pennsylvania, April 20-22, taking cognizance of the rumors and apprehensions which are abroad regarding the possible developments at Oberlin in June in the matter of the Basis of Union, wishes to inform the State Superintendents that it has taken unanimous action looking toward a wise safeguarding of the rights and peace of the churches.

The Judges of Voting are to be requested to indicate to the Advisory Committee, acting for the Executive Committee, the result of the voting by June second. If the judges find that the returns clearly indicate that the voting in one or more of the four categories is definitely short of the percentage necessary for a clear mandate to the General Council to validate the Basis of Union, the Advisory Committee, acting for the Executive Committee, will at once send the enclosed resolution to the churches with the request that all pastors immediately communicate it to the delegates representing their churches.

This resolution is the result of two full days of most careful and conscientious discussion. It has been prepared because the Executive Committee believes it is its imperative duty to take forethought and make provision to give information and such earnestly considered counsel as this emergency situation would seem to require. This resolution represents the only wise procedure the Executive Committee can recommend at this time and this resolution has been unanimously passed by that Committee.

Its purpose is (a) to avert possible serious complications within our own fellowship. It also (b) represents the Committee's realization that great numbers of our members and churches would feel it imperative that the door leading toward our brethren in the Evangelical and Reformed Church be left wide open.

The Executive Committee asks for the confidence of the Superintendents at this time. It believes that if this resolution and the spirit which we hope breathes through it are permitted to guide us at Oberlin an experience which could be grave even to the point of tragedy can be averted.

It is our earnest hope that our Superintendents will use their good offices to counsel the churches, Associations and Conferences to report promptly the result of their voting to your office, that a full and complete registration of opinion may be recorded. (And the Conference Registrars are urged to lose no time in forwarding their reports to the Judges of Voting, 287 Fourth Avenue, New York 10.)

Douglas Horton
Douglas Horton
for the Executive Committee

April 23, 1948

Document 14.
Horton's Report of the Provisional Resolution

Please return to Albert to Palm. —

THE GENERAL COUNCIL OF THE CONGREGATIONAL AND CHRISTIAN CHURCHES

TWO EIGHTY SEVEN FOURTH AVENUE NEW YORK

PROVISIONAL RESOLUTION

Resolved

That if the affirmative vote on the Basis of Union by members, churches,

Associations and Conferences as certified by the Judges of Voting on

June 1st be found to be short of 75% of the Conferences voting, 75% of

the Associations voting, 75% of the churches voting, or 75% of the mem-

bers voting, the Executive Committee send to the churches the following

statement:

TO THE CONGREGATIONAL CHRISTIAN CHURCHES

GREETINGS:

Whereas, the favorable vote of the churches of our faith and
order on the matter of The Basis of Union has fallen short of a clear
mandate to proceed with the validation of The Basis of Union;

Be it therefore resolved that the Executive Committee inform
the churches of this result;

Be it further resolved that the Executive Committee advise the
General Council that the Executive Committee is of one mind that the
General Council will best preserve the strength of the churches' life
and work and will best safeguard and protect the possibility of union
with the Evangelical and Reformed Church if no definitive action on
acceptance or rejection of the Basis of Union be taken by the General
Council meeting at Oberlin.

The Executive Committee urges and requests the delegates to the
General Council prayerfully to prepare themselves to seek God's guidance, with the hope that a way or ways may be made evident whereby we
may walk with our brethren of the Evangelical and Reformed Church in
love and by further study come, we trust, to an hour when our strength
and theirs may be made one in His service.

Douglas Horton
for the Executive Committee

Document 15.
Blanchard's Letter of 29 April 1948 to Palmer

FERDINAND Q. BLANCHARD
MINISTER
MISS LOUISE HARPER
PASTOR'S ASSISTANT AND
DIRECTOR OF RELIGIOUS ED

EUCLID AVENUE CONGREGATIONAL CHURCH
EUCLID AVENUE AT EAST NINETY-SIXTH STREET, CLEVELAND, OHIO

April 29, 1948

Rev. Albert W. Palmer, D. D.
1185 East Foothill Blvd.
Altadena, California

My dear Albert:

I want to express to you my appreciation of the articles
which you have written for the Messenger, and especially for the one
which has appeared in the recent number just received. Your statement
of the case is convincing beyond all question or debate. Also your
letters, as Moderator, have been admirable. The difficulty is, of course,
with the whole situation that people will not listen to a sane, straightforward statement of what is in the Basis and of what is involved in the
whole proposition.

The opponents persist in emphasizing certain things which
simply do not exist anywhere. I have thought that you might like to have
a brief statement of the situation as I see it to date.

The effect of the voting in the churches, with a result of
obtaining less than seventy-five per cent approval, has been, unfortunately
enough to convince a great many of the supporters of the plan that it has
been defeated. In a recent meeting of the Executive Committee at Buck Hill
Falls several of these individuals gave expression to their feeling in what
was virtually a surrender of their hope and the belief that nothing could
fairly be done at Oberlin. In the line of this conclusion the Executive
Committee decided to recommend putting off decision at Oberlin without any
clear indication of what should next be done.

I am herewith enclosing copy of a letter which I have just
sent to Dr. Goebel. This letter will give you a pretty accurate idea of

what Douglas Horton and myself and others have thought might be a possible
procedure.

The great and allimportant question is whether or not the
E. and R. people would think of this as a step forward and would be willing
to wait until it could be taken, or whether they would feel that we have
taken such action as to make it necessary to break off negotiations.

In sending this to you I would ask you particularly to
regard this statement as confidential. It would be most unfortunate if
opponents of the Merger should be apprised of it and lay plans to defeat
it in advance, if it should seem wise to present this from the Commission
at Oberlin.

If Goebel should say this would form a basis of continued
negotiations, then I think the Commission will be prepared to draw it up
in definite form and present it as the next step to be taken. And the
Oberlin Council will have it before them to decide. If Goebel finally says,
after consultation with his associates, that we cannot proceed in this way,
then we are faced with a very serious dilemma and it will need further
consideration before we shall be in a position to outline what can be
attempted and suggested at Oberlin.

Without saying anything to anybody else for the time being,
will you let me know soon what is your own thought after reading this letter
and whether you have any suggestions which the Commission might take into
consideration.

Douglas Horton has asked a committee, centering in Chicago,
which is very much interested in advancing the Merger, to make some sort of
a study of this proposition. They will, I suppose, communicate with the
Commission as to what they would do or conceive to be possible in advancing
it. Nothing will be said about this for the time being and their considerations

will be taken without giving at the present time any publicity to them.

Again let me say I shall welcome what you feel to be wise after you have thought the matter all over. I would only emphasize at the moment my feeling that we have now passed beyond the stage of doing much with arguments in favor of the <u>Basis</u> and are faced with the necessity of considering a line of action based on the fact that seventy-five per cent of the churches have not voted in favor of going forward and a great many of those who did so vote will be likely to feel we have broken faith with our projected plan if the Council proceeds in the face of the vote.

The Conferences and Associations, I feel very sure, will register the necessary seventy-five per cent. But we shall see as to that in the coming weeks.

With kindest regards, and expressing again my entire agreement with the statements that you have uttered, I am

Very sincerely yours,

FQB:mp

Document 16.
Blanchard's Letter of 6 March 1948 to Palmer

FERDINAND Q. BLANCHARD
MINISTER

MISS LOUISE HARPER
PASTOR'S ASSISTANT AND
DIRECTOR OF RELIGIOUS ED

EUCLID AVENUE CONGREGATIONAL CHURCH
EUCLID AVENUE AT EAST NINETY-SIXTH STREET, CLEVELAND, OHIO

March 6, 1948

Rev. Albert W. Palmer, D. D.
1185 East Foothill Blvd.
Altadena, California

My dear Albert:

Your letter is an excellent one, and I am very glad you are proposing to send it out.

Roberts is a human pest. If the E. and R. people should discover a few more like him and Burton, I think they would have ample ground for refusing to have any fellowship with a church that produced such specimens.

Our Commission will meet in about two weeks and prepare a Commission answer to supplement your letter.

Cordially yours,

Ferd Q Blanchard

FQB:mp

Document 17.
Palmer's Proposed Bill of Rights (18 May 1948)

A BILL OF RIGHTS FOR FREE CHURCHES;
OR
A COVENANT OF PRINCIPLES UPON WHICH CHRISTIAN UNITY CAN GO FORWARD.

1. In all efforts at genuine unity and cooperation we must keep in mind this three-fold formula:

> In all things where we agree, unity;
> In things where we differ, liberty;
> In all things, the will to be one.

2. Differences, therefore, may be as precious as unities; and so we must always seek the kind of unity which includes and provides liberty for differences. Only thus can we expect to attain "the unity of the spirit in the bonds of peace."

3. Two inseparable essentials for the unity of free churches are (a) the autonomy of the local church and (b) the effective cooperation of these churches in fellowship for mutual aid and effective service to the community and the world. Both of these must be adequately recognized, balanced and safe-guarded.

4. All organizations through which this fellowship is expressed and implemented, such as associations, conferences, councils, boards or synods, must be voluntary and autonomous - subject only to the churches which create them as vehicles of their cooperative desires and necessities. That is to say, they are to be controlled democratically from below, not autocratically from above.

5. No creedal subscription shall be required of either ministers, churches or individual members. Historic creeds should be honored for their witness to the progress of Christian thought, but a living church must not be bound by the dead hand. It has a duty, and must have the liberty, to formulate truth ever anew in the freedom of the living present.

6. The training and ordination of ministers is a concern of the candidate, who presents himself for examination and dedication to this high office; of the local church which nurtured him or which he is to serve; and also of the fellowship of churches and ministers into which he enters. All of these concerns must be properly recognized and safeguarded also in the placement of pastors and in providing for ministerial standing, pensions, etc.

7. There are degrees and intensities of unity. All unity is to some degree incomplete and federative - down to the unity of the atom. Not even the church of Rome possesses complete unity, and certainly the Quakers are not without it. Present day Congregational polity, even in churches like the Baptists and Disciples, possesses more forms and expressions of unity than formerly. This is manifestly true in our Congregational Christian fellowship - witness the rise of mission boards, a publishing house, a system of ministerial pensions, and the General Council itself. We must keep this door for more perfect union open. We must not freeze or crystalize at any stage; but, as a living organism, we must expect to grow and develop - always, of course, in accordance with our essential genius but also in accordance with the needs of the age and of the community we are set to serve. To do this we must humbly seek and await the guidance of the Holy Spirit. But to set arbitrary bounds as to where that Spirit shall lead us would be to deny the creative power of God himself to lead us into new and better ways.

A tentative draft presented by Dr. Albert W. Palmer
May 18, 1948

Document 18.
Horton's Letter of 24 May 1948
to Palmer on the Proposed Bill of Rights

THE CONGREGATIONAL CHRISTIAN CHURCHES
OF THE UNITED STATES OF AMERICA

DOUGLAS HORTON
ter of the General Council
287 Fourth Avenue
New York 10, N. Y.

24 May 1948

Dear Albert,

Your letter of the twenty-first has just this moment arrived. By this time you will have received the one I wrote to you on Saturday and will in consequence understand the issues as they appear to us to be drawn.

As I understand it, your feeling, up to the time you received my letter at least, was that we cannot appease the minority without departing entirely from the Basis of Union, and that there is some hope of getting the majority to give up its interest in the Basis of Union.

I cannot indicate too strongly that your hope for the latter is a forlorn one. In order to bring the whole business into the realm of the realistic, let me indicate what would happen if you introduce into your moderatorial address at the communion service any suggestion which would involve rejecting, tabling, or ignoring the Basis of Union. In the first place, our Commission on Interchurch Relations would repudiate the suggestion. In the second place, a score of our coming men would rise up and repudiate it. In the third place, I myself am afraid that I should be forced to do what I should loathe doing more than any words can say—publicly repudiate the idea myself.

I should be forced to repudiate it on the simple, but unequivocal basis that the adopting of the idea would be the end of the Congregational denomination—for when a company like ours decides to follow the will of the minority as over against that of the majority, the days of the free democracy are over. I think I can do no better, in order to indicate what the denomination as a whole is thinking than to quote four paragraphs from a letter I received on the same mail as yours, just now—from the Reverend Nathanael M. Guptill of Maine:

'a) To shelve the merger (or pigeonhole or table or postpone action or whatever else we call it) would be a gross malfeasance of our divine commission in this generation. It would result as did the shelving of the PE-Presbyterian merger in tremendous loss of prestige to the denomination, tremendous loss of momentum in the United Church Movement, and many other bad things not least among them being the grave insult to the E-R Synods who voted so wonderfully in favor of it.

'b) The progressively higher majorities won in Associations and Conferences above Churches prove that the folks who are interested in the fellowship of the churches within the denomination are in favor of the merger. We had votes against the merger in Maine from churches not heard from in the past ten years in any other way! The great leadership of the "anti" movement has come from a lot of decadent, self-sufficient downtown churches whose dollars could be spared a good deal better than the up and coming enthusiasm of churches on the growing edge of the denomination.

'c) Spiking the merger will spike the "World Christian Mission" plan of advance. Who wants to blister his hands and heart working for an infinitesimal sect proud of its tradition and ignorant of its destiny? We are kidding ourselves if we think all these "Federal Unionists" are going really to do something about Christian Unity. The same fellows in our Conference who were against the merger were the ones who called the WCM "Stauffacher's Folly". It is time we stopped kowtowing to the "aginers" (there was a time for that and we've worn out the olive branch) and

-2

began the grass roots job of beginning with those we have and going ahead
even if some will stay behind.

'd) Congregationalism has the choice this year (and never again, to quote
Dr. Meek) of leaping to the vanguard in the movement for united Protestantism,
of placing the stamp of our polity on the United Church so that future mergers
may leave some semblance of local autonomy, or of retiring to the ruck to join
the United Church when it comes on somebody else's terms - as inst: the Congregationalists in Canada who became Presbyterians because they were too few to
place their characteristic polity in that Union.'

In a word, you can absolutely count upon opposition to your suggestion,
and it will be the opposition of the vast majority. If your suggestion were advanced
and received the approval of the General Council, you could count upon it that many
of our present and coming leaders would seek the first opportunity to get into a
denomination which was not hamstrung by its minorities. They would withdraw, in
order the leave the denomination in the hands of the Evanston Group, whose leaders
have let it be known, at least privately, that they stand not only against the
union with the E. & R. church, but against the union of the United Church of Canada
and that of the Church of South India.

But I do not think your suggestion could win. It would call into being such
a reaction that I would genuinely fear that the Council would take too precipitant a
vote for union. There is always this danger, in any case.

Well, Albert, you see that I have been quite candid again. I am sure this is
the only basis upon which we can communicate wisely and profitably.

Let me repeat that there is no reason why we should not begin at once to
work upon a constitution--but this constitution would have to be within the frame
of reference of the Basis of Union.

The E. & R. people do not want us to do the impossible or split our denomination
in two. The simple fact is, however, that the preponderance of our denomination would
rather be associated with the E. & R. people than the Evanston Group.

Ever yours faithfully,

Douglas Horton

Dr. Albert W. Palmer
1185 East Foothill Blvd.
Altadena, California

Document 19.
Horton's Letter of 27 May 1948
to Palmer on the Proposed Bill of Rights

THE CONGREGATIONAL CHRISTIAN CHURCHES
OF THE UNITED STATES OF AMERICA

DOUGLAS HORTON
Minister of the General Council
287 Fourth Avenue
New York 10, N. Y.

27 May 1948.

Dear Albert,

Your good letter of the twenty-fourth has just reached me.

As long as you follow the course of the Christian Century editorial and do not suggest that the Basis of Union needs to be rejected, tabled, or ignored, I would raise no objection to any course of procedure you suggested. You will not get to first base, however, I am convinced on talking with innumerable people recently, if you even hint that there is a possibility of settling our problem outside of the framework of the Basis of Union.

If your moderatorial address indicates action de novo , the Evanston Meeting will use you as a front just as sure as shootin'. That dog that appears to be sleeping is playing 'possum. My hope is that he will stay on the leash. If you hint, however, that he is a dead duck (I am dragging in the whole menagerie here), I am afraid that he will turn and rend you.

Hoping that you will not do the same to me, I remain

Ever affectionately,

Douglas Horton

Dr. Albert W. Palmer
1185 East Foothill Blvd
Altadena, California

Document 20.
Horton's Letter of 29 May 1948
to Palmer on the Proposed Bill of Rights

Hotel Gramercy Park
32 Gramercy Park North
New York

As of 287 4th Av.
N.Y. 10, N.Y.
29 May 1948

Dear Albert,

If I understand your letter of the 26th in all
its parts, I agree with every word in it. The Basis of
Union must eventually be approved, but it need not be
approved till we have a Constitution in front of us--and
as soon as we have the Constitution duly adopted, the Basis
will go out of existence. It would help the cause extra-
ordinarily if in the course of your address you would witness to your belief (if it is your belief) that the union
must be effected within the framework of the ~~appr~~ eventual
approval of the Basis, but pointing out that this does not
need to happen until the Constitution is before us. This
appears to be the line the Commission will take. It has the
full approval of Walton and, apparently, even of Malcolm
Burton--but please keep it to yourself for the time being:
there are those on the Evanston committee who are simply
untrustworthy.

As for the 'Bill of Rights' (I have previously
pointed out that Massachusetts may question your original
right to the name), one man to whom I have shown it says,
'It is actually open to the criticism which has speciously
been directed against the Basis. It attempts by imprecision
and verbal juxtaposition to be satisfactory to both sides at
once.' I suppose that in so short a document you will hardly
be able to do more than generalize

My own personal criticism hovers about the
imprecision of some of the words; but I do not feel strongly
about the matter because, in so short a document, you must
almost necessarily deal in shibboleths. I'll make a few marks
on the enclosed which may be of some use to you.

Have a fine trip east!

Ever yours

Document 21.
Horton's Letter of 8 June 1948 on the "Constitution"

𝕳otel 𝕲ramercy 𝕻ark
𝟝𝟚 𝕲ramercy 𝕻ark 𝕹orth
𝕹ew 𝕐ork

As of 2⌐/ Four⌐⌐ Ave⌐⌐⌐
8 June 1948

Dear Albert,

Thank you ever so much for sending me an advance copy of your moderatorial address. You kindly ask me to criticize it, but actually I have almost no suggestions. I think it will be received with acclaim.

Parts of page 7 might be held to be a bit on the sentimental side, but of course one must not be afraid of imaginative writing. (I am speaking of page 7 of Part I).

I am sure that you will be well advised to omit the names of the seminary presidents on page 4 of Part II--if for no other reason, because of the effect on the seminary presidents not named, and their graduates.

I have nothing to add to what I have already said about the 'Bill of Rights'.

On the last page, in your own hand, you ask whether I think you might well ask for a committee to prepare a constitution. In my last letter I may have suggested that this would be a wise move: my contacts during the last ten days have convinced me that it would be deplorable. I now know that exceedingly strong leaders among us are resolutely opposed to the idea of preparing a constitution in advance, and that the E. and R. leaders are, also. The latter consideration is final with me. I can give you the reasons for the opposition when I see you.

There can be no solution of our problem outside of the framework of the Basis of Union (and where have you heard that before!) This means that the Basis must eventually be approved. I am afraid that you will have to choose between 'McConnell, Waser, Blaisdell,' et al. (not Walton, who has parted with Evanston) and the rest of us. We are not quite ready to commit the denomination to the control of men of that type of mind.

Hoping you are the same, I am

Ever thine

Douglas Horton

Document 22.
Douglass's Letter to Palmer on the Proposed Bill of Rights

The Board of Home Missions
of the Congregational and Christian Churches
287 FOURTH AVENUE, NEW YORK 10, N. Y.

TRUMAN B. DOUGLASS
EXECUTIVE VICE PRESIDENT

May 28, 1948

Dr. Albert W. Palmer
1185 East Foothill Boulevard
Altadena, California

Dear Dr. Palmer:

I am just back after nearly a month away from the office and this is the first opportunity I have had to write you since the day of our conversation in Los Angeles. You were generous enough to share with me your thinking about what may be done at Oberlin to salvage something from the merger debacle and you asked my opinion on certain proposals which you plan to bring before the General Council. I have therefore felt some responsibility for trying to give a more mature judgment about these proposals than I was able to offer at the time of our conversation.

You will recall that I expressed serious misgivings about any plan of action which anticipates discarding the Basis of Union. Those feelings of apprehension have grown into a strong conviction that an attempt to put through such a proposal would have disastrous consequences and that your own sponsorship of the plan would evoke such an outburst of resentment from the majority of delegates who will certainly be for the merger that you would lose every chance of exercising constructive and reconciling leadership.

During the past two months I have been present at meetings of four state conferences and several associations, a conference of about forty chairmen of state committees on evangelism and the members of the Commission on Evangelism, three large regional meetings sponsored by the Missions Council, and a number of gatherings in local churches. In addition I have carried on - as have you - a large volume of correspondence about the union. Granted that my own advocacy of the merger has tended to produce more frequent communication with those who are for it than with those who are against. But however much my correspondence may be weighted on the side of proponency, there is no mistaking the temper of some of our ablest ministers and lay people. Do not be misled by their gentlemanly conduct or by the fact that they have not used the methods of false statement, innuendo and vituperation of the Evanston group. They are just as determined to see this merger effected as are some of the members of the Evanston committee to block it. They are not irresponsible or reckless, but their feeling of denominational loyalty is not of a kind to hold them to a denomination which an intransigent minority is able to render impotent and disobedient to its sense of divine vocation.

It is my sober judgment that the General Council delegates who are deeply persuaded of the rightness of this union will be many more than enough to take action, under the Council's rules of voting and within the competence of that body, committing the General Council to merge with the General Synod of the Evangelical and Reformed Church. It is my judgment, further, that the Oberlin meeting will take such action, despite the consequences, unless it can be clearly shown that plans are under way which assure the consummation of the union within a year. I do not believe that your plan for presenting

Dr. Palmer - 2

a Bill of Rights, to be written ultimately into the constitution, and for turning
away from the Basis of Union to find some other platform of agreement can offer the
necessary assurances. I believe these proposals will be construed (and I must say
that while I have full confidence in your purposes the conclusion seems to me
unavoidable) as being tantamount to saying the merger is dead. The majority of
delegates to the Oberlin meeting will not allow that to be said, and they will be
deeply resentful of a scheme which they must interpret as aiming at the appeasement
of a minority in our fellowship when the price is the undoing of the work of the past
six years and the administering of an egregious insult to our E. and R. brethren
into the bargain.

When I speak of "appeasement" I do not mean that there is no room for a real and
hopeful effort at reconciliation. There are some who have voted against the union
who will change their minds when they understand the facts, and there are many who
have not voted either way who can be led to support the merger. But the method of
getting this larger support must not be one which is conducted in the vain hope of
changing those who are unalterably opposed and which goes so far in this attempt that
it actually results in defeating the union.

In your letter to the Executive Committee of the General Council you stated some of
the reasons why some members of our fellowship are against the union. I believe this
phase of the problem needs a more drastic analysis. We must be realistic at this
point or we shall be in danger of making disastrous compromises which are unnecessary
because they are futile.

Some members of our churches are opposed to the merger because they do not like the
E. and R. people. They habitually speak of them as "those square-heads", "those
immigrants", and by other terms with which I shall not assault your ears. I would
not set limits on what the Lord may do for such people, but they are not going to
be changed by the proclamation of a Bill of Rights.

Others are against the merger because it was not their idea in the first place,
because they feel they were not sufficiently consulted in the course of the negotiations, and because they see the changes which are impending in our denomination -
of which this is only one - as threatening their influence by transferring leadership
to a younger group. If these men were to be appeased by thrusting them into positions
of leadership in the merger negotiations they would be unable to carry the denomination
with them, for they have lost most of their influence.

Others oppose the union because they are unwilling to depart by a hair's breadth
from the sect type of Congregationalism. They do not wish to see our fellowship in
the main body of evangelical Protestantism. Some of them bear the scars of honorable
wounds received in doing battle for religious freedom, but because they have spent so
much of their life in one area of combat they do not realize how far other denominations have come or how remote are the positions they are still defending from the
present lines of battle. They would prefer to see Congregationalism consigned to the
position of a dwindling sect as moribund as the Unitarians rather than alter one
syllable of their ancient battle-cries.

Let us not deceive ourselves. The majority of persons in these three catagories
could not be persuaded to favor union with any other Protestant body unless we could
hit upon some extraordinary combination of circumstances in which (a) the members of
the other denomination were 90% Anglo-Saxon, (b) the idea of the union were thought
up by the leaders of the Evanston group, and (c) the statement of faith adopted by
the united church were a forthright declaration against ignorance and in favor of
Mothers' Day.

Dr. Palmer - 3

I sadly confess that while I never doubted we should meet some opposition on such grounds, there is more of it than I calculated at the start. We shall not change the minds of most of these persons; but they are, I am glad to say, a very small minority in our denomination.

The larger body of the opposition is composed of persons who have been misinformed by the well-financed campaign of the intrasigents, disturbed by rumors and fears so vague that there has not been time to analyze and allay them, and confused to the point of believing that unpleasant controversy can be avoided by killing the merger around which the controversy has centered.

It is my judgment that these reasons for opposition can be dealt with much more effectively in terms of the Basis of Union than by presenting a new document, writing a constitution, or coming forward with the unilateral proffer of a Bill of Rights.

You have spoken of the problem in semantics created by the centering of emotions and prejudices upon the name "Basis of Union" and of the need for a new document which will be free of these encumbering associations. If we understand that the attitude of the E. and R. people is still an important factor in the merger negotiations I think we shall have to recognize that the putting forth of "A Bill of Rights for Free Churches" will create problems in semantics which are even more unhappy than those we now have on our hands. The E. and R. people will feel they are being given a lecture aimed at instructing them in an understanding of their Christian liberties. They will be forced to the inference that in our view they cherish their liberties less than do we, their rights are of a lower order than our rights, and their churches something other than free. We must also recognize that the meaning of "free churches" in the tradition of British independency is quite different from the connotation of that term elsewhere. To many of our E. and R. brethren the expression "free churches" means churches which have in fact rejected their evangelical protestant heritage in favor of some vague form of humanitarianism or deism. If we are going to give heed to semantics let us include in our semantic concern the other party to these merger conversations.

There is another and probably more cogent reason for being dubious about introducing a bill of rights or proceeding to write a constitution without the control of the Basis of Union. The plain truth is that an attempt to effect any major alteration of the Basis of Union will involve much more hazard to its "congregational" principles than a determined and vigorous program of education aimed at answering the absurd and groundless criticisms of that document. Each successive revision of the Basis of Union has nailed down more securely its espousal of essential Congregationalism. At every point where the option was between this congregationalism and something else the Joint Commission chose the congregational way. Dr. Richards is correct when he says that the E. and R. members of the committee "yielded everything." They have yielded much more than we had a right to ask or expect. To discard the Basis of Union or undertake to write a constitution without the safeguards furnished by the Basis of Union would be to open again the many issues which from our point of view have been so favorably settled. I believe that if we were to work over the ground again the E. and R. people, having watched our flounderings during the past year and having seen the threat to the integrity of the denomination which a determined minority has been able to offer, could ask some very penetrating questions about our form of church life which we should be embarrassed at trying to answer.

I realize that there is the appearance of impudence in seeming to set my own judgment against yours in this matter. I have written this letter only because you did me

[343]

Dr. Palmer - 4

the courtesy of asking for my opinion and because I did not have time to think the
question through during our conversation in Los Angeles. If we were dealing with the
same facts I should be sure that your judgment was more likely to be right than mine.
If I have any facts which you do not possess they have been acquired simply by knocking
about the country and talking with many people of our churches. After reflecting on
what you said to me during our conversation I have had the feeling that you have
underestimated the seriousness and resoluteness of the majority of our fellowship who
favor the union. They are not going to accept counsel which implies defeat or any long
postponement of the union. If they are not offered some straight-line course of action
leading to the early effecting of the merger they will not be intimidated by threats
of schism and will devise action of their own which I am sure will seem to you
precipitate and unwise. Those who really care for our fellowship are not going to
allow its future to be determined by the people who wrote that letter to the E. and R.
ministers. Your plan for discarding the Basis of Union is in effect a plan for retracing
the journey of the last six years and starting again from the beginning. Unless I have
entirely misread the mind of our denomination such a proposal will not be acceptable
at Oberlin.

There is little profit in trying to assign responsibility for the failure to get the
required affirmative vote in all categories. All of us who are for the union are at
fault - for underestimating the opposition, for giving much of our time to other
matters of less importance, for failing to act with more promptness and skill to
attempt a reconciliation of differences. In my humble opinion, however, the one body
which might have changed the situation is the Executive Committee of the General
Council. While there was no vote of precise instruction, certainly the whole mood and
action of the Grinnell meeting was a mandate to the Executive Committee to promote the
union. This it has not done. It has been so tender of the feelings of two or three
of its members who are against the union that its position has been one of benevolent
neutrality, and in contrast with the aggressiveness of the Evanston group the impression
which the Committee has made on the denomination has been largely negative.

In addition - and here I must ask you to treat this letter as confidential but feel
that as Moderator you ought to know the facts - one of the executive officers of the
General Council, being opposed to the merger, has been able in a hundred individually
small but cumulatively disastrous ways to sidetrack and hinder effective action. At
a time when Douglas Horton desperately needed executive help he has had non-cooperation
and hostility in his own office.

The point of the foregoing paragraph is not to assess blame but to indicate what can
be done. Let the General Council clearly instruct the Executive Committee to promote
the merger. Let the Executive Committee act on these instructions. Free the Committee
from its paralyzing doubt about spending denominational money for education and promotion. Forget about trying to win the leaders of the Evanston group and get into the
field with effective counter-measures for dealing with the mis-statements and appeals
to fear which have been disseminated. Explore further the possibility of getting
agreement on a few simple interpretations of the sections of the Basis of Union which
have seemed ambiguous - a line of exploration which the irreconcilables have rejected
but which we already know will satisfy some of the more reasonable among the present
opponents of the union. Provide further opportunity for voting (the opponents have
generally got out a heavier vote than the pros and have even revived dead churches
which they could influence to vote negatively.) Let these things be done for only one
year and we shall have substantially more than the desired 75% affirmative vote in all

[344]

Dr. Palmer - 5

categories. Meanwhile the Evanston group will move rapidly toward dissolution.
Indeed its leaders have already brought so much discredit upon themselves that I am
persuaded a number of churches which voted in the negative a few weeks ago would
report a very different result if they were to vote again tomorrow.

Those of us who are in favor of the union need to remember that it has not been
rejected by the denomination. The Congregational Christian people are for this
merger, and by a substantial majority. They will provide an overwhelming majority
if they are given a chance. With the issue so nearly decided let us not make the
tragic mistake of taking unilateral action at the risk of losing everything.

Faithfully yours,

TRUMAN B. DOUGLASS

TBD/db

ack
6/11/48

Document 23.
Blanchard's Letter to Palmer on Plans

FERDINAND Q. BLANCHARD
MINISTER
MISS LOUISE HARPER
PASTOR'S ASSISTANT AND
DIRECTOR OF RELIGIOUS ED.

EUCLID AVENUE CONGREGATIONAL CHURCH

EUCLID AVENUE AT EAST NINETY-SIXTH STREET, CLEVELAND, OHIO

June 1, 1948

Rev. Albert W. Palmer, D. D.
1185 East Foothill Blvd.
Altadena, California

My dear Albert:

There have been some developments in the situation as regards the Merger, and I feel that you ought to know about them and understand them as fully as possible. It may be that you have heard something as to what has been done, but let me set down briefly the course of events in the last few weeks.

At a meeting of the Executive Committee in Buck Hills Falls in April the reports from the voting of the churches was to the effect that we definitely had not secured from either category a seventy-five per cent vote in approval of the Merger. As a result of this, the so-called Evanston Group, who were present by their distinguished representatives, were insistent that we should announce at once that the merger had failed and turn to something, I do not know what, that they would propose. The opponents of the Merger on the Executive Committee and a number of those who were favorable to it, but who had apparently lost their nerve completely because of the reports of the voting, forced through a resolution to the effect that if there was nothing happening to the contrary, the Executive Committee should advise the superintendents that they would recommend at Oberlin that no action be taken upon the Basis of Union, this due to the fact that churches and members had not given a seventy-five per cent vote.

The Commission has been at work independently, not bound by any action of the Executive Committee. We thought at first it might be possible to state certain explanations and interpretations of the Basis, upon which people

seemed to have trouble and to secure from the E. and R. representatives an
agreement, unofficial of course, that these interpretations, in their judgment,
were valid. We were nearly of one mind in the conviction that if the Council
at Oberlin in any wise was like that at Grinnell, the plan of union could be
carried through as it had been set up. However, with the attitude of the
Executive Committee so definite, and the fact that the opponents of the union
evidently were determined to make every possible use of the fact that the
seventy-five per cent had not been secured, charging that it would be bad
faith to go ahead in the light of this fact, we have been inclined to feel that
it would not be wise, indeed, to push through the Merger on the basis of the
prepared Basis of Union, even accompanied as it would be by the explanation's.

Personally, I have come to this conviction with reluctance.
Indeed, I have hardly come to it at all. But in this respect I am clearly in
the minority and the judgment of the outstanding members of the Commission on
our side is that we had better not let the Council push through the measures
because it might easily result in a deep cleavage of our denomination.

We have, therefore, worked out a plan which takes account of
certain things. First, that the vote of churches and members has not been up
to the figure that we desired. Secondly, that much of the opposition has
centered around the fact that no constitution was suggested, and supposedly this
fact aroused fear as to what might eventually develop.

We are therefore proposing at this time to place before the Council
a recommendation that we do not take definite and final action at Oberlin, but
gather up a new group, perhaps, to formulate a constitution on the basis of the
principles which have been laid down. And at the time the Council meets in 1950
the opponents of the measure will have no reason to question us to what is
explicitly implied.

I give you this in the barest outline because the Commission's final recommendation has not been put into shape, and also because we want to be sure that the E. and R. people agree with this. Horton and I are to meet them this week here in Cleveland and go over the proposal with them.

May I suggest that you do not speak to anybody about this plan of the Commission now. Would you simply say that you know that we are working definitely to propose something which will be a forward step and which will be as far as possible, except for the adoption of the Basis of Union, from an abandonment of the efforts for merger.

Before we come to Oberlin there will be a chance to put all this definitely before you so that you will know what is in progress. It is, however, at this time exceedingly important not to give to those who are so violently in opposition an outline of what we shall we shall propose. They will make use of it, if possible, to discredit it in advance. Therefore we are saying nothing to anybody outside of the Commission and hoping to work out something which cannot be reasonably refused and which will be a measurable satisfaction to those who want to see the merger effected fully and wish it might be done at Oberlin.

I will be glad to write you more in advance of Oberlin and certainly to talk things over fully before the Council. Knowing your interest in the matter and being confident of your desire to see action taken, I have nothing, of course, to hold back, but do not want to state what can be done at this moment until the final approval of it is given by the E. and R. people and our own Commission. We must get together on this, and all of us who believe that the Merger is good should have in mind a plan upon which there can be a complete union of effort.

With all kindest regards and best wishes,

Cordially yours,

FQB:mp

Document 24.
Buschmeyer's Letter to Churches on Voting

TO THE CONGREGATIONAL CHRISTIAN CHURCHES   June 7, 1948

GREETINGS: The Judges of Voting upon the proposed Basis of Union between the Evangelical and Reformed Church and the Congregational Christian
Churches have just reported the following totals to the Executive Committee
of the General Council and we hasten to pass them on to the Churches of our
Fellowship, requesting the Pastors to communicate the full information of
this letter to their delegates to the General Council meeting in Oberlin,
June 17-24.

		Resolution #1	Resolution #2
Churches	For	2,576 (65.5%)	2,818 (78.3%)
"	Against	1,352	781
Members	For	144,221 (63.3%)	147,680 (76.2%)
"	Against	83,503	46,108
Conferences	For	32 (94.1%)	31 (91.2%)
"	Against	2	3
Associations	For	152 (80%)	163 (94.2%)
"	Against	38	10

          Believing it to be its duty to give some kind of counsel to
the Churches of our Fellowship in this emergency situation, the Executive
Committee has given careful thought to the problem of achieving the highest
permanent values out of the negotiations carried on thus far, and now passes
on to our Churches and delegates the following resolution:

          "Whereas, the favorable vote of the churches of our faith and
order on the matter of The Basis of Union has fallen short of a clear mandate
to proceed with the validation of The Basis of Union;

          "Be it therefore resolved that the Executive Committee inform
the churches of this result;

          "Be it further resolved that the Executive Committee advise
the General Council that the Executive Committee is of one mind that the
General Council will best preserve the strength of the churches' life and
work and will best safeguard and protect the possibility of union with the
Evangelical and Reformed Church if no definitive action on acceptance or
rejection of the Basis of Union be taken by the General Council at Oberlin.

          "The Executive Committee urges and requests the delegates to
the General Council prayerfully to prepare themselves to seek God's guidance,
with the hope that a way or ways may be made evident whereby we may walk with
our brethren of the Evangelical and Reformed Church in love and by further
study come, we trust to an hour when our strength and theirs may be made one
in His service."

          It is hoped that the Commission on Interchurch Relations and
Christian Unity will have an analysis of the voting by Churches, associations,
and Conferences, to be mailed to delegates before they leave for Oberlin. If not
received prior to your leaving this analysis will be on hand for your consideration at Oberlin.

          The Commission is receiving and considering possible alternate
courses of action by the General Council meeting in Oberlin, and will make its
supplementary report, with a recommended procedure, when the Council is assembled.

          Wishing you Grace, Mercy and Peace, *Fred S. Buschmeyer*

          Fred S. Buschmeyer, Chairman for the Executive Committee

Document 25.
The Oberlin Interpretations

Synod and ratified by the Conferences in collaboration with the Associations and Congregations.

XI. Revisions and Amendments

Revisions and amendments of the Basis of Union while it is in force before the adoption of a constitution may be made by consent of ninety per cent of the members of the General Synod of the United Church of Christ duly assembled.

The Interpretations of The Basis of Union

(a) The Basis of Union calls for a union of the General Council of Congregational Christian Churches and the General Synod of the Evangelical and Reformed Church to form the General Synod of the United Church of Christ.

(b) The constitution for the United Church of Christ provided for in Article IV-A of the Basis of Union: (1) will not come into force until it has been ratified by two-thirds of our churches voting; (2) is to be based on the principles set forth in the Basis of Union; (3) is in no wise to abridge the rights now enjoyed by the churches; (4) will define and regulate as regards the General Synod but describe the free and voluntary relationships which the churches, associations, and conferences shall sustain with the General Synod and with each other.

(c) The Basis of Union calls for a union of the Boards of Home Missions, the Boards of Foreign Missions, the Annuity Boards, the Councils for Social Action, and similarly all related Boards, commissions, agencies, and instrumentalities of the two denominations.

(d) Churches, associations, conferences and the General Synod, being self-governing fellowships, possess autonomy in their own spheres, which autonomy is acknowledged and will be respected.

(e) Synods, conferences, associations and churches are to retain their present status until they are united by their own action and when mutually agreeable.

(f) Congregational Christian churches do not go out of existence at the time of the union of the two communions. In consummating this union the Congregational Christian Churches and the Evangelical and Reformed Church are uniting without break in their respective historic continuities.

(g) The United Church of Christ will be a union of two denominations joined in fellowship and cooperation without involving any invasion of the rights now enjoyed by local churches or congregations.

(h) With the constituting of the General Synod of the United Church of Christ, the General Council of the Congregational Christian Churches [and the General Synod of the Evangelical and Reformed Church] will remain in existence in order to fulfil necessary legal functions, but shall transfer to the General Synod all of its functions which do not for legal reasons need to be retained.

Document 26.

Horton's Letter of 7 May 1948 to Palmer

En route from Kansas City, Mo.
to Billings, Mont.
7 May 1948

Dear Albert,

I have often wished during the last two years that New York
was a bit closer to Altadena--but this time even such a proximity would
not have helped, for I am in the midst of a mad four-weeks' race from one
conference to another, speaking at their annual meetings and being over-
taken by my correspondence only here and there. Your letters of April
19 and 28 reached me ten days or so after they were sent, and though I
immediately set about securing the answers for which you asked, I cannot
even yet tell you the whole story.

John Scotford has, I believe, sent you his unofficial totals
of the voting. His very last report places the affirmative vote of the
churches at 65.4%. It may possibly work up to 66 2/3 %, a very large
majority but not large enough.

As for having Jim Fifield appointed an 'Accredited Visitor'
to Amsterdam, the moment I received your letter I telegraphed John Phillips,
who is the chairman of the committee making the nominations. The four
Accredited Visitors had already been appointed, but I thought some adjustment might be made. But John has been silent as the grave.

I have two suggestions to make. (1) If Jim will go as an
ordinary visitor, I shall see to it that he is shown every courtesy. If
he is at all interested in this, I shall ask that literature be sent him.
(2) There might be a chance to have him go as an accredited visitor not
on the Cong'l Christian quota. I shall write to Hank Leiper about this
immediately. I fear that the chances here are slim, however.

I have never had in my possession a copy of the second Evanston
letter to the E. and R. ministers, though I have read it. It was like the
former one--clever, filled with half-truths, insidious. The effect it had,
however, may be judged from the fact that the E. and R. synods are voting for
the Basis almost unanimously.

(each)
I have talked with Jim before about having a competent commission
go over the administration of the denomination. I am all for it. I have
wanted Jim on our Executive Committee but the closest I have come to it is
the prospective election of his brother. I should want him on the constitutional committee for the United Church (though I do not know that he would be
elected). In any case I think your idea (and his) about calling for such a
commission as would be composed of expert organizers, the very kind that
Jim could pick out, himself being their chairman, is top-hole.

I shall ask the office to send you a copy of the proposed
program, if it has not been already sent you. I do not have it here.

Fred Fagley has sent me a copy of his response to your letter of the 24th. In thinking over the actions taken at Buck Hill Falls I should emphasize some features that Fred does not have so fully in mind. I am sure that he was thinking of the Evanston group when he spoke of the Christian forbearance of the opponents—that is, Hansen and McGiffert, who did not lose their heads. Malcolm Burton was also there, and so was Ted Shipherd.

Surely Fred is unrealistic in even hoping that there may be no debate upon the subject of the proposed union at the General Council. There will be present there at least a 2-to-1 and probably a 3-to-1 (possibly even a 4-to-1) majority in favor of the Basis, and they are not going to be muzzled by anybody. I have come to realize this in visiting the various conferences of the western Middle West.

I think it fair to say that though there are notable exceptions the men of spiritual power and insight, old and young, but especially young, stand for the Basis. If the Basis should be tabled it would be positively calamitous for Congregationalism. Some of our strongest leaders would leave us, on the ground that we are no longer Congregational. The departure of our ministers into Episcopalianism and other communions which seem to have a purpose (as I think I have pointed out before) would be accelerated. Already three young men from one seminary alone have written me that they are not interested in Cong'l'm if by its actions it denies its proud statements. These proponents will demand that nothing be done at Oberlin which can be construed by the world as a repudiation of the Basis.

In great confidence may I say that the Commission is now proposing to lay the enclosed motion before the Council (after the motion has been thoroughly gone over by E. and R. as well as our own leaders) to be acted upon not at Oberlin but at a meeting of the Council to be called in connection with the International Council at Wellesley in June 1949—or at the regular meeting of the Council in 1950. Several of the opponents of the Basis have approved the motion, since it makes it plain as a pikestaff that the Basis is Congregational in polity. Even some of the Evanstonians like the fine lawyer, Mr. Morgan of N.J. and N.Y., have done so. The Commission has not exposed its hand to the Evanstonians in general, however—certainly not to Hansen and McGiffert, though they are bound to hear about the matter soon.

Would you think it wise to talk this whole matter over with Jim Fifield and get his reaction? We should like to have him suggest improvements for the motion and then support it. That would be an immense help. If we do not do something of this sort, the proponents of union may take the bit in their teeth and vote the union at Oberlin then and there. That, I am convinced, would be unwise. I leave the whole matter of deciding whether or not to lay this before Jim to you. Blessings on you!

I am not sure that Fred Fagley knows about the plans of the Commission. I should not mention them in writing to him. He has been wonderfully loyal, but no one could call him enthusiastic about the union.

Ever grateful for you, I am

Yours

Douglas Horton

Dr. Albert W. Palmer

Document 27.
Scotford's Letter to Palmer on Voting

REPRESENTING
THE CONGREGATIONAL CHRISTIAN
C H U R C H E S

Editor
JOHN R. SCOTFORD
287 Fourth Avenue
New York 10, N. Y.

Published Monthly By
THE PILGRIM PRESS
14 Beacon Street
Boston 8, Mass.

April 29

Dear Dr.Palmer:

I take it that you are not unreceptive to some facts concerning the Merger voting

So far nine R&R synods have voted, all favorable and by large margins.

As of this morning our count is 1,822 for to 1,020 opposed, which is 64.8% favorable. This will improve. The churches which took their time are for the most part voting approval.

I have not totalled the popular vote, largely because neither Massachusetts nor Illinois have given us the figures, although they have reported the vote by churches.

The association vote stands at 50 for to 11 against. In Iowa the churches voted 73 to 86 against, while the associations voted seven to two in favor. In Illinois the associations stand five to five, with the churches 113 to 115. When one considers that Chicago only counts as one, this is interesting.

An interesting pattern is emerging. The strongest negative vote will be that of individuals, then at the church level. The associations will be strongly favorable, and the conferences and the Council more so.

I believe that the explanation of this is simple. We have many church members and churches who do. not know much about the denomination or how it works. On the other hand, the churches and people who attend the association and conference meetings are much better informed.

Apparently I am the only person who has been following the church by church returns closely. I also believe that I know as many of the local churches as done anyone. In addition, I have had church by church analyses from Colorado, Missouri, Middle Atlantic, and New York. In these states the bulk of the negative votes have come from marginal churches that cooperate only sporadically if at all with the denomination. In Indiana, Maine, Southern Illinois, the small churches have been the negative ones. Ultimately we hope to have a statistical study of this.

[353]

I have a number of signed statements from superintendents and pastors as to what actually happened. The pastorless and part time churches and many of those served by pastors from other denominations were defenseless against the propaganda sent to the clerks by the Evanston committee and others. They were "confused" and their fears played upon.

Now, departing from facts to opinions, I am willing to grant that there are sincere elements in the opposition. Some of this is natural conservatism. Some of it is a nostalgic attachment to a Congregationalism which is gone. A more considerable element is the leadership of the pastors of some of the larger churches. This is the reason for the negative vote in Iowa and Michigan. Wisconsin and Pennsylvania are special cases.

This is borne out by the state totals. Michigan, Pennsylvania, and possibly Iowa are the only hopeless states. Wisconsin, Indiana, and Maine are teeter-tottering.

I have two thoughts. Through ADVANCE and DAILY ADVANCE I am planning to lay the facts before our people. This is as it should be. Curiously, in the three areas where the opposition controls the machinery, the facts are being with held -- Chicago, NorthernIllinois and Intermountain.

If a way could be found to give the negative churches a little education as to what it is all about, there would be no difficulty in getting the 75%.

The final returns from Wisconsin have just come in. When I get them digested I will append a revised statement. The only other area from which there are many negative votes to be counted is Michigan.

Cordially yours,

John R. Scotford

Document 28.
Article in December 1947 Issue of Advance

Is the Plan of Union Presbyterian?

ALDEN S. MOSSHAMMER

How 'PRESBYTERIAN' IS THE proposed *Basis of Union?"* asks the Editor of *ADVANCE.* Having served for more than four years as the examiner in Presbyterian polity for the Presbytery of Morris and Orange, permit me to greet with a hearty chuckle, if not a loud guffaw, the use of the word "Presbyterian" to describe the *Basis of Union!* I have read every word of the document and I can find nothing "Presbyterian" in it.

Look first at the conception of the basic unit in the church and of denominational organization.

In the Presbyterian Church, the basic unit, as the name implies, is the Presbytery. In direct contrast, the *Basis of Union* states that "the basic unit of organization of the United Church of Christ is the Congregation; that is, the local church" (III, A). This is strictly Congregational; to a Presbyterian it resembles heresy! As long as the local church remains the unit, the concept is that of Congregationalism or Independency.

To a Presbyterian "the church" is the denomination; the local congregation is but a branch of a tree. Presbytery is the basic unit with oversight of all the churches in its bounds. The

local church, theoretically, has no real existence except in relation to Presbytery, to which it is subject, and of which it is an integral part.

There is a marked difference, also, between the denominational structure proposed in the *Basis of Union* and that of the Presbyterian Church just as there now is in Congregationalism. That difference lies in the word "authority."

The Presbyterian Church operates as a system of lower and higher church courts, or "judicatories" each with authority over the court next lower. The local church is governed by a Session, elected by the congregation; the Sessions are subject to the rules and judgments of Presbytery; the Presbyteries to their Synods; and the Synods to the General Assembly. The Session of a local church, for example, must transmit to the congregation every benevolence appeal which has been approved by any higher court—Presbytery, Synod or General Assembly. The mandates of the higher courts must be carried out, and the local church must operate according to Presbyterian law.

Nothing of this kind exists in the *Basis of Union.* The "autonomy" of Congregations, Associations, Conferences and the General Synod is respected, and the rights now enjoyed by Congregations are "in no wise abridged." (Cf. III, I) As long as there is "auton-

ALDEN S. MOSSHAMMER is a birth-right Congregationalist who was pastor of the Hillside Presbyterian Church of Orange, N. J. for six years, but who has now returned to the fold as pastor of Faith Church, Springfield, Mass.

Dec. 1947

omy," the denominational organization remains that of Independency, or Congregationalism. In the Presbyterian system, freedom is subordinate to authority and organization. The *Basis of Union* reaffirms the Congregational idea that freedom is superior to organization, and conserves the concept of free churches in fellowship. Significantly, freedom of worship, education and other freedoms are guaranteed. (Cf. III, C. I)

THE MOST IMPORTANT difference, however, is that decisions by any denominational body under the *Basis of Union* "are advisory, not mandatory." (III, G) This is completely contrary to Presbyterian procedure. Decisions handed down by a higher court, or judicatory, in the Presbyterian Church are mandatory. They constitute Law. The right of appeal, complaint, or reference by an individual to Congregations, Associations, Conferences and ultimately to the General Synod, (III, G), however, is akin to Presbyterian usage. But as long as decisions are merely "advisory" the power of Presbyterianism does not exist.

It should be noted, also, that the real units in the *Basis of Union* are the local church, the Conference, and the General Synod The Associations "may" be organized by churches through their ministers and delegates. Now the Association parallels the Presbytery in the two denominational structures. Presbytery is the unit in that church with very real power. The Association under the *Basis of Union* is even weaker than in present Congregational practice. It "may" be organized and then only for

fellowship, mutual encouragement and inspiration. (III, B) It has no power, no authority, and in terms of denominational machinery is probably a fifth wheel.

A further important distinction concerns the ownership and operation of church property. In the Presbyterian Church the property of a particular church, including the manse (parsonage), is held by Presbytery. No purchase, sale or indebtedness can be negotiated without the approval of Presbytery. This gives Presbytery great power over the local church, and in practice, prevents a local congregation in a moment of disaffection from severing its connection with the denomination. The *Basis of Union*, wisely or unwisely (depending on the point of view!), leaves all power over property in the hands of the local church. (Cf. III, H)

The *Basis of Union* will strengthen Congregationalism by recommending procedures to protect the standards for its ministry. There is nothing Presbyterian about it!

The above contains the first half, and then the last paragraph, of this article in the Dec. 1947 magazine, "Advance".

Document 29.
Conversation between Max Strang and Rev. L. W. Goebel (23 June

MEMORANDUM OF CONVERSATION had be-
tween Rev. L. W. Goebel and Max Strang, in the Harvey Restaurant, Union Station, Chicago, Wednesday morning, June
23, 1948.

The meeting with Rev. Mr. Goebel was by the sheerest coincidence. We had not previously met; I had not seen him
before he spoke to the General Council on Monday morning,
June 21.

When we had introduced ourselves; he remarked that he
was born in Dubuque; that his mother was a Haeberle; and
that her family were members of the First Presbyterian church,
of Dubuque.

We soon entered upon conversation regarding the proposed
merger between the E&RC and the C-C churches, and the
action, on the matter, which the General Council had just taken
at Oberlin.

I said, in the course of the conversation, inter alia that I
was very unhappy over the way the merger had been handled,
both before, and at the General Council; that I felt it very
unwise to try to merge two fellowships seemingly so widely
divergent as the E&RC and the C-C's; that it would have been
wiser to have followed the recommendations of the Executive
Committee, and the moderator, Dr. Palmer, that this Council
take no definitive action on the merger; that I felt that the
Council had entered upon perilous ethical grounds, and sowed
seeds of discontent, when it disregarded the implied assurance
in the Basis of Union that the merger would not be voted if it
failed of a 75% favorable vote in any of the four categories;
that the provision in paragraph (4), of the revised report of
the Commission on Interchurch Relations and Christian Unity
was merely a means by which the Council could determine as
sufficient any ratio of percentage it chose; that the statement of
Lincoln's, "No question is ever settled until it is settled right,"
was appropriate, for I felt that the merger question had not
been settled right by this Council; that Goebel's words to the
Council were harsh; that, in the language of the reporter of
the Cleveland Plain-Dealer, the delegates were "stunned" by
them; but, that I admired his candor, wished our own Congregational leaders had been as frank, and felt that probably there

was more to be·feared from them than from the leaders of the E&RC.

Mr. Goebel said, in substance: That he was sorry I felt as I did about the merger; that the E&RC was a liberal, democratic Church; that the Constitution of the E&RC was patterned after the Constitution of the U.S. through emotional appreciation of the liberty found in the U.S., rather than through any desire to impose a rigid, formal body of law; that he had been amazed to discover the degree of authority exercised by the C-C state superintendents; that he felt that the insistence of some in the C-C c's upon freedom was an insistence upon freedom to do as they please; that he had not known a group· as obstinate, selfish, and dictatorial as the C-C c's; that the E&RC had at every step made concessions until they had given up practically everything; that the E&RC did not wish to unite with a divided C-C fellowship; that he hoped—he thought—the merger would be consummated; that if the merger failed, he wished the E&RC to be known for the ecumenical church it is; and the C-C c's to be known for the provincial fellowship it is.

Continuing, pro and con, he said that candor compelled him to speak bluntly and plainly to the Council as he did on Monday morning; that as far back as last February, certain interpretations of the Basis of Union were considered by some individuals of the E&RC meeting in Cleveland, and were accepted by them; that the Council of the General Synod of the E&RC, however, could not regard such interpretations, revisions, or alterations of the Basis of Union as official; and that any such, which were given a status of parity with the Basis of Union, would make it necessary to re-commit the Basis of Union, with such interpretations, revisions, or alterations, to the synods of the E&RC for a vote; that formal resolutions to this effect were sent in February to the Commission on Interchurch Relations and Christian Unity. (I have the rather definite impression, from Mr. Goebel's remarks, that some of the interpretations, etc., considered in February, were in substance, if not in phraseology, the same as those presented to the Council at Oberlin by the Commission on Interchurch Relations and Christian Unity)

Further, Mr. Goebel said that, some two weeks prior to the meeting of the General Council, at the request of Dr. Horton, he sent to Horton, at Horton's address at Oberlin, a copy of the above-mentioned resolutions, with a letter, in which he repeated that reservations, interpretations, or comments, made equal with the Basis of Union, would require recommitment of them to the synods of the E&RC, and would delay final action on the merger until 1951, and that might mean abandonment of the merger.

I asked Mr. Goebel why, if the Commission on Inter-church Relations and Christian Unity were informed of the foregoing facts, and Horton knew of the consequences to the E&RC proceedures of the adoption of the Meek amendment, or similar reservations, they sat silent, and allowed the Council to adopt the Meek amendment, and to express its feeling of the achievement of unity and community in a tumultuous display of emotion, when both the Commission and Horton knew that it was falsely founded, the answer given by him was, "Perhaps that was why I was asked to speak to the Council."

I insisted that our leaders had not acted with candor; that they should have told the Council of these facts before the Meek amendment was adopted, and not left the information to be given by someone outside our fellowship after the Council had acted; that a matter of such import demanded utter candor and fullest confidence; that men of honesty must deal honestly with each other; and I wondered if any other vital information had been withheld from the C-C c's, or were being withheld. To this Mr. Goebel remained silent.

Mr. Goebel requested me not to quote our conversation; that it would put him "on the spot"; I replied that I did not wish to embarrass him by quoting him; that I would not do so unless I conscientiously felt it necessary to do so.

Document 30.
Evangelical and Reformed Church
Resolution of 29 September 1948

E & R SEPTEMBER 28th RESOLUTION

"The Evangelical and Reformed Church, having by action of the General Synod and the Synods approved the Basis of Union, rejoices that the General Council of the Congregational Christian Churches at its meeting in June 1948 with practical unanimity has also approved the Basis of Union.

"For its own clarification, the General Council of the Congregational Christian Churches furthermore adopted a series of interpretations which it declared to be in harmony with the spirit and purpose of the Basis of Union.

"The General Council of the Evangelical and Reformed Church recognizes the right and privilege of the General Council of the Congregational Christian Churches to interpret the Basis of Union according to its own understanding. The Evangelical and Reformed Church, however, interprets the adoption of these interpretations as not binding it or the United Church to any traditional polity for the present or for the future.

"We hope that the union may move forward to a speedy and satisfying conclusion and that the Constitution of the United Church may, through the guidance of the Holy Spirit and the experience of the new Church, not merely develop a compromise of two former polities but may bring a new polity and place of organization to the United Church.

"We find ourselves in complete harmony with the General Council of the Congregational Christian Churches in its 'desire for larger union with other denominations, in the conviction that where a common faith in Christ unites us historical confessions and polities shall no longer constrain us to go our separate ways.'"

Document 31.
The 1947 Basis of Union—Pages 1–10 and 19–20*

The Basis of Union

of

The Congregational Christian Churches

and

The Evangelical and Reformed Church

First issued in March 1943 with subsequent revisions in August 1943, March 1944, October 1944, September 1945, October 1946 (not printed), and November 1946 (not printed).

Now finally revised at a meeting of the Joint Committee held at Cleveland, Ohio, on January 22, 1947, and presented for official action by the two communions.

*Details of merger of boards, pages 11 through 18, are omitted as irrelevant to this book. Most details were temporary and were for a transitional period or have not been followed anyway.

THE JOINT COMMITTEE

Congregational Christian	*Evangelical and Reformed*
FERDINAND Q. BLANCHARD, Chairman	GEORGE W. RICHARDS, Chairman
-SIMON A. BENNETT	ROBERTS R. APPEL
WILLIAM F. BOHN	JOHN C. GIESER
MRS. HENRY B. DAVIS	L. W. GOEBEL
NOBLE STRONG ELDERKIN	G. W. GRAUER
DAVID K. FORD	JOHN R. C. HAAS
HAROLD B. FRAME	NEVIN C. HARNER
DAVID MCKEITH, JR.	JOHN LENTZ
CHARLES C. MERRILL	JOHN W. MUELLER
J. CHESTER MOLYNEUX	S. D. PRESS
WILHELM PAUCK	PAUL N. SCHAEFFER
HERMAN F. REISSIG	PAUL M. SCHROEDER
FRANK MILTON SHELDON	
RUSSELL HENRY STAFFORD	
ALFRED GRANT WALTON	

The present members of the Joint Committee desire to express their grateful appreciation to their predecessors on that committee for their very effectual labors and to the representatives of the Boards and others for assistance without which the work could not have been completed.

Table of Contents

PROCEDURES

The Congregational Christian Churches

In March, 1947, the Congregational Christian Churches intend through the Conference offices to send the Basis of Union to all of their delegates to the General Council inviting them to meet by Conference groups as soon as possible thereafter to discuss the Basis and appoint from each Conference group one of their number as a representative to advise the Executive Committee of the General Council in person at its next meeting as to whether or not to send the Basis officially to the churches.

On April 30, 1947, at Columbus, Ohio, the Executive Committee will meet with these representatives sent by the Conference groups of General Council members and decide whether to send the Basis of Union officially to the Conferences, Associations, and churches.

If that decision is affirmative, it is proposed that before April 1, 1948, the churches and their members, and before June 1, 1948, the Conferences and Associations, vote approval or disapproval of the Basis of Union.

In late June 1948, at the regular meeting of the General Council, the delegates will vote, on the basis of the previous votes taken by the Conferences, Associations, churches and members, on the question of effecting the Union.

It is recommended that the General Council vote approval of the Union if seventy-five per cent of the Conferences voting, seventy-five per cent of the Associations voting, seventy-five per cent of the churches voting, and seventy-five per cent of the members voting have already approved the Basis of Union.

The actual union would probably follow in the early Autumn of 1948, the first step being the official uniting of the General Council of the Congregational Christian Churches and the General Synod of the Evangelical and Reformed Church. This ceremony would take place in some appointed city and other gatherings celebrating the union would probably be held in other important centers throughout the country.

The Evangelical and Reformed Church

The Basis of Union will be presented to the General Synod at its triennial meeting at St. Louis, Missouri, July 9-16, 1947. If adopted by a two-thirds vote of the members of the General Synod voting it shall be submitted to the thirty-four Synods. If two thirds of the Synods vote approval the General Council shall declare it adopted.

The Committee on Closer Relations with Other Churches shall then request the General Council to call a special meeting of the General Synod to conclude whatever business it needs to transact. This meeting shall be held at the same time and place as a similar meeting of the General Council of the Congregational Christian Churches. Then the General Synod of the Evangelical and Reformed Church and the General Council of the Congregational Christian Churches shall meet in joint session in order to consummate the union. The Chairmen of the Committees on Union of the two Churches shall announce the vote of the Congregational Christian Churches and of the Synods of the Evangelical and Reformed Church, and the United Church of Christ shall be constituted by prayer and the election of officers.

Basis of Union

of the

Congregational Christian Churches

and the

Evangelical and Reformed Church

Adopted by the Joint Committee 22 January 1947

PREAMBLE

We, the regularly constituted representatives of the Congregational Christian Churches and of the Evangelical and Reformed Church, moved by the conviction that we are united in spirit and purpose and are in agreement on the substance of the Christian faith and the essential character of the Christian life;

Affirming our devotion to one God, the Father of our Lord Jesus Christ, and our membership in the holy catholic Church, which is greater than any single Church and than all the Churches together;

Believing that denominations exist not for themselves but as parts of that Church, within which each denomination is to live and labor and, if need be, die; and

Confronting the divisions and hostilities of our world, and hearing with a deepened sense of responsibility the prayer of our Lord "that they all may be one";

Do now declare ourselves to be one body, and do set forth the following articles of agreement as the basis of our life, fellowship, witness, and proclamation of the Gospel to all nations.

I. NAME

The name of the Church formed by this union shall be UNITED CHURCH OF CHRIST.[1]

This name expresses a fact: it stands for the accomplished union of two church bodies each of which has arisen from a similar union of two church bodies.[2] It also expresses a hope: that in time soon to come, by further

---

[1] If the name "United Church of Christ" seems presumptuous, it should be remembered that any good general name must seem so, since it would apply equally well to other groups. A name, however, quickly becomes a mere means of classification, and it is hoped that the world will soon come to know that the Churches uniting under this name do not pretend to be more than they actually are.

(The purpose of this and other footnotes in this instrument is purely explanatory. They are designed to throw light on the text, but are not part of the Basis of Union.)

---

[2] See the brief history appended to this Basis of Union.

4

union between this Church and other bodies, there shall arise a more inclusive United Church.

II. FAITH

The faith which unites us and to which we bear witness is that faith in God which the Scriptures of the Old and New Testaments set forth, which the ancient Church expressed in the ecumenical creeds, to which our own spiritual fathers gave utterance in the evangelical confessions of the Reformation, and which we are in duty bound to express in the words of our time as God Himself gives us light. In all our expressions of that faith we seek to preserve unity of heart and spirit with those who have gone before us as well as those who now labor with us.

In token of that faith we unite in the following confession[8], as embodying those things most surely believed and taught among us:

We believe in God the Father Almighty, Creator and Sustainer of heaven and earth; and in Jesus Christ, His Son, our Lord and Saviour, who for us and our salvation lived and died and rose again and lives for evermore; and in the Holy Spirit, who takes of the things of Christ and shows them to us, renewing, comforting, and inspiring the souls of men.

We acknowledge one holy catholic Church, the innumerable company of those who, in every age and nation, are united by the Holy Spirit to God in Christ, are one body in Christ, and have communion with Him and with one another.

We acknowledge as part of this universal fellowship all throughout the world who profess this faith in Jesus Christ and follow Him as Lord 'and Saviour.

We hold the Church to be established for calling men to repentance and faith, for the public worship of God, for the confession of His name by word and deed, for the administration of the sacraments, for witnessing to the saving grace of God in Christ, for the upbuilding of the saints, and for the universal propagation of the Gospel; and in the power of the love of God in Christ we labor for the progress of knowledge, the promotion of justice, the reign of peace, and the realization of human brotherhood.

Depending, as did our fathers, upon the continued guidance of the Holy Spirit to lead us into all truth, we work and pray for the consummation of the Kingdom of God; and we look with faith for the triumph of righteousness and for the life everlasting.

III. PRACTICE

A. The basic unit of organization of the United Church of Christ is the Congregation; that is, the local church.

---

[8] This confession expresses the content and meaning of the faith held generally by the members of the two uniting communions. It is not to be considered a substitute for any confession of faith which may be used in any congregation today. Like the ampler statement called for in Article IV, Section F, it is designed to be a testimony, and not a test, of faith.

B. The Congregations, through their ministers and through delegates elected from their membership, may organize Associations for fellowship, mutual encouragement, inspiration, and such other functions as may be desired.

C. The Congregations, through their ministers and through delegates elected from their membership, constitute Conferences for fellowship, counsel, and cooperation in all matters of common concern. The Conferences exist to make cooperation effective (a) among their Congregations and (b) between their Congregations and the General Synod, the Boards, commissions, agencies, and instrumentalities[4] of the Church.

D. The Conferences, through delegates elected by them from the membership and ministers of the Congregations located within their respective bounds, constitute the General Synod.

E. Officers, Boards, councils, commissions, committees, departments, agencies, and instrumentalities are responsible to the bodies that elect them.

F. The government of the United Church is exercised through Congregations, Associations, Conferences, and the General Synod in such wise that the autonomy of each is respected in its own sphere, each having its own rights and responsibilities. This Basis of Union defines those rights and responsibilities in principle and the constitution which will be drafted after the consummation of the union shall further define them but shall in no wise abridge the rights now enjoyed by Congregations.

G. Individual communicants have the right of appeal, complaint, or reference to their Congregations, Asssociations, Conferences, and ultimately to the General Synod. Ministers, Congregations, Associations, and Conferences have similar rights of appeal, complaint, or reference. Decisions rendered in consequence of such appeals, complaints, or references, are advisory, not mandatory.

H. Each Congregation, Association, and Conference has the right of retaining or adopting its own charter, constitution, by-laws, and other regulations which it deems essential and proper to its own welfare. This right includes the holding and operation of its own property.

I. The freedom of worship and of education at present enjoyed by the Congregations of the negotiating communions will be preserved in the United Church. Other freedoms at present enjoyed are not hereby abridged.

J. Men and women enjoy the same rights and privileges in the United Church. It is recommended that at least one third of the members of the national administrative bodies be women.

K. Baptism and the Lord's Supper are the recognized sacraments of the Church.

---

[4] The Basis of Union employs both the word "agencies" and "instrumentalities" in order to meet legal requirements.

6

IV. Functions of The General Synod

A. The General Synod shall initiate action for the preparation of a constitution of the United Church. This constitution shall be based upon the principles set forth in this Basis of Union. When prepared, it shall be submitted to the General Synod; and the General Synod shall declare it in force when it shall have been ratified by not less than two thirds of the former Congregational Christian churches voting, and by not less than two thirds of the former Evangelical and Reformed Synods.

B. The General Synod shall elect its officers and assign them their duties.

C. The General Synod, directly or through an executive committee, commissions, and other committees, shall carry on the general work of the Church which is now conducted by the General Council of the Congregational Christian Churches and the General Synod of the Evangelical and Reformed Church; and through the instrumentality of Boards, commissions, and other organizations as needed, shall meet the responsibilities of the Church for foreign missions, home missions, education, publication, the ministry and ministerial relief, evangelism, stewardship, social action, and institutional benevolence.

D. The General Synod shall have power to receive overtures and petitions; to give counsel in regard to cases referred to it; and to maintain correspondence with other communions.

E. The General Synod shall promote the reorganization of Conferences. Associations, and Synods into Conferences and Associations which shall be constituted on a territorial basis and enjoy a status similar to that of the former Conferences, Associations, and Synods. This ' reorganization shall be effected by the Conferences, Associations, and Synods concerned, with the counsel and confirmation of the General Synod[5].

F. If and when the Basis of Union is regularly adopted, the General Synod shall appoint a commission composed of an equal number of representatives of the two uniting communions to prepare a statement of faith based in principle upon Article II of this document, which shall be submitted for approval to. the General Synod, Conferences, Associations, and Congregations. This statement shall be regarded as a testimony, and not as a test, of faith.

G. The General Synod shall meet in regular sessions, determine their time, place, frequency, and program, and provide for extraordinary sessions as may be necessary.

---

[5] It is expected that the Conferences and Synods will take the first steps necessary to this reorganization as soon as practicable after the consummation of the union, forming non-competitive units without overlapping boundaries capable of continuing all the work carried on by the present Conferences and Synods, together with such other work as may prove to be desirable. The formation of Associations, as deemed advisable, would follow.

H.   The executive committee of the General Synod shall be called the Executive Council. Its functions shall correspond to those of the present Executive Committee of the Congregational Christian General Council and of the present General Council of the Evangelical and Reformed General Synod. While it shall not be charged with the administration of the Boards and other agencies and instrumentalities of the communion, it shall be its duty to consider their work, to prevent duplication of activities, to effect all possible economies of administration, to correlate the work of the several organizations, including their publicity and promotional activities, so as to secure the maximum of efficiency with the minimum of expense. It shall have the right to examine the annual budgets of the several national organizations and have access to their books and records. It shall make report of its actions to the General Synod at each stated meeting of that body and present to that Synod such recommendations as it may deem wise for the furtherance of the efficiency and economical administration of the several organizations. It shall study the relative needs of these organizations, including the Conferences, and recommend the apportionment percentages for the distribution of benevolent contributions.

I.   For the interim between the effecting of the union and the adoption of the constitution, the membership of the Executive Council shall be twenty-four, with equal representation of the uniting communions[6].

J.   This Executive Council shall have a budget under its control, with income for it derived from the present sources of revenue of the General Council of the Evangelical and Reformed Church and the Executive Committee of the General Council of the Congregational Christian Churches. It shall carry out faithfully all obligations of both of these bodies and conserve as separate funds all funds of both bodies until otherwise provided.

K.   There shall be a central receiving treasury for all funds contributed to the General Synod and all the national agencies and instrumentalities. Each Conference will decide whether its Congregations shall be encouraged to send their moneys for these organizations direct to the central treasury or through the Conference treasurers.

L.   No attempt will be made to set up a detailed plan for the solicitation, collection, and disbursement of missionary, benevolent, and administrative funds before the union is effected, but the General Synod shall be requested at its first meeting to appoint a special committee adequately representing all interests to deal with these matters and to report at a later date. In any plan it is understood:

1.   That all property rights and trust funds shall be scrupulously protected as provided in Article IX, Sections A and C, of the Basis of Union.

2.   That an adequate budgetary system will be established which will be voluntary in character on the part of the Congregations, Associations,

---

* Paragraphs describing arrangements for the interim between the consummation of the union and the adoption of the constitution, while constituting part of the Basis of Union, are printed in smaller type to distinguish them from the rest of the text.

8

Conferences, and Synods but in which due emphasis will be placed on the moral responsibility of all to support the general work of the Church.

M. Pending the report of the committee to be appointed by the General Synod and until new policies are adopted, present practices in apportionment allocations, per capita assignments, and kindred matters shall be maintained.

N. The choice of location of headquarters for the United Church of Christ shall be left until after the union is effected.

V. CONFERENCES, ASSOCIATIONS, AND SYNODS

Until, according to Article IV, Section E, it is otherwise determined, the Conferences, Associations, and Synods shall continue; and each shall conduct its business in its own way. Whatever action is submitted to them by the General Synod shall be disposed of in the same way as these bodies respectively disposed of such action by the General Council of the Congregational Christian Churches or the General Synod of the Evangelical and Reformed Church prior to the union.

VI. MINISTERS AND CONGREGATIONS

A. The ministers of the two communions shall be enrolled as ministers of the United Church. Candidates for the ministry, after the union, and until a standard method is provided by the constitution, shall have the same status, and be licensed or ordained as ministers by the Associations or Conferences and Synods in the same way, as before the union. The standard method shall provide for ordination by authorization of the Conference or Association and normally upon the call to a Congregation. Similarly the formal induction of a minister into his parish, which is recommended as normal procedure, shall be by authority of the Conference or Association at the request of the Congregation.

B. A minister of another denomination shall not be accepted by any body of the United Church in which ministerial standing is held without recommendation from the body to which he belongs; if, however, a denomination refuses to recommend a minister in good and regular standing, he may be accepted after proper examination by the Conference or Association in which his standing would be held.

C. The calling of a minister to a Congregation is a concern of the Church at large, represented in the Association or Conference, as well as of the minister and the Congregation. Ministers and churches desiring to maintain a system of pastoral placement in which the Conference or Association shall have little or no part, shall be free to do so; but the recommended standard of denominational procedure shall be one in which the minister, Congregation, and Conference or Association cooperate, the Conference or Association approving candidates, the Congregation extending

9

and the minister accepting the call. The new communion will appeal to all Congregations not to call or dismiss their ministers, and to all ministers not to respond to calls or resign, until the Association or Conference shall have given approval. In all relationships between minister and local church or Congregation, the freedom of the minister and the autonomy of the church are presupposed.

VII. MEMBERS

All persons who are members of either communion at the time of the union shall be members of the United Church. Men, women, and children shall be admitted into the fellowship of the United Church through baptism and profession of faith according to the custom and usage of each congregation prior to the union. When they shall have been admitted, they shall be recognized as members of the United Church.

VIII. ORGANIZATION OF BOARDS

[*This article has been ratified (subject to the adoption of the entire Basis of Union by the negotiating communions) by the Executive Committee of the Congregational Christian General Council, by the Evangelical and Reformed General Council, and severally by the governing authorities of all Boards, agencies, and instrumentalities involved.*]

A. The Boards, commissions, and other agencies and instrumentalities shall proceed to correlate their work under the General Synod as rapidly as their charters, constitutions, property rights, the effectiveness of their program, and the laws of the State will permit. In the original personnel of the Boards, commissions, and other agencies and instrumentalities, when consolidated, due representation shall be given to each of the consolidating communions.

B. At each regular meeting of the General Synod each Board and commission shall submit for review a report of its operations during the time elapsed since the last regular meeting of the General Synod.

C. Except in the case of the Pension Board, the members of the Boards shall be nominated and elected by the General Synod. They shall be represented through corresponding members, with voice but without vote, in the General Synod itself. They shall elect their own officers. The executive committees or other governing groups of the Boards shall have a sufficient number of members to provide for geographical distribution, representation of both of the uniting Churches (*see Section A above*), and the inclusion of persons qualified to render specific services, as for example in the field of investment, medicine, education, etc., as the Boards may require.

D. The American Board of Commissioners for Foreign Missions and the Board of International Missions shall be united under the name of the AMERICAN BOARD OF COMMISSIONERS FOR FOREIGN MISSIONS[1].

---

[1] It is the intention of the present American Board to amend its Charter and By-laws to conform to those of the Board of the United Church.

10

IX. Legal Obligations

A. The property rights of all bodies such as Congregations, Associations, Conferences, Synods, and corporations shall be scrupulously observed.

B. The theological seminaries, colleges, academies, denominational boards, benevolent institutions, and other corporations shall be controlled under the terms of their respective charters and other governing documents. Those institutions, however, which were under the supervision of the national bodies of the uniting communions shall, at least until the constitution is adopted, pass under the supervision of the General Synod. While they are under the supervision of the General Synod, the interests of the previously supervising groups shall be properly recognized.

C. Due protection shall be given all trust funds, including pension funds.

X. Approval and Implementation of The Basis of Union

A. The Basis of Union shall be submitted to the General Council of the Congregational Christian Churches and the General Synod of the Evangelical and Reformed Church. Each shall proceed according to its own polity[14] in the approval or disapproval of the Basis of Union. When the Basis has been approved by the regular action of the two bodies, each shall designate an equal number of its membership, approximately three hundred, with power to represent it at a joint meeting which shall constitute the first meeting of the General Synod of the United Church of Christ.

B. The joint meeting being duly called and assembled, to it the final report of the action of the communions upon the Basis of Union shall be made; and by joint resolution it shall be declared that the union of the communions is effected at that time, the General Synod of the United Church of Christ being the successor to the General Council of the Congregational Christian Churches and the General Synod of the Evangelical and Reformed Church, the joint meeting becoming the first meeting of the General Synod of the United Church. Then the delegates shall be led in a constituting prayer, effect an organization by the election of officers, and proceed to the transaction of business. From the time of the organization of the General Synod of the United Church until a constitution of the United Church has been adopted, this Basis of Union shall regulate the business and affairs of the United Church.

C. At the joint session referred to in the foregoing paragraph when the Union shall be formally effected, such action shall be taken as will unite the General Council of the Congregational Christian Churches and the General Synod of the Evangelical and Reformed Church: the further union of Conferences, Associations, Synods, and other bodies within the uniting communions shall proceed with the approval of the groups concerned, according to the principles laid down in this Basis of Union.

------

[14] See Procedures, p. 3.

19

D. The General Synod of the United Church of Christ at its first meeting shall also take any and all appropriate steps necessary to insure the continuity and to effect the consolidation of the Boards, commissions, and other agencies and instrumentalities as described in Article IV, Section C, and to make effective an interim plan for their consolidation and operation, as more explicitly set forth in Article VIII.

E. The General Synod at its first meeting shall be made up of representatives elected as set forth in Article X, Section A; but at subsequent meetings, until a constitution shall have been adopted, the General Synod shall be composed of delegates elected by the present Conferences and Synods, or their successors, one delegate representing each three thousand communicants or major fraction thereof, so that the total number will be about six hundred.

F. Upon the consummation of the union the general officers of the former Congregational Christian General Council and the former Evangelical and Reformed General Synod not connected with the Boards shall become the staff of the General Synod of the United Church of Christ until other arrangements are perfected by the General Synod.

G. Revisions and amendments of the constitution shall be made by the General Synod and ratified by the Conferences in collaboration with the Associations and Congregations.

XI. REVISIONS AND AMENDMENTS

Revisions and amendments of the Basis of Union while it is in force before the adoption of a constitution may be made by consent of ninety per cent of the members of the General Synod of the United Church of Christ duly assembled.

20

Document 32.

The Decision in the Groton Lawsuit, June 25, 1980

1.

THE DECISION IN THE GROTON LAWSUIT, JUNE 25, 1980

On the five following pages is printed the decision on the merits in the Groton case mentioned at the
end of Chapter 2. This forms the third portion of
Judge Hendel's decision and is the only part rendering
findings regarding the United Church of Christ. The official listing of this case is:

NO.   39165

‾JOSEPH A. COPP, ET AL   SUPERIOR COURT

VS.   NEW LONDON JUDICIAL DISTRICT

HORACE L. BARNUM, ET AL   JUNE 25, 1980

Part I. of this decision has to do with whether
the courts may properly consider such a case. As Judge
Hendel stated, "The first issue to be considered is
whether any of the relief sought by the plaintiffs may
be granted without resolving ecclesiastical questions."
Judge Hendel held that the case could be considered.

Part II. of the decision dealt with the issue of
res judicata stemming from the Cadman, Burlington and
other cases. Curiously Judge Hendel held that res
judicata and collateral estoppel did apply but he went
on to hand down a decision on the merits in addition.

The author of this book believes that the decision
regarding res judicata misinterpreted what was actually
decided in the Cadman Case, as a very careful reading
of the entire decision of the Michigan Supreme Court in
1966 would show. But since the decision on the merits
was also handed down there would be no purpose in appealing the res judicata issue, and the attorneys for
the Plaintiffs were convinced there was no point in
having any appeal.

Following Part III of the decision, which is
quoted in full on the next five pages, Judge Hendel
decided:

IV.

For the reasons stated above, the court
renders judgment in favor of defendants on all
counts of plaintiffs' complaint.
              (s) Hendel, J.

[373]

III.

Although the findings made above that this action is barred by res judicata and collateral estoppel is dispositive of the matter, in view of the considerable time and resources already invested in this litigation, the court believes that it would be appropriate to render a decision on the merits of the issues of fact and law which have been presented.

The first of these issues is whether the assets and properties of the Church have been unlawfully diverted from the charitable uses and purposes to which they had been devoted. Section 17-2 of the Connecticut General Statutes provides that all transfers for public and charitable use "shall forever remain to the uses to which they were granted, according to the true intent and meaning of the grantor, and to no other use whatsoever." Unrestricted gifts to churches are "to be devoted to the general purposes of the donee as authorized in its charter." New York East Annual Conference v. Seynour, 151 Conn. 517, 521 (1964). Thus, there must be a showing that contribution of Church funds to the U.C.C. in some way violates the general purposes authorized in the Church charter to support plaintiffs claim that S 47 -2 is being violated.

Plaintiffs maintain that contribution of Church funds to the U.C.C. violates the prohibition contained in Article X of the Church Constitution against influencing legislation or desseminating propaganda. In Section II, above, this court has already decided that the evidence presented by plaintiffs is insufficient to show that such contributions to the U.C.C. constitute a violation of Article X.

The Plaintiffs also claim that the authority of

the U.C.C. is inconsistent with the autonomy of the
Church. They lay great emphasis on the fact that Paragraph 22 of the U.C.C. Constitution provides as follows:

> Actions by, or decisions or advice emanating
> from, the General Synod, a Conference or an
> Association, should be held in the highest
> regard by every local church.

Plaintiffs find this position incompatible with Article
II of the Church Constitution, which provides that the
Church "cannot accept as authoritative the advice, decisions or other actions of any other body." An obligation to hold a decision or advice in "the highest regard"
however, is far different from an obligation to accept
a decision as authoritative, and as long as the Church
is not bound by U.C.C. decisions, the Church's independence is preserved.

Plaintiffs also complain that the U.C.C. inter-
feres with local Church independence by its involvement
in the ordination, selection and dismissal of ministers.
The U.C.C., for example, certifies to the standing of
a minister in the U.C.C., checks credentials of ministers
and reviews contract provisions and financial arrangements between ministers and local churches. Plaintiffs
acknowledge, however, that a local church may reject
such assistance if it so chooses.

Plaintiffs suggest that the U.C.C. exercises a degree of control over the selection of ministers by
virtue of its power to deny certain benefits to ministers. However, the evidence establishes that conformity to the U.C.C.'s rules is necessary only to functioning within the U.C.C., not to functioning as an
independent church. Ordination as a minister of the
U.C.C., for example, is necessary only for that minister
to act within the U.C.C.; it is not necessary for his
service to his local church. A minister's lack of stand-

ing in the U.C.C., or inability to participate in an
Association of the U. C. C. ministers or lack of freedom to move to certain other churches would seem to be
matters of co(n)sequence only to a congregation which
desired to be an integral part of a larger church.

Plaintiffs further argue that a local church is
not completely free to select any minister of its
choosing when the by-laws to which its members have a-
greed establish detailed rules for the selection. Yet
the selection must be considered free where the guidelines are voluntarily adopted and followed and the congregation may abolish such guidelines.

Of great significance with reference to the question as to whether membership in the U.C.C. is inconsistent with local church autonomy is the testimony of
plaintiff's witness, Reverend Burton. The evidence establishes that Reverend Burton was very familiar with
the merger of the Congregational Church into the U.C.C.,
including the protracted and complicated deliberations
and negotiations which finally resulted in the adoption
of the U.C.C. Constitution. He was also thoughly familiar with the Church Constitution.

Reverend Burton testified at length, and in great
detail, on many sections of the U.C.C. Constitution,
including, among others: the provision relating to the
holding "in the highest regard" by every local church
of actions, decisions or advice of higher bodies discussed
above; provisions relative to elections of delegates by
a local church to higher U.C.C. bodies; provisions relating to the conferring of standing on a U.C.C. Conference,
on a local church and on a U.C.C. minister; provisions
relating to U.C.C. officers and higher U.C.C. bodies;
and provisions relating to ordination of ministers and
termination of pastorates. After completing such tes-

5.

timony, Reverend Burton responded to question put to
him by the court, as follows:

> THE COURT: (W)hich, if any, of those provisions
> (of the U.C.C. Constitution) are absolutely
> binding upon the local church?
>
> THE WITNESS: I would say that these are mat-
> ters of pressure rather than of binding.
>
> THE COURT: Well, now, you are saying none
> are binding?
>
> THE WITNESS: I wouldn't say that any of
> those are binding the way that they are now.
> But they could be made binding by an
> amendment.
>
> THE COURT: At this time none of these provi-
> sions of the Constitution are binding on the
> local church?
>
> THE WITNESS: I would assume that's what the
> language means at present.

Following this acknowledgement by Reverend Burton
that none of the provisions of the U.C.C. Constitution
which he reviewed were binding on a local church,
plaintiffs elicited testimony from Reverend Burton to
the effect that U.C.C. usurpation of local church autonomy could result from paragraph 88 of the U.C.C. Constitution, which vests the power to amend the U.C.C. Constitution in the General Synod and the Conferences,
rather than in the local churches.

The U.C.C. Constitution, however, clearly disallows
any power over local churches, when, in Paragraph 21 it
states:

> The autonomy of the local church is
> inherent and modifiable only by its own action.
> Nothing in this Constitution and the By-laws of
> the United Church of Christ shall destroy or
> limit the right of each local church to continu
> to operate in the way customary to it; nor shal
> be construed as giving to the General Synod, or

6.

to any Conference or Association now, or at any
future time, the power to abridge or impair the
autonomy of any local church...(emphasis supplied)

Moreover, the power to amend the U.C.C. Constitution is expressly limited in Paragraphs 50, 60, and 61,
as follows:

> The General Synod has the following powers,
> provided, however, that no power vested in the
> General Synod shall invade the autonomy of Con-
> ferences, Associations and local churches, or
> impair their right to acquire, own manage and
> dispose of property and funds:....
>
> j. To amend this Constitution as
> hereinafter provided; and
>
> k. To adopt by-laws for the United
> Church of Christ and, as hereinafter
> provided, to amend them.

Based upon the clear provisions and intent of the
U.C.C. Constitution, the court cannot accept plaintiffs'
argument that the U.C.C. Constitution hypothetically
could be amended in the future to affect the property or
inherent autonomy of a local church.

Moreover, speculation about hypothetical situations
is unwarranted. Connecticut courts are limited to consideration of justiciable controversies: Tellier v. Zar-
nowski, 157 Conn. 370, 373 (1969); and should not answer
abstract questions or render advisory opinions. McGee
v. Dunnigan, 138 Conn. 263, 268 (1951)

Based upon all the evidence during the trial and
the arguments of law made by the parties on the merits
of the present action, the court holds that the U.C.C.
does not have the ability to bind the Church or to demand contributions from the Church in violation of the
charter of the Church, and, therefore, the U.C.C. cannot
usurp the authority or the property of the Church.

Document 33.
A Bill of Rights,
submitted by Dr. Henry David Gray for Paragraph 21

1.

A BILL OF RIGHTS
(Submitted by Dr. Henry David Gray for Par. 21)

PREAMBLE

Congregational Christian Churches, in their wider
relationships, recognize all churches that worship and
serve the God and Father of our Lord Jesus Christ as
parts of Christ's catholic church and as having mutual
duties subsisting in the obligations of fellowship.
Therefore, these Churches do maintain the scriptural and
inalienable right of each Church to self-government and
administration; and do covenant that this General Synod
shall never exercise legislative or judicial authority,
nor consent to act as a council of reference.

Congregational Christian Churches are related to on
another, and to their wider agencies in a responsible,
free fellowship. The particular Church voluntarily
elects delegates to meetings of wider bodies, and takes
responsibility for the work undertaken by those delegates, with the usual Congregational reservation; namely
that what is undertaken must win the support of the
Churches, and that the Churches must win the support of
their members. The wider bodies are expected to be sen-
sitive to the will of the Churches, and, on the association and conference level, are directly controlled by
delegates from the Churches and by directors elected by
those delegates. Responsible freedom, at its best,
means voluntary sensitivity to the will of the Churches
on the part of the wider bodies.

A Congregational Christian Church writes or chooses
its own statement of purpose, belief, covenant, or creed
adopts its own constitution, or other governing rules;
and is subject to no external ecclesiastical authority
for the substance of them.

A Congregational Christian Church sets its own
standards for membership.

A Congregational Christian Church orders its worshi
as it believes to be most fitting.

A Congregational Christian Church administers the
sacraments and holy rites on conditions and after such
manner as it chooses so to do.

A Congregational Christian Church adopts and follows its own program of education, fellowship, community
service, missionary action, music, pastoral work, and
kindred religious and civic activities.

8.

A Congregational Christian Church calls its minister,
sets his compensation and tenure, and makes all other
arrangements directly with him.

A Congregational Christian Church may request that
a council (association or vicinage) either "install" or
"recognize" its minister. The council may withhold "recognition" or "installation" or may give counsel, but
the final decision as to whether or not the candidate
will be its minister rests with the local church.

A Congregational Christian Church, in its own right
and by itself, may license and ordain candidates for its
own Christian ministry.

ORIGIN OF THE ABOVE STATEMENT

According to a letter to me from Dr. Henry David
Gray dated Mar. 1, 1978, the above Bill of Rights was
set forth on the request of Judge William Maltbie, who
was chairman of the sub-committee on the United Church
of Christ Constitution charged with drawing up Paragraph
21. It was intended as a preamble to the Constituion,
in a form that could not be amended.

This Bill of Rights sets forth the Congregational
concept of the church in far more sweeping and thorough
fashion than the mere word "autonomy" would suggest.
People in the United Church of Christ are in danger of
losing the vision, the breadth, and the depth of their
Congregational roots and heritage.

Actually this Bill of Rights had a long history.
About 20 ministers and Hartford Seminary professors
worked this over on May 24, 1956 - before the Omaha
Council meeting. Prior to that the Los Angeles Association, under Dr. Gray's leadership had a similar proposal
even before Dr. Albert Palmer came out with his Bill of
Rights in May of 1948, as discussed in Chapter 11.

Dr. Gray states that Judge Maltbie came to him
twice. Apparently Judge Maltbie had received a copy
of this Bill of Rights after someone had, as Dr. Gray
says, "emasculated it." Judge Maltbie asked Dr. Gray
to re-write it. "This I did", says Dr. Gray, "simply by
putting back all the excised rights. We phoned Fred
Meek, who was also on the # 21 Committee and found that
he agreed with the wording which included all the rights."

In a second meeting with Judge Maltbie, "There
followed an intense discussion of # 21. Judge M. favored
the retention of all the rights of the Churches, and
suggested the Preamble format in which I subsequently
prepared them (2/26/60)". (Dr. Gray's letter of Mar. 1)

Index

Abbott, Alexander H., xi, 42, 64, 66, 84, 124, 197, 199
Adams, Judge C. B., 246, 256
Advance, 52, 35, 139, 144, 223–25, 356, 357, 358, (see also *Daily Advance*)
Adventure in Liberty, 69, 70, 72, 73
Alexander, John H. See note under Howell D. Davies.
Allentown Spiritual Conference, 81, 82, 104
Amendments to U.C.C. Constitution, 21 ff.
Archibald, Warren S., 280
Atkins, Gaius Glenn, 36, 69, 70, 72, 73, 177

Bailey, Harold, xvii
Bailey, Steven, 49, 57
Barth, Barthian, 49, 50, 54, 55, 57
Barton, Wm. E., 101, 133 ff.
Basis of Union, 9, 10, 35, 62, 75–77, 80, 89, 97, 128, 138–39, 193, 197, 198, 199, Appendix 360–371
Bill of Rights, H. D. Gray, 378–79
Bill of Rights, Palmer, 217, 218, Appendix 334
Blanchard, Ferdinand Q., 34, 93, 127, 128–9, 144, 148, 156, 158–59, 160–218, Appendix 308–09, 330–32, 345–47
Blinn, Oscar S., 201
Boards of Pastoral Supply, 174–76
Bradshaw, Dr. Marion J., 42, 54, 280
Bridges, Ronald, xii, 34, 35, 126, 247
Brown, Hugh Elmer, 43, 53
Buck Hill Falls, 229 ff., 235–38
Burton, Charles E., xi, 101
Buschmeyer, Fred, 212, 310 on *Comments*, 348 on Voting
Bushnell, Horace, 182
Butman, Harry R., 44, 260

Cadman Lawsuit, 4, 11, 36, 136, 285–86
Cadman, S. Parkes, 174
Chatterton, S. Read, 208
Christian Church (Disciples of Christ), 17
Christus Victor, 51, 53, 285
Cleveland, Council of 1949, 280, 282

COCU, 2, 18, 19, 58
Comments of Jan. 1948, 211, 311–12
Committee for the Continuation of the Congregational Christian Churches, xiv, xvi, 265, 280
Committee of Fifteen, 264
Committee on Free Church Polity, 95, 141
Commission on Interchurch Relations, 90, 92, 127
Conn, Howard, 36, 313, 315
Congregational Historical Society, 7
Congregational Library, Boston, 139
Congregational Polity, 60, 95, 140, 189
Congregationalism "B," 72
Constitution for Congregationalism? 221
Constitution of the E. and R. Church, 60, 63, 94, 141, 197
Council for Social Action, 46, 47
Cover-up, 9

Daily Advance, (1944) 86; (1946) 125–26
Davies, Howell D., p. 44. Dr. Davies, who took charge of the office of the Committee for the Continuation of the Congregational Christian Churches in Chicago from June of 1950 to the time of his death in October 1962, did not come into the picture until June of 1949—a few months after the Cleveland meeting of 1949. He was, however, a member of the Interim Committee mentioned on page xvi of the Foreword and handled the affairs of the new Missionary Society as well as the office of the Continuation Committee. Another member of that Interim Committee, not mentioned in the book but very active in anti-merger work, was Rev. John Alexander, who later became the first moderator of the National Association of C.C. Churches and its Executive Secretary in 1970.

[381]

Meek, Fred, 139, 232
Merrill, Boynton, 249, 250, 252
Michigan Supreme Court, xv, 5
Mid-Winter Meeting of 1948, 210
Missionary Boards, 195

National Association of the
Congregational Christian
Churches, xvi, 5
Neo-orthodoxy, 49
New Haven General Council, 66
New London Association of
Congregational Churches and
Ministers, 63, 64, 66, 67

Oberlin Council, 10, 35, 193, 242 ff.
Oberlin Interpretations 33, 35, 105,
185, Appendix 349
Office For Church Life and
Leadership, 3, 7
Organic Union, 48

Palmer, Albert W., 6, 35, 51, 96, 197
ff., 213–27, 235, 239, 244–45,
Appendix 320, 321, 334
Paragraph 21, 1, 2, 21, 22
Pauck, Wilhelm, 34, 53, 64, 65
Penner, Al, 221–23
Philips, John M., xii, 233
Philo of Alexandria, 55, 56
Pilgrim Deeds and Duties, 285
Pilgrim Fellowship, 110
Plan of Union with Presbyterians,
285 ff.
Polity of E. and R. Church, 141–42
Polity of the U.C.C., 143 ff., 148 ff.,
172–73, 189, 190
Pope, Liston, 251
Potter, Rockwell Harmon, 135
Presbyterian, 5, 60, 95
Pro-merger Committee, Oberlin,
246, 248
Pro-merger Committee, Mid-winter
Meeting, 211, 222
Proposals of 1705, 283, 284
Proposed motion for Oberlin,
Appendix 216–18

Res Judicata, 5
Richards, George W., 32, 54, 107,
121, 145–49, 196
Roberts, S. T., 214
Rouner, Arthur A.,Sr., 42
Russell, Joseph J., 44

Saybrook Synod and Platform, 283
Schroeder, Paul, 224, 225, 277–78

Scotford, John, xii, 32, 110, 221, 223,
240, 246, Appendix 352–53
Scott, Philip, 126
Scribner, Frank S., 33, 109, 120, 125
Seminaries, 9
Shaping of the United Church of
Christ, The, See Gunnemann
Shipherd, Theodore M., 41, 42, 64,
66, 92, 97, 103, 108, 197
Simpson, Clifford, 147–48
Stafford, Russell Henry, 109
Stamm, Frederick K., 171–72
Steinbrink, Judge Meier, xiii, xiv,
36, 192
Strang, Max, 44, 45, 257, 260, 279,
Appendix 356–58
Suggestions from Connecticut
group, 319

"That they all may be one," 48

U.C.C. Constitution and By-laws, 3,
Chapter 2, p. 16 ff., 198
Vallon, Michel, re Barth, 56, 181,
184
Voting on B. of U., 194, 229–30

Wagner, James E., 32, 52, 105, 185
Walton, Alfred G., 35, 209
Waser, Raymond A., 281
Watergate, 13, 279
What Really Happened at Oberlin,
252
Wheelock, Arthur, 267–68
White, Hugh Vernon, 86, 115
Wise, John, 284–85
Wood, Loren E., 32